17-8

The Popular Book

A HISTORY OF AMERICA'S LITERARY TASTE

The Popular Book

A HISTORY OF AMERICA'S LITERARY TASTE

BY JAMES D. HART

Berkeley and Los Angeles

UNIVERSITY OF CALIFORNIA PRESS

1963

University of California Press
Berkeley and Los Angeles, California

Cambridge University Press
London, England

An abridged version of Chapter 1 appeared under
the title 'A Puritan Bookshelf' in Vol. I, No. 1, of
The New Colophon, copyright 1948.

Printed in the United States of America

To Ruth

Acknowledgments

The study of a subject as large as the relation of America's popular reading to its social background could not have been pursued without a great indebtedness to the research of scholars and commentators on many of the special elements concerned in this general matter. The Bibliographical Checklist contains brief citations of the sources which provided specific data or proved particularly suggestive. To state the nature of my obligation to each would prove cumbersome in a work whose spirit runs counter to the use of footnotes and an extensive, formal bibliography. I cannot, however, leave the matter of sources without stating that I am deeply sensible of my debt to the research of many persons whose works are noted in this appendix.

I am, of course, also indebted to Lewis Bayly, Thomas Paine, William Hill Brown, G. P. R. James, Grace Aguilar, Elizabeth Stuart Phelps, Henry Wadsworth Longfellow, Samuel L. Clemens, Charles Major, Harold Bell Wright, Percy Marks, and Hans Fallada for the headings of the following chapters that were first used as titles on their books. These titles, popular in their own times, now seem the most accurate brief statements of the tastes prevailing in the periods when they were first published.

Finally, it is a pleasure to express my appreciation to my sister and my brother-in-law, Mr. and Mrs. Joseph M. Bransten, to Professor George R. Stewart, and to Mr. David Randall, who read the manuscript and offered many valuable suggestions.

J. D. H.

Berkeley, California
4 January 1950

Contents

The Popular Book

A HISTORY OF AMERICA'S LITERARY TASTE

Chapter 1

The Practice of Piety

Knowledge and entertainment in the portable form of books came to America with its first colonists, and reading, for profit or pleasure, has ever since been an integral part of the life of this land. When the Pilgrims prepared to board the *Mayflower*, they spent their last days on English soil checking provisions needed for settlement in a wilderness across the ocean. While considering supplies they met the familiar problem of selecting a few books to take to a 'desert island.' Most bibliophiles who treat this question as a parlor game make their choice from fiction, poetry, and drama. If really faced by the issue they would quickly scuttle belles-lettres in favor of books explaining how to get along in an uninhabited place. Most particularly would they choose works describing the region to be settled. This is exactly what the Pilgrims did. A vessel of 180 tons like the *Mayflower* has little room for the niceties of life; its cargo must be picked as carefully as its crew. The raw materials for building a new civilization may include books but the books must be useful.

First the Pilgrims turned to the works of Captain John Smith, who had explored the New England coast in 1614. Smith himself had asked to ship on the *Mayflower* as guide and counselor, but Bradford and Brewster had not looked with favor upon this contentious adventurer, this so-called Admiral of New England. No, they tartly told him just before sailing, it is cheaper to buy your books than to hire you—a decision that Smith contends cost them a 'wonderful deal of misery.' So Smith stayed home writing unsought advice to 'unexperienced planters of New England,' while the first colonists spent time on deck, in their narrow cabins, and later on land, reading and discussing Smith's *Description of New England,* whose great map clearly showed the harbor of Plymouth and gave to it the name the Pilgrims retained. They had with them also Smith's book entitled *A Map of Virginia,* describing by word and by chart the region to which their grant directed them.

Thomas Dermer's account of his explorations in New England just six months before the Pilgrims put into Plymouth was another book valuable to the new settlers. Bradford acquired it in June 1620, the month the *Mayflower* was chartered, and because of it he may have led the Pilgrims to settle in New England instead of Virginia, to which they were ordered. Plymouth was free of Virginia's established Anglican Church and English government, two good reasons for selecting it, but even better was Dermer's exhortation: 'I would that the first plantation might hear be seated, if ther come to the number of 50 persons, or upward.' Bradford quoted these words approvingly and echoed Dermer's commendation of 'the richest soyle, and much open ground fitt for English graine.' Surely during the days of their long voyage the Pilgrims must have thought about Dermer's advice just as they probably scanned the account of Gosnold's expedition, to which Bradford referred in his *History,* along with James Rosier's *True Relation,* and some other records of early New England exploration.

The seventy adults aboard the *Mayflower* may have welcomed writings of Smith, Dermer, and other voyagers, but the twenty-six so-called Saints who emigrated for religious reasons turned to the Bible as the fundamental guide to the reefs and shoals of this world. They brought Bibles, both great and small. The Geneva Bible was probably most common, because the Separatists admired its marginalia, but it is likely that they had copies too of the new King James version, and some of the more scholarly voyagers may have had texts in Hebrew, Greek, and Latin. Whatever other books they regretfully left behind, without the Bible they would not travel. It was truly their Book of Books, with them always in mind and in print. In it resided the source of all laws, the only firm knowledge of good and evil, to be read in the light of its pure reason and in the ecstasy of grace which it imparted. The importance they attributed to the Bible was indeed the basis of the split between Separatists and Anglicans, the reason why the Pilgrims left their homeland. To the Anglican, Scripture was to be reinforced by other authorities, but those who opposed the Established Church saw the Bible as the only revealed word of God, containing the complete, final, and absolute code for all matters spiritual and civil. Without the Bible the devout voyagers would have felt themselves faced not only with the 'hideous & desolate wildernes' that frightened Bradford, but with chaos itself.

Most of the other emigrants, if they could read, were the sort who could take a book or leave it alone. Though the *Mayflower* had room for a pet spaniel and a mastiff bitch, books must have been considered by many to be but idle matters, better fit for an established commonwealth than for a band of pioneers. Some hands hired as navigators and mariners may have owned a few of the eleven texts later recommended in Captain John Smith's *Pathway to Experience necessary for all young Seamen.* Samuel Fuller, serving the Pilgrims as physician and surgeon, presumably brought along some treatises on physics, blood-letting, and simple pathology, perhaps William Vaughan's *Directions for Health,* compiled some years earlier for Newfoundland settlers, and *Joyfull Newes Out of the Newe Found Worlde,* the standard work on America's medicinal plants. The adventurers who were not of the company of Saints probably did not hesitate long in choosing to bring a stout pair of boots instead of a calf folio, but there were many men among the Pilgrims and their more powerful successors, the Puritans, who soon felt the need to import Bibles and other books.

As the years passed, carvers and joiners, masons and blacksmiths, weavers and tailors arrived to furnish other goods, but few could provide the texts needed for a proper understanding of holy living and holy dying. And so those who knew the value of the written word collected libraries in the wilderness. One such was Elder William Brewster, the only Pilgrim who had attended a university.

When William Brewster died in 1643, he left a book collection valued at £42, while the remainder of his estate was worth but £108. Brewster's inventory shows that he owned 323 English books, 64 works with Latin titles, and two bundles of small books not fully identified. Time and place allowed neither haphazard nor luxurious book buying, yet Brewster owned thirteen duplicates, suggesting that his personal library may also have been intended for the community. Seventy-five per cent of these books were published before the *Mayflower* set sail and could have been brought on that ship, but more likely they were imported later as examples of the works he and his fellows knew at home and yearned to have with them again. Brewster also had new books, indicating that he kept in touch with ideas circulating in England after the Pilgrims' departure, for his library contained publications of every year but two between his arrival in 1620 and his death in 1643.

Over two-thirds of Brewster's books dealt with religion, helping laymen better to understand the Bible, answering ethical problems, and clarifying theology and ecclesiastical polity. Among the rest were several legal texts to help establish a commonwealth, and a few scientific works such as an herbal, studies of surveying, and even one on the cultivation of silkworms. The assortment of fifty-four miscellaneous books also included Machiavelli's *The Prince,* Bacon's *Advancement of Learning* and his *Declaration of Treasons of the Earl of Essex,* two of Prynne's Puritan pamphlets, Robert Cawdrey's collection of moral aphorisms, a geography, Richard Rich's *Newes from Virginia,* a Latin poem in honor of James I, and Thomas Dekker's *Magnificent Entertainment Given to King James* upon his accession to the throne. Eight of the books contained descriptions of the New World. Among the twenty-four historical works were *The Swedish Intelligencer,* a popular narrative of the Protestant champion, Gustavus Adolphus, and Camden's *Britannia* in its original Latin edition, which Brewster's executors valued at three shillings, the current price of a pair of shoes. Brewster even accumulated fourteen books of poetry. Among them were Ainsworth's translation of the Psalms; the later poems of George Wither, written in order 'that all Persons, according to their Degrees and qualities, may at all times be remembered to praise God'; William Hornby's *The Scourge of Drunkenness;* a book entitled *Prosopopoia,* presumably Spenser's vigorous satire on church abuses and court evils; and Richard Johnson's *Golden Garland of Princely Pleasures and Delicate Desires,* a typical Elizabethan miscellany of lyrical poetry.

Brewster's was the largest library in the Plymouth Colony, but nearly all the Pilgrims owned some books as the years brought them greater wealth and more leisure. Even the peppery little captain, Miles Standish, at his death left about fifty books along with his fowling piece, three muskets, four carbines, two small guns, and sword and cutlass. On the whole, his interests were secular, for he never joined the church of those Saints whom he originally served as a mercenary soldier, but he owned several Bibles, some collections of sermons, Calvin's *Institutes,* a Psalm Book, and some catechisms. His more worldly works included half a dozen history books, Homer's *Iliad,* an herbal, a dictionary, and Pierre de la Primaudaye's *French Academy,* a collection of essays that served as the seventeenth-century equivalent of a one-volume encyclopedia. Like a good soldier he read Caesar's campaigns in the *Commentaries,* and he had at his bedside Bariff's treatise on artillery.

While the Plymouth planters were slowly and painfully building their colony, extending trade, planting crops, accumulating livestock, and even adding to their store of books, their dreams of establishing the firmest English settlement north of Virginia grew more and more disturbed. In mid-June of 1630 John Endicott's little settlement at Salem suddenly grew to formidable proportions when the *Arbella* put in at the North River harbor with the largest and wealthiest passenger list yet seen in those parts. From her cabins came men of substance and standing and from her holds rolled forth over 20,000 gallons of wine and beer, as well as other goods in like proportion. The fleet that followed the wake of the *Arbella* that year brought to the Massachusetts Bay some thousand settlers, three times the number that had straggled into Plymouth in a decade. They were a different kind of colonist too. The Pilgrims, poor in all but their faith, were considered fanatics by the wealthier, more firmly settled Puritans. The Massachusetts Bay leaders had wealth and property to preserve, strong hostages to radical thought unknown to the Pilgrim fathers. Plymouth's Governor Bradford had been a workingman at home, but John Winthrop, Governor of the Massachusetts Bay Colony, had been lord of a manor at Groton, where he employed twenty servants.

With a force of this sort the Pilgrims could not long compete. Their economy was upset by the loss of Indian trade to their stronger neighbors, whose increased prosperity from farming, fishing, and ship building further weakened the old colony's prestige. Two years after the arrival of the *Arbella,* the Puritans had six settlers to every one at Plymouth, and their followers had spread out to found Boston and half a dozen other communities. For half a century more the Plymouth Colony continued feebly on its own, but in 1684 it was finally drawn into the circuit of the Massachusetts Bay Colony, whose path it thereafter followed.

When the *Arbella* sailed into Massachusetts Bay there was already a library there greater than any in Plymouth, except Elder Brewster's. This was but chance, yet chance of a sort that is symbolic. The library belonged to William Blackstone (or Blaxton as some spelled it), a crotchety Puritan clergyman who established himself on a neck of land called Shawmut by his only neighbors, the Indians. There he dwelt in a little cottage surrounded by his 186 volumes, among them three Bibles and

eleven Latin folios, all probably brought with him from Emanuel College. Blackstone was thoroughly irritated when Winthrop disturbed his
quiet reading, but like others he had to yield to the stronger and richer
newcomers who bought his rights to the land. In 1635 he crated his books,
bought some cows with the money awarded him, and, riding astride one
of them, removed to an equally secluded spot thirty-five miles south,
where he continued to live a quiet life, cultivating his garden, tending
his stock, and reading his books.

Blackstone was an unwitting harbinger of things to come, for he was
a university man and a book collector in Boston before there was any
Boston. Fifteen years after Winthrop's arrival, some 130 university
alumni were settled in the northern colonies, mainly around Boston. This
meant that New England had more than one university graduate to every
two hundred people, probably as great a ratio as could be found in England itself. To this learned group the Bay slowly began to add its own
graduates from Harvard College, founded in 1636. During the seventeenth century Harvard enrolled almost 600 students, so that proportionately more of the population was sent to the Puritans' sole institution of
higher learning than is today sent to all New England colleges.

In the very first days of colonization each minister was given ten
pounds to start his religious library, and records show that other highly
educated men were adding books to the homes that began to cluster
around the Bay. The literary level of plainer people was high enough to
suggest they also bought books when they had enough money. Literacy,
at least as defined by the ability to write one's name on an official docu-
ment, appears to have run between 89 and 95 per cent in Massachusetts
and Connecticut from 1640 to the end of the century. Of course this estimate fails to account for slaves, indentured servants, and even most hired
men, who had little occasion to meddle with deeds and petitions. It also
excludes most women. Of the few women who had official business between 1635 and 1656, 42 per cent were able to sign documents; their
number increased to 62 per cent between 1681 and 1697. Estimating literacy by a study of official documents may give too high a score, but this
method of judgment probably compensates for itself when applied to a
period in which writing was considered a rather sophisticated subject to
be learned after graduation from the hornbook, the primer, and some
acquaintance with the Bible as a text.

Probate records confirm literacy studies, for 60 per cent of the estates
noted in Middlesex County between 1654 and 1699 contained books, all

but 8 per cent including more than the Bible. In Essex County, mostly frontier at this time, 39 per cent of the estates listed between 1635 and 1681 included books, though 19 per cent of these had only Bibles, while in Salem more than a third of the estates recorded to 1700 included some books besides the Bible. Even these figures fail to give a full picture of the spread of reading, for in those days large private collections were treated virtually as public libraries, so general was the borrowing by the poorer from the wealthier.

The inventories of estates listed books because they were considered valuable property, frequently worth noting by title. A man often owned but one book, and that 'an old Bible,' 'a great Bible,' 'a small Bible,' or just a plain 'Bible.' Sometimes the sole piece of reading matter is more fully described, as in the estate of the Providence miller who owned 'an old Bible, some lost and some of it torne,' assessed at nine pence. Men who had no other books frequently owned as many as half a dozen copies of the Book. One cannot tell for certain what texts followed the Bible in popularity, because records are few and misleading. Small collections, the sort that furnish a guide to popular reading, are often casually described as 'Books, bottles, and odd things, 12 shillings,' or 'one pound in bookes, sackes, and ladders.' But it appears that excluding schoolbooks and the Bible, the most common work was a Book of Psalms, and following in popularity was one of the treatises by Calvin or some other favored divine, with catechisms ranking third in demand.

America's first best seller was also the first piece of literature wholly of its own making—the so-called *Bay Psalm Book,* printed in 1640 at the newly established Cambridge press. One might think this the last book for which New Englanders would feel a special need, since the Psalms were available in their many Bibles, in prose and metrical versions separately published, and in the Book of Common Prayer. But not even Ainsworth or Wither furnished a translation and verse setting wholly satisfactory to men attempting to adjust their lives to the injunctions of Holy Writ. To follow the Lord's will one must know His literal words, and so the Puritan text was based on the belief that 'Gods Altar needs not our pollishings.' The emphasis was on 'Conscience rather than Elegance, fidelity rather than poetry, in translating the hebrew words into english language, and Davids poetry into english meetre.' The popularity of the work proved the soundness of the criteria, though one may wonder whether the 1,700 copies of the first edition were all sold in New England. In 1640 there were perhaps 3,500 families in the northern colonies, every other one of which would have had to buy a copy to warrant the *Bay Psalm Book's* speedy sales. As the Separatists in Plymouth and the Puritans in some outlying plantations would have none of this Boston work, there were probably only as many families amenable to the *Bay Psalm Book* as there were copies in the first printing. Surely some of these families had neither the money nor the inclination to buy the book. Presumably, a good part of the first printing was sold to Puritans across the Atlantic. Certainly it was popular abroad as well as at home, for the next century and a quarter saw at least fifty-one editions published in New England, England, and Scotland.

The Puritans read religious books, but then so did any cultivated man of the day. The library of an Englishman or a Virginian would be likely to have about the same religious texts as that of the New England settler, for though theology might vary, piety was the cornerstone of culture. Between a third and a quarter of the books in the libraries of Southern colonists were religious; somewhat more than a quarter of the books published in England between 1666 and 1685 dealt with religion; 32 per cent of the books imported by a Boston dealer from 1682 to 1685 fell in the same category. New Englanders were not unusual in their tastes. They differed from other colonists mainly in the great emphasis they placed on reading and owning books. Southern colonists had fewer books than New Englanders, because in the South, where literacy was lower and class divisions sharper, there were but few middle-class readers. At one end of the social scheme were the five thousand slaves settled in the colonies by 1700; at the other were the plantation owners, of whom five held almost four hundred of these Negroes in bondage; and in between much of the population consisted of indentured and formerly indentured servants. The Southern colonists lived on widely separated plantations (by 1685 Virginia's population, smaller than that of a contemporary London parish, was spread over an area greater than England itself), and without cities they had no popular centers for the development of intellectual life. Lacking a cohesive pattern of schools and churches, printing houses and booksellers, a large reading public could not develop. Nevertheless, the Bible was a common possession. John Smith and other founders of Jamestown in 1607 had ousted one of their captains, Edward Maria Wingfield, as an atheist, because, as he admitted, 'I carried not a Bible with me,' thus implying that ownership of the Book of Books was mandatory for a leader and expected of all seventeenth-century readers in the South as well as in New England.

All told, there were probably never more than 20,000 volumes in Virginia at one time, and that at the end of the century. They were gathered into better than a thousand private libraries, but, generally speaking, only the man of some wealth could afford more than two or three books. Ordinary men found the Bible, the Book of Common Prayer, and a good work on practical piety useful in a land where settled parishes were rare and ministers scarce or poor, but more religious works they did not need. Sharing the heritage of England's established religious beliefs, the Southerners outside of Maryland were not embroiled in doctrinal dispute, which made New Englanders import and print books. If the ethical sentiments were suitable, the writings of Calvinists, Quakers, or Catholics were as acceptable as those of Anglicans. For most Southerners it was enough to have one work outlining a practical way to achieve exemplary conduct in this world and salvation in the next. As one of the Southern colonists said, they were 'more inclinable to read men by business and conversation than to dive into books.'

The actual number as well as the proportion of religious works was higher in New England's book collections, but that is to be expected in a region where frequently the cultivated man was the minister and where libraries, though numerous, were small, for the smaller the collection the greater the percentage of basic, that is religious, books.

Religious books were not only for serious contemplation in the study; they were part and parcel of everyday reading. Samuel Sewall saw nothing unusual in spending part of a Saturday outing to Dorchester reading Calvin on the Psalms while his wife picked cherries and raspberries. Like other great theologians, Calvin was an arbiter to whom the New Englanders turned for judgment on even the small details of daily life. When Sewall learned that a friend had cut off his hair to put on a wig, he remonstrated and 'pray'd him to read Tenth Chapter of the Third Book of Calvin's Institutions,' pointing out that God having ordained the color and texture of our hair, it was not for us to meddle in His doings. For similar great and small reasons the writings of the English educators and divines, John Preston, Richard Sibbes, William Perkins, and William Ames, were equally popular as refinements of Calvin's sweeping theology, and many a Puritan read Anglican texts so that he might better refute his enemies.

The New Englander frequently spent an evening by the light of the chimney fire reading Foxe's *Book of Martyrs*, that dramatic account of Protestant sufferings. Its vigorous and moving stories had the excitement of fiction, yet imparted a feeling of virtue to readers laboring to per-

petuate the faith for which these men and women died. The work was
to be found in libraries numbering but a hundred books, and a small
Massachusetts settlement looking for a minister in 1650 held out as bait
the use of a local citizen's copy of Foxe's tome. It was a long book that
would last many a winter evening, and length was pleasing to the New
Englanders, who purchased Joseph Carryll's 1,200-page *Exposition upon
Job,* a folio that furnished both the theory and practice of patience. The
Book of Martyrs, appealing to all classes, continued to be a common and
popular work in New England throughout the century. Like Foxe's work,
Pilgrim's Progress was a kind of Bible for the layman. Its pious guidance
to salvation was animated by vivid characters, dramatic situations, and a
moving allegory. At one and the same time it was an exciting tale and
a religious work viewing man's progress through life in Puritan terms.
Readily comprehensible to the naive reader, the work was perfectly
suited to the interests and abilities of the common New Englander. In
1681, only three years after the first English publication, the Cambridge
press issued its own edition of *Pilgrim's Progress.* To reprint a new work
so soon was an unusual honor, and Bunyan appears to have been quite
right when he declared that the colonists looked upon it with a 'much
loving countenance.'

Although the average New Englander bought books expounding the
intricacies of theology and the subtleties of ecclesiastical polity, he probably turned more often to practical guides to godliness. As a stout middle-
class citizen he wanted his books to be purposeful, and the highest purpose was to explain to man the ways in which God bade him walk
through life. The most popular rationale of religious behavior was Lewis
Bayly's *The Practice of Piety,* one of the few books thought to warrant
the pains of translation and publication in the tongue of the Massachusetts Indians. Bayly's pocket-size work was just what the common man
needed. It summarized doctrine, acted as a manual of Biblical interpretation, furnished select prayers and meditations, enumerated hindrances
to piety, contrasted the regenerate and unregenerate man, cited examples
of divine judgment against sinners, gave a key to knowledge of one's own
possibilities of salvation, and was even said to be a good antidote to
witchcraft. With it in hand any reader could deal directly with God and
be pretty certain that all would work out well.

A first cousin to *The Practice of Piety* and almost as frequently found
on New England shelves was *An Alarm to Unconverted Sinners* by the
English minister Joseph Alleine. This book supposedly sold some 20,000

copies in England and the colonies under its original title, but hit its full stride when a shrewd publisher reissued it as *The Sure Guide to Heaven.* Under that irresistible caption another 50,000 copies are said to have been sold. Although Edmund Calamy was a bit too enthusiastic when he declared, 'No book in the English tongue (the Bible excepted) can equal it for the number that hath been dispers'd,' it was certainly popular even as late as 1717, when Samuel Sewall gave a copy to each deputy of the General Court, presumably without ironic implications.

Still another book of wide and long-lived popularity was *The Great Assize* by Samuel Smith, a leading Presbyterian preacher in England during the Commonwealth. His careful inquiries into human actions and his guidance to godly conduct so appealed to New Englanders that Boston's leading bookseller imported forty copies within a single year. Smith's work was actually a collection of sermons, a form of reading matter extremely pleasing to the average man of the day. In part sermons furnished the knowledge and guidance later generations obtained from public lectures, magazines, and newspaper editorials, for many of them were hoards of practical knowledge, furnishing answers to the ideals, hopes, and fears of New England's bourgeois society, which listened to sermons on Sundays and in the midweek, at holidays and special events, and over the bodies of the great and the lowly.

That the early New Englanders' interests were not limited to religion is indicated by the books they imported. They sent not only for works that would guide them along righteous paths, but also for those that would help them subdue the wilderness. Books on farming and stock raising, on industry, science, shipping, surveying, and military affairs were what they needed and read. Sawmills, brickworks, breweries, and shipyards grew up in the larger towns, their founding and running described in some of the books the New Englanders read. Very early Bible-quoting Yankee skippers carried lumber, furs, fish, and other native products across the seas, bringing back such exotic merchandise as rum, sugar, and Negro slaves. These Puritans learned seamanship by experience and by expert guidance from the texts they read. Of one shipment of 109 books sent to Massachusetts, 56 dealt with nautical matters, the most popular being Richard Norwood's *Application of the Doctrine of Triangles in the use of the plain Sea-Chart,* imported into Boston by the dozens and the scores. Though an occasional treatise on such esoteric subjects as cryptography or the alchemic properties of virgins' milk and crows' heads found its way into the hands of the learned, the common man insisted that his books be practical.

The books the average Puritan read, no matter how diverse their subject matter, reveal the contours of a mind shaped by social and religious forces affirming the principle that success in this world is an earnest of salvation in the next. The dissenting Puritan mind was in great part a religious expression of the middle-class struggle against a luxurious nobility having regard neither for toil nor for temperance. Their humble economic background having taught the Puritans the need for sobriety and daily work, they labored in the world, accounted prosperity a mark of divine approval, and relished books like William Perkins's A Treatise on Vocations, which declared that commercial success was granted to those whom God favored.

Perkins's treatise on the gospel of work and others like it affected general literary tastes, for books were often judged by the amount of help they furnished the reader in his quest for worldly advancement. Most popular of all mundane books was the almanac. It could not promise redemption, but because its information on the changes of sun, moon, tide, and weather could assist an agricultural and maritime people, there was a New England Almanac even before there was a New England psalm book. Other compendia of facts, such as Bacon's Advancement of Learning and his Essays, were highly esteemed because they offered advice on practical matters. And many New Englanders bought history books for the same reason, undoubtedly nodding their heads in approval when they read in the popular Sir Walter Raleigh's History of the World that 'wee may gather out of History a policy no lesse wise than eternall; by the comparison and application of other mens forepassed miseries, with our owne like errours and ill deservings.' The desire for practical books extended even to manuals on polite behavior, for these founders of new colonies needed printed guides to instruct them in the amenities appropriate to men but recently come to worldly success. Among the books dedicated to this end was The Academy of Compliments, of which seventeen copies were imported within six months by one bookseller so that Bostonians might have letter models, speech formulae, a glossary of difficult words, and even an anthology of 'Songs and catches à la mode' all in one binding. Elder Brewster, seeking similar counsel, found a Renaissance Italian handbook and the Puritan Robert Cleaver's plainer Godly Form of Household Government the answer to his needs, while Governor Bradford preferred Gouge's Domestical Duties, which warned him against calling his wife such nicknames as 'Ducke, Chicke, Pigsnie, &c,' and furnished him other sober advice on the running of a seemly home.

One of the clearest indications of the New Englander's reading tastes is found in five invoices addressed to John Usher, Boston's leading book-seller. Between 1682 and 1685 this bookseller imported 3,421 books from one English dealer. Since there were a dozen other booksellers in Boston during those years and since Usher probably imported books of which we have no record, these shipments cannot be taken as a fully representative sample of New England's book buying. Still, 3,421 books (exclusive of those printed at the Cambridge press) intended for some 75,000 people in the northern colonies, of whom perhaps but 7,000 lived in Boston, furnish fair evidence of the trends of Puritan literary taste and ample indication that New England had an avid reading public.

The titles listed in Usher's invoices are very sketchy, but a little study can group them roughly into twenty categories, yielding the following information about the New Englander's literary demands:

Religious (Sermons, catechisms, aids to piety, concordances, etc.)	1,096
School Texts	1,004
Bibles and Psalm Books	428
Romances and light fiction	162
Navigation	150
Books of practical morality, essays, general philosophy, etc.	94
Modern English poetry	81
Medicine	65
Law	61
Classics (Presumably not used in schools)	43
History	32
Jest Books	28
Dictionaries	15
Astronomy	11
Military	11
Cookery	5
Biography	5
Geography	4
Travel	3
Unidentified	123
	3,421

Although the listing is not so clear as one would like,* it does reveal some surprising matters. The fourth largest category, running nearly

* The categories are not exact, for the invoices are often open to question and there may be some errors in assigning books to their proper spheres. Some of the

to 5 per cent, is comprised of romances and light fiction. The titles are
hardly those one would expect in a sober Puritan library, yet Boston was
a big port and to it came sailors and adventurous travelers whose literary standards were not molded by the Mathers. During the 1680's Usher
sold fifteen copies of *Argalus and Parthenia,* the work of Francis Quarles,
whose translations of the Psalms and short devotional poems were much
admired by the Puritans. Still, Usher probably needed no such round-
about reminder in his sales talk, for his customers without similar excuse
bought six copies of *The Most Pleasant History of Tom a Lincoln* and
half a dozen of *Jack of Newberry.* Their religious interests and concern
with demonology stretched pretty far if these were the reasons leading
them to buy three copies of *Venus in the Cloyster, or The Nun in Her
Smock,* and sixty-six copies of *The History of the Damnable Life and
Deserved Death of Dr. John Faustus.* And surely no utilitarian interest
in shoemaking caused them to buy twenty-nine copies of *The Pleasant
History of the Gentle Craft. A Discourse containing Many Matters of
Delight, very pleasant to read, set forth with Pictures, and Variety of
Wit and Mirth.* And what is one to make of the two copies of *The London Jilt, or the Politick Whore; shewing all the artifices and stratagems
which the Ladies of Pleasure make use of, for the intreaguing and decoy-
ing of men; interwoven with several pleasant stories of the Misses' ingenious performances?* Was it material for sermons or was it only erotica?
Whatever it was thought to be, *The London Jilt* would probably have
sold more than two copies if Usher's reorder had not been returned
marked 'out of print and not to be had.'

Romances seem odd fare for readers who generally insisted that their
literature be didactic, but authors, editors, and printers lured them on
with sanctimonious prefaces and dedications that put a moral veneer on
worldly tales. Without conscious hypocrisy the Puritans may have been
assuaged by the belief of Francis Meres that 'as Bees out of the bitterest
flowers . . . doe gather the sweetest hony: so out of the obscene and
wicked fables some profit may be extracted.' Such rationalization probably eased the minds of New Englanders when they went to the book

so-called religious books may have been intended for school use, since one cannot
make a clear distinction between catechisms for the child and the adult. Likewise,
some of the classics may have been ordered for school use, although the subjects and
the small numbers of each title indicate that they are probably assigned to the proper
category. Even if the 123 unidentified titles (less than 4 per cent of the total) could
be eliminated altogether, the proportions of the various groupings would not be much
changed.

section of Usher's general merchandise store to buy Mlle de Scudéry's *Clélie,* Sidney's *Arcadia, Guy of Warwick, Pharamond,* and similar romances. The Puritan's conscience was evidently not outraged by jest books either, for although the admired William Perkins specifically warned against the reading of 'merry ballads and bookes, as Scoggin,' Usher sold eight copies of *Scoggins Jests* with a foreword that declared 'there is nothing beside the goodnesse of God, that preserves health so much as honest mirth.'

Another large division of Usher's imports is the group of eighty-one books of modern English poetry. If Usher's invoices are a fair guide, poems were in greater demand than medical or legal texts. The New Englanders evidently enjoyed the English collections of the day, buying copies of *The Jovial Garland, The Crown Garland, The Garland of Delight,* and similar anthologies of witty and amatory poems. Commonplace books kept by Harvard undergraduates indicate that the contemporary love lyric was popular, for the boys copied passages from Cowley's *Mistress,* Herrick's 'Gather ye rosebuds,' Cleveland's poetry, Beaumont's lyrics, a great deal of Spenser, some lyrics by Shakespeare, and both prose and poetry by Sir Philip Sidney. Usher stocked four copies of *Paradise Lost,* but that represented only a drop of his poetic offerings, which even included the works of the licentious John Wilmot, Earl of Rochester. The Puritans read profane love poems, light lyrics, and droll verses, yet they seem to have considered poetry primarily as an intense medium for the communication of spiritual or worldly wisdom. Rhythm and imagery were generally desirable because they aided the understanding or memory, but the Puritans looked less to Parnassus than to Zion, the Mount of God. Most of the poetry they read was hortatory or didactic, even though it ranged from Thomas Heywood's *Hierarchy of the Blessed Angels* to Sir Richard Blackmore's *Prince Arthur,* and included the verse of Herbert, Wither, and Cowley, as well as Du Bartas's epic on the creation, which was enjoyed both for its subject matter and for the encyclopedic learning crammed into its verses.

The New Englander's attitude toward poetry is best illustrated by his own publications. Next to the *Bay Psalm Book,* the most famous was *The Day of Doom,* a long theological work by Michael Wigglesworth, the minister of the church at Malden. This doggerel Dante illustrated the conventional New England view of poetry by writing his epic of the Last Judgment in ballad meter, which was familiar to readers accustomed to broadside ballads hawked on the streets for a few pennies every time an unusual event occurred. The ballad did very well to celebrate severe snowstorms, rivers that overflowed their banks, captured pirates, and hanged criminals. Why should it not do for a longer, more serious work? 'He is the best artist,' Wigglesworth proclaimed, 'who can most clearly and familiarly communicate his thoughts to the meanest capacity,' and so he adopted the familiar jog-trot of the ballad. A more sophisticated aesthetic might find the rhythm poorly suited to the subject, but Wigglesworth knew his audience: the 1,800 copies of the first edition were mostly sold within the year, allowing the author to make a trip to Bermuda on his profits. Within a decade two more editions were published, and for a century after the first printing of 1662 *The Day of Doom* was sold as a book or broadside in New England. If the first edition was sold in New England alone, it must have reached every twentieth person; if it sold throughout the colonies, one out of every forty-five people (men, women, and children) could have owned a copy, a sale comparable to some two and a half million in the United States of the 1940's. This circulation is out of all proportion to other books, and it may be supposed that many of the copies were shipped to the mother country. But wherever it was sold, the sulphurous title and jingling verses attracted more buyers in one year than that other Puritan epic, *Paradise Lost*, found in twice that time.

According to Usher's invoices, schoolbooks were almost as much in demand as religious works, as might be expected of a people whose faith depended on an enlightened ministry and laity able to read and interpret the Bible. Massachusetts in 1642 required that every child be taught enough reading to understand the principles of religion and the laws of the land. Five years later the school law ungrammatically demanded 'that every township in this jurisdiction, after the Lord hath increased them to the number of fifty householders, shall then forthwith appoint one within their town to teach . . . to write and to read.' In many towns this statute was evaded, but its spirit was obeyed in course of time through the wide distribution of *The New England Primer*, the first in America's great trinity of schoolbooks that includes Webster's Speller and McGuffey's Readers. Probably first compiled in 1683, the *Primer* ranked next to the Bible in popular distribution. At one time, for example, a Boston bookseller stocked nearly five hundred copies, all of which were read, dog-eared, and shredded out of existence by successive students, so that fewer than 1,500 copies remain of the six to eight million probably printed during the first century and a half of the *Primer's* publication, and the earliest dated issue now known is the Boston printing of 1727. Penmanship, mathematics, and bookkeeping were obviously secondary subjects. Of the thousand texts Usher imported, only forty-five were arithmetic books, and but seventeen attempted, as one title described it, to have *The Young Lad taken from the Writing School, and fully instructed . . . in all the Mistries of a Merchant.*

Their love of books must have been great to induce men as poor as most of the colonists to buy so many volumes. In the quarter century between 1640 and 1665 small books seem to have cost somewhere between two and four shillings, while folios were worth a great deal more. The highest salary paid to any minister around Boston in 1657 was £100, and the average was £65, a good part of it generally paid in produce. Nathaniel Rogers, the pastor at Ipswich, was obviously unusual in leaving an estate of £1,497, including a library valued at £100, but many of his fellow divines possessed libraries proportionately as large for the size of their estates. Samuel Eliot Morison estimates that some ten thousand different titles made their way to New England's bookshelves before 1700. Their quantitative range probably extended from several thousand copies of the Bible and nearly as many catechisms, through several hundred copies of the more popular works of Puritan divinity, down to a single one of the more esoteric works.

Lacking public libraries, New Englanders bought their books from local merchants and borrowed from one another. From 1642 to 1661 Boston had only one bookseller, but in the 1660's there were two, in the 'seventies there was a jump to nine, and in the 'eighties there was another great rise to seventeen, of whom fifteen were still in business during the last decade of the century. The increase was out of proportion to the growth of New England's population, which rose from some 18,000 to almost 100,000 during this period, and Boston, which had not yet got around to naming its streets, had far more than a normal share of bookshops for its 1,500 inhabitants in 1640 or for its 7,000 at the end of the century. The booksellers ranged from those who carried a few volumes among their general merchandise and printers who sold their own publications, to retailers whose stocks of books numbered into the thousands. Michael Perry's shop had 5,802 books in 1700, extending from a single folio Bible to 106 dozen copies of a popular catechism. Books were bought directly from English dealers too, though most imports were made through local merchants. When John Dunton, the London bookseller, arrived in Boston in 1686 he supposedly came to collect £500 owing on past orders. Dunton's accounting cannot be trusted any more than his story of a ten-month stay in New England, which actually lasted but half that time. Yet even if his £500 were also pared in half, the sum represents about 1,500 volumes at prevailing retail prices, and it cannot be supposed that all the books he had sold New Englanders had gone unpaid. During his visit Dunton set up stores in Boston and Salem, collected £400 in silver for his old and new sales, and left with the amount owed him reduced to £300. Book business was obviously brisk.

The first colonists had looked upon books as expensive though desirable commodities, whose worth had to be weighed against the many other goods needed from England. Their sons and grandsons in the wealthier and better settled towns did not have so many choices to make in deciding between a book and another import. A learned divine like Cotton Mather might accumulate a great library of 3,000 volumes, but the sailor, farmer, or merchant owned books too. Riffling through a peddler's pack or the stalls of a general merchandise store, even an average citizen of the 1690's found that books would help him prepare for the afterworld, meet the problems of daily life, and divert his idle hours. This attitude was well illustrated time and again in the diary of Samuel Sewall. Though wealthier and more learned than most men, Sewall held to these prevailing beliefs, feeling that books were the nicest and most persuasive of all worldly objects.

When Sewall's wife died, he fixed his eye on Mrs. Denison as a likely successor. To her he gave 'Dr. Mather's Sermons very well bound' and a 'Psalm Book neatly bound in England with Turkey-Leather,' along with some almonds, shoe buckles, and miscellaneous bric-a-brac. Although her answer was 'No,' Samuel was not discouraged about the efficacy of books. He found Mrs. Tilley to be a more amenable widow, willing to say 'Yes' after receiving only the copy of Cotton Mather's *Ornaments for the Daughters of Sion* which he had given his first wife seventeen years earlier. Unfortunately, the simple Mrs. Tilley lived but seven months as Mrs. Sewall. The widower now turned his attention to Mrs. Winthrop. He laid the groundwork of this romance with a copy of Willard's *The Fountain Opened*, an unsuccessful publication whose remaining stock he bought twenty years after its printing. Tips to Mrs. Winthrop's servants, a piece of ginger cake 'wrapped up in a clean sheet of paper,' and several volumes, including an *Account of the State of the Indians on Martha's Vineyard* and Preston's *The Church's Marriage and The Church's Carriage* (which cost him six shillings) had no effect. Indeed,

Mrs. Winthrop turned his own book against him when he objected to buying a periwig, which she considered a prerequisite to their marriage, for she quoted Preston that ''twas inconvenient keeping out of a fashion commonly used.' Realizing that he was getting nowhere with Mrs. Winthrop, Sewall turned to the widow Ruggles of Brookline, to whom he presented a copy of 'Mr. Moody's Election Sermon' bound in marbled boards. Mrs. Ruggles seems to have been no bibliophile either, so six months later Sewall was calling on Mrs. Gibbs of Newtown, with a copy of Cotton Mather's *India Christiana,* 'very well bound, gilded on the edge, inscribed to her with my own hand.' A book by Mather turned the trick again, for Mrs. Gibbs consented, and thereafter Sewall's book buying was for their joint collection.

The range of Judge Sewall's interest in books, as in women, was wider than that of his more conventional neighbors, but his point of view on either subject would have been considered quite normal. One required helpmates through this life, and to this end books were nearly as important as human beings. The New Englander, even in the most desperate days of early colonization, was never a man of but one book. The Bible answered fundamental needs in all problems encountered on the walk through life, but every book had its place in helping to meet all the travail and pleasure of the long and winding path from the cradle to the grave.

Chapter 2

The Age of Reason

A century after the *Mayflower* put into Plymouth harbor the Americans were well settled on their land. They had carved it into thirteen colonies and pushed its frontier into the mountains. Inland a new generation of pioneers struggled in the austerity of the wilderness, but in scattered settlements along the coast men had leisure to enjoy the comfortable variety of town life. In a hundred years, more or less, the seaboard colonists worked themselves out of their narrow, heavy-laden pattern of life to achieve a culture comparable in refinement to that of provincial England. Few cities of the empire could surpass those of America. Boston still dominated other settlements, its population increasing from 7,000 to 17,000 during the first fifty years of the eighteenth century. Philadelphia, with little more than half as many people at the opening of the century, very nearly equaled Boston at the midway mark, and by 1800 was as large a city as Liverpool. No wonder that a proud citizen wrote:

> Europe shall mourn her ancient fame declined
> And Philadelphia be the Athens of mankind.

The residents of New York, Newport, or Charleston could have substituted the names of their home towns in this couplet with some improvement of meter and no harm to the sense. Even though but 5 per cent of the population lived in these five cities, from and through them came the manufactures and ideas that prevailed elsewhere. Their docks received the foreign cargoes and their shops made the native products that provided refinements for the hinterland. They were the keystones to the cultures that were slowly being joined to make a distinctive American civilization.

As yet there was no uniform culture throughout the colonies, but the English was dominant. The English language, school system, formal literature, and balladry led all others. If in New York the colonist could buy Dutch books at almost any stationer's shop and if in Pennsylvania he could find texts written for the German, Swiss, and Scotch-Irish immigrants, alongside such popular Quaker works as Penn's *No Cross, No Crown*, the prevailing books were those which, allowing for a slight lag, the English were reading at home. And those books most in demand, though still utilitarian, were more and more worldly in their conception of what it was useful to know.

The settled towns were growing not only British but sophisticated. There seems to have been no outcry in 1722 when a Harvard students' club publicly debated 'Whether it be Fornication to lye with one's Sweetheart (after contract) before Marriage?' Even if that practice did not become established, lesser sins became popular in the old citadel of Puritanism. In the 1730's Boston had over a hundred and fifty licensed drinking houses, a few gaming resorts without license, a public billiard room, and a dancing master. By 1772 Boston imported 6,000 packs of playing cards for a population of fewer than 18,000 inhabitants.

Just as tailors and wigmakers advertised that their goods were of the latest English mode, so the elite of the coastal cities proclaimed its manners followed the English fashion. For this society were printed colonial editions of such works as *The Lady's Preceptor* and for its domestic help such manuals as Eliza Haywood's *A Present for a Servant-Maid* and Hannah Glasse's *Servants Directory*. In the 'seventies high society studied the graces through the writings of Chesterfield, while simpler folk aped them secondhand, even though some said his morals were as bad as those of Clarissa Harlowe's Lovelace. The early settlers had considered manners synonymous with morality, but these eighteenth-century people learned from Chesterfield that social deportment and ethics were separate affairs. A year after the *Letters* were issued in England, New York published its own four-volume edition, which was several times reprinted, and so highly was its author esteemed that a bookdealer sold the *Memoires* of Cardinal de Retz by advertising it as 'recommended warmly by Lord Chesterfield.' Chesterfield's work was frequently reissued in abridged and expurgated form and to the great Lord was also attributed the older *Family Companion; or the Oeconomy of Human Life,* another treatise on polite behavior, first published by Franklin in 1751 and reprinted some forty times during the remainder of the century.

An urban society developing a high standard of refinement and looking to England for cultural guidance and social stability had need of many books besides those on etiquette. Educated people usually imported long or erudite texts, which American printers could not afford to publish or which American book buyers wanted in editions more elegant than those produced on colonial presses. But by 1755 ten colonies had twenty-four presses, and Lawrence Wroth estimates that that year they ran off 1,200 different titles, almost one for every thousand people. This variety permitted great opportunities for selection of different kinds of books. In the cities the book business was brisk. Boston opened sixteen new stores in the first decade of the century and soon introduced book auctions as well. As early as 1730 the Bay Colony capital with its five newspapers was acknowledged to be a center of English publishing and bookselling second only to London. Soon a dealer like John Mein needed a full page of the *Massachusetts Magazine* to advertise the books 'just imported,' which rounded out his stock of 9,000 volumes. Philadelphia, with five bookstores in 1742, had thirty in the 1770's, and James Rivington, one of the proprietors, proclaimed that he was ready to furnish 'Country Shopkeepers . . . with a very great variety of . . . Books.' Even a little town like Annapolis had a bookseller as early as 1700, and, not much later, 58 per cent of Maryland's free whites owned books. Of course there were more people who could and would read Captain Charles Johnson's lives of the highwaymen than Dr. Samuel Johnson's *Lives of the Poets,* but as an English commentator observed of America, 'the common people are on a footing, in point of literature, with the middle ranks of Europe. It is scarce possible to conceive the number of readers with which even every little town abounds.'

The taste for reading, having become established in the eighteenth-century town, slowly spread out toward the lonely clearings to the west. About 90 per cent of the people lived on isolated farms or in rude communities hacked from the forest, their secular reading usually limited to such works as *The Farmer's Companion* or Jared Eliot's *Essay upon Field-Husbandry,* for pioneer settlers obtained books of general interest only infrequently and by chance. Yet, in addition to *Husband-man's Guides,* peddlers hawked chapbooks, almanacs, and such sure-fire sellers as *Pilgrim's Progress*. Traveling through the countryside, sometimes bartering new books for old, the tradesmen occasionally left more sophisticated fare in some small settlements. So it was that the effete William Byrd, journeying in the backwoods of North Carolina in 1732, expressed no surprise at coming upon a copy of Gay's *Beggar's Opera*, produced but four years earlier in London.

The increased reading public could not always find enough copies of favored books available or enough shillings in their purses to buy them. The solution was the subscription or circulating library established in Philadelphia by Franklin before it was known in London. In midsummer of 1731 he got 50 subscribers to pay 40 shillings each to a Library Company, which imported 84 volumes to circulate freely among the members, each member pledging 10 shillings more a year for additions.

Franklin's scheme was soon imitated in other colonies. Most of the libraries charged a flat sum for membership, which could be afforded by few outside the merchant and professional groups, but some poorer people also used the libraries, paying their fees in grain, butter, or flax. The length of time members were allowed to keep books varied according to the length of the text or the distance of their homes from the library. A big folio was generally loaned for a month; a small work the size of a current novel, for a week. In the 'sixties one Boston library with 1,200 volumes announced that it was prepared to 'amuse the man of leisure, to afford an elegant and agreeable relaxation to the minds of men of business and to insinuate knowledge and instruction under the veil of entertainment to the fair sex.' Another petulantly advertised that the failure to return books tended 'to frustrate the very establishment, and, instead of a *Circulating*, to render it a *Stagnated* Library.' Still, business was generally good. At the beginning of the Revolution there were as many circulating libraries as colonies. By then the common man was using them, and even as early as 1772 the librarian of Franklin's old organization remarked that 'for one person of distinction and fortune, there were twenty tradesmen' who frequented this library. Before the century was out, the circulating library was so firmly established as a business that other shopkeepers, indeed even two Boston milliners, were adding rental books to their stock in trade.

In circulating libraries and bookstores historical studies were popular, for the colonists, with their growing worldliness, were curious to learn how man had governed his affairs in the past and how the mundane problems of society might be met without divine assistance. As the century wore on private libraries containing more than half a dozen titles generally had some history book among them. When a Philadelphia printer in 1770 published Robertson's *History of the Reign of Charles V*, he proudly announced he set 'a price so moderate the Man of the Woods, as well as the Man of the Court' might own it, and several newspaper editors felt they could attract buyers with serializations of Robertson's *History of America*. Just as Rapin's *History of England* was one of the books in the £4 estate of a Baltimore ironmaster (who in addition left his heirs only clothes, a penknife, two razors, and an ink pot), so Smollett's *History of England,* published cheaply in parts, was to be found in many a modest home. It arrived there, too, without the wonderful expedient of the British publisher who sent every English parish clerk a half-crown as compensation for distributing prospectuses through the church pews.

Ezra Stiles, the New England divine, showed an outmoded point of view in declaring, 'Voluminous Writing is not necessary to History. The History of the World may be contained completely in one Quarto Volume, especially of such a small world as this.' Most of his contemporaries did not agree. As Gibbon remarked, 'the historian was crowned the taste or fashion of the day,' and he might nearly as well have referred to the colonies as to England when he declared with authorial hyperbole, 'my book was on every table, and almost on every toilette.' True, there was some objection to the *Decline and Fall* as an anti-Christian work extolling 'infidel principles' and a 'martial spirit,' but, though the president of Harvard had to announce 'Gibbon's History was never thought of' for the curriculum, it was commonly found in private collections alongside Clarendon's *History of the Rebellion,* Bishop Burnet's *History of My Own Times,* and the chronicles of Hume, Goldsmith, Smollett, and Voltaire.

For a more specialized audience legal studies gave a further feeling that man might bring order into the world by his own logic. The first English edition of the *Commentaries* by the new Oxford professor Blackstone sold a thousand copies in America, preparing the way a few years later for a Philadelphia printing which had an advance sale of 1,400 copies. There were but a few hundred professional lawyers in the colonies at the time, so the book must have been popular among legislators and laymen with property to protect, such as the New York merchant who declared that Blackstone 'brought that Mysterious Business to some System.' The frequent appearance of the book in inventories of small estates confirms the observation of a leading English bookseller that 'in no branch of his business, after tracts of popular devotion, were so many books as those of the law exported to the plantations.'

Refined society also took to reading poetry, though most folk preferred simpler fare. In part, the interest in poetry was another result of man's search for inspiration from human rather than divine sources; in part it was simply a following of British style and a susceptibility to the same kinds of literature that pleased Englishmen. So it was that when Queen Caroline took up the Wiltshire bard, Stephen Duck, and made him into a courtly nightingale, American colonists hurried to buy over 1,200 copies of his mediocre verse. Yet, by and large, reading was considered as entertainment or as a utilitarian pursuit, even if this utility extended to the area of manners. The special language and meter of poetry set it off from the plain reader's area of pleasure and only a few poems were obviously useful. The older poets, including even Milton, were not much read, and though an individual like Thomas Buckingham had a copy of *Comus* with him in 1711 when marching with the Connecticut troops to New York, he was a minister in a class apart from the general reader. So far as Milton was known to Americans, it was generally as the author of *Paradise Lost;* and presumably Pope's *Essay on Man* was thought to be a better poem in justifying the ways of God to man.

The eighteenth-century mind was pleased by Pope's neat, easily read versification of ideas essentially suited to prose. He was the poet who more than any other filtered down to a general audience. His books were widely imported from England, forty-five editions of his *Essay on Man* were printed in America between 1747 and 1799, and snatches of his verse appeared in almanacs and journals. Pope was invoked like a god, or at least a muse, his poems quoted or imitated in magazines and newspapers to support any issue to which the lines could be made appropriate. Schoolmasters used Pope's verse to teach grammar and morality at one and the same time, but if the juvenile mind was better acquainted with Isaac Watts' *Divine Song for Children,* adult Americans generally preferred Pope's poems to Watts' *Horae Lyricae.* Mather Byles, a Boston versifier, wrote to Pope, 'We read you with Transport, and talk of you with Wonder.' Franklin, when ordering six sets of Pope's works in 1744, declared, 'That poet has many admirers here . . . Your authors know but little of the fame they have on this side of the ocean. We read their works with perfect impartiality, being at too great a distance to be biased by the factions, parties, and prejudices that prevail among you.' And somewhat later David Humphreys, a Connecticut Wit, observed, 'Every poet

who aspires to celebrity strives to approach the perfection of Pope.' Even
lesser English satirists like Charles Churchill had some favor, as is indicated by the 2,200 advance subscriptions a Philadelphia printer obtained
in 1769 for Churchill's works. The more vigorous and comic satire of
Samuel Butler's *Hudibras* had a wide audience, particularly in the South,
where Louis B. Wright finds it had a greater popularity than any other
poem. New England necessarily was less likely to look kindly upon this
scornful picture of Puritanism, yet the Hartford poet John Trumbull
popularized its style in his widely read *M'Fingal*.

Only in the last quarter of the century did the growth of a feminine
reading public affected by the sentimental novel bring softer, more emotional and elegiac poetry into demand. Goldsmith's *Deserted Village*,
first issued in Philadelphia in 1771, required twelve American editions
and many imports before 1800. Still more popular was Thomson's sweetly
tranquil depiction of the countryside in *The Seasons*. It was a favorite
with heroines of sentimental novels and with the young ladies who emulated the bucolic musings of these fictional characters. Even Franklin
wrote his London agent, 'Whatever Thomson writes send me a dozen
copies of. That charming poet has brought more tears of pleasure into
my eyes than all I ever read before.' From Thomson to the pensive *Elegy
in a Country Churchyard* and the more mournful 'Graveyard Poets' was
but a step, and a step easily taken by many readers who bought the eight
American editions of Young's *Night Thoughts* and the twelve of Blair's
The Grave, along with many copies imported from England. As one
young lady commented, 'We all seem'd in the pensoroso style,' and another, upon hearing her home was burned during the Revolution, remarked that if the Bible and *Night Thoughts* were spared she would not
grieve for the rest of her books.

Literature was not wholly restricted to the printed word. A people
growing more worldly were now willing to accept the once reviled drama.
By 1716 Williamsburg had a theater, and in 1736 the students of William
and Mary were producing Addison's *Cato* at the same time as Charleston's Dock Street Theatre opened with Farquhar's *Recruiting Officer*.
Thomas Kean's company played Philadelphia in 1750 and moved on to
New York, where their repertoire included dramas by Shakespeare, Congreve, Dryden, Gay, Lillo, Farquhar, Otway, and Addison. In a town
of fewer than 20,000 people a consecutive run of 24 different plays was
a triumph. By 1761 the theater had invaded Rhode Island, the most
liberal of the New England colonies. The manager, armed with a letter

of recommendation from the Governor of Virginia, still considered it expedient to produce *Othello* as 'A Moral Dialogue, in five parts, depicting the evil effects of jealousy and other bad passions, and proving that happiness can only spring from the pursuit of virtue.' So that nobody would feel he had spent good money to attend the Devil's Chapel, the moral dialogue in five parts was gratis, but spectators paid for the concerts between acts. The emotional effect of plays was widely appreciated and at Valley Forge, Washington raised the morale of his troops with a performance of *Cato*, Addison's dramatization of the stand for liberty against the tyranny of a Caesar.

Plays were even more widely known in print than on the stage. Lillo's *George Barnwell*, for example, appeared serially during 1732 in *The New England Weekly Journal*, soon after its London production, while Dodsley's *Toy Shop* was published in Virginia and South Carolina newspapers. In the 'thirties a Boston bookseller advertised the dramas of Aphra Behn and some Restoration comedies. The small town of Salem in 1760 imported for its Social Library copies of plays by Lillo, Gay, Mrs. Centlivre, Dodsley, Steele, and Farquhar. Gaine's New York bookstore in 1761 featured George Colman's newly published *The Jealous Wife*, along with copies of Vanbrugh's *Provok'd Wife*, Shakespeare's *King Lear* and *Tempest*, an adaptation of *The Taming of the Shrew*, and plays by Rowe, Dryden, and others currently popular in England. Goldsmith's *She Stoops to Conquer* was published in New York and Philadelphia in 1773, the same year it appeared on the London stage, and Garrick's *Irish Widow* was printed in the colonies just a year after its production in England.

Shakespeare, given an amateur production in 1730, was known to some Americans even before the opening of the century, when at least one copy of a play by him was recorded in a private collection. By 1722 there was a set of his works in the New England *Courant* library, Harvard catalogued Rowe's edition the following year, at Philadelphia in 1744 Dr. Hamilton picked up a copy of *Timon* (probably Shadwell's adaptation), Franklin's circulating library included Shakespeare in 1746, and before the century was out Dr. Johnson's edition was printed in Philadelphia. Allusions to Shakespearean lines (particularly the 'To be or not to be' soliloquy) in the Revolutionary War propaganda of both sides assume the public had some knowledge of the dramatist's works. Over 15 per cent of New York's and Philadelphia's performances from 1766 to 1768 were Shakespearean plays, and, in all, fourteen different dramas by Shakespeare were produced in the colonies before the Revolution.

Although Timothy Dwight, the Connecticut minister and poet, declared that 'to indulge a taste for play-going means nothing more or less than the loss of that most invaluable treasure, the immortal soul,' plenty of Americans, accepting the drama along with other worldly pleasures, were now seriously beginning to doubt whether the divines alone really knew all the answers about men's souls. The prevailing intellectual movement was from revelation to rationalism, from supernaturalism to science. Among the texts that helped confirm these new points of view the most widely read included Addison and Steele's *Tatler* and *Spectator* papers. Addison declared his desire was to have it said that he 'brought philosophy out of closets, schools, and colleges, to dwell in clubs, assemblies, at tea-tables, and in coffee-houses,' and this, it appears, is approximately what he and Steele did in the colonies, as in England. The average educated American found the sentiments of *The Tatler* and *The Spectator* just those he would have liked to frame for himself. The influence of Addison and Steele was to be seen in every American journal, just as their works were displayed in every bookshop. When a provincial political dispute rocked New York in the 1730's, the adherents of both sides rushed into newspaper controversy imitating or quoting Addison and Steele; when Franklin taught himself to write, it was by modeling his style on that of *The Spectator;* and when he founded his *Courant,* the very first words echoed Addison's introduction to *The Spectator.* College boys and rural parsons alike subscribed to the paper or bought the collected volumes. Jonathan Edwards treasured them along with his divinity texts; Cotton Mather noted in his diary that he contemplated 'sending some Agreeable Things to the Author of The Spectator.'

It is just as well that Mather did not carry out his intention, for he ran the risk of a rejection. His was essentially a mind of the last century, and *The Spectator* was representative of a new period. Dr. Johnson, Defoe, Swift, Locke, Pope, and Paine were the kinds of authors now wanted in England, Old and New. When Dr. Johnson scornfully remarked, 'The Americans! What do they know and what do they read,' an American acquaintance promptly replied, 'They read, Sir, the *Rambler.*' In South Carolina, a Charleston bookdealer was advertising Defoe's works in 1733. *Gulliver's Travels* was obviously well known throughout the colonies, for newspaper editors felt their public would understand when they spoke of political enemies as 'this Yahoo' or 'these Lilliputians.' Comments about Swift's book turn up in widely different situations during the 'seventies. A Boston schoolgirl wrote in her diary that a cousin 'lent me Gulliver's

Travels abbreviated, which aunt says I may read for the piece was de-
sin'd as a burlesque upon the times in which it was wrote.' A thousand
miles away in the wilderness of Kentucky, Daniel Boone read the book
by campfire and named a stream Lorbrulgrud, after the capital of
Brobdingnag.

This changing taste of Americans is synopsized in the advertisements
of bookstores. In 1731 Bradford's Philadelphia store featured only religious texts, but by 1736 the books he billed were *The Spectator, The
Tatler,* Steele's *Guardian,* the English *Cato's Letters,* and only one religious treatise. Two years later, Franklin, who understood the times, was
advertising that his store sold *The Guardian,* Locke's *Essay concerning
Human Understanding,* Pope's *Homer,* Swift's *A Tale of a Tub,* Dryden's
Fables, and a four-volume set of Rabelais. People who had with Addison
and Steele made a rational survey of man's manners and foibles, and who
had read Swift's virulent denunciation of human institutions grounded on
his belief that 'I am in all opinions to believe according to my own im-
partial reason' were of a mind to investigate themselves and the world
about them with increased common sense. A virile grasp of facts and a
rational use of them were what many enlightened readers desired of their
books. As they observed a logic in man's actions and a reasonable relationship in natural events, these readers bit by bit grew skeptical about
the old explanation of events as sportive providences of an inscrutable
Deity. The terrible earthquake that rocked New England and New York
in the mid-century was still, in parsons' tracts and sermons, accounted
but another symptom of divine irritation, yet readers might find other
pamphlets whose geological data would shake their minds as much as
their bodies had been buffeted by the temblor itself. Observation was
beginning to defeat authority. Men were willing enough to retain God
as an original first cause of earthquakes or anything else, yet many were
beginning to believe that through scientific investigation rather than
through the words of inspired prophets they might learn how the mechanism of His created universe worked.

In part the new attitude toward God and nature was caused by new
theories; in part it was the ironic result of a desire for a more intellectual
approach after all passion was spent in the last emotional upheaval of
Calvinism, known as the Great Awakening. Frenzied clamoring for salvation absorbed almost the whole psychic energy of the people from the
mid-1730's to '40's, but the duration of the revival was as brief as it was
intense. During those years religious books were in great demand. Be-

tween 1739 and 1741 the evangelical sermons of Whitefield were more often printed than the works of any other author, foreign or native, religious or lay. At the beginning of the century, Cotton Mather's books had circulated in numbers out of proportion to his popularity, because he gave them away at a rate of six hundred a year, but no divine needed to worry that he would not be read during the revival years when people throughout the colonies were overcome by raptures of regeneration. But if the people were held in an ecstasy of fear and atonement for a decade or so, they were also divided into sects whose theological differences were not always so sharp as their mere acceptance of schism, and finally they were exhausted. Their minds were open for new ways to look upon God and the world.

Newton was the most inspiring guide in this search to rule out mystery, for his mathematical observations banished miracles by illustrating general principles of a natural law. Although Newton's works were included in several libraries patronized by the wealthy upper classes, only a few plain citizens like Thomas Godfrey, the Philadelphia glazier, knew his *Principia Mathematica* first hand. But Newton's theories on an immutable and universal natural law were widely popularized through almanacs, through abridgments of the sort that the Marquis de Chastellux was surprised to find at a Massachusetts inn during the 1780's, as well as through Addison and other easily read authors. Science was not, as the Reverend Thomas Prince contended in his analysis of the 1755 earthquake, trying to lead man 'out of the mighty Hand of God.' Rather, science was helping man to understand that there was a natural order, whose laws, designed by God, could be discovered through human reason instead of through a superstitious centering of religious affections on a sole book—the Bible. That was why Mason Weems, the itinerant parson and bookseller, could honestly write his Philadelphia publisher, 'For my sake—for your sake and for God's sake send me *instantly* 200 copies' of Goldsmith's *History of the Earth, and Animated Nature.*' The people agreed with Weems's sense of urgency, for between Alexandria and Norfolk, Virginia, he sold nearly a thousand copies within a twelvemonth. Goldsmith's hack work, the encyclopedic studies of 'Sir' John Hill, and other popular scientific treatises sold well throughout the colonies, so that Horace Walpole's comment, 'natural history is in fashion,' was a fair though unintentional description of taste in the colonies as well as in England toward the end of the century.

Foreign books, widely available in translation, also contributed to the move toward rationalism. Perhaps most popular were the unorthodox works of Voltaire. Bookstores from Albany to Baltimore advertised imported editions over a long period of time, subscription libraries commonly owned them, newspapers and magazines often reprinted excerpts, and before 1800 separate works were issued by six of America's bookselling printers. Voltaire's *Philosophical Dictionary, Candide,* and various histories were examples of the kind of acute common sense and vigorous criticism of church and state that pleased many people at the time. The versatility he showed in touching on ideas in which Americans were interested led a few of the wealthiest or most cultivated to watch for everything he wrote. 'Has Voltaire published any late tracts?' Charles Carroll of Maryland inquired of an English friend in 1771, explaining that he owned everything but that which might be very recent. Another Baltimore resident, Mr. Parkin, had seventy volumes of Voltaire's works in his home along with seventy-six by the French naturalist Buffon; the liberal Jonathan Mayhew of Martha's Vineyard, though he could not endorse Voltaire's religious views, declared he read him 'with high delight'; and even the orthodox Calvinist pastor, Ezra Stiles, declared that 'Voltairs profane Philos. Dictionary has some instructive remarks.'

Voltaire may have been the most popular French author, but no single book of his seems to have been so well read as was Fénelon's *Télémaque.* This political novel written to instruct a king's grandson that monarchs exist for the people, and not the other way around, was a tract welcome to colonists whose parents had rid themselves of a king claiming to rule by divine right and who themselves were already objecting to a parliament that taxed but did not represent them. Even after the American Revolution, Parson Weems could write from Virginia that 'Telemaque Eng. & French are *much much wanted.*'

Rousseau's works were advertised almost as widely as those by Voltaire and Fénelon, though his fiction was better known than his pure theory, and Montesquieu's writings, particularly the *Spirit of Laws,* were frequently imported in French and British editions as well as being extracted in newspapers. Whatever foreign books were read, the evidence is that they, like those of English origin, were generally liberal or at least rationalistic in point of view.

The French authors known to the colonists were, on the whole, those who confirmed or extended ideas set forth by English philosophers and political theorists. Supreme among these Englishmen was John Locke. Private and circulating libraries up and down the coast were stocked with his writings, colleges used his works as texts, and booksellers seemed always to have a London edition for sale. The complete works were fairly common, but most popular of all were the *Essay concerning Human Understanding* and the *Treatises of Civil Government*. Refuting the belief in innate ideas, Locke's *Essay* lucidly and systematically showed that knowledge was a product of the mind reflecting upon sense impressions derived from the outside world. This thesis that man requires only his own experience and reason to understand his place in the universe dealt a terrible blow to orthodox scriptural revelation and the Calvinist ideas of predestination.

The scientists, headed by Newton, showed that nature worked by certain general edicts; the philosophers, led by Locke, taught that man's knowledge of truth depended on observation instead of subjective belief. The two together opened the way for deism, leading extremists to see the cosmos as a mechanism originally wound up by God and thereafter run by such immutable and understandable laws as that of gravity, their creator merely standing by as a 'Passive Policeman.' To the deists this proved that God did not perform adventitious miracles, the reasons for which were only vaguely revealed to certain people banded together in a certain church. Locke may have been the most widely read single source of deism, but the natural scientists of England, the French philosophers, and the theologians like Blount and Tindal were among the many other writers whose books brought deism to the land.

In England, deism reached a climax in the early part of the century, but America, because of a normal cultural lag and various native forces— such as the Great Awakening—did not fully feel its effect until somewhat later. True, deistic literature seeped into the country early enough to warrant the publication in 1734 of *A Short and Easy Method with the Deists*, and most of the men who became leaders of the Revolution were early inclined toward deism. Jefferson, though profoundly religious, was deistic in his belief, as was Franklin; Adams was hardly orthodox, and Paine, of course, was determined to make his an age of reason in religion. When the time came to write a federal constitution, the mundane preamble had nothing conventional to say about the blessings of an almighty God; the first amendment specifically declared that there should be 'no law respecting an establishment of religion'; and at the very end of the century Washington declared in a statement to Tripoli (perhaps meant only for export to Mohammedans) that 'the government of the United States is not in any sense founded upon the Christian religion.'

The President's statement may have been extreme, but the intellectual tone of the latter part of the century was opposed to revealed Christianity. When new colleges were founded, such as the University of Pennsylvania in 1751 and King's College in 1754, there was no thought that they should be used primarily to train the clergy. Matters were presumably no better in the older institutions of learning. Whitefield, visiting Harvard in 1740, found that 'bad books are become fashionable.' Of course, he was a biased reporter who by 'bad' meant simply Tillotson and Clarke, both rationalists, one an Archbishop of Canterbury in the past century, the other a writer against out-and-out deism. And if the students did read them it must have been from private copies, for Tillotson was not withdrawn from the college library for nine years (1732-41) and Clarke slumbered in the stacks between 1739 and 1741. Perhaps Whitefield's fears were merely a bit premature, for by 1794 even the students admitted they could observe a tendency toward skepticism; the administration found the trend so strong that it gave each undergraduate a copy of Bishop Watson's *Apology for the Bible,* an answer to Thomas Paine, several times reprinted in this country. At Yale the drift to deism was even worse, if we can believe Lyman Beecher, who observed that in 1793 the 'college was in a most ungodly state. The college church was almost extinct.' In the second half of the century only a third of the graduates entered the ministry. Beecher, one of the devout, declared that the boys 'read Tom Paine and believed him . . . most of the class before me were infidels, and called each other Voltaire, Rousseau, D'Alembert, etc.' From the University of North Carolina one boy wrote home in 1795 that the students' favorite reading was Paine's *Age of Reason,* and that Locke's *Essay concerning Human Understanding,* Gibbon's *Decline and Fall,* and Helvétius's *On the Human Mind* circulated widely. Because such inclinations were common on American campuses, the faculties of Rhode Island College, Queens College, and Union College sponsored baccalaureate addresses on the theme that Biblical revelation was superior to deistic philosophy.

By the 'seventies deism was fairly well established in the minds of the more sophisticated city people and began to infiltrate the back country. John Adams remarked that deistic literature 'circulated with some freedom' in Worcester and similar country towns. A little later, Mason Weems, when writing his publisher for stock with which to found a Virginia bookstore, warned, 'let the Moral and Religious be as highly dulcified as possible. Divinity, for this climate sh^d be very rational and lib-

eral.' But there were plenty of conservative people throughout the country who were horrified at the ideas of deism. When a Northampton resident ordered Hume's *Essays* and Leland's *Views of Deistical Writers* from
a Boston bookseller, he arranged their delivery with all the surreptitious-
ness attaching to contraband traffic, and when another New Englander
had the misfortune to die with a copy of Ethan Allen's *Reason the Only
Oracle of Man* in his bedroom, the book was viewed by hundreds of
people as 'an awful curiosity,' while his unhappy minister admitted 'a terrible opposition to me fixed in the minds of the devout and ignorant mul-
titude.' In Goshen, New York, there were, however, enough people interested in deism to warrant the village storekeeper's request that Allen
exchange a few copies of his book for credit in general merchandise.
Even if Goshen was an unusual town, deistic ideas slipped into the villages through the medium of almanacs and newspapers, for, from the
time of Franklin to that of Freneau, these city-bred sheets were generally
rationalist and frequently unorthodox in their ideas. As the Reverend
Robert Hall wrote in an English sermon reprinted in this country when
it was thought necessary,

Hume, Bolingbroke, and Gibbon addressed themselves solely to the more polished classes of the community, and would have thought their refined specula-
tions debased by an attempt to enlist disciples from among the populace. Infidelity has lately grown more condescending; . . . having at length reached its
full maturity, it boldly ventures to challenge the suffrages of the people, solicits
the acquaintance of peasants and mechanics, and seeks to draw whole nations
to its standard.

Anti-deist tracts such as Hall's helped call attention to these heterodox
works. Most people knew deism, as their descendants came to know Communism, only through the attacks upon it, until curiosity led them to investigate a particularly notorious book or two. The work that created the
greatest noise of all was Tom Paine's *Age of Reason*, which called out at
least thirty-six different replies, as well as leading some booksellers to
advertise unrelated texts like *The Pious Christian* as a 'very valuable book
in spite of Deism, Tom Paine, and the Devil.' Heroines of novels were
even enlisted in the anti-Paine campaign. One of them, in a novel published in 1795, upon being asked by her fiancé to read Paine, replied,
'I am chagrined and mortified beyond expression to find the man, whom
I have esteemed more than any other, has imbibed sentiments which
must separate us forever.' Such strictures may have kept a few timorous
swains from reading Paine, but there were enough hardy fellows to re-

quire publishers to issue eight different editions of *The Age of Reason* in 1794 and another seven the following year. Two more editions appeared in 1796, in which year the second part, with its sensational attack on the Bible's inconsistencies, was often sold separately; for from France Paine sent 15,000 copies of this part to supplement the circulation of native editions. Sales were so brisk that the book peddler Weems, even though he was a parson, could not resist turning a quick penny by stocking *The Age of Reason*, though he said he always sold the Bishop of Llandaff's reply as an antidote. If advertisements and comment are any criteria, it was among the most widely read books at the end of the century and certainly the most popular of all deistic texts.

After the period of *The Age of Reason*, Volney's *Ruins*, an elementary analysis of comparative religion, was probably the most read of deistic works. Translated from the French by Jefferson and by Joel Barlow (who was responsible for the first printing of Paine's book), Volney's treatise was published in three American editions. To supplement them, 1,200 copies of a translation made in France were shipped to New York in 1803, and alert booksellers imported many copies from the six British editions published before 1808. The last and most militant of the deists was Elihu Palmer, whose *Principles of Nature*, supplemented by his two magazines and several deistic societies, attracted a fair number of followers in the larger cities. Deism had changed from an intellectual and rather aristocratic movement to one attracting a fairly large general public, but by the end of the century, when Palmer was active, it quickly dwindled to a cult for cranks championing quaint ideas such as Palmer's campaign to tax bachelors because as a class they were responsible for unmarried motherhood.

The maladjusted city people who temporarily embraced Palmer's fervid deism and other ill-assorted isms found their emotional needs better satisfied by a new wave of evangelical religion, which with all the familiar paraphernalia of revivals swept over the country at the end of the century. Free thinking and rational deism reached their apex during the 'nineties, when identified with the republican principles of the French Revolution, but as Americans became outraged at the excesses of the Revolution, the support for deism collapsed. Where Ethan Allen once wrote 'My affections are Frenchified,' and summoned a good deal of sympathy on that account, an author in 1800 could hope to win sales by advertising her novel in this fashion:

> This volume to the reader's eye displays
> Th' infernal conduct of abandoned man;
> When French philosophy infects his ways,
> And pours contempt on Heav'n's eternal plan.

The Reign of Terror numbered American deism among its victims. Godless intellectualism was smothered under the opprobrium directed at all things French during the period of Adams's administration. The century that had begun by introducing rationalism ended by ostracizing deism as one of its principal tyrannies. Rationalism itself was not dead, but its sphere was once again that of the pure and applied sciences, untouched by the common folk, who now turned either to a revival of conservatism or to romantic escape.

Chapter 3

Common Sense

Americans of the eighteenth century became increasingly concerned with establishing themselves in this world rather than in the one to come. When Franklin in 1734 issued *Every Man his Own Doctor* and two years later published *Every Man his Own Lawyer,* he knew what practical men needed and wanted; and there was ironic significance in his humorous announcement that he would soon print a book titled *Every Man his Own Priest.* Men living on a frontier might need books telling them how to heal physical or legal wounds without professional aid, but Franklin implied that these publications had a greater meaning: they taught that a man could make of himself what he wanted.

These eighteenth-century colonists were interested in improving their lot, personal and social, that they might more fully obtain what were called natural rights. As Jacob Duché observed in 1772,

The poorest labourer upon the shore of the *Delaware* thinks himself entitled to deliver his sentiments in matters of religion or politics with as much freedom as the gentleman or scholar . . . Such is the prevailing taste for books of every kind, that almost every man is a reader; and by pronouncing sentence, right or wrong, upon the various publications that come in his way, puts himself upon a level, in point of knowledge, with their several authors.

For readers of all classes political realities were crowding out religious revelations. The shift showed itself in the way Americans looked upon all aspects of their scene, even upon that common feature of the landscape—

the Indian. The red man was at no time clearly understood by the colonists, who appropriated his gifts in agriculture, medicine, and forest fighting as readily as they seized his lands; but the nature of the misunder-
standing changed as the whites' basic philosophic ideas shifted. The early
colonists looked upon the Indians as the Devil's children, to be Chris-
tianized if possible; otherwise to be killed or driven out so that the land
occupied by Satan might come into the hands of the godly. The colonists
of the eighteenth century did not generally consider the Indian innately
wicked but thought that, though he had been molded by his environment,
he could be reshaped by the whites for their own political purposes.
Treaties were made with his 'nations,' and his history and character were
studied that better use might be made of him. To woo the red man the
Americans tried even such dubious practices as entertaining ten Cherokee
chiefs at a New York production of Shakespeare's *Richard III* in 1767.
Even though the Indian's origins were sometimes still explained in quaint
Biblical terms that made him a descendant of the Lost Tribes of Israel,
his more recent folkways and beliefs were seriously studied, not as anthro-
pology, but as part of the science of politics. By the middle of the century books began to appear with such titles as *The Importance of Gaining the Friendship of the Indians to the British Interest* and *Enquiry into
the Causes of the Alienation of the Delaware and Shawanese Indians
from the British Interest.* These works accorded the Indians their new
position in the eyes of the whites: that of a people who held the balance of power in the century's interminable colonial wars among England, France, and Spain. Where the Indian could be prevailed to throw
his weight, there might victory lie. Victory was no longer conceived in
terms of the Indian's own soul but in terms of his lands and fighting
power serving an imperial and colonial scheme. No wonder that young
George Washington, acting temporarily as book salesman, sold two hundred copies of *The American Savage: How He May Be Tamed by the
Weapons of Civilization* in and around the small town of Alexandria,
Virginia.

Washington's brief bookselling career might have been even more
profitable had he vended some of the narratives known as Indian Captivities. Actually or ostensibly autobiographical accounts, often by poorly
educated people, these books described the narrator's capture, the cruel
march into the wilderness, the brutalities he suffered while living among
the Indians, and his eventual escape. Captivity literature was enormously
popular. Almost five hundred different titles belonging to this genre have

been collected by the Newberry Library and numerous editions were
printed of the most appealing works. Mrs. Mary Rowlandson's narrative,
first issued in 1682, had a fifteenth edition in 1800 and *The Redeemed
Captive,* telling the adventures of John Williams, was issued eight times
between the first edition of 1707 and 1800. Another popular example was
Jonathan Dickinson's *Journal; or, God's Protecting Providence,* describing how this Quaker and his family were seized by Spanish-allied Indians
who spoke vehemently of the 'English Son of a Bitch.' Every year saw
several of these books published or reissued and read by people as diverse
as William Adams, who carried Williams's book to Yale when he registered in 1730, and village housewives of the kind Mrs. Rowlandson was
herself.

Different readers found different meanings in the captivities, but most
of all the point of view of the authors themselves changed. The early
narratives are motivated by a pious faith, their details but part of an
essentially religious experience: a trial of the Christian spirit. In later
accounts, as Roy Harvey Pearce points out, the central figure no longer
views himself as a pious sufferer of God's inscrutable wisdom; he now
sees himself as a person malignantly oppressed by the fiendish enmity of
the Indian allied to the French or Spanish. Eventually, when this political bias was no longer a psychic need, the captivity degenerated into a
simple blood-and-thunder shocker. Even as late as the 1820's when Mary
Jemison's *Narrative* was widely read as a kind of pulp thriller, the captivity and torture story was a best-selling type of literature, and its popularity lasted until the dime novel was created. All the while the Indians
and their captivities remained realities, except in a few narratives padded
or falsified by hack writers, but if the facts did not change, the interpretations did. What happened to the white and Indian relation was merely
symptomatic of what was happening to the century's general shift from
religious to political interests.

Needing knowledge of civil affairs more than theological edification,
Charles Carroll of Maryland was representative of the general colonial
mind when in 1764 he wrote his English agent: 'I shall be obliged if you
Direct your Book Seller to Send me in yearly about fifteen or twenty
Shillings of the Best Political Pamphlets, but none of Religious Contro-
versy.' Three years later Carroll specifically asked for 'a Collection of the
Most Interesting Tracts which were Published in England or America on
the Subject of Taxing the American Colonies or Regulating their Trade.'
Carroll had more money and a better education than most Americans of

his time, but his basic interests in reading were in keeping with theirs. Like many plainer colonists, Carroll turned to Locke for guidance. The *Essay concerning Human Understanding* helped free Americans from a Deity known only through Biblical miracles and an organized church; his *Treatises of Civil Government* prepared them to be receptive toward a declaration of political independence. The *Treatises* formulated principles applicable to the current situation, since the colonists felt that Parliament was violating the natural rights inherent in Locke's concept of a compact between governor and governed. The popular almanac maker Nathaniel Ames summed up the situation in 1774 when he pointed out, 'As it is unpardonable for a Navigator to be without his charts so it is for a Senator to be without His which is Lock's Essay on Government.' If senators got their charts for the ship of state directly from Locke, plenty of the ordinary seamen also learned their political navigation from him. Harrington, Algernon Sidney, Shaftesbury, Hume, Berkeley, the prose works of Milton, and particularly Pufendorf's *Law of Nature and Nations* were read, but Locke's *Treatises* were more popular than all of these together. Locke was known to the average reader as no other political philosopher was, for not only were his own works widely read, but his essential ideas were echoed in the newspapers, pamphlets, sermons, speeches, and almanacs of the time.

The almanac was directed at the common man. One editor admitted our business is looked upon by many as low and vulgar, yet there are no Works so essential to the Well-being of the community.' He was quite right, since almanacs made information about current intellectual and social movements available to everybody. Young Nathaniel Ames's almanac of 1766 pictured the colonists happy 'under as good a King as ever reign'd,' but six years later he was extolling John Dickinson, 'The Patriotic American Farmer,' for defending the colonists' natural rights 'with Attic Eloquence and Roman Spirit.' *Bickerstaff's Boston Almanack* in 1769 printed a portrait of John Wilkes above open volumes by Locke and Sidney 'in whom,' it declared, 'the Spirit of the antient Republics revived.' The almanacs did more than open these volumes in portraiture, for they sometimes printed extracts indebted to their ideas, along with selections from such favorites as Addison, Steele, and Pope. In the decade prior to the outbreak of hostilities at Concord, almanacs were readying farmers for rebellion. The essential facts of current history were published, significant public documents and political tracts were synopsized, economic grievances were cited, snippets of patriotic poetry were printed,

and, finally, in 1775, some almanacs even got around to instructions on
how to make gunpowder at home. They were the plain man's abstracts
and brief chronicles of the time. As one maker declared, 'we are read by
Multitudes who read nothing else.' *Poor Richard Improved* sold some
10,000 copies a year, while Ames's more popular compilations circulated
an average of 60,000 copies annually between 1725 and 1764, bought at
the beginning of this period by one of every eleven, and at the end, by
one of every thirty-three people in the colonies.

Almanacs and weekly newspapers were two of the media to which
eighteenth-century readers turned for political guidance. They were
equally accustomed to the pamphlet, a form intermediary between the
book and the periodical, for it had long been used to circulate all kinds
of reading matter from sermons and orations to instructive essays. The
pamphlet had a perfect format for texts needing more space than newspapers could furnish, such as John Dickinson's *Letters from a Farmer in
Pennsylvania,* a conservative objection to British policy, or the *Votes and
Proceedings of the American Continental Congress,* which had thirty-
two printings in 1774. Simple political arguments sometimes appeared in
both forms, either first serialized or later extracted by newspapers, but
the pamphlet remained essentially the medium for considered thought
while the newspaper more often printed propaganda. Still, as one poetical
commentator observed in 1764:

> Pamphlets have madden'd round the Town,
> And drove poor Moderation down.

The most inflammatory statements or most sensational descriptions of
current events spilled out of pamphlets and newspapers into broadsides.
Handbills tacked on tavern walls, trees, or posts by night were more violent than newspapers, for printers, like authors, remained safely anonymous, and simple, vigorous statement appealed to those illiterates who
gathered around while more educated friends read the broadsides aloud.
Sometimes a text might appear in all three forms, but, by and large, there
were three different reading publics, each with its own medium.

After the battle of Lexington and Concord the pamphlet with its rea-
soned arguments dropped off in popularity. The time for analysis was
past; energies were given to the practical affairs of war. As one of the
North Carolina delegates to the Continental Congress noted early in 1776,
'we have searched almost every Booksellers shop in this City for pamphlets but have made a poor Collection, few are Written, none read, since

the appeal to arms.' Writers and readers were busy with practical affairs; type and paper were scarce; channels of circulation were interrupted by battles; and, with the depreciation of currency, prices for manufactured goods shot out of the common man's reach. Not even a single newspaper managed uninterrupted publication; two of the three magazines of the period went out of business and the third was stillborn. College library buildings were maltreated when used as barracks and hospitals, their books lost or, as the president of the College of Rhode Island complained, rendered 'very ragged and unsightly.' Private libraries were sometimes pilfered by soldiers of both armies, and occasionally they were deliberately destroyed by the British or lost by fire. Even though dealers with Royalist leanings in British-occupied towns managed to import the latest English books, the average American read less during the war. In 1775 when hostilities broke out, American printers issued 852 publications, but in 1781, the year of Cornwallis's surrender at Yorktown, their publications numbered only 371. Between these two extremes the quantity of publication varied with the degree of active warfare.

Only a very few works had sufficient appeal to receive wide circulation. One was John Trumbull's *M'Fingal*. Written in easy Hudibrastic couplets, this rollicking satire on the Tories was issued in a forty-page pamphlet late in 1775. The amusing burlesque was quickly pirated and hawked by peddlers and chapmen, so that a friend of the author complained that it appeared in an 'uncooth' form 'to catch the Vulgar by a low price.' Few pamphlets had a success of that sort, for few could be so easily read and few were desirable enough to make Tom, Dick, and Harry part with their hard-earned pence.

A week or two after the publication of Trumbull's poem there appeared another pamphlet which had an even more unusual success. It was a direct and sober piece of prose titled *Common Sense,* signed simply 'By an Englishman.' Thomas Paine's pamphlet was perfectly suited to the temper of the times, when towns on either end of the seaboard—the present Portland, Maine, and Norfolk, Virginia—had been burned to the ground by the British. It did not make jovial fun of the Tories, as had Trumbull; instead, in clear images and simple statements it reduced a complicated subject to one definite point: the colonists must declare their independence from Great Britain. Paine's argument, as he himself said, is 'as straight and clear as a ray of light . . . I bring reason to your ears, and, in a language as plain as ABC hold up truth to your eyes.' Only a few months before its publication, Franklin was able to state that he had never heard an expression in favor of independence 'from any person, drunk or sober,' and Washington, even after the battles of Lexington and Concord, had declared that 'one might set me down for everything wicked' if he prosecuted the war in order to achieve colonial independence. Except for comments by John Adams, Paine's was the first unqualified argument for political independence. But events of the preceding weeks had prepared people for the brilliant and forceful appeal Paine published on January 10, 1776. Within three weeks a second printing of *Common Sense* was needed; before the end of the month another edition was announced, with many copies 'already bespoke, one thousand for Virginia' alone. Edition after edition came off colonial presses. By the end of March over 100,000 copies were sold. America had never known such a popular book and not since its time has any book had such a quick or widespread sale relative to the population. One copy was sold for every twenty-five people in the colonies—men, women, and children— Whigs and Tories alike. It was the one great subject of conversation, outside the war, whose very purpose it helped to change. Two weeks after publication General Lee wrote to Washington, 'Have you seen the pamphlet "Common Sense"? I never saw such a masterly irresistible performance. It will, if I mistake not . . . give the "coup-de-grace" to Great Britain.' The day after the letter was received, Washington remarked that the brutality of the British campaign and 'the sound doctrine and unanswerable reasoning contained in the pamphlet "Common Sense" will not leave numbers at a loss to decide upon the propriety of separation.' Six months after Paine's pamphlet was issued in Philadelphia the same city witnessed the signing of the Declaration of Independence.

The autumn of 1776 was a black season for the Continental Army. It was defeated at Long Island, forced to retreat from New York, lost a battle at White Plains, and surrendered the redoubts at Fort Washington and Fort Lee; its Commander in Chief was put to flight with his ragged forces through New Jersey and across the Delaware. Paine, participating in the events, determined to change them with his pen if he could not with his sword. A month after the retreat from Fort Lee he finished another pamphlet and helped in its printing. It appeared just after Washington had privately admitted, 'if every nerve is not strained to the utmost to recruit the new army with all possible expedition, I think the game is pretty near up.' Paine's new pamphlet, *The American Crisis,* spoke in a different tone. With an incisive and stirring style he declared,

These are the times that try men's souls. The summer soldier and the sunshine patriot will, in this crisis, shrink from the service of their country; but he that stands it *now*, deserves the love and thanks of man and woman. Tyranny, like hell, is not easily conquered; yet we have this consolation with us, that the harder the conflict, the more glorious the triumph.

It was a wonderfully appealing call to arms. Two days after publication, Washington had the text read before his regiments drawn up in ranks. Another two days later Washington led his troops back across the Delaware and on to the victories at Trenton and Princeton.

During the next seven years of war and protracted peace negotiations Paine continued pamphleteering. At every critical point he wrote an issue of *The American Crisis,* each a separate pamphlet opposing compromise or exhorting fellow Americans to further endeavors, until finally, just eight years after the Battle of Lexington, he issued his last statement, calling for a strongly unified government. During all the war years he was America's most popular author, and his pamphlets were more widely read than any other writings. His defense of the French Revolution in *The Rights of Man,* like his deistic text, *The Age of Reason,* had many readers in the 'nineties, but they were not so numerous as those who composed his following during the Revolution, for the earlier writings were considered patriotic, the later, wildly radical.

Very different in spirit and style from Paine's pamphlets on *The American Crisis* were *The Federalist* papers, the only other series of political exposition to receive a wide reading. These eighty-five essays by Hamilton, Madison, and Jay, published under the appealing and concealing name of Publius, were issued at the rate of three or four a week in New York newspapers over an eight-month period from the fall of 1787 through the spring of 1788, and were soon the talk of the town. Achieving their purpose of persuading the voters to ratify the Constitution, they were collected in a two-volume edition which had a wide sale, though their more solid reputation did not come until the nineteenth century, when they were often reprinted as a fundamental exposition of American constitutional government, incidentally proving that one generation's light reading often becomes another's heavy text.

The Revolution won, the people had an opportunity to read more than tracts for the times. Zealous believers in democracy insisted that intellectual activities should be open to all, for a republican government demanded a literate and enlightened public. As one magazine contributor put it,

From public schools shall general knowledge flow,
For 'tis the people's sacred right—to know.

The spread of popular education brought about huge sales of textbooks, dictionaries, and spellers. Most popular of all was Noah Webster's *American Spelling Book* (at first more elegantly entitled *A Grammatical Institute of the English Language*), which sold some 24,000,000 copies between the date of its publication in 1783 and that of its author's death in 1843, becoming the best seller of all American books. Substantial revision kept the famous 'Blue Back Speller' in style, so that even after Webster's death it continued to be distributed through schools at the rate of a million a year and had reached a total sale of about 70,000,000 by its centennial anniversary. Webster continued his job as schoolmaster at large to America by producing in 1806 his *Compendious Dictionary of the English Language*, but though the ever-augmented work has had a long and honored life, it started off slowly with a first edition of 2,500 copies that took thirteen years to sell out.

This expanding enlightenment of the public after the war showed itself in ways as diverse as the enthusiasm for deism and the simple spread of journalism. Between 1783 and 1790 the number of newspapers almost doubled, amounting to ninety in all by the end of the period which also saw the establishment of the first successful dailies. Finances were still shaky and the raw materials for printing hard to get (one enterprising New Hampshire printer told children he would exchange a copy of *Robinson Crusoe* for four pounds of rags with which to make paper), but books were widely printed and quickly sold. An English visitor may have stretched a point or two, as is the custom of travelers, when he declared in 1789 'there are few publications that cannot be purchased here,' implying this state of abundance existed even in little towns. Nevertheless, he was on the right track. Publication which had dropped to a low of 360 pieces of printing in 1782 jumped to 802 in 1790. Shipments of English books and American reprints increased tremendously to answer the pent-up demand for new reading matter, stifled by the non-importation agreements of the 'seventies and the succeeding war. A considerable quantity of literature began to be available to the reading public, and publishers and booksellers as well as educators made conscious attempts to increase that public.

Chief among those who wrote what he felt the public should have, and sold it to them himself, was Mason Locke Weems, the self-styled Pastor of Pohick Church. He knew not only what people should have, but what they wanted, for both his own inclinations and his book-peddling, begun in 1792, taught him a lot about general reading interests. Weems was a shrewd salesman, capitalizing on his supposed position as Washington's one-time pastor. Branching out from the selling of other men's almanacs by the tens of thousands, he issued his own *Lover's Almanac* and, then, in 1799, *Weems' Philanthropist; or, A good twenty-five cents worth of political love powder,* urging the partisans of Jefferson and Adams to cease factional war. This book, like his *Immortal Mentor: or, Man's Unerring Guide to a Healthy, Wealthy, and Happy Life,* bore opposite its title page a recommendation from Washington, probably the first example of the use of testimonial endorsement in American book advertising. In three days Weems sold 350 copies of *The Philanthropist,* and he did as well with *The Immortal Mentor,* which was almost immortal itself, going into edition after edition. Next came *Hymen's Recruiting Sergeant; or, The New Matrimonial Tat-too for Old Bachelors,* which, he declared, was 'much admired by the best Critics in Alexandria where last week I sold 8 gross in one day & an half.'

That same summer of 1799 Weems got his best idea of all. With typical enthusiasm he sent his publisher the sketch of a biography of Washington, including a crudely drawn frontispiece inscribed with the wonderful echo of Shakespeare:

> Go thy way old George. Die when thou wilt
> We shall not look upon thy like again.

Old George co-operated as nicely as ever he did in endorsing a Weems book. He died on December 14th, just ahead of the publication of Weems's biography. Hearing the sad news, the Pohick pastor commented, 'Washington . . . is gone. Millions are gaping to read something about him. I am very nearly primed and cocked for 'em.' They were indeed gaping and he was truly primed. The very first time he went on the road with his book he reported to the publisher that 'the people are tearing me to pieces . . . I can sell 10,000 copies in *Virginia alone.*' He had estimated the public taste perfectly. The new nation wanted new heroes. Some of the Revolutionary fathers—like Jefferson—were still alive; others —like Tom Paine—were in disgrace. Washington, newly dead, was just right. The nation was waiting for him to be memorialized in the terms of Light-Horse Harry Lee's Congressional resolution: 'first in war, first in peace, first in the hearts of his countrymen.' Weems had a good thing and he knew it. As he traveled around the country selling his biography, he told new yarns about Washington, testing them on prospective customers, incorporating in new printings those that struck the people's fancy. Six years and five editions after the first publication of *The Life and Memorable Actions of George Washington,* he included the famous cherry-tree story. The tree wasn't chopped down, as later embroidery on this apocryphal anecdote has it, but by George's little hatchet it was 'barked so terribly, that I don't believe the tree ever got the better of it.' Even if people evidently felt that the harm to the tree should have been more severe, they cherished what Weems called 'the tough question' which 'the old gentleman' addressed with 'much warmth,' and the 'inexpressible charm of all conquering truth' with which the six-year-older 'bravely cried out, "I can't tell a lie, Pa; you know I can't tell a lie. I did cut it with my hatchet."'

A steady stream of new editions flowed from the presses for thirty years; at least eighty-four different printings had appeared by 1829, when Weems's portrait of Washington began to be looked upon as a quaint work worth reissuing only for antiquarian interest. Though in the intervening years Weems himself hawked four thousand copies of Chief Justice Marshall's monumental biography of Washington, it attracted only a small fraction of the readers that the cherry-tree book had. At last Weems was supplanted by Harvard's first history professor, Jared Sparks, whose laudatory *Life of Washington,* issued in 1837, averaged two printings a year for ten years. But even the scholarly biographies of Sparks, George Bancroft, and Washington Irving never found the audiences that Weems knew.

Weems was the plain people's Plutarch. He never hit another subject so good as Washington, but his succeeding biographies of Franklin, Penn, and Francis Marion, the 'Swamp Fox' of the Revolution, had many devoted readers. His work on Franklin had to compete with the subject's own *Autobiography* and, considering such opposition, it did well. Even the biography of the South Carolina General Marion sometimes sold at the rate of five hundred copies a month and, as the shrewd biographer-bookdealer noted, 'for cash.' Indeed, Weems appears to have established Marion as a hero; as George R. Stewart points out in his *Names on the Land,* only after the publication of the biography were towns named for Marion. Weems was the most popular biographer of his day because he knew what the rising public of middle-class readers wanted. He emphasized the homely virtues of honesty, duty, industry, temperance, and fru-

gality which they respected and he presented these values in the form
of lively anecdotes whose subjects appeared—as well they might—like
characters in a work of fiction.

The reading public traveled a long and winding road through the
eighteenth century before it reached Weems. Its mind at the outset was
dominantly British and centered on the religious values of an earlier
colonial period. The common people's lives were still narrow, as poor in
cultural interests as they were in money. The pressure of daily work left
little time for reading even to those who had the education for it. As they
passed through rationalism and revolution the people changed. Their eyes
were no longer focused so intently on the hereafter as on the scenery
around them or the pitfalls directly ahead. The people grew in numbers
and their cultural heritages were different, even though they were spoken
of as blended into something called 'American.' Their long progress was
attended not only by changes of ideas, which seeped down from more
sophisticated leaders, but also by practical, utilitarian inventions. When
common men were given the Franklin stove and the spermaceti candle
for even light, they could read without hugging the hearth of a shadowy
room, faces flushed and backs cold. At the outset of the century-long
journey, books were, to a great extent, the property of ministers, public
officials, and other professional men whose duties involved them in
'required reading.' By the end of the century, thousands of people had
acquired a taste for reading. Their interests were indicated by the books
they made their own, for they created best sellers of Tom Paine's *Common Sense*, arguing for the independence of America, and of Weems's
biography of their country's first President. The public's tastes and abilities were not always equal to those of its social betters, and a cultural
cleavage marked the Americans at the opening of the nineteenth century.
But if the majority of the people were often reading books different from
those selected by the more worldly and more learned classes, they were
reading, and reading widely.

Chapter 4

The Power of Sympathy

The eighteenth century not only developed a new reading class, it also produced a new form of literature for this class. Quite appropriately this form was called simply the novel.' The term was the same as that which Boccaccio gave to his short prose narratives, but it was especially suitable. The eighteenth-century novel was really an innovation; it was the product as well as the favorite text of the rising bourgeoisie.

When Addison in 1711 described the library of a typical young lady of the day he included in it the long-winded romances of Mrs. Manley, Mlle de Scudéry, and Honoré d'Urfé, the very sort of works to be found in the collection that the Boston widow Mrs. Nathaniel Greene left behind her in 1728. If Addison had written later in the century or Mrs. Greene had clung to life a few years longer, these libraries would have been full of novels rather than fancifully inflated romances. The change came almost overnight after Samuel Richardson issued his *Pamela* in 1740. Here, for the middle class, was something to read that was both easy and edifying. It had none of the romance's rarefied atmosphere, distant setting, fantastic circumstances, or aggrandized characters. It was fiction about people with whom ordinary readers could readily identify themselves. The New York serving girl whose mistress gave her a domestic's manual designed as 'a sure means of gaining both love and esteem,' could imagine those states of affection more easily attained by reading herself into the place of Pamela, with her mistress dead and the lady's son desperately and dishonorably enamored of her. The lady herself could forget domestic duties for a while, sighing with vicarious pleasure at the travails of Pamela, who, though a servant, was first of all a woman. Benjamin Franklin knew his business when he followed the London printer Richardson by publishing *Pamela* in 1744, for imported copies had already sold well in the colonies.

As the land grew more settled and the reading public more extended, the demand for novels surpassed that for any other type of literature. In the new, comparatively full security and leisure of town life there was time and ease for an appreciation of the novel's sophisticated refinements. The current emotional religious revivals inculcated an enthusiasm for its strong feelings and vivid scenes. The novel was molded to the needs and desires of middle-class minds; its interests were theirs. Although the average person in the average situation was virtually unknown to its pages, neither character nor plot was so fantastic that it was beyond the usual daydreams of people in the middle and somewhat lower stations of society. A patchy knowledge was able to cope with anything the novelist had to say, and a rudimentary taste appreciated his way of saying it.

Fiction filled America's bookshelves during the latter half of the century. In the forty-five years between Franklin's publication of *Pamela* and the printing of America's first home-grown novel, the public depended on English imports, with but fifty-six American reprints of foreign fiction to help meet the growing demand. Even during the Revolution, when novel publishing declined in England, Royalist booksellers in cities occupied by the British imported 'in the Fleet' eight-volume sets of *Clarissa Harlowe* and series of prints 'representing the principal actions' of Pamela's life. From 1789 to the end of the century imports jumped tremendously and local publishers alone turned out over 350 different foreign novels and 37 American ones, several in many editions.

Novels were expensive for the average reader. Shorter works in paper wrappers could be had for as little as 37½ cents, but in 1798 an American novel sold for a dollar 'handsomely bound' and a half dollar more when 'elegantly bound.' Captain John Davis noted in his travels around the country that 'Americans expect quantity in a book not less eagerly than in other merchandise.' He was right. Nearly all novels were in two volumes, many ran to three, and the full *Clarissa* required seven or eight. Many people wanted to read these novels, but usually only once, and the prices were too high for that. Their proper home was the circulating library. By the end of the century it had become a middle-class institu-

tion, no longer the property of wealthy merchants, who began to speak
of the libraries as 'slop-shops of literature.' When Royall Tyler, the New
England lawyer-turned-author, wrote an introduction to one of his novels
in 1797, he noticed with somewhat greater enthusiasm, 'in our inland
towns of consequence, social libraries had been instituted, composed of
books designed to amuse rather than to instruct.' The result in America
as in England, as the London bookseller Lackington observed in 1791,
was that

> the poorer sort of farmers, and even the poor country people in general, who
> before . . . spent their winter evenings in relating stories of witches, ghosts,
> hobgoblins, &c. now shorten the winter nights by hearing their sons and daugh-
> ters read tales . . . If John goes to town with a load of hay, he is charged to
> be sure not to forget to bring home 'Peregrine Pickle's Adventures,' and when
> Dolly is sent to market to sell her eggs, she is commissioned to purchase 'The
> History of Pamela Andrews.' In short all ranks and degrees now READ.

Novels were the reading matter of the lower middle class which rose
to prominence after the Revolution, of nearly all the younger generation,
and of women of every age and station, but older, more sober, or more
religious citizens were generally horrified at the degradation of morality
and intellect that they associated with fiction. The novel, it was widely
said, softens the mind, unfitting it for more solid reading and, what was
worse, 'pollutes the imaginations.' Does it not, one critic asked, give
young people 'false ideas of life'? To which another could only answer,
'it renders the ordinary affairs of life insipid.' Still others thought that it
corrupted wholesome republican virtues by encouraging the imitation of
foreign amenities: 'the leer, the affected anguish, the yawn of feigned
ennui, the pert titter.' It was that to which the serious twenty-year-old
John Quincy Adams objected when he confided to his diary, 'Nancy is
about seventeen . . . she has read too many novels; her expressions are
romantic . . . a few years may cool her down to an agreeable sensible
girl: now, it may suffice to say, she is young.' More matter-of-fact members of the older generation asked people to 'calculate the number of
actual hours expended in a large family' on novel reading, and come up
with a sum of time that should have been put to practical use. Worst of
all, another critic remarked, was that 'a "novel-reading female" expects
attention from her husband, which the cares of the business will not
permit him to pay.' No wonder that an English article, 'Novel Reading
a Cause of Female Depravity,' was reprinted in America several times
after its original London publication in 1797, and that the Harvard au-

thorities in 1803 determined the principal commencement address should
be directed against the dangers of fiction.

To forestall such attacks, some American novelists took to embellishing
their title pages with statements that theirs was a tale of truth, so that
Mrs. Foster's popular *Coquette*, which had at least thirteen printings,
bore the subtitle, 'A Novel Founded on Fact.' Others followed the cue
of William Hill Brown, who declared in his preface to *The Power of
Sympathy* that his fiction was written to expose a particular vice and
promote a specific virtue. And still others tried to eliminate foreign competition and answer native criticism at one and the same time by stating
that only when the American girl reads an English novel is she 'insensibly
taught to admire the levity, and often the vices, of the parent country,'
which 'excites a fondness for false splendor; and renders the home-spun
habits of her own country disgusting.' Some admitted that the moral fiction of America 'is enough to give one the vapours' but counted on such
chauvinist signatures as 'By a Lady of Massachusetts' to sell their books;
they pleaded with readers to turn from licentious foreign fiction and not
permit 'an American production to be consigned to oblivion, or criticized
with rigour.' Critics sometimes played both sides against the middle. In
June of 1801 the *Philadelphia Repository and Weekly Register* attacked
fiction as 'one great engine in the hands of the fiends of darkness,' and
next month blandly featured the first installment of a novel by 'a young
gentleman of Philadelphia.' Circulating libraries adopted no such mealy-
mouthed attitudes, and figuring that the best defense was a good offensive, a Boston bookseller echoed Richardson in advertising his works as
likely 'to Cultivate the Principles of Virtue and Religion in the Minds of
the Youth of Both Sexes.' The New York dealer Caritat in the preface to
his enormous list of novels vehemently printed the statement that

The mere novel reader will probably be found more alive to distress, more refined, more *companionable*, than the wholly unlettered rustic, who is generally
coarse, brutal, and unfeeling. The eye [that] fills with tears at fictions, it may
be fairly presumed will drop the kindly shower at real distress . . . I had rather
see one of the lower class peruse these mischievous books, than with newspaper in hand, plunging into the gulph of politics, and losing his health, his
substance, and his senses at the Ale-house. The decrease of drunkenness in this
country is, perhaps, owing to the introduction of circulating libraries, which
may be considered as temples erected by literature to attract the votaries of
Bacchus.

No matter what the attack or defense, the novel suited the taste of the
times, and people read it. Even as early as 1744 Dr. Hamilton observed

that at a Boston book auction *Pamela* was a best seller alongside *The Marrow of Modern Divinity*. Richardson's *Pamela* was by far the most popular of all fiction, followed by his other novels. As a contemporary English critic remarked, 'Pamela is like snow, she covers everything with her whiteness.' American women, like their English sisters, had volumes of *Pamela* in their libraries, Pamela fans in their hands, and Pamela engravings on their walls. Booksellers sold spurious sequels and thin parallels as well as travesties, but the genuine Richardsonian article did best of all. His account of a servant girl's rise to high position had the didactic purpose and moral outlook on which the middle class prided itself; the book proved that virtue is tangibly rewarded, and at the same time it had titillating descriptions of an adolescent girl constantly agonizing on the verge of sexual experience. What could be better? *Pamela* could be read for several reasons and enjoyed for all. Jonathan Edwards read *Pamela* and gave it to his daughter, who, though she found it a bit long, admitted, 'there is certainly many excellent observations and rules laid down that I shall never repent my pains.' And like all who had read through the four volumes she could sniff at those who knew but the abridged versions, which another critic called 'just the recreation of an hour or two for a sofa-lolling miss on a summer's afternoon.'

Richardson's *Clarissa Harlowe* was a fine complement to *Pamela*. It showed how an innocent girl caught between the machinations of her unfeeling family and the wiles of a determined rake is led to nervous collapse and seduction. As a warning against the 'Misconduct Both of Parents and Children' it pleased stern moralists, like the New Englander, Judith Sergeant Murray, who considered that *Clarissa* deserved a place 'for literary excellence, above the Iliad of Homer, or any other work, ancient or modern,' and who, though sharing her grandfather's 'invincible aversion to novels,' quite agreed with his practice of having his family read *Clarissa* and the Bible alternately. And again like *Pamela*, *Clarissa* could be enjoyed for other reasons too. Many American readers would have agreed with Lady Bradshaigh when she admitted to Richardson, 'If I was to die for it, I cannot help being fond of Lovelace. A sad dog! why would you make him so wicked and yet so agreeable?' It was for reasons closer to those of the English than the American lady that the North Carolinian, James Iredell, took to the novel. He chanced upon it while making a social call, 'during some part of which I fear I was a little rude, for happening to take up Clarissa Harlowe, I could not quit it.' Two days later he purchased it for fifty American shillings (say, $6.25) and confided to his diary, 'In the afternoon went early to my office, and could not resist the temptation of reading a little in Clarissa.' The private office was evidently the only place Iredell felt safe with the treasured novel, for a few evenings later he remarks, 'Would have read Clarissa, but did not care to show the book lest it might have been borrowed from me.' With such faithful followers not uncommon in America, critics tended to be less severe with Richardson than with other novelists, for though he depicted vice, Pamela, Clarissa, and Grandison were paragons of virtue. One timorously declared, 'I am not equally pleased with all Richardson's writings; yet so multifarious are his excellencies, that his faults appear but specks, which serve as foils to display his beauties to better advantage.' And it was a daring young lady who, after admitting that Pamela 'is a very good girl, and as such I love her dearly,' could state, 'I must think her very defective while she allows herself that disgusting liberty of praising herself' and 'by criticising Mr. Locke, has taken the liberty to dissent from that admirable author.'

Richardson's popularity as a novelist was surpassed by no one, for even though Defoe's *Robinson Crusoe* had nineteen editions between 1775 and 1796, his fiction for adults—*Captain Singleton, Moll Flanders,* and *Roxana*—had no American printings. Richardson waited only four years to be published in this country, but fifty-four years and a great many English novels flowed through American presses before Fielding's *Tom Jones* had an American title page. However, Fielding had enough admirers finally to warrant three American editions of *Joseph Andrews* and nine of *Tom Jones.* There was, for example, Dr. Hamilton, who in 1744 picked up a copy of *Joseph Andrews* in Philadelphia and rated it 'a masterly performance'; or James Iredell in North Carolina who admitted to 'a great regard for Mr. Fielding's character and some of his writings'; or even the twelve-year-old Anna Green Winslow, who wrote in 1771, 'I have bestow'd no new year's gift, as yet. But have received one very handsome one, viz. the History of Joseph Andrews abreviated. In nice Guilt and flower covers.' Still, if a Maryland bookseller within eighteen months during 1771 and 1772 imported fifteen copies of *Tom Jones* to only a dozen of Richardson's works and if one Pennsylvania circulating library loaned *Tom Jones* forty-three times to twenty times for *Pamela* and ten for *Sir Charles Grandison,* most readers considered Fielding a very poor second to Richardson. Except for Brackenridge, whose *Modern Chivalry* seems to have had a moderate popularity, no American novelist showed a deep indebtedness to Fielding. Smollett had

a far smaller following. Like Defoe, Fielding and Smollett were better
suited to men than women, and the novel was essentially woman's possession. Women were its readers, as a New York bookseller recognized in
heading an advertisement, 'To the Ladies: Novels for Winter Evening
Amusements.' Women were also very often the writers of novels; more
than a third of the American fiction published before Cooper's *Precaution*
in 1820 was by women and the average was still higher in England. For
this 'generation of Amazons of the pen,' as Dr. Johnson called it, Fielding, Smollett, and Defoe were too rough and direct. The simpler minds
of the new reading class preferred emotion to bluff humor and frank description. For sentiment they were suited and sentiment they demanded
after Richardson taught them what it was.

The emotional exaggeration in Pamela's prolonged scrutiny of her feelings and the implicit argument that persistent purity eventually over-
comes vigorous vice were the two main marks of the sentimental novel.
It was emotionalism with an ethical ideal. As Dr. Johnson said, 'Why,
Sir, if you were to read Richardson for the story, your patience would
be so much fretted that you would hang yourself. But you must read
him for the sentiment, and consider the story as only giving occasion to
the sentiment.' Sentimentalism was a grand thing; it allowed you to phi-
lander with your feelings and yet preserve a clear conscience, for, though
it heightened the emotions, it had a moral purpose, such as the preser-
vation of female virtue. The dramatist George Colman thought it no
wonder the novel that was '. . . sentimental is the style,' for it was
'So chaste, yet so bewitching all the while.' Its cumulative effect was
intended to be moral, yet,

> Plot and elopement, passion, rape, and rapture
> The total sum of ev'ry dear, dear chapter.

In America, as in England, the sentimental novel swept everything
before it. *Pamela* had hundreds of daughters, and readers loved them
all. A visitor to Caritat's circulating library remarked,

Its shelves could scarcely sustain the weight of *Female Frailty, The Posthumous
Daughter,* and the *Cavern of Woe;* they required the aid of a carpenter to support the burden of *Cottage on the Moor,* the *House of Tynian* . . . They possessed alluring, melting, irresistible titles: such, for instance, as *Delicate Embar-
rassments, Venial Trespasses, Misplaced Confidence.*

They were, he says, 'called for by the young and the old; from the tender
virgin of thirteen, whose little heart went pit-a-pat at the approach of a

beau, to the experienced matron of three score, who could not read without spectacles.' No wonder that Parson Weems grumbled when his publisher expected him to peddle Jonathan Edwards in those days. 'I wrote to you,' he complains, 'begging for sweet prosperity's sake that you w^d send no more of such books, but send rather, "fine sentimental Novels."'

Sentiment was all the rage. In New York the sentimental dramas of Kotzebue flourished on the stage, and in 1797 the *American Moral and Sentimental Magazine* was founded. Even before its day, periodical fiction employed the stock sentimental characters: hardhearted parents; a girl about to be seduced; a lover who is generally a rake, and is just as generally reformed too late by his victim; and a long-suffering wife abused by an evil husband. And the events in which they are involved were always told for the ostensible purpose of conveying a moral, so that its aim, as one magazine put it, was 'Blending the Useful with the Sweet.' The titles might be flamboyant but the subtitles were moral—'The Fatal Effects of Curiosity,' 'The Rewards of Virtue,' or 'The Fatal Effects of Seduction.' Thus, for example, in 1784 one magazine printed 'The History of Auretta,' telling of a young lady who, to escape the unromantic match planned by her father, goes to visit her beloved 'Mr. Wendall.' She loses her way in the dark, and Mr. W., assuming that some horror has occurred, writes a neat little poem and then commits suicide. Auretta, lacking a lover, goes back to take advantage of her second-best offer from the man her father had selected. Unfortunately, she finds him dead too—he has taken poison upon hearing of the reason for Mr. Wendall's death. The point of this melancholy tale is amply set forth in the subtitle: 'The Fatal Effects of Impatience.'

The same sort of thing went on in the novels. Hannah Foster's *The Coquette*, a tale of a girl's seduction, elopement, and death in childbirth, was advertised as teaching 'The American Fair' a lesson: 'Let them despise, and forever banish the man, who can glory in the seduction of innocence and the ruin of reputation.' One popular novelist gave a recipe for pleasing fiction: 'remember to mix a sufficient quantity of sighs, tears, swooning hysterics, and all the moving expression of heart-rending woe . . . Be sure you contrive a duel; and, if convenient, a suicide might not be amiss.' The only important ingredient omitted in this recipe was the letter. Here again Richardson set the style. His epistolary form allowed the writer to string incidents together loosely, which was helpful to the untried authors of sentimental fiction. Fielding's architectural construction demanded more than the amateurs could give. One American novelist frankly cried out, 'A fig for your plots and unities of design,' which he called 'fetters to pathos and sublimity.' Letters were easier to write and besides they were the perfect form for the sentimentalists to use in revealing their characters' innermost feelings. What their hearts felt, their pens wrote—instantly. Whole books, patterned after *Pamela* and *Clarissa*, were written as letters, sometimes even as one long single letter. Mrs. Bleecker of Albany told her *History of Maria Kittle* in a 17,000-word epistle, which at one point was sufficiently confusing in time and sequence to make her admit that perhaps the reader was 'alarmed at my silence about Mrs. Kittle; I think we left her reposing under a tree.'

All such epistolary novels had two outstanding pieces of furniture: the bed and the writing desk. The villain had his eye on the former, the heroine, on the latter. Any incident that created goose pimples just as surely called for a goose quill. 'I am unfit to write, yet fly to my pen, for a mitigation of my harassed mind,' one heroine confesses. Another writes as she lies dying, for even though her lifeblood is ebbing she still has plenty of ink. Still another appears to write in the midst of a terrible struggle to preserve her virtue, for she describes the actions of her attacker in the present tense and in such a way that the gaping reader never knows what will happen next. Evidently she fended off the villain with her left hand while her right described his dastardly doings. It was write, write, write all the time for these poor girls. One of Charles Brockden Brown's heroes marveled, 'How you can maintain the writing posture, and pursue the writing movement for ten hours together, without benumbed brain, or aching fingers, is beyond my comprehension.' Some of the men were only a little behind the women in their addiction to penmanship. One gifted fellow—it is true he recorded his feelings in a journal rather than in letters—lost his right arm midway in his career as a soldier, but he quickly learned to use his left and went on scribbling. What these heroes and heroines needed was a ball-bearing pen that could write under water. It seems amazing that the quill sufficed to indite their endless letters, showered as they were with cascades of tears.

Under Sterne's influence, the pages of novels became even damper. Richardson had fostered sentimentalism, but Sterne nourished her weaker sister, sensibility. Sentimentalism had a conscience and, on the whole, confined herself rather strictly to the domestic virtues. But sensibility moped in the moonlight, gave herself to ecstatic titillation of the affections, and felt that just as eyes were made for seeing, emotion was its own excuse for being. Its credo was art for heart's sake. Sensibility allowed one to feel deeply about any situation without having compunctions that something must be done to rectify it. To enjoy one's own feelings was an end sufficient in itself. No cause was needed proportionate to the sensibility one expressed; indeed a great cause rather argued that one's powers of sensibility were obtuse. The refined sensibility trembled at the slightest irritation, pleasurable or painful; middle-class women relished the novel of sensibility because it allowed them to affect a tender, ladylike delicacy. As Harriet Lee wrote in her novel, *Errors of Innocence*, sensibility, 'tho' originally deriv'd from the passions, is meliorated into something gentler,' and even its normal expression of tears was rarefied into something more delicate. Tears became 'lucid emanations,' 'glittering globes of chrystal,' 'pure drops of celestial sensibility,' and other such evanescent stuff.

In his novel, *The Emigrants*, Gilbert Imlay, lately a captain in the Revolution, could brush aside a tear and write perfectly seriously about a fly: 'Go, thou little innocent thing. You shall not a moment longer be confined, for perhaps already have I robbed thee of joys, which the exertion of my whole life cannot repay.' This was undoubtedly the high watermark of sensibility in American novels, but Sterne left his impression on much of the fiction written and read here by adulterating the typical Richardsonian plot with a heightened refinement of feeling. Seven editions of *A Sentimental Journey* were printed in America between 1768 and 1795, and a selection of *The Beauties of Sterne* had five Boston and Philadelphia printings. 'Fugitive pieces' were separately issued, and in 1774 Sterne became the first novelist to have a collected edition of his complete works published in the colonies. *The Massachusetts Magazine* seems to have appointed itself Sterne's official American guardian. Its stories were generally weak echoes of *Clarissa*, but one of its essayists, declaring himself 'all over Sternefied,' expressed the tone of the periodical that reprinted parts of *Tristram Shandy*, original contributions 'in the Shandean manner,' and Dunlap's play, *The Father; or, American Shandyism*. But Massachusetts was not the only place in America to cherish Sterne. While Mrs. Rowson, at one time a Bostonian, published a novel, *The Inquisitor; or, Invisible Rambler*, as an avowed attempt to 'write in the style of the inimitable Sterne,' a New Yorker paid his debt to the master in an operetta, *Sterne's Maria;* another New Yorker, a smart bookseller, obviously capitalized on *A Sentimental Journey* by advertising a travel account as 'one of the most pleasant books of observation that ever came from a writer of sensibility,' and the North Carolinian James Iredell observed that in his region 'we were all reading Shandy.' Everywhere Sterne was the rage. Only severe moralists were incensed at his emotionalism, and they knew they were fighting a losing battle against popular taste. It was indeed a harassed gentleman who wrote to *The New England Quarterly* in 1802,

I suppose few writers have done more injury to morals than Sterne. Formerly if a man felt a passion for the wife or mistress of his friend, he was conscious at least, that, if he persisted in the pursuit, he was acting wrong; and if the Novel Writer invented such a character, it was to hold him out as an object of detestation and punishment. Now this is so varnished over with delicate attachment and generous sensibility, that the most shocking acts of perfidy and seduction are committed not only without remorse, but with self-complacency.

Sterne was the high priest of sensibility, but Goldsmith stood close to him in the hierarchy that included Rousseau; Mackenzie, the author of *The Man of Feeling;* and Brooke, who wrote the curious *Fool of Quality.* *The Vicar of Wakefield* was reprinted in Boston in 1769, just three years after its first appearance in England, and copies of this and foreign editions were widely scattered through the colonies. It is true that one circulating library loaned out the *Vicar* only half as often as *Tristram Shandy,* but Parson Weems, always a good judge of books, included Goldsmith's work as one of the two titles in his 'sundry *best* novels' that sold most rapidly in Virginia during 1803. Many American authors seem to have been influenced by Goldsmith, and not a single native novel appeared during the century without some mark of sensibility.

The opponent of the novel found Richardson and his followers bad, Sterne and his worse, but most deplorable of all was the cult of Goethe's *Werther.* When the three combined, as they very often did, the solid citizen was truly outraged. *The Sorrows of Young Werther* was first printed in America in 1784, though copies had been imported earlier from England, and within five years there were seven native editions, based on three different translations. Goethe's novel was quickly followed by *Werter to Charlotte* and *A Description of the Tomb of Werter,* two English poems published in Philadelphia in 1787; by the apocryphal *Letters of Charlotte,* reprinted six times in this country after 1797; by a dramatized version of *The Sorrows,* entitled *Werther and Charlotte,* produced in New York, Boston, and Charleston; as well as by several imitative novels, both foreign and native, such as *The Slaves of Passion; or,*

The Fruits of Werter and *Eleonora; from The Sorrows of Werter,* which flaunted their debt in the titles.

Following *Werther,* the novel of sensibility assumed a pathological taint, for it made suicide the current vogue in fiction. Self-destruction was a final and excruciatingly pleasant turn of the screw to put pressure on the reader's feelings, so that Ophelia Shepherd, a character in *The Power of Sympathy,* America's first novel, committed suicide after being seduced, but did not die before she had time to tell posterity that as death came closer her 'sensibility became more exquisite.' On Ophelia's bedside table, next to the last unsealed letter, lay the approved trademark of heightened sensibility—a copy of *The Sorrows of Werther.* Even a heroine who continued to live, like the one in *Ferdinand and Elmira,* by the Maine novelist Mrs. Wood, considered it a 'want of delicacy to be cheerful.' The readers of *The Power of Sympathy* and similar novels were probably mainly feminine and upper class, for ladies had the most time to cultivate their sensibilities.

The style of melancholia was encouraged, not only by the novels of the day but by the graveyard school of poetry then so popular; and it was expressed by the non-writing female in the funereal painting which refined young ladies affected. They loved to draw nothing so much as a weeping willow trailing its boughs over an obelisk or an urn, and they adorned themselves with 'mourning jewelry,' made from the plaited and powdered hair of a dead loved one. It was at these affectations, in part engendered by the *Werther*-like novel, that critics aimed their attacks. 'We sometimes,' said one of these faultfinders, 'see instances of young ladies who weep away a whole forenoon, over the criminal sorrows of a fictitious Charlotte or Werter, turning with disdain, at two o'clock, from the sight of a beggar.' Yet there were also plainer women captivated by what *The Massachusetts Magazine* called the 'fiery spirit of enthusiasm and overflowing sensibility' of *Werther.* John Davis, the Englishman who traveled through this country between 1798 and 1802, in one of his novels remarks upon the *Werther* craze in a passage that may be more factual than fictional. His hero, stopping overnight at a Newark tavern where he finds several sentimental novels, 'asked the girl in waiting whether she read any of these love-inflicting volumes. She replied with a coquettish air that she slept every night with the Sorrows of Werter under her pillow. I could hardly restrain my laughter,' Davis writes, 'but discharging the bill, bade my novel-reading nymph farewell, whose susceptibility amused me.'

It was another Charlotte than Goethe's whose story was to be found under the pillows of most young American girls. Though her beloved did not commit suicide, but only 'to the end of his life was subject to severe fits of melancholy,' and though her seduction and later travail were not told in the form of letters, the short life of Charlotte Temple was that of the typical sentimental heroine. To some degree she seems to have existed in fact, but her real life has long since been lost in the mists of fiction created by Susanna Haswell Rowson's enormously popular *Charlotte Temple: A Tale of Truth,* first published in 1791. Mrs. Rowson, a former actress who later settled down as head of the Young Ladies' Academy in Boston, wrote four volumes of poetry, two plays, some textbooks, and eight novels, but *Charlotte Temple* eclipsed all of them, and all other novels as well. It was neither better nor worse than dozens of other sentimental novels whose stock characters, rambling but hectic plots, emotional crises, linguistic prudery, refined style, and moralistic tone it paralleled. But it was the most popular of all eighteenth-century novels in America. Its appeal in part rested on the American setting, and the piquancy attached to a plot based on fact, both characteristics of Mrs. Foster's *Coquette,* the runner-up to *Charlotte* in popularity. There was, besides, a real grave in New York marked 'Charlotte Temple,' to which sentimental admirers might bring flowers and tears by moonlight. Lacking these qualifications in England, the novel had no such unusual success there. It was first printed in America in 1794, and had but three editions before the turn of the century. Then it really got under way. By 1805 sixteen editions had been printed; people were buying this novel rather than borrowing it for only a few days from circulating libraries. Parson Weems felt the sale would be even greater if the price could be reduced still further. 'Remember the Nimble ninepence is better than the slow shilling,' he wrote the publisher in a letter complaining that at $62\frac{1}{2}$ cents a copy it took him four years to sell his allotment of 2,000 copies from the third edition. He admitted that was a pretty good sale, but nothing compared with what it might be if the book were better priced. 'Why,' he grumbled, 'no offense to that poor Girl, the horse farriery sells as well.' As the century wore on, the horses were left at the post, for Charlotte went through well over two hundred editions, according to her bibliographer, R. W. G. Vail. Prices dropped and so did Charlotte's morality in garbled and unauthorized editions, one of which billed her as 'The Fastest Girl in New York.' Her child was a chip off the old block, for Mrs. Rowson's sequel, *Lucy Temple,* tells how Charlotte's illegitimate daughter nearly married her own brother, a story so enthralling that thirty-one editions of her life have been located, and probably several more were read to pieces. No character had had a success like Charlotte's in America before, and none surpassed her until Mrs. Stowe created Uncle Tom.

Charlotte's popularity was the more remarkable because by the time she appeared on the literary scene a new type of fiction was in fashion. It was called the Gothic novel, a general term that covered any romance of terror, usually dealing with the supernatural. Horace Walpole's *Castle of Otranto* had started the style as far back as 1764, but not until Mrs. Radcliffe's *Mysteries of Udolpho* and other horror tales were published in the 'nineties and M. G. Lewis's fiendish tale of *The Monk* appeared in 1796, did the Gothic become the prevailing mode. Most of their followers employed their settings: antique lands dotted by picturesquely ruined Gothic castles or moldering abbeys and convents, properly partitioned into dungeons, underground passages, and haunted chambers, elegantly furnished with rolling balls of fire, animated portraits, statues given to nosebleeds, or simply with groaning ghosts, all of which served to terrify abducted girls, erring wives—and readers. The story itself, as a contemporary critic remarked, was told with a 'bloated magnificence of diction, extravagance of imagination and wild eccentricity of adventure.' Young ladies delighted in these melodramatic adventures and their Byronic heroes, telling one another that their fears at such scenes and such goings on were proof of the delicate sensibilities they still cherished. Others simply found these novels a new form of escape from their own humdrum lives, allowing them vicariously to experience thrilling adventures. From the middle class of America to the Middle Ages of Europe was a wonderfully exciting journey, when made through the medium of a Gothic novel. Royall Tyler even implied that it had another use, for with lifted eyebrow he observed that, 'Dolly the dairy maid, and Jonathan the hired man, threw aside the ballad of the cruel step-mother, over which they had so often wept in concert, and now amused themselves into so agreeable a terror with the haunted houses and hobgoblins of Mrs. Ratcliffe, that they were both afraid to sleep alone.'

With such wondrous and varied appeals the Gothic novels did well. A contemporary critic observed that 'Otranto Ghosts have propagated their species with unequalled fecundity. The spawn is in every book shop.' It was in every circulating library too—by 1799 Caritat had forty-five different examples—and abridgments or brief, clumsy imitations of the full three-volume works were sold by chapmen as shilling shockers, the grandfathers of the dime novel. The Gothic novel moved onto the stage too. William Dunlap, who always capitalized on every turn of taste, in 1794 produced his *Fontainville Abbey*, an adaptation of Mrs. Radcliffe's *Romance of the Forest*, which he followed with *Ribbemont, or The Feudal Baron*, and *The Man of Fortitude;* and in 1798 New York saw the first of the dramatizations of 'Monk' Lewis's work. The new style in fiction was accompanied by a general appreciation of art and architecture of the Middle Ages, and in 1800 one daring virtuoso built his country house after a Gothic design, the first of many to punctuate a landscape previously occupied by classic or native forms.

Perhaps the first full-length Gothic novel by an American was Charles Brockden Brown's *Wieland*, published in 1798. The dark and brooding atmosphere was genuinely Gothic, as were the titular character's fanaticism and madness, the disembodied voices that harried other characters, and the general shambles of murder and death by spontaneous combustion. Brown had simply moved the scene to the United States, showing, as he said in the introduction to his next novel, *Edgar Huntly*, that 'the caverns of America's hills supplant the Gothic vaults of Europe, and the red-skin proves no less terrifying than the spectre of the castle.' There were, however, readers who still felt that a Gothic novel wasn't Gothic without a castle, and as one American author remarked, 'a castle without a ghost is fit for nothing but to live in, and were it generally the case, the poor novelist might starve and the bookseller publish sermons.' One who saw to it that he didn't starve on that account was Isaac Mitchell, a Poughkeepsie editor, who during 1804 published serially in his newspaper the novel that later appeared in book form as *The Asylum, or Alonzo and Melissa*. Mitchell's Gothic tale was fully equipped with a crenelated castle set in Connecticut, inhabited by ghosts and the heroine, who was confined there to keep her from marrying the penniless Alonzo. Mitchell furnished his novel with everything readers of sensibility or Gothic taste could want, and so popular was it that not only were eleven editions demanded, but it received the dubious compliment of an almost verbatim plagiarism, *Alonzo and Melissa, or the Unfeeling Father*, cavalierly signed by one Daniel Jackson, a teacher at Plattsburg.

The eighteenth century had three principal fashions in fiction—the sentimental tale, the novel of sensibility, and the Gothic romance. The first two were markedly similar; the latter tended to merge with them in several ways; and the epistolary style, though most common to the first, was used in all. In general, their periods of popularity ran in the order cited, yet one did not succumb completely as another came into being. The earlier either fused with the later, dropped slowly out of favor, or was issued for a lower-class public, which relished it in cheap abridgments and reprints while the stylish world took to the newest mode. Those accounted best sellers survived their initial vogue, for the larger body of book readers continued to buy them long after sophisticated readers considered them old-fashioned. Nevertheless, in the course of time, they all become antiquated. To paraphrase Maria Edgeworth's criticism of the novels that preceded hers in popularity, readers could not remain breathless continually, with mouths wide open through three volumes. The public finally tired of the eighteenth-century novels' exaggerated emotionalism, and what Caritat called their 'spun-out superfluities.' During their day they had been challenged by the moralistic educational tales of Mrs. Inchbald and her successor, Thomas Day (his *Sanford and Merton* lingered on for what it called the 'instruction of juvenile minds'), and by exotic Oriental tales furbished with Gothic horror, but the only serious challenge they ever met was time. A reader found that he could take just so much of them, and though he might return with pleasure to Sterne, Goldsmith, and Goethe, or perhaps even to an abridged Richardson, he could not stomach the imitators. Their own intensity was too great. They had either to be heartily accepted or completely rejected; there could be no halfway appreciation. If they weren't thrilling they were only fantastic. If they weren't appealingly sentimental they were only meretricious. And so, though the types of fiction popular in the eighteenth century lingered into the opening decades of the nineteenth, they were loved only by an unsophisticated class of readers who had not yet been jaded by their profusion. In time, these readers too were surfeited.

Chapter 5

The Ancient Regime

The nineteenth century was America's era of expansion. In 1790 the nation numbered something short of four million people; before 1820 the figure had doubled. Though native Americans and immigrants were leaving the seaboard for the frontier, urban centers grew too, and New York City's population nearly quadrupled. The nation's 200 newspapers of 1800 mushroomed to about 375 in 1810. A quarter of a century later there were some 1,200 of them, three times as many as either England or France printed. Sixty-five were dailies, with an average circulation of a thousand copies each. Naturally, newspapers and magazines were more widely read than books, as they have been ever since in America, but the book-reading public was growing too. With increased education, 91 per cent of the adult whites became literate. For them hundreds of new printing offices sprang up. Printing from plates instead of type began in 1812, soon followed by inexpensive cloth binding; both processes helped to bring books more quickly and inexpensively to the new reading classes. The public-library movement was still unborn, but so-called Mechanics and Apprentices Libraries came into being. By 1825 those in the four largest cities had twenty times as many books as could be found in 1800 in all the nation's semi-public collections. These libraries and the booksellers' shops were for the most part filled with English works. A typical dealer's advertisement in 1801 listed 400 titles, 250 printed in England, and only a very few of the remainder written by Americans. Samuel Goodrich, the Boston publisher, estimated in 1820 that three-quarters of the books Americans bought were of English origin. In the early years of the century, bookdealers opposed a tariff on printed matter because America could not furnish enough books for the expanded reading public. As printing became a big business, they fought against the importation of English books but still clamored for the works of English writers because, without copyright and royalties, they could be sold at better profit. Either way, English authors were favored.

Before the first decade was over, the most popular new literature was Scott's poetry. To it the American reading public responded enthusiastically, having been prepared for Scott's exciting and picturesque verse romances by the sentimental emotionalism of Richardsonian novels, the more primitive sensationalism of *Werther* and the Gothic novel, the nature poetry of Thomson, and Burns's rustic Scottish minstrelsy, of which seven editions were printed in America before 1807.

The impulses that made the public ready for romanticism and Scott were more than literary. Romanticism's philosophic concepts, emphasizing idealism, imagination, boundlessness, and greater personal freedom, may have been theories unknown to average American readers, but they were what many experienced first hand, whether as individualists in the East's nascent capitalistic enterprise or as pioneers on the westward-moving frontier. The spirit of the times was idealistic because a confident people felt they had a manifest destiny ahead of them. As early as 1800 they were pushing west from Kentucky, Ohio, and Tennessee, states only recently carved from the wilderness; in 1803 a whole new empire was added through the Louisiana Purchase, to become the basis of thirteen new states 140 per cent larger than the original thirteen; and a year later a Kentuckian could declare his neighbors were 'full of enterprise . . . Mexico glitters in our eyes.' Americans exulted when 'Tippecanoe' Harrison quashed Tecumseh's rebellion, when Andrew Jackson closed the second war against Great Britain with the resounding victory at New Orleans, and when Lewis and Clark's overland voyage to the western shores brought word of the stretches waiting for American conquest. The continent was being conquered in other ways too. Eighteen years after Fulton's *Clermont* made its first commercial voyage, 125 steamboats were plying America's rivers. Soon the land was scored by the railroad's steel ribbons, and the staccato voice of the telegraph called from settlement to settlement. Two centuries after the landing at Plymouth, Webster celebrated the Pilgrims by declaring, 'New England farms, houses, villages, and churches spread over and adorn the immense extent from the Ohio to Lake Erie and stretch along from the Alleghany onwards, beyond the Miamis, and towards the Falls of St. Anthony . . . Ere long the sons of the Pilgrims will be on the shores of the Pacific.' Everywhere, the atmosphere of time and place exhorted Americans to romanticism, though they might know neither the word nor its meaning.

The romantic temper wanted heroic action, rich color, and exciting pageantry. These it found simply and melodiously set forth in Scott's poems, whose romanticism was glamorous and emotional rather than bookish or intellectual. Discussing 'the general intoxication' with Scott, the publisher Samuel Goodrich observed,

these productions seized powerfully upon the popular mind. Everybody could read and comprehend them. One of my younger sisters committed the whole of the Lady of the Lake to memory, and was accustomed of an evening to sit at her sewing, while she recited it to an admiring circle of listeners. All young poets were inoculated with the octa-syllabic verse, and newspapers, magazines, and even volumes, teemed with imitations and variations inspired by the 'Wizard Harp of the North.'

Even the stage was indebted to Scott's poems; the Philadelphia dramatist James Nelson Barker successfully adapted *Marmion*, using it as a medium for patriotic views during the War of 1812. Of *The Lay of the Last Minstrel, Marmion*, and *The Lady of the Lake, The American Review* declared, 'no poetical works . . . have been more widely circulated or read with more avidity in this country.' Copies were imported rapidly, so that *The Lady of the Lake* was to be found in Lexington, Kentucky, only a few months after it was first issued in Edinburgh. Presumably it circulated here even among some Indians, for Dickens in his travels between Cincinnati and Louisville later met a Choctaw chief who remembered the opening of *The Lady of the Lake* and the great battle scene of *Marmion* very clearly. Everywhere Scott's poetry was read enthusiastically and committed to memory. There are accounts of its first generation of readers reciting passages of vigorous description or idealistic sentiment many years after its original popularity, so that even as late as the 1860's, when *The Lay of the Last Minstrel* was an established classic, Raphael Semmes said he was influenced to resign from the United States Navy and follow the Confederacy because of his recollection of the lines beginning, 'Breathes there the man, with soul so dead . . .'

Scott's later poems were neither so fine nor so appealing as his first three, and when the fresher and more passionate romanticism of Byron appeared, Scott was displaced as the popular favorite. At first the interest in Byron was partly an aping of the English vogue that followed upon the publication of *Childe Harold* in 1812, for America had no need of a laureate of impassioned revolt and melancholy negation. Some Americans, however, were fascinated by the poet's glamorously turbid life, for his haughty pride and eccentric morality titillated an adolescent society just beginning to feel its way into a more sophisticated cultural world. Although Samuel Goodrich noted that the pulpit 'thundered against Byron's poems,' and one printer refused to stereotype the wicked works, the less rigorously moral public was entranced by Byron. To readers reared on fiction about the man of feeling, Byron, in his person and his poetry (which were inextricably merged in the public mind), was a man of sensibility for whose melancholy, macabre mysteriousness and licentiousness the Graveyard Poets, the Gothic novelists, and the sentimentalists had all prepared the way. To an even wider public, less concerned with such ideas, Byron's narration was pleasing. The vigor of his declamatory verse suited America (whose character he lauded in passages on Daniel Boone), and his descriptions delighted a people given to celebrating the rugged grandeur of their national lands.

Byron himself was somewhat surprised at this enthusiastic public, which accepted even his juvenile verses, for he told the publisher George Ticknor he 'wondered that our booksellers could find a profit in reprinting the *Hours of Idleness*.' The *New England Galaxy* measured the American public more accurately than Byron, even though it tortured metaphors by declaring in 1818: 'Everything from the poetical mint of his Lordship passes current and is bought up with little less avidity than our merchants in the China trade buy Spanish milled dollars.' Between 1811 and 1830 no less than forty-eight editions of Byron's writings were printed in America and selections of his verse were commonly found in magazines and newspapers. *The Portfolio* of December 1813 and January 1814 went so far as to reprint all of *The Giaour,* and on the Kentucky frontier the *Western Review* published *Mazeppa* and the first part of *Don Juan.* Publishers raced one another to issue his new books. So great was the profit to the edition first on the market that Carey and Lea of Philadelphia worked thirty compositors day and night to get *Don Juan* out in thirty-six hours after the proof sheets arrived from England; *Manfred* was said to have been received, printed, bound, and published all in one day. Captain Marryat, who toured America in 1839, was told by the publishers that between 150,000 and 200,000 copies of Byron's poetry had been sold in America, and he was inclined to believe it when he found sets of Byron in two log houses of the small Michigan village of Sault Ste. Marie. Mrs. Trollope in her usual caustic tone declared that Byron's popularity was attested by the fact there had been named for him a New York settlement consisting of but a warehouse and a liquor store. When Byron met his early and romantic death in 1824 the newspapers of the country, particularly in the South, blossomed with poetical tributes. The courtly Alexander Everett wrote a fifty-page critique for the nation's leading magazine, *The North American Review,* opening with the sentiment that 'The death of Lord Byron, without depressing the price of stocks or affecting the election of President, has produced a deep and general feeling of regret throughout the country.'

John Quincy Adams, a Byronic versifier himself, was elected President and the stock market continued bullish on America, but there was no poet to take Byron's place after his death. Keats and Shelley had no popular following, for their ideas, subject matter, and even their verse forms were too extreme for the public. Wordsworth and Coleridge, whose *Lyrical Ballads* were issued in America in 1802, found Joseph Dennie, the leader of the conservative Federalist literati, their only champion, and even he turned against them later, to declare in 1809 that 'Wordsworth stands among the foremost of those English bards, who have mistaken silliness for simplicity, and with a false and affected taste, filled their pages with the language of children and clowns.' The wording and the spirit of his criticism indicate he was influenced by Byron's satirical comments in *English Bards and Scotch Reviewers,* which may have directly persuaded the public to ignore Wordsworth and Coleridge. Although another edition of Wordsworth appeared in 1824, he did not reach a wide audience until he was safely crowned Poet Laureate in 1843. American poets fared no better. In 1818 Freneau, the most distinguished of all, learned from his publisher that after nine years the thousand copies of his latest edition were not quite sold out and that 'the demand here has ceased.'

The poets who were widely read during and after Byron's reign were all British. One of the most popular was Thomas Campbell. His declamatory love of liberty and his romantic descriptions of nature pleased those who admired Byron, and his high moral tone delighted those whom Byron shocked. He 'uniformly consecrated his fine talents to the interests of morals, humanity, and freedom,' the *Analectic Magazine* declared enthusiastically, and his *Pleasures of Hope* was endorsed by *The American*

Monthly Magazine as having 'that refinement which should characterize
the nineteenth century.' *Gertrude of Wyoming* was particularly popular
because it appealed to nationalism: its subject was a Revolutionary War
incident in which the English made a very poor showing and its setting
glamorized the American landscape. His sentiments being considered
appropriate to the young as well as the mature mind, Campbell was reprinted in school readers and elocution manuals. As N. P. Willis said,
'The school-boys have him by heart, and what lives upon their lips will
live and be loved forever.' The statement is marked by Willis's usual
exaggeration, but a few of Campbell's lines still linger in the American
memory, such lines as 'Coming events cast their shadows before,' ' 'Tis
distance lends enchantment to the view,' and 'Spare, woodman, spare the
beechen tree,' the latter better known through the American G. P. Morris's
plagiarism.

Samuel Rogers had a good American following, as did Bernard Barton,
the English Quaker whose verses were frequently reprinted by Philadelphia publishers, but the only other poet to rank with Campbell and
just behind Scott and Byron was Tom Moore. The public that welcomed
The Lay of the Last Minstrel was almost equally glad to hear the harp
that once through Tara's halls the soul of music shed. Like Scott, Moore
was a national poet making use of native balladry. As his biographer,
Howard Mumford Jones, observes,

Moore presented in his small person the union of music and verse, of folk tradition and courtly accomplishment which the age had read in Ossian, in Scott,
in novel and historical romance. In a sense Moore did not merely 'belong' to the
romantic movement; he incarnated it. He sang at one and the same time the
rights of the people and the glories of ancient kings, the pangs of romantic love
and the sympathy of nature.

Wordsworth, thirty-five years after his first poems were published, told
Moore that he had scarcely earned £1,000 from his many verses, while
Moore estimated he had made twenty times as much during a somewhat
briefer period. The ratio of earnings was indicative of their relative popularity, in America as well as England. Moore's sales here were not even
harmed by his scornful trip through the States, which he described as

> . . . One dull chaos, one unfertile strife
> Betwixt half-polished and half-barbarous life.

He continued for a long period to appeal to the sentimental taste of the
times, and the public that had welcomed Byron's *Giaour* and *Bride of*

Abydos took to the rococo pedanticism of *Lalla Rookh,* Moore's lengthy
oriental romance in prose and verse, as it had taken to his brief and
tuneful melodies. To own it and have it on the parlor table was the prevailing fashion, and even a heroine of fiction, such as one who appeared
in a Rhode Island magazine, carried 'that beautiful poem Lalla Rookh'
to the trysting place where she was to meet her beloved, for presumably
he alone could make her lift her eyes from Moore's purple pages. The
vogue lasted a long time, and as one American magazine noted, 'His
popularity seems to have increased with every publication.' According to
the New York editor, Cornelius Mathews, his favor did not wane until
1840 when 'Tom Moore was forgotten amid the sweeter melodies of
Tippecanoe and Tyler too.'

While Byron, Campbell, and Moore were attracting readers, Scott as
a novelist came back with greater force than before. From 1814, when
Waverley appeared anonymously, to 1832, when the last of the *Tales of
My Landlord* was issued, his novels were the most popular of all American pleasure reading. At least one new romance or collection of tales
appeared annually (except in the two years prior to his death) and countless editions of them flowed off the presses to eager readers. The century's first great writer of fiction, Scott presented with a new vigor all the
qualities that had appealed to readers of earlier novels and of his own
narrative poems. Uniting the attributes of prose and poetry, his historical
romances presented the pageantry of the past, the adventure of heroic
life, the beauty of spacious scenery, and a dramatic conception of human
relations, all more exuberantly and firmly realized than in any other contemporary works of literature.

A few critics grumbled because 'such splendid powers of imagination
and intellect were bestowed by Providence for some higher purpose than
novel writing,' fearing Scott tended to absorb time that might have gone
to pious literature, but most custodians of public taste were glad, as one
said, that 'the sickly pictures of . . . circulating library novels' were
being replaced by 'the energetic and manly fictions of Sir Walter Scott.'
Catharine M. Sedgwick, a novelist and arbiter of taste, declared of *Kenil-
worth,* 'I salute it with as much enthusiasm as a Catholic would a holy
relic.' Some reviewers even reached a kind of rapture, in which *The Port
Folio* critic of *Ivanhoe* declared he really could not appraise the novel,
because upon completing it he felt that he was awakening from a dream
of the days of Richard the Lion Hearted. But no matter what the critic

might say, the public could hardly wait for each new work by the anonymous 'Wizard of the North.' Samuel Goodrich said of Scott,

The appearance of a new novel from his pen caused a greater sensation in the United States than did some of the battles of Napoleon, which decided the fate of thrones and empires. Everybody read these works; everybody—the refined and the simple—shared in the delightful trances which seemed to transport them to remote ages and distant climes, and made them live and breathe in the presence of the stern Covenanters of Scotland, the gallant bowmen of Sherwood Forest, or even the Crusaders in Palestine.

John Hay recalled that on the Kentucky frontier his father and other pioneers saddled their horses and rode from a neighboring county to the principal post town of the region when a new novel by the author of *Waverley* was expected. On the seaboard, James Fenimore Cooper's daughter Susan and her Westchester friends watched for ships said to be bringing a new Scott romance among their cargo.

An audience of this sort made competition among publishers so keen that it helped break up their joint association for fair trade practices. With a Scott novel at stake any practice was considered fair. One American firm succeeded in planting workmen in Ballantyne's Edinburgh printing office to obtain galley proofs as soon as they came from the press, to be rushed to the United States by fast ship, apportioned among several printing houses so that compositors all over the city could work on them night and day and get them ready for printing, binding, and shipment by chartered stagecoach. Even when the business was regularized to the degree of purchasing rather than pilfering advance sheets, the same speedy system was maintained because the authorized publisher, Mathew Carey, feared another edition might be issued more rapidly by some other devious scheme. In 1822 when he was hurrying *The Fortunes of Nigel* to press, Carey had nine printing plants in Philadelphia and one in New York simultaneously setting different parts of the book in type. Every hour counted with a public so intense. In 1823 Carey wrote Constable, the English publishers,

We have rec'd 'Quentin Durward' most handsomely and have the Game completely in our own hands this time. In 28 hours after receiving it, we had 1500 copies sent off or ready to go . . . The opposition Edition will be out in about 48 hours after they have one of our Copies but we shall have complete and entire possession of every market in the Country for a short time.

Sometimes a great part of the first printing was snapped up by local readers buying directly from the publishers, and out-of-towners had to wait. *The American Monthly Magazine* declared that when *Rob Roy* was ready for issue, 'the doors of the publishers [were] thronged as soon as the anticipated pleasure was known to be lying in boards upon their stalls'; and of the first printing of 9,000 copies of *Woodstock*, 8,000 were sold on the day of publication. But generally Scott's novels were distributed throughout the country with as much speed as they were printed. So it was, for example, that *Woodstock*, issued in England during May 1826, was for sale in three New Orleans bookstores by June.

Because of these immense sales and because no royalties had to be paid to an author who was not an American resident, Scott's novels could be sold more cheaply here than in England. *Woodstock*, for example, cost 31 shillings 6 pence in England but only a dollar and a half in America, and prices dropped a good deal lower as soon as pirated editions came on the market. In course of time, novels other than the latest sold at seventy-five cents a copy and a whole set of twenty-six volumes could be bought on the installment plan at twenty-five cents a week for six months, or for five dollars outright. 'Could Sir Walter Scott have obtained a copyright in the United States,' Captain Marryat declared in 1839, 'it would have been worth to him by this time £100,000.' So great was Scott's popularity that some people even opposed the publishing practices of the day enough to wonder if the remarkable author ought not to receive some money for his American-issued works. When he ran into financial difficulties the *New York American* wrote an editorial, copied as far off as New Orleans, suggesting that Congress pass a law granting Scott and Scott alone the privilege of copyright for a sufficient period to recoup his losses.

Adaptations of Scott's novels, critical works about them, and biographies of the author had their day too. An anonymous dramatization of *Guy Mannering*, first produced in New York in 1818, had at least twenty revivals in that city alone. *Ivanhoe*, brought to the stage in 1820, the year the novel was published, continued to be played in various Eastern cities off and on for twenty years. A production of *Anne of Geierstein* was so elaborate that the stage was remodeled to accommodate sixteen horses in its battle scene. During twelve years—1820-32—New Orleans saw seven of Scott's novels and two of his poems dramatized in English (some, like *Rob Roy*, having as many as thirty performances), and the French theaters of the same period produced plays based on four of his novels and one of his poems. Donizetti's *Lucia* became a favorite opera; all over the nation parlor pianos held romantic sheet music from the opera or inspired by Scott novels in general, and two plays—*Lucy of*

Lammermoor and *Ravenswood*—were adapted into English from the Italian libretto. Scott-like novels, both American and foreign, had a good audience. Lockhart's *Life of Scott* sold more copies in America than in England, despite its revelation that America's love of Scott was not wholly requited; and Irving's impressions of *Abbotsford and Newstead Abbey* struck the public as a perfect combination of author and subject.

All Americans read and revered Scott, but the South was especially enthusiastic about him. From Virginia to Texas thirty-five towns were named Waverley. Many Southern children were christened Rowena, Ivanhoe, or even Walter Scott; plantations were known as Waverley, Deloraine, and Melrose; and steamboats were called *Rob Roy* and *Lady of the Lake*. The romantic sensibilities of the South were undoubtedly stimulated by Scott and the social system may have been buttressed by his pictures of medieval society, but some critics have contended that his effect was even deeper. Mark Twain felt that in the South

the genuine and wholesome civilization of the nineteenth century is curiously confused and commingled with the Walter Scott Middle-Age sham civilization . . . But for the Sir Walter disease, the character of the Southerner—or Southron, according to Sir Walter's starchier way of phrasing it—would be wholly modern, in place of modern and medieval mixed, and the South would be fully a generation further advanced than it is . . . For it was he that created rank and caste down there, and also reverence for rank and caste, and pride and pleasure in them.

Scott may have been responsible for the pseudo-Gothic architecture of the Louisiana state capitol and the florid literary style of Southern magazines, as Mark Twain also suggests, and he may even have introduced the word 'chivalry,' which was unknown to the regional vocabulary before his time, but Scott did not create the tobacco and cotton crops that made for a plantation system and a wide cleavage of classes; and he did not invent the cotton gin that made slavery profitable. The Connecticut Yankee Eli Whitney unwittingly did more to shape the Southern economy and social structure in the nineteenth century than Sir Walter Scott could ever have accomplished through all his fine and stirring words. The Waverley Novels may have helped make some of the men think of themselves as proud knights fighting for a romantic ideal, and Scott's code of chivalry may have contributed toward the exaggerated respect for ladies, yet such matters were but the decoration on a way of life whose foundations were more firmly sunk in economic realities.

Although only four or five of Scott's novels dealt with the Middle Ages, the South thought of him as the romancer of chivalry. When he died the

Louisiana Courier asked sadly, 'Who shall now depict the feudal castle—the time worn turret—the feats of warrior knights—the conflicts of the tournaments—the battles against the infidels?' Although there was no longer a Scott to paint such pictures, the Southern patricians enjoyed a kind of juvenile imitation of them in the tournaments they instituted in the 1840's. Nothing quite like their tilting with lances at a suspended ring was to be found in Scott's pages but the spirit of the contest was his. A South Carolina newspaper announced one as copying 'closely in dresses and arrangements . . . those that Ivanhoe witnessed'; contestants frequently took such titles as Waverley, Ivanhoe, The Disinherited Knight, and Peveril of the Peak; Sir Walter's name figured in the orations delivered to the winning 'knight'; and the affairs were furbished with Queens of Honour, pseudo-medieval costume, and all the other trappings of romance identified with a Scott tourney. Even in the serious contest of the Civil War Scott may have had some part in influencing Morgan, Mosby, and others to become intrepid cavaliers on horseback, dashing behind enemy lines with plumes waving; but that kind of warfare made sense for other reasons in a country where boys were trained to the saddle and where they lacked heavy munitions. If Scott did not shape Southern culture, he surely appealed to the region in which, during the bitterest days of the war, the *Richmond Examiner* could editorialize, 'While it is not for the South to fight with any mean advantage, it is time for her to abandon those polite notions of war which she has got from the Waverley Novels.' Even in defeat the South seems to have turned to Scott, who in contributing both 'clansman' and 'fiery cross' to the English language apparently stirred the founders of the Ku Klux Klan. Scott was influential because his fiction was in accord with the region's general attitude of mind. Like took to like, and his popularity was as much an effect as a cause of the South's aristocratic and chivalric bias.

When Scott died in 1832 the *Richmond Enquirer* published the sad news in an issue heavily bordered in black, such as is usually reserved for the death of a President. But the enjoyment of his books continued, for though occasionally children had to be prodded to read Scott because he supposedly inculcated a knowledge of history painlessly, it was not until half a century after his death that he was considered a 'classic' rather than a popular favorite. There were times during his own half century of greatest popularity—from the 'twenties to the 'seventies—when he was challenged by his imitators and successors, but always he came out on top in the realm of the historical novel that he had made his own. According to *The Southern Quarterly Review*, Bulwer-Lytton became 'Scott's legitimate successor and unvarying rival' during the 'thirties and 'forties. Bulwer's occult tale, *Zanoni*, published almost simultaneously in bound form and in two newspaper 'extras' selling for six cents a copy, was said to have reached some forty to fifty thousand Americans, and the *Southern Literary Messenger* contended *Pelham* swept over Scott's popularity like a wave: 'as the old Byronic enthusiasms had put Scott's verses out of fashion, so did the new threaten to dispose of his immortal prose romances.' It was during this period that Harriet Martineau observed in her *Society in America*, 'Scott is idolized, and so is Miss Edgeworth, but I think no one is so much read as Mr. Bulwer. I question whether it is possible to pass half a day in general society without hearing him mentioned.' Sometimes Bulwer was mentioned with asperity because of the loose morality of his brilliantly fashionable novels, but his varied types of fiction, following popular fads, were generally well received. *The Last Days of Pompeii*, going far behind Scott's medievalism to bring classic times into the realm of historical fiction, had the strongest and longest popularity. Its heroine was even honored by having a mining town named in her honor, for at the height of the Bulwer craze, Bedbug, California, was rechristened Ione.

Another successor of Scott was his protégé G. P. R. James, a prodigious writer of romances. Even students of James cannot quite agree on how many books he wrote (the number seems to have been between the high fifties and the mid-sixties), but it is agreed they all sold well. Some years saw as many as seven different books come out under his name, most of them running to two or three volumes. They began to appear in 1829 and continued until his death in 1860. The very titles indicated their nature, for among his many popular books were such works as *The Robber, The Smuggler, The Gentleman of the Old School*, and *Lord Montague's Page;* some used proper names whose mere mention evokes thoughts of intrigue and romance: *Richelieu, Darnley*, and *Agnes Sorel*. Most symptomatic of his own interests and those of a whole school of American readers is the title of one novel—*The Ancient Regime*—redolent of the adventurous romance found only in days that are gone, the time of wonders whose passing creates nostalgia for bright promises that remain unfulfilled.

James's romances of chivalric adventure had a good formula and for a long time neither he nor his readers saw any reason to change it. Statistics show that no less than seventeen of his novels open with a 'solitary

horseman' or 'a party of cavaliers' riding through a romantic landscape
as a sultry summer day draws toward evening, and the rest of the sword-
and-cloak doings followed a regular pattern to an established happy conclusion. *The Knickerbocker* playfully contended that when its reporter
was asked by James, 'Are my works read in America?' the answer was,
'Your *work*, I presume you mean, why, my dear Sir, it is published once
a month regularly by one of our great publishers and always with a new
title.' Actually, the success of every one of his novels was 'always the
same and tremendous,' his publishers declared. So sure was the sale of
any work by James that in those rough-and-tumble days, one firm went
to the length of breaking into Harper's offices in the hope of snatching
a James manuscript. To take advantage of such popularity James moved
to the United States for a while, hoping to collect full royalties as a resident, but though he was turned off with substantial payments instead,
he did have the pleasure of learning 'that upon an average my works had
a sale of seven thousand more than those of any other author,' and that
Harper's considered him far more valuable property than their other
great English author, Thackeray.

The success of Scott and other historical and local-color romancers,
such as Jane Porter (her *Thaddeus of Warsaw* and *The Scottish Chiefs*
attracted many readers) and Maria Edgeworth, inspired Americans to
follow their lead. During the 'thirties Americans were busily founding
historical societies and making anthologies of regional literature; a combination in the form of native historical romances was logical. Publishers
were something less than enthusiastic about the works of American authors which, because of royalty payments, had to sell at a third to a half
more than those by Englishmen, but critics and some of the public hope-
fully called for an American Scott. During the period of national expan-
siveness following the War of 1812 and the semi-centennial celebrations
of the Revolution, there was a demand for American historical novels to
present patriotic subjects and local scenes. Critics who liked novels but
who still felt a taint attached to 'mere fiction' contended that if a historical romance were written and set in America it would probably be
pure. Therefore, they cried, let us have our own *Waverley*. Besides, did
we not have a finer and grander tradition, they said, and why should we
continue our dependence upon the British when two wars had proved
our superiority and freedom? Material was plentiful, they pointed out;
there waiting for the pen of the novelist were the Indians, the Pilgrims,
the French and Indian Wars, the Revolution, and our vast and rugged

scenery. Why, said one reviewer, 'compared with some of ours, Scottish rivers are but brooks, and Scottish forests mere thickets.' Rufus Choate delivered an oration at Salem amply described in its title, *The Importance of Illustrating New-England History by a Series of Romances Like the Waverley Novels,* and statesmen of other regions were as loud in demanding chauvinistic fiction about their native areas. Cooper, in 1821, was the first to answer these calls with his Revolutionary War romance, *The Spy,* soon followed by the beginning of the Leather-Stocking Tales and *Lionel Lincoln,* which he announced as the first of thirteen romances, one about each of the colonies and its part in the Revolution. During the decade of the 'twenties almost a third of the novels written by Americans dealt with the colonial period or the Revolution, and even though critics sometimes casually disposed of half a dozen native works in a single review as 'imitation Waverley Novels,' the fad lasted through the 'thirties, when 20 per cent of the American-written novels made use of local history. J. P. Kennedy's *Horse-Shoe Robinson,* which turned Scott's aristocrats into Virginia cavaliers and his Highlanders into frontiersmen, had four editions within a year, and other historical tales of the 'thirties, such as William Gilmore Simms's *The Yemassee,* Daniel Pierce Thompson's *The Green Mountain Boys,* and James K. Paulding's *The Dutchman's Fireside* had a great many readers. Even *Nick of the Woods,* by the popular playwright, Robert Montgomery Bird, though issued in the middle of the financial crisis of 1837, eventually had twenty-three editions in English, four in translation, and a popular melodramatic dramatization. As late as 1883 Mark Twain in *Life on the Mississippi* could refer to the leading character in Bird's novel as though he would be known to all educated readers.

Of all these and many other historical novelists, Cooper alone was accorded the distinction of being called 'the American Sir Walter Scott.' Though in those days this was equivalent to saying that an author had written 'the great American novel,' it was, according to Cooper, 'a term that gives me more disgust than any other.' His first work, after an amateurish fling called *Precaution,* was *The Spy.* Two weeks after it appeared the surprised publisher wrote Cooper, 'it has succeeded over and beyond my own expectations,' and when he quickly followed the first small printing with an issue of 3,000 copies, this also was exhausted in two months, requiring another of 5,000. Three years later came *The Pioneers,* the first of the series about Natty Bumppo, which is said to have sold 3,500 copies on the day of publication. The next year *The Pilot* had a

great success, following in the wake of Scott's *The Pirate*, which Cooper
purposefully attempted to outdo. *The Last of the Mohicans*, issued in
1826, sold out its first 5,000 copies so rapidly that the publisher decided
it should be stereotyped so that more printings could come as quickly as
demanded. He optimistically had plates made of all Cooper's novels,
'which,' as he told the writer, 'has not happened to any living author of
works of fancy.' The next of the Leather-Stocking series, *The Prairie*, and
the next sea story, *The Red Rover*, did well, but in 1829 came *The Wept
of Wish-ton-Wish*, a novel about King Philip's War, which was a failure
because Cooper neither really understood nor sympathized with his
Puritan characters. The barbarous title must have scared away some
readers too. Cooper's great popularity was at an end.

Cooper lost his public partly because in the 'forties taste shifted from
the romance of adventure to the elegance of Bulwer and the sentiment
of Dickens. But Cooper was mainly responsible for his own waning popularity. His novels after *The Wept of Wish-ton-Wish* were the products
of seven years of travel abroad, which had changed his views about the
values of both American and European society in such a way as to dis-
appoint his audience and eventually alienate it. After 1830 he was
damned first for dispelling the glamor of European feudalism in his tedi-
ously doctrinaire trilogy, *The Bravo*, *The Heidenmauer*, and *The Heads-
man*, which ran counter to the Scott attitude. Next he was damned for
attacking the abuses of democracy in his satires, *The Monikins*, *Home-
ward Bound*, and *Home as Found*. The public was further irritated by
his pungent social criticism and his fights with the people of his home
town and the national press over matters varying from ancestral property
rights to a reinterpretation of heroes in the War of 1812. Now instead
of being called America's Scott he was popularly nicknamed Effingham
Cooper, after one of his characters who was considered aristocratically
un-American. Cooper still had a greater public than most novelists
(*Satanstoe*, for example, sold over 6,000 copies in three months), but his
work no longer had the following he once knew. Although he completed
the epical Leather-Stocking Tales with *The Pathfinder* and *The Deer-
slayer* and wrote sixteen more novels, including some of his best, the
critics and public alike generally attacked or neglected him. As a prominent editor of the time, Sarah Josepha Hale, said in reviewing *The Deer-
slayer*, 'He mistook his course when he turned aside from the legitimate
province of fiction to sneer at and condemn those to whom he was
inimical.' His *Ned Myers*, a realistic sea story unlike his earlier romances

and in the tradition of Dana's popular *Two Years Before the Mast,* was a momentary favorite, selling 10,000 copies within a year, but most of his works fared poorly. Although from 1842 onwards the novels were brought out at twenty-five cents a volume in a bid for sales, the publishers, who had lost $2,600 on *The Monikins* and had sold only 1,700 of the 4,000 copies of *Mercedes of Castile,* found that even price cutting could not redeem Cooper's great popularity. His day was over. Scott's sales mounted all through the 'forties and 'fifties, but Cooper had killed his own popularity. Only after his acrimonious disputes were forgotten was he revived as a boy's favorite to have about 50,000 copies of his various books sold annually during the 'sixties. Later he became a major figure in the study of American literature.

The only American writer whose popularity preceded Cooper's, rivaled it at its most brilliant period, and outlasted it was Washington Irving. *Salmagundi,* his youthful satirical essays written with his brothers and a brother-in-law, and his burlesque antiquarianism in the Knickerbocker *History of New York* appealed to a local audience and gave him a great reputation even beyond his home city. His whimsical, good-humored raillery at the city's history, tinctured with a fascination for the quaint ways that were gone, struck just the right note for the city that in rapidly outgrowing its past was beginning to feel a self-conscious need of discovering its traditions. His fictitious chronicler, Diedrich Knickerbocker, pleased the public fancy and just as *Salmagundi* coined the name Gotham for the city, so the name of a forgotten Dutch family from Albany suddenly became a symbol of New York. Before long there was a Knickerbocker School of writers, a *Knickerbocker Magazine,* and even more mundane organizations such as a Knickerbocker insurance company, steamship line, bakery, and ice factory. The book 'took with the public,' as Irving remarked, 'and gave me celebrity.' He admitted, 'I was noticed, caressed & for a time elated by the popularity I gained,' and he found that the $3,000 from the book was earned more pleasantly than the salary from his family's hardware business. Still, he continued with the firm, meanwhile entering into military, political, and social activities, with only an occasional piece of writing, such as an edition of Campbell's poetry, to keep his pen busy.

In 1815 he set sail for England to take charge of the family business there, but when it went into bankruptcy three years later he stayed to earn his living as a professional author. He had been impressed by the beauties of the English countryside as he saw it through his own eyes

and through those of the romantic poets and of Scott, who was his literary passion, and it was this scene that in part formed the background
for his next work. *The Sketch Book* was a great success; its first printing
of 2,000 copies was quickly sold. The dreamily poetic mood, quiet antiquarian interest, and picturesque legendry appealed to a public accustomed to Scott and searching for an interpreter of its own past. Although
Irving lacked the vigor and amplitude of Scott or Cooper, just as he
lacked the philosophic introspection of the intellectual romanticist, his
work had the patina of romanticism cherished by the public. His purpose, Irving wrote, was 'to escape . . . from the commonplace realities
of the present, and lose myself among the shadowy grandeurs of the
past,' which is just what his plum-pudding-and-holly tales of England
and his pastel-colored creations of an American folklore perfectly succeeded in doing. His gently humorous sentiment and graceful evocation
of quaint and distant times in 'The Legend of Sleepy Hollow,' 'Rip Van
Winkle,' and other tales delighted his contemporary public. After the
publication of *The Sketch Book* readers looked forward to another work
by their new favorite, and the *New York Evening Post* declared, 'There
is as much anxiety for its appearance, as there would be for a novel of
Scott's or a poem of Byron's.' *Bracebridge Hall*, which followed after
two years, was no disappointment, for even if an astute critic like Maria
Edgeworth remarked that 'the workmanship surpasses the work,' the
public, seeing that it was in the style and tradition of *The Sketch Book*,
eagerly accepted its romances of Merrie England and of Dolph Heyliger,
a new addition to American legendry. Not until his next work, *Tales of
a Traveller*, did many readers notice the thinness of Irving's sequels to
The Sketch Book, yet, as his biographer Stanley Williams has remarked,
'Indeed, it was his eminence which made the inferior *Tales of a Traveller*
so glittering a bull's-eye for the critics.' *The Conquest of Granada* and
The Alhambra, a sort of Spanish *Sketch Book*, recaptured the public,
which guessed that the latter work had sold some 20,000 copies; for, according to Williams, 'it was the fashion to compare the circulation of
Irving's writings with those of Byron and Scott.'

Finally in 1832 Irving returned to his native New York after a seven-
teen-year absence abroad. He came back like a conquering general from
war. At the very moment when his only rival, Cooper, was going into
eclipse, Irving shone most brightly. He had been gone so long that the
mere fact of his return made him seem more important somehow, almost
as though he were his own beloved Rip Van Winkle come back to the

native city he had celebrated and helped make famous. A great reception and public dinner was given him at the City Hall, and those who could not have the privilege of listening to the windy after-dinner eulogies and the author's modest reply read them eagerly in the newspaper. Here was the man whose writings they had for years been collecting on their shelves, along with books by Scott and Byron, yet he was alive, and, moreover, American, an American who had received the seal of English approval, even of Scott himself. Plaster of Paris busts of Irving were sold by the hundreds, and at $15 apiece, for Irving was a national hero to be enshrined in the parlor. He was the symbol of American culture, the author who was also a gentleman, the writer who had made money and traditions alike, and who was as much respected abroad as he was at home.

Irving's next books were popular too, for he now turned his attention to the one scene he had left untouched that was bound to please the American public. Taking as his criteria those that the people themselves established—the belief in the nation's manifest destiny and the rugged individualism of the pioneer—Irving celebrated the West in his *Tour on the Prairies* and the fur-trading empire of the nation's wealthiest citizen in his *Astoria*. In a period about to pick up the great slogan, 'Go West, Young Man!' and already dallying with thoughts of running the national boundary out to Oregon, any volume on the West was likely to be popular; one from Washington Irving was a natural success. It was, as Philip Hone, a leading figure of New York, said, 'the very best kind of light reading,' for the charm lay in Irving's easy, graceful manner of describing 'events of ordinary occurrence to the settlers of the great West, but matters of thrilling interest to comfortable citizens who read them in their green slippers, seated before a shining grate.' Irving began his career concocting graceful legendry for a people hungry for traditions of past time; he ended it vicariously thrilling a people anxious to extend their dominions in space. Although he himself was a quiet, contemplative, and sophisticated gentleman, his main themes were in sympathy with the interests and desires of the plain men and women of his own time, and they rewarded him by making him their most popular American author.

Chapter 6

Home Influence

As America approached the century's halfway mark the great middle class began to look around and realize it had a 'manifest destiny' as great as that of the nation itself. With the increase in industrial prosperity the cities grew. East of the Mississippi and north of the Mason and Dixon line more and more people began to crowd into the settled communities, which, though they contained new slums, also contained new wealth. Financial and cultural extremes were tremendous but they tended to melt at either end into the large, fluid body called the middle class. Members of this vaguely bounded, constantly increasing focal point emulated upper-class standards, but their sophistication was softened and transmuted by subconscious memories of lower-class mores. Establishing its own compromising criteria, this new *bourgeoisie* told the lower class to aspire to them, and called the upper class to account for transgressing them. Though it was the middle class, it was also the ruling class. Aware of its social responsibilities, it extended the principle of public education so that, at least in the North, free education through high school began to be fairly common. The middle class established or supported libraries to which mechanics of the working class might turn for edification. It trebled the number of subscription libraries between 1825 and 1850. It sponsored lyceums, which by the 'forties numbered into the thousands, bringing men and women face to face with the speakers and writers who represented the great cultural guides of the middle class itself. Its inventive genius and money-making interest created machine-made paper and printing presses that turned out thousands upon thousands of impressions an hour. It congratulated itself that through the penny newspaper, the periodical, the Sunday School tract, and the cheaply bound book it was bringing culture to the masses. Early in the 'fifties, *Harper's Magazine,* one of the new organs of middle-class culture, could proudly proclaim, 'Literature has gone in pursuit of the million, penetrated highways and hedges, pressed its way into cottages, factories, omnibuses, and railroad cars, and become the most cosmopolitan thing of the century.' At the same time a Southern critic commented: 'The almost universal ability to read and the consequent love of reading have developed in this nation especially an immense middle class of ordinary readers of average intelligence. The great middle class,' said this critic, presumably referring to its readers only, 'is composed four-fifths of women in as much as the hard-worked men of the day have little leisure and less taste for anything beyond the counting room.'

One of the greatest inventions of the middle class was the new woman. She, the men frankly and fondly admitted, was their arbiter in affairs that might be called cultural. Her power was of a sort no ruling-class woman had ever possessed before. Men were busy with money-making, politics, and all the other so-called practical affairs of the day; women took over the arts, social deportment, and domestic standards. As the *Token of Friendship,* issued from Boston in 1844, declared, 'Home is the empire, the throne of woman. Here she reigns in the legitimate power of all her united charms. She is the luminary which enlightens, and the talisman which endears it. It is she who makes "home, sweet home." ' Though some women were marching out into fields sacred to men and in 1848 dared organize the first Woman's Rights Convention, most knew and cherished their place. 'We are not for learned ladies,' announced Mrs. Kirkland, in an article on 'The American Ideal Woman,' though she did champion the cultivation of 'every faculty.' And another spokesman, Sarah Josepha Hale, asserted that women being weaker in a physical sense were obviously stronger in a moral one, and should preserve that strength pure, untainted by the market place and the political campaign.

The ideal woman of the mid-century still resembled her ancestors, Pamela and Clarissa and the heroines of a hundred other sentimental novels, but she was much changed. She was not so fragile as her grandmother affected to be. Though still possessed of a delicate sensibility, she neither fainted nor wept so much and was less given to simpering displays of emotion. She was still inclined to believe that 'frailty thy name is woman' was an encomium, yet her lugubrious sensitivity was less adolescent. Her unceasing domestic duties and exquisitely sensitive appreciation of the beauties and horrors of the world made her prone to illness, which she presumably fought with high nobility. To indicate that she was ill and therefore pure she often employed 'whitening powders,' which gave her a prefabricated pallor as notable as the artificial suntan her granddaughters affected a century later to show that they were wholesome and natural. Dumas's novel *Camille* and its popular dramatizations may have encouraged the conception that a taint of tuberculosis moved men to erotic thoughts. At any event, the 'decline' was considered extremely attractive, but most generally it was associated with the sainted mother to whom passion is alien. Her refinement might make of her a delicate female, but her morality made her also a genteel woman. She did not approve her rowdier sisters who asked for education and voting rights equal to those of men, but she was nevertheless more woman than female. She stood on her own two legs, though she blushed even to call them limbs and hid them carefully behind voluminous skirts. She possessed a strong mind, its strength coming from full knowledge of her own sphere. The home was her domain, which she ruled in part by cultivating self-abnegation. Anyone outside this sphere was either more or less than a woman: either a feminist or one of those dark, passionate exotics who seem to stray from Latin countries and into American novels of the time as a contrast to decent domesticity. Something more than a mere housewife, something less than a Lucy Stone, and far from the insipid heroine of the late eighteenth century, America's new ideal woman was a subject remarked upon by all visitors to this country. James Silk Buckingham, one of the Englishmen who came to discover the land of the middle class, summed it up when he said that the 'leading features' of the American woman were 'domestic fidelity, social cheerfulness, unostentatious hospitality, and moral and religious benevolence.'

The middle-class lady, only newly arrived in her responsible position, needed guidance. As her husband might learn to use his talents most profitably from a phrenological reading of the bumps on his head, so she might learn to use her new-found wealth and leisure from the studied reading of an etiquette book. If one journalist, Edgar Allan Poe, could declare of phrenology, 'It has assumed the majesty of a science,' another, Catharine Maria Sedgwick, could insist that with etiquette book in hand one might become genteel in far less than the conventional three generations, 'too slow a process in these days of accelerated movement.' This was the age of the etiquette book, and an admittedly incomplete enumeration by the historian Arthur M. Schlesinger discovers 'aside from frequent revisions and new editions, twenty-eight different manuals appeared in the 1830's, thirty-six in the 1840's, and thirty-eight more in the 1850's—an average of over three new ones annually in the pre-Civil War decades.' The etiquette books of one generation may become the joke books of the next, as Clifton Furness points out, but in the mid-nineteenth century this type of writing was sufficiently respected to enlist the services of even such well-known authors as Lydia Huntley Sigourney, Miss Sedgwick, and Timothy Shay Arthur; and it had a large enough following to warrant Irwin Beadle's publication of a *Dime Book of Practical Etiquette*.

One of the things the etiquette books taught was proper behavior in the parlor, for the parlor was the most sacred shrine of the middle-class temple—Home. Here a union was effected between domesticity and culture, the twin deities of the middle-class woman. On the polished mahogany or marble-topped table, located in the very center of the room, lay a book, for all readers of etiquette manuals knew that to have a book on the parlor table was a passport to culture. The book, of course, need not be read; it was merely a symbol. It proved that its cultivated owner loved the arts enough to spend good money on them, and, for a few dollars, allowed her to assume something of the character of the patron generally associated with society of wealth and breeding. For those unable to show their devotion to culture by attending such displays as Jenny Lind's concerts, the ballets of Fanny Ellsler, or the violin recitals of Ole Bull, the gift book on the parlor table was an acceptable substitute. As the name implies, gift books were generally not purchased by their owners. They were, to use the fancy term of the day, 'bestowed' on a suitable occasion, such as Christmas, New Year's Day, a birthday, or even a funeral. The middle-class sentimental attachment to holidays could most genteelly be celebrated by the donation of a handsome anthology of appropriate stories, poems, and pictures known as the gift book. For that reason no such book was complete without a mezzotinted wreath, a chromolithographed garland, a scroll, or a sunburst in which the donor might inscribe his and the recipient's names and a suitable sentiment in copperplate handwriting. As many as sixty different gift books appeared within a year, and, all told, some thousand

such keepsakes were issued between 1825 and the Civil War years.
A luxuriously refined appearance was their main requirement, and though
almost every great American author of the day contributed to these
anthologies, they existed principally for the elegant color plates and steel
engravings to which the text often served merely as explanation.
Publishers generally spent three times as much on the so-called em-
bellishments as on the printed matter and twice as much again on the
bindings of watered silk, flamboyantly stamped gilding, embossed
leather, or varnished papier-mâché with inlaid mother-of-pearl. These
Dew Drops, Gems of the Season, and *Books of Pearls* were truly what
Lydia Sigourney called them: 'luxurious literature.' And yet a more
astute contributor, Robert Southey, was also right when he observed
that they were 'schools for Novelists, male and female.'

For the gift book Poe wrote stories whose lush decoration and hyper-
emotionalism were well suited to the spirit of these annuals, yet his
Tales of the Grotesque and Arabesque, published in a small edition in
1840, two years later had not earned enough to pay for the printing.
Authors of popular novels frequently graduated from the annuals, their
refined sentiment and elegant diction being carried over into the full-
length fiction of the day, but there the resemblance ended. The gift book
was clearly understood to be ornament, no more fit for daily reading than
the horsehair sofa or the polished table of the heavily curtained parlor
were suited to everyday use. For reading the family wanted a book in
which it could be absorbed for some time, one to hold it together as a
harmonious intellectual unit evenings on end after early supper. Just as
Foster's 'Old Folks at Home' was a favorite song and *The Home Journal,
The Fireside Monthly,* and *Arthur's Home Gazette, A Journal of Pure
Reading* were popular periodicals, so the book that was to be successful
generally had to stay within the imaginative bounds of the family, avoiding any subject or language that might be improper for the growing
child to hear or the mother to read aloud. Women looked upon fiction as
a medium for bringing culture to the family, a culture very nearly
synonymous with morality. Though the scene might be fanciful, the
language speciously unnatural, the emotion heightened, still the novel
that was liked was the one that was 'improving,' or at least moral. If
it taught a lesson, for example that an honest man or woman will rise
in station; if it brought one a greater appreciation of God's handiwork—
nature; or if it somehow imbued one with the desire to live a purer,

more purposeful life, it was particularly suitable to reading aloud in the family circle.

For these purposes fiction was the most satisfactory form of literature. It did not fly off into the misty idealized world of poetry and yet it was not hobbled to the dull reality of texts. It occupied a middle ground between poetry's heightened sentiment and the text's severe intellectualism, a compromise pleasing to the middle class. It allowed scope to the pure imagination and yet it was bounded by a purpose. And so though biography and history, travel and theology, poetry and essays all had some readers, the largest public turned to the novel.

In 1835 when publishers divided their stock into sixteen categories, 64 new novels and tales were issued, while poetry, history, and biography together numbered only 61 new works. Nearly half of these novels were by Americans, about as many as had appeared in the decade from 1810 to 1820. From 1820 to 1830 Americans issued 109 different fictional works of their own and then, with the period of the novel firmly established, they more than tripled this number from 1830 to 1840. From 1840 to 1850 they really hit their stride and issued almost a thousand different novels and tales. With the growth of the middle-class reading public the book business had become big business. Only $2,500,000 worth of books were manufactured in this country in 1820; by 1850 the value of book publications was set at $12,500,000.

'The task of the novel writer of today is much more arduous than . . . thirty years ago,' declared a New York reviewer in the 1830's, for he found that 'there are as many good critics of novels now as there were readers of them formerly. The public taste has grown nice.' The reviewer was right about the number of readers but he was right about taste only if he used the word 'nice' to mean squeamish rather than discriminating. By the 'forties the novel was getting to be nice as Nelly. It had been taken out of the hands of a Cooper and put into those of women who resembled Cooper's feminine characters, stigmatized by Lowell as being flat as the prairies and sappy as the maples. Because women were the rulers of the home and home was where the novel was read, fiction came more and more to concern itself with women and their special world. It excluded business (husbands daily disappeared from fiction to enter some remote, uncharted world where they earned money); it neglected politics (civic affairs and the structure of a democracy were seemingly impolite parlor topics); it was ignorant of social movements (incoming immigrants and westward-moving pioneers were merely quaint characters used for contrast with the normal middle class); and ethical or theological problems were viewed only in the simplest Sunday School terms.

As a magazine of the day declared, 'The privilege of deep research is man's right; with it we have no wish to interfere,' but fiction it claimed as 'woman's appropriate sphere, as much as the flower-garden, the drawing room, and the nursery.' First as readers, then as writers, women took over the novel. The style of these women was as 'fine' in its superlative decoration as the bindings in which their gift-book contributions appeared or as the pen names they chose. Their subject matter was simple enough though. It was essentially the life of the home, the way of the household. A severe structure or a complex plot was too much for most of these writers; instead, from the episodes of family life they spun stories that had one or two simple themes: the womanly concepts that submission to God's will brings its own happiness or that virtuous deportment creates a happy home and a better social status. Other popular fiction of the day suggested characters and situations. From Bulwer came the drawing-room scene, purified and Americanized; from Dickens, the pathetic bride, the orphaned child, and the kindly eccentric character; from Charlotte Brontë, a watered version of the Jane Eyre-Rochester relation; from Mrs. Gaskell, the sense of quiet rural life. But more important than all these influences was the one original component: the normal background of domesticity. Adulterate the style and the story as they would, these women revealed clearly enough that they knew one thing—their own homes. Their plots were romantic and so was their point of view toward life, but their minor details and setting were realistic. A more professional novelist like Mrs. Gaskell appreciatively observed how 'These American novels unconsciously reveal all the little household secrets; we see the meals as they are put on the table, we learn the dresses which those who sit down to them wear . . . we hear their kindly family discourses, we enter into their home struggles, and,' she concluded as thousands of contemporary readers would, 'we rejoice when they gain the victory.'

Though the 'fifties saw the publication of three novels by Hawthorne—*The Scarlet Letter, The House of the Seven Gables,* and *The Blithedale Romance*—and three by Melville—*White-Jacket, Moby-Dick,* and *Pierre* —as well as such other distinguished works as *Walden, Leaves of Grass,* and *Representative Men,* none of these sold the way the women's books did. All of them together probably did not in that decade add up to the sales of one of the more popular domestic novels. Fred Lewis Pattee appropriately calls these the 'feminine fifties.' In a period whose world of popular fiction was essentially unfurnished outside the home, a novel about whaling, which moreover concerned itself with the essential nature of evil, was inevitably not for a wide public. Only sixty copies of Melville's *Moby Dick* survived the burning of Harper's warehouse in 1853, but these presumably satisfied the demand for ten years, since the book was not reissued until 1863. The reprint, even though it moved faster than an average of six copies a year, did not sell enough to warrant a third printing before 1892.

Hawthorne was a success compared with his neighbor Melville, but a failure by more usual publishing standards. He too was given to allegory, and, as Poe pointed out, he could not hope to attract many readers until he was willing to 'get a bottle of visible ink, come out from the Old Manse, cut Mr. Alcott, hang (if possible) the editor of "The Dial," and throw out of the window to the pigs all his old numbers of "The North American Review."' In *The Scarlet Letter* Hawthorne made a halfhearted move in that direction by bulking out his romance with a pleasant, realistic introduction about the Customs House in which he worked. Though it had little enough to do with the story, many critics agreed with the one who thought it 'more piquant than anything in the book.' This introduction and some gossip about the raciness of the novel's subject helped sell the first edition's 2,500 copies very quickly. One reviewer wondered querulously, 'Is the French era actually begun in our literature?' Another contended he knew where some of the public came from. Traveling on a stagecoach he heard a group of girls tittering about the book. 'These school girls,' he thought, 'had done injury to their young sense of delicacy, by devouring such a dirty story; and after talking about it before folk, inadvertently, they had enough of Mother Eve in them to know that they were ridiculous and that shame was their best retreat.'

The Scarlet Letter invaded the field of popular books for a moment and the strange domestic life of *The House of the Seven Gables* interested over 6,500 book buyers the next year. On the strength of this following, *The Blithedale Romance* was issued in June of 1852 with a printing order of 5,090 copies and a reprint the next month of 2,350 copies. Soon the sales stopped dead. A novel set in a Fourierist colony and concerned with the individual's relation to society was too abstract for a large public. It was in keeping with current interest in improvement but it was too 'gloomy,' too 'psychological,' and too burdened by ideas, as contemporary reviewers stated.

A year after *The Blithedale Romance* appeared, Thoreau discovered that his *Week on the Concord and Merrimack Rivers* had sold only 219 copies since its publication in 1849. When his publisher returned the remainder, Thoreau wryly mused, 'I have now a library of nearly nine hundred volumes, over seven hundred of which I wrote myself.' While Thoreau was contemplating his books in his own home, Fanny Fern might have walked into any genteel parlor along the eastern seaboard and seen her books, for in that year of 1853 she sold 70,000 copies of just one work, *Fern Leaves from Fanny's Portfolio*. And that same year G. P. Putnam wrote Hawthorne his royalties on *Mosses from an Old Manse* amounted to $144.09, explaining that 'the last two semi-annual accounts were passed over by our bookkeeper simply because the amount was small.' Parenthetically, to prove some Putnam books did sell, he casually mentioned that Susan Warner, the author of *The Wide, Wide World*, received from us for six months' sales $4500.' It was a poor time for Concord literati, a good one for the ladies. Thoreau calmly considered the unopened packing cases of his books, commenting quietly, 'Is it not well that the author should behold the fruits of his labor?' But Hawthorne simply exploded,

America is now wholly given over to a d——d mob of scribbling women, and I should have no chance of success while the public taste is occupied with their trash—and should be ashamed of myself if I did succeed. What is the mystery of these innumerable editions of the 'Lamplighter,' and other books neither better nor worse?—worse they could not be, and better they need not be, when they sell by the 100,000.

The mystery of Maria Susanna Cummins's novel, *The Lamplighter*, was no mystery at all, except to Hawthorne. It was a moralistic romance about an orphan girl befriended by the appropriately named lamplighter, Trueman Flint, and later taken into the home of a kindly woman accidentally blinded in youth by a brother who then ran away in remorse. When the orphan becomes a young lady and marries her childhood sweetheart (he has become a financial success) and discovers her benefactress's brother (he turns out to be the orphan's father), and they all move into substantial houses, the great reading public had just such a novel as it liked. The main characters were women—women who overcome all sorts of dilemmas through Christian fortitude and faith that eventually establishes them securely in prosperous middle-class homes, tangible symbols of an eventual call to heavenly mansions. It is no wonder the novel sold 40,000 copies in eight weeks.

Hawthorne might not understand *The Lamplighter*, but he meekly confessed in his very next letter to Ticknor,

I bestowed some vituperation on female authors. I have since been reading 'Ruth Hall'; and I must say I enjoyed it a good deal. The woman writes as if the Devil was in her; and that is the only condition under which a woman ever writes anything worth reading . . . Can you tell me anything about this Fanny Fern? If you meet her, I wish you would let her know how much I admire her.

Hawthorne wasn't the only man to admire Fanny Fern, though few knew that she was really named Sarah Payson Willis and was the sister of N. P. Willis, the popular journalist. She was in her mid-forties when she achieved success, a vivacious, coquettish woman hiding a blowzy face behind a stylish veil, but nonchalantly revealing the foot and ankle that dapper young men about town declared wonderfully well turned. Her head was a mass of curls and had been, in fact, ever since school days when she tore up a copy of Euclid to make curling papers; her whole manner was as lively as the brisk sketches she wrote. It was not her flighty yet florid style but a personality shining through her prose that impelled readers to tell the author, 'I like your writings and I like you.' Neither essays nor stories, her rapid-fire sketches dealt with different subjects—119 of them in a 400-page book—but carried one clear mood throughout. Compounding sentiment and satire, pathos and puns in a strangely personal blend, they conjured up a feeling, told a brief anecdote, sketched the vignette of a romantic landscape, outlined a quaint character, or served simply to set forth an animated moral. She was almost the only member of the generation's sorority of sentimentalists who had a sense of humor.

Within a year Fanny Fern published three books, selling 180,000 copies of them, equivalent to a sale of more than a million copies to the population of the 1940's. In 1855 her first novel appeared, the sanctimonious autobiographical study entitled *Ruth Hall*, so much admired by Hawthorne. It pictured the heroine (that is the author) as 'a model wife, a model mother, a model widow, a model saint,' every way in which a woman could be a model, and other characters (all clearly recognizable as relations and associates) as fiends. 'It has sold universally,' said *Harper's* (by which they meant 50,000 copies in eight months), 'and that profoundly interesting question whether Ruth Hall is Fanny Fern has been debated from the Penobscot to the Mississippi.' There wasn't much doubt who Ruth Ellett Hall was meant to be and there was less that her brother, Hyacinth Ellett, who 'recognizes only the drawing-room side of human nature,' was the author's brother, N. P. Willis. This dandified journalist, whom Oliver Wendell Holmes described as 'something between a remembrance of the Count d'Orsay and an anticipation of Oscar Wilde,' was no longer so popular as he had once been, but his sentimental prattle and cleverly turned stories were just feminine enough to make him a serious competitor of the lady authors of the day. Fanny herself was untroubled as week in and week out for sixteen years she collected anywhere from a hundred to a thousand dollars for her columns in Bonner's *New York Ledger* and had the satisfaction of seeing a full-page advertisement in the rival *Herald* filled from margin to margin with the single repeated sentence, 'Fanny Fern writes only for the Ledger.' She knew that she was one of the principal reasons why the *Ledger* had a circulation close to 400,000.

Among Fanny's real rivals were the Warner sisters, Anna and Susan. Susan was the more popular, that is as a novelist. One look at her spare equine face distinguished by a pair of eyes set not quite evenly in her head, a thin determined mouth, and hair brushed tightly behind large ears proclaimed her a spinster by nature. She liked to think of herself as another Jane Eyre, though no Rochester ever came her way. All her emotion was channeled into novels. Her first, *The Wide, Wide World,* was the most popular, though its own first entrance into the world came near being its last. Harper's returned the manuscript with the single word 'Fudge' written across its opening page. Putnam would probably not have touched it either had not G. P.'s mother picked it up and insisted on its publication. 'Providence will aid its sale,' she said. Providence wasn't necessary when there were thousands of Mrs. Putnams in America, all eager to buy a novel about a motherless girl who lives with a cruel aunt, is protected by a kindly farmer, learns what a really Christian home can be through her friendship with the local minister's daughter, and, though only fourteen, is most affectionately regarded by the minister's son, who is himself a divinity student. By 1852 the book was in its fourteenth edition, and in 1853, three years after publication, it was earning the author $4,500 for one of her semiannual payments, as Mr. Putnam gratuitously pointed out to Hawthorne. Even years later *The Wide, Wide World* continued to attract weeping readers at home and abroad, readers as different as Martha Finley Farquharson, author of Elsie Dinsmore's endless saga, and Vincent van Gogh, the great Dutch painter.

Another of Fanny Fern's competitors, and one right inside the magazine that sponsored Fanny, was the lady who rejoiced in the name of Mrs. Emma Dorothy Eliza Nevitte Southworth. Her novel, *The Hidden Hand,* published serially in the *Ledger,* was said to be the most popular work the paper ever printed and went on to greater favor in bound form and in forty different dramatizations, three of which played simultaneously in London. Though more sensational than Fanny, Mrs. E. D. E. N. Southworth was no less sentimental, even though her scenes strayed from the confinement of domesticity. Her settings were often wild landscapes of narrow mountain roads and fearful chasms, more indebted to the Brontës than the Blue Ridge where they were nominally located. She realized that she used them constantly, for in one novel, *Cruel as the Grave,* she blandly wrote, 'It was one of those fearful passes so frequently to be found in the Allegheny Mountains, and which I have described so often that I may be excused from describing this.' There was a dreadful sameness about her Maryland and Virginia plantation houses, too. They were fantastically idyllic, their young girls all beautiful and delicate, their young men all gallant and chivalrous, and their Negroes always happy and kindly, employing a dialect never spoken south of a vaudeville stage. She did a good deal to contribute to the myth of the South as it appeared in later novels. Her characters were two dimensional, her situations few and constantly repeated, her plots melodramatic, and her incidents arranged neatly toward a properly edifying conclusion, but she insisted that all her fiction was based on true events. Whenever she realized that reality had been stretched a bit out of shape, she would attempt to set all right with the reader by inserting an asterisk in her story that directed attention to the bottom of the page where one might read the simple and presumably reassuring words: 'A fact.' She loved to enter right into the novel, frequently speaking in the first person or catching the sleeve of her 'Dear Reader' to call attention to a particularly significant moral injunction. She continued on in this way for a hundred volumes, and evidently it was a good way, for even as late as 1936 one publisher still printed 27 of her novels and another admitted, though somewhat regretfully, that he had copies of 62 of them in stock. *The Hidden Hand, Ishmael,* and *Self-Raised* (the latter two really one novel) were her most popular works, but everything she wrote had a wide circulation. She was such a favorite that English publishers bought advance sheets of her works for quick reprinting, while in this country her publisher had to advertise that novels by any Mrs. Southworth other than the one initialed E. D. E. N. were products as spurious as Smyth Brothers or Smith Sisters Coughdrops.

Publishers in the 'fifties learned to welcome any woman who turned up at their offices with a novel in bulky manuscript under her arm. For example, Alice Cary, the Ohio poetess whose verses were praised by Whittier, gave up the lyric to plunge into the savannahs of fiction, in whose dank undergrowth Fanny Fern blossomed, Grace Greenwood put forth her *Greenwood Leaves,* and Fanny Forester (carefully nurtured by N. P. Willis) watched her *Alderbrook* average three editions a year between 1847 and 1850. Alice Cary's *Clovernook* took up a small patch of popular interest in 1852, and other women who cultivated their gardens of fiction included: Louisa May Alcott (she began her literary career in 1854 with *Flower Fables*); Mary Jane Holmes (who eventually sold 2,000,000 copies of her endless series of novels, which publishers bound up in lots of 50,000 copies at a time); Ann Sophia Stephens (who went on to write the first dime novel about the West); Sarah Josepha Hale (who added several novels to her achievements as author of 'Mary Had a Little Lamb,' editor of *Godey's Lady's Book,* and compiler of a 900-page *Woman's Record, or Sketches of all Distinguished Women from the Creation to 1851*); Elizabeth Oakes Smith (her novel, *The Newsboy,* went through twelve printings in 1854), Caroline Lee Hentz (her various novels sold 93,000 copies in three years); Louise Chandler Moulton (who in 1859 proudly entitled her third book *My Third Book*); and such phenomena as Harriet Beecher Stowe and Augusta Jane Evans, who deserve fuller treatment elsewhere.

And then there were the English women who wrote proper middle-class novels of domesticity, sometimes as popular with the lady readers of America as their own home-grown products. Dinah Maria Mulock's *John Halifax, Gentleman,* essentially an edifying tract in fictional form, was widely read; for somewhat different reasons, so was Charlotte Brontë's first novel. Its theme and its treatment were too fervid for the home, but young girls like the Lowell millhands dreamed of being another 'Jane Erie,' as they called her. Charlotte Yonge's *Heir of Redclyffe,* presenting British family life and a hero who held to the more emotional aspects of the Oxford Movement, drew tears from many American girls, as it did from Jo, their fictional counterpart in the tremendously popular *Little Women.* George Eliot had a following that was centered on *Adam*

Bede and *Silas Marner,* her more moral tales of life among plain people; for her theory of art that 'faithful representing of commonplace things' furnishes 'the raw material of moral sentiment' was pleasing to the American lady's mind. Among the most popular imported novels by women was Grace Aguilar's *Home Influence: A Tale for Mothers and Daughters,* which vividly contrasted the effect upon character of home backgrounds, good and bad. It was published in the United States and England in 1847, and its rapid British sale of thirty editions was probably matched in this country. The author's introductory statement that her 'aim has been to assist in the education of the HEART, believing that of infinitely greater importance than the mere instruction of the MIND' could not have been better if written by an American lady herself.

An occasional intrepid male wandered into the lists of fictional best sellers, like the delicate Donald Grant Mitchell, who masqueraded under the pseudonym Ik Marvel and was the subject of many a feminine sigh. His *Reveries of a Bachelor,* on the borderline between fiction and essay, used Fanny Fern's technique of tying short sketches together by mood and a thin thread of continuity. They recounted the sentimental musings of a young but confirmed bachelor as he sat before the open fireplace, slippers on his feet, dog by his side. The Bachelor had not a worry in the world, so he had to imagine some. He toyed with the thought of marrying and finding himself tied to a shrew, the thought of marrying and finding his wife dead one day when he returns to their dear, little, imaginary home, the thought of marrying and having his daughter and son predecease him. His agonizing was exquisitely neurotic and delighted the women who wanted to be both mother and wife at the same time. Tantalized by this masculine author, all wanted to marry him and prove his thoughts on wedded life wrong, or perhaps they wanted to marry him so they might be the darling spouse whose fevered brow he stroked and whose chilled hands he took into his own. The Bachelor dreamed even of the South Seas and praised *Typee,* but Melville was too exotic for most ladies (and, besides, did he not swim with the undressed Fayaway?); so though four editions of *Typee* were sold in three years, the women over a long period required fifty pirated editions of the *Reveries of a Bachelor,* in addition to the million copies sold by the authorized publisher.

Of course the Bachelor was not the only man whose books were read. There was Joseph Holt Ingraham, a precursor of dime novelists turned author of religious romances, who singlehanded accounted for nearly

10 per cent of the fiction titles published during the 'forties. But his thrillers were mainly sold on trains and steamboats to be read by traveling men. His was the public that lived on such shocking accounts as the *Awful Disclosures* of Maria Monk, the sensational fabrication of a notoriety seeker. Her account of supposed residence as novice and nun in a Montreal convent told how monks and nuns lived together, had children, and murdered them. It titillated the prurient-minded and appealed to the anti-Catholic bias of the period.

Very much the same public read the lengthy sensational novels of George Lippard, a Philadelphia eccentric whose most notorious work was variously known as *The Monks of Monk Hall* and *The Quaker City*. It was a leader among the class of books that Robert Louis Stevenson noticed during his first trip to America, belonging to what he called 'the Penny Messalina school of literature . . . marked by sickening, inverted snobbery.' Lippard's exuberant attempt to show the evils of the present social system through lurid accounts of upper-class orgies, rapes, murders, tortures, and general terror attracted a goggle-eyed public, which in five years caused the author to issue what is labeled—perhaps too enthusiastically—a twenty-seventh edition. Then there was Solon Robinson's melodramatic tale of social reform, *Hot Corn*, which sold 50,000 copies in six months, but as the subject of his exposé was life among New York's poor, he attracted less attention than Lippard, for the degradation of the needy proved less intriguing than the vices of the wealthy.

Sylvanus Cobb, Jr., was another sensational author. He began writing for Bonner's *Ledger* in 1856, flanked by Fanny Fern, Longfellow, Bryant, Mrs. Stowe, Tennyson, and Dickens. For thirty years he had a contract (at $50 a week) calling for a novelette every eight weeks and a minimum of two short pieces a week. Altogether, he figured he contributed 124 long serials, 862 short stories, and 2,143 'scraps,' running from two to six pages each. So jealous was Bonner of his exclusive rights to Cobb's work that for a long time he would allow none of the fiction to be issued in book form, though Bonner himself often reprinted the serials. Cobb was the most consistently read of all the period's novelists and his *Gunmaker of Moscow* probably had an American public second only to that of *Uncle Tom's Cabin*, but he did not see his stories in book form until late in life. He appealed mostly to the dime novel readers, one of whom wrote for him an elegy as appreciative as any occasioned by the death of a writer of the time:

Sylvanus took *his* hero where a hero ought to go,
In scrapes an' awful dangers where he seemed to have no show;
He drowned him, shot him, scalped him, but every reader knew
Sylvanus knew his business well and he would pull him through.
He bruised him, banged him, buried him, an' did a han'some job,
But still we knew the chap was safe with ol' Sylvanus Cobb.

Popular as he was, Cobb was scorned by the more cultivated and the more genteel readers of his day. Oliver Wendell Holmes described part of his public: 'My landlady's daughter . . . Aet. 19. Tender-eyed blonde. Long ringlets. Cameo pin. Gold pencil case on chain. Locket. Bracelet. Album. Autograph Book. Accordion. Reads . . . Sylvanus Cobb, Jr., while her mother makes the puddings.'

The same readers who looked down upon Cobb also disdained melodramatic foreign writers. If a domestic novelist wanted to show a character as evil she had but to insinuate into the character's possessions a copy of a French novel and all was perfectly clear to the reader. Mrs. Trollope declared that earlier French authors like Voltaire and Rousseau were 'known more as naughty words than as great names,' and she might have said the same thing more strongly about modern French novelists. The French were generally considered licentious and irreligious, and the recent Revolutions of 1830 and 1848 only proved them to be a flighty, dangerous people. Though a New England magazine developed the syllogism that French society was immoral and since literature was the expression of society, therefore 'French literature is immoral,' French books were considered exciting and interesting by some mature minds. The costumed romance of *The Three Musketeers* and *The Count of Monte Cristo* was popular in the 'forties as a kind of French *Waverley*, but generally when the public thought of French fiction it did not have Dumas in mind. The French, it had to be acknowledged, were sophisticated, and the middle-class women who bought *Godey's Lady's Book* to examine its hand-tinted pictures of the latest styles in *haute couture* were also intrigued by its reprints of rather mild French fiction.

The men who liked sensational stories and those women who cultivated upper-class sophistication between the early 'forties and the late 'fifties allowed French tales to seep in with domestic novels to replace Scott and his followers. This drift in taste can be measured by the activities of Henry William Herbert, a hackwriter moving with the literary demands of the day. Previously an author of historical romances, Herbert, in the late 'thirties, began to add to his stock in trade many translations of novels by Sue, Dumas, and other contemporary Frenchmen. His rendering of Sue's *The Wandering Jew* contained the statement that the work was 'utterly subversive of social morality.' Despite what seems a tongue-in-cheek warning, the book was as popular as Herbert and his publisher had expected, pleasing the many Americans who had read Maria Monk or who resented the wave of Irish Catholic emigrants sweeping into American politics. So Herbert translated and America read these novels. Generally they were read outside the sanctity of the home. The British traveler, Sir Charles Lyell, tells that in 1849 as he was crossing 'the pine barren between Columbus and Chehaw,' a news vendor came through his railway car calling out, ' "A novel by Paul de Kock, the Bulwer of France, for twenty-five cents! All the Go! More popular than *The Wandering Jew!" '* And Hinton Helper in California during the early 'fifties found the yellow-backed volumes of DeKock and Sue the miners' most popular reading. DeKock's works, essentially flamboyant newspaper serials, were taken as serious descriptions of French society, no better and no worse than George Sand's novels, which outside the Transcendentalist group were generally considered to be as lax in morals as the lady herself. In course of time she came to be considered in somewhat more kindly fashion because of her earnest desire for social improvement, for this was a theme of much fiction ranging from *The Lamplighter* to *Hot Corn*, but such sentiment as she had for the oppressed was not enough to make her as popular as one who wrote about them with a heart that was pure as well as an eye that was sentimental.

The British novelists were another matter. A middle class desirous of being cosmopolitan found that the fiction of such Englishmen as Bulwer and Disraeli, though not altogether proper, did impart a knowledge of high society life purer than that of the French. The demand was so great that not only did book publishers carry on a war as brisk as that which earlier centered on Scott's work, but periodicals now entered the great game of piracy. With fewer problems of format and composition and without any problem of binding, such journals as *Brother Jonathan* and *The New World* were able to print a whole English novel in a gigantic 'extra' hawked on the streets for a dime or so, often several days before the books were ready for distribution. These sleazily made novels captured the out-of-town trade because they could be mailed at rates reserved for newspapers, but eventually competition became so fierce that it overfed the market. Then a tacit agreement was made that the firm that first contracted with an English author for advance sheets had a proper priority.

Of all English novelists Dickens was most widely read. He had a sympathetic understanding of the very type of people who read him. His mind and his heart were as optimistic, aspiring, and moral as those of his American readers. Like them, too, he had a tender interest in improvement and reform. While always possessing a firm grasp on reality, his stories had a pathos or humor that was essentially sentimental in an age given to sentiment. The high coloring of plot and character and the absence of any serious body of thought made the novels easily understandable. Their vitality and intensity aroused as much enthusiasm in America as in England.

Mr. Pickwick and Sam Weller, Oliver Twist and Fagin, Little Nell and her grandfather, Barnaby Rudge and Dolly Varden, Nicholas Nickleby and Smike were all familiar to American readers when Dickens made his visit to this country in 1842. He came mainly to see Cairo, Illinois, the site of an ill-fated canal company in which he had invested and lost many royalty checks, but his trip turned out to be a triumphal tour. Americans had once waited on New York's docks for the final number of *The Old Curiosity Shop,* shouting at the approaching steamer, 'Is Little Nell dead?' Now they gathered to welcome her creator. Nine days after his arrival Dickens wrote to a friend,

I can give you no conception of my welcome. There never was a King or Emperor upon the earth so cheered and followed by the crowds, and entertained at splendid balls and dinners and waited upon by public bodies of all kinds. I have had one from the Far West, a journey of two thousand miles! If I go out in a carriage, the crowd surrounds it and escorts me home; if I go to the theatre, the whole house (crowded to the roof) rises as one man, and the timbers ring again. You cannot imagine what it is. I have five public dinners on hand at this moment, and invitations from every town and village and city in the United States.

The great Boz Ball given in New York on 14 February not only showed that the young author was America's favorite valentine but its elaborate decorations were a clear example of the middle class displaying its wealth for 'cultural' purposes. Every inch of the Park Street Theatre, where the ball was held, was festooned and embellished for the great occasion. Portraits of eight Presidents of the United States were almost lost in a decorative scheme that included American and British flags, garlanded medallions enwreathing the titles of Dickens's works, a vast painting of the author over which hovered an eagle gripping some laurel in its beak, twenty vignettes portraying scenes from the novels, and a great curtain that was a facsimile of the *Pickwick Papers'* frontispiece. When parted it revealed a dozen tableaux in which living statues portrayed scenes from Dickens's books, Washington Irving in England, and Dickens himself in his hour of American triumph.

Dickens found the store windows of every city he visited almost as lavishly decorated with his portrait as the Park Street Theatre, and newsboys in the streets cried out the titles of his books. The 'Entire Works of Boz' were available in pamphlet form at twenty-five cents each or five dollars for the set. Almost everybody could afford to own his writings and all who knew them considered him the ideal British author. Smarting under the attacks of Captain Hall, Mrs. Trollope, and other scornful English visitors, the nation expected their idol Dickens would write a book to offset the others. As one commentator observed, 'We have been trolloped—let us be *bozzed.*' Bozzed we were all right when *American Notes* was published later in the year. The *New York Herald* reprinted the whole book less than twenty-four hours after the first English copies arrived. Within three days 50,000 copies were sold, but people who read them were piqued at his occasional uncomplimentary remarks and even more angered at the slurs that ran through *Martin Chuzzlewit,* issued in 1843. Still Dickens's works remained popular. *A Christmas Carol,* published the year after his visit, was issued without copyright for six cents and probably sold more copies here than in England, where it cost the equivalent of $2.50. His novels were dramatized (eventually every one of them, and six of his stories appeared on the American stage), and during the 'fifties the popular songs included 'Dora and Agnes,' suggested by *David Copperfield,* and 'Florence,' inspired by *Dombey and Son.* A series of good novels following one after the other during the 'fifties atoned for the unkind remarks he had written about his hosts. The payments to Dickens for priority in receiving advance sheets of his novels furnish a good criterion of his continued popularity. From American publishers he received £400 for *Bleak House* in 1852 and £1,250 for *Great Expectations* in 1861; and by 1870 Harper's contracted to pay £2,000 for *Edwin Drood,* which Dickens did not live to finish. *The Knickerbocker Magazine* even considered that the period after his visit was 'the very hey-day of the renown of this great master.' When Dickens returned twenty-five years after his first visit, his public was as great and as enthusiastic as ever. Thirty-one different editions of his collected works were issued in 1867, the year that he took home over $100,000 earned by a long series of readings from the books that captured America's heart.

When Thackeray arrived in 1852 for his lecture tour, his fellow traveler, Eyre Crow, declared 'the "American Notes" had dampened the enthusiastic ardour of the Yankees, who now hung out no bunting.' Actually, Dickens had long since been forgiven and other English novelists were not neglected because of his few unkind words. It was Thackeray himself who did not attract bunting. He had published three of his great novels— *Vanity Fair, Pendennis,* and *Henry Esmond*—but the fact that his many other works had been scattered around and issued under several pseudonyms kept the public from knowing his name thoroughly. Besides, Thackeray was too restrained to attract a great public; he was hostile to sentiment, and he was satirical. His characters did not capture the affections of the reader, his plots were not intense, and his moral point of view required a degree of sophistication greater than a really wide public possessed. Though he certainly had a following, it was small by comparison with Dickens's. He was entertained at dinners public and private until he complained his tour was one long, unbroken case of indigestion, and he saw his books hawked through railway cars for twenty-five cents, but the public never made a hero of him. He himself figured that for every copy of his books five by Dickens were sold in America. *Harper's* Easy Chair declared that this was a period marked by 'the Henry Esmond-Thackeray fever,' but this view was probably conditioned by the fact that the magazine was serializing *The Newcomes* over the devastatingly long period of two years.

Like the nation, the popular novel of the mid-century dreamed and sentimentalized. Fiction, it was said, was meant to inspire, to exhort one to a fuller and finer life. Subconsciously its readers found in it a compensation for unachieved ideals. Its characters and their involvements were of the sort with which middle-class readers could identify themselves, and heroes and heroines who conducted themselves according to accepted bourgeois ethics always made their way onward and upward in this world or achieved an earnest of salvation in the next. These popular novels had a thesis, sometimes explicitly stated, as in anti-slavery and temperance fiction; more often it was a hollow echo of prevailing folkways. Like the other arts, fiction belonged to the middle class. Paintings of the day appealed to the aspiring generation by celebrating the vast beauties of our national scene, by unrolling miles of canvas whose panoramas gave a knowledge of foreign cultures, or by depicting charming genre scenes of domestic felicity. Statuary of the day was refined, even though undraped. But, as in the novel, it all depended on the right way of looking at the subject. The beholder of Horatio Greenough's pseudo-classic conception of George Washington was not supposed to see a Virginia gentleman masquerading in a loose-hanging toga that covered his body only below the umbilicus. He was to notice that Washington's right hand gestured to the heavens and his left held a sheathed sword pointed downwards. Obviously the statue portrayed the moral virtues putting aside military force. And as for Powers's *Greek Slave,* though the attractive lady of marble wore no clothing but a pair of flimsy chains, still everybody could see, as one minister put it, 'the Greek Slave is clothed all over with sentiment.' No stouter substance could the generation desire. It was essentially the fabric from which its art was made, a material most successfully tailored to the desires of the middle class in the fiction written by the women of its own society.

Chapter 7

The Gates Ajar

While middle-class ladies were busy fashioning their homes into the land of heart's content, the nation at large was also cleaning house. Emerson, trying to explain America to Carlyle in 1840, wrote, 'We are all a little wild here with numberless projects of social reform. Not a reading man but has a draft of a new community in his waistcoat pocket.' For two decades, until the Civil War united men in a greater and more pressing cause, the natural religion was perfectionism, isolated in hundreds of special cults. The nation indulged in one long holiday crusade. Fervid optimism was the prevailing mood.

Diverse forces were breaking established molds, leaving the nation wide open for those who wished to promote new patterns. Mexican War soldiers and adventurous frontiersmen were changing the very contours of the nation, thus promoting a feeling of boundlessness. The new mechanics of industrialization and improved techniques of communication and transportation gave men the feeling they could also tinker with their social system and their psyches to reach a worldly paradise more rapidly and securely. Discovery of coal and oil in the East and gold in the West seemed to prove that equal treasures waited to be mined within the individual. The sudden surge of immigrants discovering freedom and opportunity in this new land symbolized for the native-born the individual's release from restraint. Everywhere examples gross as earth exhorted optimistic Americans to find the millennium immediately. The exuberant means included phrenology and free love, hydropathy and health foods, mesmerism and spiritualism, socialism and communism, feminism and pacifism, temperance and anti-slavery crusades, and scores of new sects and colonies. If only the right new way were followed, surely, it was said, the path would lead quickly to a home-grown Utopia.

Tracts for the times were common, but for people accustomed to novels much of the propaganda was cast in the form of fiction. A caustic journalist inquired, 'Do you wish to instruct, to convince, to please? Write a novel! Have you a system of religion or politics or manners or social life to inculcate? Write a novel!' So many earnest souls took this advice that the historian Motley (himself an unsuccessful novelist) grumbled, 'Certainly the world should be reformed, but not entirely by novel writers.' Most critics and readers disagreed with Motley, like the reviewer who ecstatically noted that Mrs. Oakes Smith's *Bertha and Lily, or The Parsonage of Beach Glen* had 'in it, at times, a tinge of *transcendentalism;* yes, and of *spiritualism* too; to say nothing of a strong flavor of *Swedenborgianism,* all through.' Even ministers could be found to declare, 'Instead of carping against light literature it were better to charge it with truths and influences, purifying, profound and enduring, and send it abroad as a mission of love to mankind.'

The novelist with a thesis had a good chance of popularity, so long as his cause was not merely a personal cult or crotchet. If identified with the temperance crusade he found himself at the very center of the major reform movements. Since criminals were often drunkards, since irreligion and intemperance were considered to go hand in hand, and because it was noted that children reared by drinking parents were poorly educated and unfit to become part of an intelligent electorate, the temperance advocate was welcomed by almost every worthy person.

No one could avoid hearing of the temperance movement. By 1834 one strongly centralized organization, led by schoolteachers, church groups, and medical societies, claimed a million members in its 5,000 local units. Then in 1840 a rival league, the Washington Temperance Union, was formed. Its members were mostly reformed drunkards instead of the socially conscious leaders of each community. Their appeal rested on lurid tales of reformation and Cold Water Army parades, in which children, with the superiority of the untempted, chanted in high-pitched voices:

> We, Cold Water Girls and Boys,
> Freely renounce the treacherous joys
> Of Brandy, Whiskey, Rum, and Gin;
> The Serpent's lure to death and sin:

Wine, Beer, and Cider, we detest,
And thus we'll make our parents blest;
'So here we pledge perpetual hate
To all that can Intoxicate.'

Although these revivalist tactics were condemned by conservative reformers as examples of 'emotion supplanting reason,' the temperance
movement grew. In 1838 Massachusetts passed an anti-saloon law forbidding the sale of less than fifteen gallons of liquor, more than even an
unreformed Washingtonian could drink at one time. Though the statute
did not stay on the books long, Maine in 1851 tried the experiment of
total prohibition, which one temperance novelist hailed as 'the law of
Heaven Americanized.' By 1855 thirteen states in New England and the
old Northwest had adopted some kind of law prohibiting or restricting
liquor sales. Since they resulted from minority pressure, the acts were
soon evaded or overruled, but enough people believed in them to make
a wide, if specialized, reading public for temperance novels.

Over 12 per cent of the novels published in America during the 1830's
dealt with temperance, and though they were mostly brief tracts disguised as fiction and distributed free, they had a great circulation. Even
as late as the Civil War years, the American Temperance Union shipped
two million pieces of propaganda (much of it fiction) to the army and
navy, where soldiers and sailors probably read it in lieu of anything
better. The temperance tale was as simple and highly colored as the
Currier and Ives print of 'The Drunkard's Progress,' its structure often
only a step-by-step chart of an inebriate's life. Tragedy ran riot in these
tales. It was well understood that he who drank was bound to die by
disease, accident, murder, or suicide before the last page was reached.
Bloated corpses with staring eyes were common around the drunkard's
house in a temperance novel, though an occasional body just exploded
into nothingness by spontaneous combustion. Even pure children died
as a result of parents' dereliction. Generally they died gracefully, as in
Walt Whitman's novel, *Franklin Evans* ('not written for the critics,' he
said, 'but for the people'), in which the child's last action is to give a
temperance tract to the guilty member of the family: 'the uplifted hand
fell suddenly into the open palm of her brother's, depositing the tiny
volume there. Little Jane was dead.' Sometimes their deaths were more
gruesome: in one tale a drunk mother rocked her baby near the hearth and
accidentally dropped it into the open fire. To all but the most zealous
reformer the death of these little children could not have been unadul-

terated tragedy. They were such prigs as to make Little Eva seem a
hoyden by comparison. There was, for example, Charlie Plimpton, the
young hero of *The Little Cider Merchant,* who liked to illustrate the virtues of water by pointing out that it alone was fit 'to penetrate unfelt into
the subtlest tissues, and without causing the slightest jar, to flow among
the finest, most sensitive and most hair-like vessels.'

Among the most popular temperance novelists was the Boston anti-
quary, Lucius Manlius Sargent. His first tale, *My Mother's Gold Ring,*
was issued in 1833; within six years its title page proclaimed '113th thousand.' It set a pattern for fictional mothers who gave their sons gold rings
as a reward for abstinence, leading to such accounts as T. W. Brown's
Edward Carlton, in which, when Edward finally did take a drink, it was
with a thirst so long stifled that in fiercely grabbing the glass 'the ring
upon his finger snapped in two pieces.' Sargent's tale was held by reformers to be an antidote for children who read Fielding or even Scott.
Even more exemplary was Timothy Shay Arthur, who wrote some hundred moral tales and tracts in favor of the cause. Single-handed he produced over 5 per cent of all the volumes of fiction published in the 1840's.
By 1860, according to publishers' statistics, a million copies of his books
had been printed. Most popular of all was his lurid *Ten Nights in a Bar-
Room,* issued in 1854. William W. Pratt's dramatization with the sentimental song, 'Father, dear father, come home with me now,' kept the title
alive for many years, just as the 'Tom shows' increased the notoriety of
Mrs. Stowe's novel. Arthur's prose was on a level with the illustrations
prepared for his novels. One picture in his *Six Nights with the Wash-
ingtonians* shows a husband at dinner table inducing his wife to try some
wine. He waves the bottle above his head, leers at his wife like a white
slaver finding a new inmate for his bordello, and extends a glass regard-
less of her timorous gesture of arrest. A maidservant looks on slightly
bemused (perhaps she has her own bottle in the kitchen), and from the
wall a portrait of George Washington leans from its frame pop-eyed at
such goings on. That things are badly conducted in this home is obvious
from an incident dimly glimpsed in the corner of the illustration: a mouse
seems to have the household cat by the tail.

The temperance novelist with his injunctions to vow perpetual celi-
bacy or to 'slay yourselves, rather than give your right hand to wine-
bibbers in the bonds of wedlock' was obviously too fanatical to attract
a normal reading public. The average person was more apt to look upon
the subject as did Hawthorne, who in 1855 wrote to his publisher:

I made a convert to total abstinence yesterday. It was a sea-captain who has fallen into dissipated habits; I preached to him with such good effect that he asked me to draw up a pledge, which he signed on the spot . . . On the strength of this good deed, I thought myself entitled to drink an extra glass or two of wine in the evening, and so have got a little headache.

Reform was in the air and one could not avoid it, but except for a particularly striking novel or two, its fiction was generally read only by extremists.

Only one reform movement became a national issue. In 1826, when the first big temperance union was founded, there were already a hundred anti-slavery societies. Their cause grew slowly, but because it touched political and economic realities it interested all the people. The Compromise of 1850, strengthening the old Fugitive Slave Law, brought home the meaning of slavery to Northerners who had known it only as a problem in theory. Of course, thousands of printed pages had discussed the problem, and there had been pleas for the Negro in novels like Hildreth's *The Slave; or, Memoirs of Archy Moore* (which went through seven editions in eleven years), but before 1850 most Northerners found the subject comparatively abstract or distant. Now they were ready for a novel that would dramatize the issue of slavery in contemporary terms. Harriet Beecher Stowe, who had graduated from the gift book and the temperance novel, approached the subject in a spirit suited to the times. When she began her work she wrote, 'The Carthagenian women in the last peril of their state cut off their hair for bow-strings to give to the defenders of their country; and such peril and shame as now hangs over this country is worse than Roman slavery, and I hope every woman who can write will not be silent.'

Mrs. Stowe raised her voice in the *National Era*, a Washington anti-slavery journal, which published *Uncle Tom's Cabin* between June 1851 and April 1852. The first advertisement of the new serial announced its length as approximately that of Mrs. Southworth's *Retribution*, for about anything concerning a novel Mrs. Southworth could stand as a criterion. The second installment was pared down to make room for a story by Grace Greenwood, but after the novel really got going there was no woman writer anywhere in America who could challenge Mrs. Stowe.

In March 1852 the serial was published as a two-volume book. Five thousand copies were printed, and to the publisher's surprise they sold out in two days. Within three weeks 20,000 copies were sold. Everybody read this powerful and controversial story, even though the more sophis-

ticated saw that it suffered from the usual defects of contemporary feminine fiction. Its plot structure with two thinly connected stories was
clumsy; both stories were crassly sentimental and hortatory, and the writing was speciously fine. But the book had power because, for all her
faults, Mrs. Stowe was a natural-born storyteller with a graphic ability to
present character and situation. 'My vocation,' she said correctly, 'is
simply that of a *painter* . . . There is no arguing with *pictures,* and
everybody is impressed by them, whether they mean to be or not.' Her
thesis attracted readers but she held them by her strong, simple portraiture; her sentiment, both of pathos and humor; and her dramatic
handling of suspense. It is not surprising that, subject aside, *Uncle Tom's
Cabin* completely eclipsed *Henry Esmond,* which appeared the same
year, but it is remarkable that such a fastidious reader as Oliver Wendell
Holmes found Mrs. Stowe's work more engrossing than that of her
master, Dickens.

On June 29, 1852, Henry Clay died, still believing that his compromise
would hold the union together. But by that month *Uncle Tom's Cabin*
had sold 75,000 copies and was beginning to play a significant part in
stirring up old issues. It appeared in an election year, and one in which
the people for the first time could express their reaction to the Compromise of 1850. Its effect was never intended by the author. She had carefully made her evil characters Northerners and her noble characters
Southerners, indicating that most Southerners had a patriarchal kindliness toward their slaves though the system as system was bad. She was
sure the Southerners would see the wrongs and release their Negroes
from bondage. Instead they were so infuriated that a Mobile bookseller
was run out of town for stocking the book, while Mrs. Stowe herself received threatening and scurrilous letters, and even a package containing
an ear cut from the head of a Negro.

The controversy naturally increased interest in the book. At Andover
Theological Seminary, where they were both faculty wives, Mrs. Stowe
replaced the elder Elizabeth Stuart Phelps as the literary figure of the
day. Mrs. Phelps's *The Sunny Side* had sold 100,000 copies within the
year of 1851, but Mrs. Stowe's two-volume *Uncle Tom's Cabin* sold that
number in five months of 1852. In California miners were renting the
book for two bits a day. Closer home there were twenty Uncle Tom songs
on the market, including one in which Whittier rhymed 'Eva' with
'grieve her' and 'river.' Down South the children countered by chanting:

Go, go, go,
Ol' Harriet Beecher Stowe!

In September George L. Aiken's dramatization, the most popular of
many, opened an initial hundred-night run in Troy, New York, and soon
the stage versions, even more melodramatic than the novel, were helping
sell the book. By November 120,000 copies had been sold, and a manufacturer of parlor games cashed in on the excitement by vending 'Uncle
Tom and Little Eva,' a game played with pawns that represented 'the
continual separation and reunion of families,' according to the producer.
Month after month four power presses were kept busy day and night
(except Sundays), two hundred bookbinders had found what looked to
be permanent jobs, and the publisher still ran behind orders. By the end
of the year 200,000 copies had been sold in this country, the price varying, according to edition, from $2 to 37 cents, supplemented by a special
Christmas issue containing 'one hundred superb engravings and an elegant steel-portrait of Mrs. Stowe.' The year 1853 saw a condensation for
children titled A Peep into Uncle Tom's Cabin, an edition in German
issued for immigrants, and another in Welsh, and by the time of the first
anniversary 305,000 copies of the regular American editions had been
sold. That number (adjusted by eliminating Southern population, which
included almost no customers) is equivalent to a sale of more than
3,000,000 copies in the United States of 1947. If one could give proper
consideration to literacy levels of the two dates and improved systems of
book distribution, the sales figures would appear even more striking. Imitations or attacks upon Uncle Tom's Cabin had a vogue too. Hildreth's
The Slave and Sarah Josepha Hale's twenty-five-year-old Northwood, or
Life North and South were reissued. Mrs. Hale rushed out a new novel,
Liberia, and at least fourteen pro-slavery authors met Mrs. Stowe head-on
with novels bearing such titles as Uncle Robin in His Cabin in Virginia
and Tom Without One in Boston and Aunt Phillis's Cabin; or, Southern
Life as It Is.

Year after year Uncle Tom's Cabin continued to be read, abetted by
many things—the stage versions; Mrs. Stowe's Key to Uncle Tom's Cabin
(which sold 90,000 copies within a month of publication); Dred, a complement to her more famous novel, showing the demoralizing influence
of slavery upon the whites; and the general fervor of the times as they
moved closer to the 'irrepressible conflict.' Although she never wrote
another great popular success, after 1853 any book with her signature had
a sure sale of at least 150,000 copies.

'Yankee wives have written the most popular antislavery literature of the day,' declared Hinton R. Helper, a North Carolina author, considering the work of Harriet Beecher Stowe. 'It is well enough for women to give the fiction of slavery,' he continued, 'men should give the facts.' And so he wrote *The Impending Crisis of the South: How to Meet It,* the peculiarly effective attack of a Southerner upon his own region. Northern publishers couldn't see any profit in this flat, verbose work, and Harper, Appleton, and Scribner refused the manuscript. Southern publishers would have none of it on the grounds that it would violate a law against printing material having 'a tendency to excite discontent or stir up insurrection amongst people of color.' Finally, in 1857, Helper found a New York book agent willing to issue it at the author's risk. The work attracted only moderate attention at first, selling 13,000 copies within the year.

Though Helper hated slavery, he had no love for the Negro, and his book did not greatly interest the humanitarians. Appealing to the nonslaveholding whites to whom it was dedicated, *The Impending Crisis* was a lengthy argument to prove that slavery, being incompatible with mechanization and industrial diversification, the twin sources of Northern strength, necessarily arrested Southern economic and cultural advancement. This conception of the Southern social system as enslaving white men along with black obviously appealed to some middle-class whites below the Mason and Dixon line, since a North Carolina town publicly burned ten copies and a farmer of Alexandria, Virginia, was arrested for owning the seditious work. *The Impending Crisis* was not the kind of book that could be answered by what its author called 'pictures of the beatitudes of plantation life' which had been painted as replies to *Uncle Tom's Cabin.* Helper had to be met on his own statistical grounds. When this value was realized, a group of prominent Republicans drew up a testimonial stating that 'no other volume now before the public . . . is, in all respects, so well calculated to induce in the minds of its readers a decided and persistent repugnance to slavery.' Then they took action, printing a *Compendium of The Impending Crisis* (a 214-page book in itself), selling or distributing 142,000 copies as propaganda during the 1860 campaign. Lincoln considered the work had contributed so greatly to his election that he rewarded Helper with the consulship at Buenos Aires.

When the long-pent-up hostilities finally broke into open war, public interest naturally turned from novels and texts fulminating against slavery in general to the kind of books that every war brings: novels about soldier life, autobiographies of Army nurses and others with unusual war experiences, biographies of military officers and heroes, journalistic narratives of campaigns, simple studies of strategy and tactics, accounts of past wars, and exuberant theories on ways to win the present war. Propaganda of fact and fiction continued, but it was now more concerned with immediate events.

Of all the propagandists for the North, Parson William G. Brownlow was the most sensational and the most successful. A vituperative circuit-riding Methodist of east Tennessee, Brownlow was less interested in doctrinal dispute and political theory than in personal abuse. Through a fervid sequence of violent contention he had become opposed to what he called the 'corrupt Democratic party of the South' and accordingly to the doctrine of secession. When war broke out he was arrested for treason, jailed in Knoxville without trial, and proved himself such a cantankerous martyr that the Confederate States decided it preferred to give him a safe-conduct pass to the Union, where he might prove less of a bother to the South.

Arriving in the North in March 1862, Brownlow found himself a well-known figure in demand as a speaker at recruiting rallies and other public gatherings. He toured the whole Union as far west as Chicago, and everywhere, as he reported, his 'gabble was not only listened to, but loudly cheered.' With high-strung energy he peddled patriotism by proclaiming,

If I had the power, sir, I would arm and uniform in Federal habiliments every wolf, and panther, and tiger, and catamount, and bear, in the mountains of America; every crocodile in the swamps of Florida and South Carolina; every negro in the Southern Confederacy; and every devil in Hell and Pandemonium . . . This war, I say to you, must be pursued with a *vim* and a vengeance, until the rebellion is put down, if it exterminates from God's green earth every man, woman, and child south of Mason and Dixon's line.

A shrewd New York publisher soon realized that this kind of vituperation would sell as well in books as on the lecture platform, and in May 1862 there appeared a fat volume with the copious title, *Sketches of the Rise, Progress, and Decline of Secession; with a Narrative of Personal Adventures Among the Rebels*. Or at least that is the way the title page read. The binder pared this wordage so that the spine simply read: *Parson Brownlow's Book*. By that title the work became famous. It was as good a title as any, for the 458 pages of text were a hodgepodge of materials held together only by the Parson's fiery temperament and were interesting mainly because of his personal notoriety. Into his hastily compiled book he crammed editorials written in 1860 and 1861 for his *Knoxville Whig;* part of a diary composed in jail; an irrelevant but at least a dispassionate account of the climate, topography, and soil of east Tennessee; a lengthy 'proof' that God favored the North because statistics (Brownlow probably learned their value through reading Helper) showed that He had given the North a larger population and more industry; and, wherever a bit of white space remained on these pages, there were brief but scurrilous denunciations of Southern leaders and their actions. Crammed into all this text were lurid engravings of Confederate atrocities.

Brownlow admitted that 'extreme fastidiousness of taste may, perhaps, shrink with oversensitiveness from some of the language I have employed,' but he insisted that only 'a sword and thrust style' would suit the subject. The people agreed. Within a year they bought more than 75,000 copies. For those who liked this sort of propaganda but couldn't afford the big book, there was issued the same year a fifty-cent account of *Brownlow, the Patriot and Martyr Showing His Faith and Works, as Reported by Himself;* and if that proved too expensive, a loyal American might buy a twenty-five-cent pamphlet presenting a *Portrait and Biography of Parson Brownlow,* or the printing of a speech in which he told how Confederate soldiers rode through Knoxville after the Battle of Bull Run, holding aloft decapitated heads of Union troops. Finally, the Parson dwindled even further in price and rose in fame as the subject of Beadle's dime novel, *Parson Brownlow and the Unionists of East Tennessee.* In the world of cheap books 1862 was so definitely the Parson's year that anything with his name seems to have sold, from a 'Parson Brownlow Quick Step,' with his fiery face glowering from the cover of the sheet music, to *Miss Martha Brownlow; or the Heroine of Tennessee,* in which one Major W. D. Brownlow described how the 'lovely and accomplished daughter of the celebrated Parson' defended the Stars and Stripes against Confederate soldiers intent on ripping the flag from her home.

Through reports of his speaking tours and the writings by and about him, the name of Brownlow was encountered in print almost as often as that of Lincoln. The Parson's notoriety was further extended when he accompanied General Burnside in the recapture of eastern Tennessee. There the Army set him up as editor of a revived *Knoxville Whig,* to which he added the subtitle, *and Rebel Vindicator.* Brownlow's speeches and writings next carried him to election as Tennessee's governor on the day that Lincoln was inaugurated for a second term, and finally, in 1869, put him in the Senate. Not only did Brownlow make a hero of himself but he established his home region as such a glamorous setting that when the Boston author, John T. Trowbridge, published *Cudjo's Cave* in 1864, he found a ready audience for his novel. Essentially a book for children, this story of conflict between anti-slavery Southerners and the Confederates of eastern Tennessee had a wide reading public among adults; the *American Literary Gazette and Publishers' Circular* declared that 'within three days after it appeared the edition ran to the tenth thousand.'

Another novel widely read during the Civil War was Victor Hugo's *Les Misérables*. His *Notre Dame de Paris*, issued in America in 1834 under the more sensational title of *The Hunchback of Notre Dame*, did not find a wide audience until *Les Misérables* appeared in the stormy days of the Peninsular Campaign, when the Southern forces were sometimes derisively called 'Lee's Miserables.' Editions were printed behind both Confederate and Union lines, and, despite the scarcity of paper, a year after publication 120,000 copies were said to be in print. A reliable publisher stated that though book sales in general were dropping off, he received an order for 25,000 copies of *Les Misérables* from a single wholesaler, and another publisher advertised in May 1863 that his particular edition had sold 30,000 copies within a month. By 1864 *Les Misérables* could be bought in editions ranging from an 'elegant' half-calf volume priced at $10 to a 'popular' paper-covered pamphlet hawked on streets and trains. Catharine Sedgwick contended, 'The book is everywhere.' Its sensationalism appealed to a public accustomed to Sue, its sentimental sympathy for the poor attracted readers of Dickens, and the scenes of the Battle of Waterloo and fighting at the French barricades interested a war-torn public. Since it was about five times the size of an average novel, *Les Misérables* also afforded readers a long escape from their own problems into a substantial and thrilling piece of fiction.

A long book was a good buy during those expensive days, and if it had an historical setting offering an extended escape from or explanation of current events, its chances of popularity were great. Joel Tyler Headley's bulky two-volume *Napoleon and His Marshals*, which had had a tremendous sale at the time of the Mexican War, was revived with success in 1861. Another popular study of the past was Macaulay's *History of England*. The first two volumes issued in 1849 had been popular, for some

60,000 copies were sold in pirated printings that brought the price down to fifteen cents each. But when the next two volumes appeared in 1861, at a price that never got below twenty-five cents apiece, some 200,000 copies were sold within a few months. Macaulay himself was puzzled 'how it should be acceptable to the body of people who have no kings, no lords, no established church, no tories, nay, I might say, no whigs, in the English sense of the word.' But as a leading historian of the time his work had an interested public. The stern pressure of events temporarily forced people to an increasing sobriety and they found in Macaulay a champion of common-sense conservatism who could be opposed to Carlyle, the great English expositor of transcendentalism.

Though the war made people hardheaded, ample sentiment remained; now, however, it was focused less on generalized schemes for mankind's improvement and more on patriotism, the yearning for peace, and religious faith, particularly on speculation about the afterworld to which so many young sons and husbands had been untimely sent. Edward Everett Hale, a Unitarian clergyman of Boston, expressed perfectly the patriotic idealism of the period in *The Man Without a Country*. First printed in the *Atlantic Monthly*, the story was reissued as a pamphlet two years later, in 1865, and had a wide sale. Dramatizing a Confederate sympathizer's statement that he did not wish to live in a country tolerating Lincoln's administration, Hale created the character of Philip Nolan, whose similar sentiments made him more famous in American folklore than his prototype, Ohio's Congressman Vallandigham. And the account of how Nolan during his enforced exile read Scott's lines:

> Breathes there the man with soul so dead
> Who never to himself hath said,
> 'This is my own, my native land'

probably etched the passage from *The Lay of the Last Minstrel* more deeply in America's mind than the whole of the Scott vogue ever did. No author expressed the yearning for peace as clearly as Hale stated the patriotism of the times, but the desire for such a work is evidenced by several books touching on the theme and by the success of the song, 'When this Cruel War is Over,' which as the most popular sheet music of the time sold almost half a million copies upon publication, outdistancing even 'When Will My Darling Boy Return?' and other similar lyrics.

Religious themes had always been prominent in American novels and poetry and, of course, religious books always outsold all others in that wide area loosely lumped under the heading 'nonfiction'; but they grew even more popular as faith was tried by losses on the field of battle. The winter of 1863-4 brought about a great religious revival and the reading of religious books accordingly increased. The American Bible Society at the advent of the war split into two groups, but the accounts of the larger is typical of both. The New York group, which in 1860-61 distributed 700,000 Bibles and Testaments annually, four years later was distributing a million and a half copies. The records of The American Tract Society show a greater increase. In 1861 the Society distributed 6,700,000 pages of pious literature, but in 1865 it scattered abroad 109,-000,000 pages in its various tracts. Increased interest in testaments and tracts was attended by larger sales of belles-lettres with religious themes. In the 1830's the Boston clergyman, William Ware, found what was then considered a wide public (eight editions in seventeen years) for his *Zenobia,* dealing with the struggles of early Christians, and Joseph Holt Ingraham's epistolary romance, *The Prince of the House of David,* had a great sale in the 1850's, but the sales records of both authors were eclipsed by those of writers on religious themes whose works were published during and directly after the Civil War.

Women were the most popular novelists bent upon justifying the ways of God to man. First in point of time, and perhaps first too in sales, was a young Southern lady, Augusta Jane Evans. Her novel, *Beulah,* published when she was but twenty-four, had as its theme a girl's discovery of the frailty of philosophy and the strength of religious faith. Thrusting aside the books of such transcendentalists as Emerson and Carlyle, Beulah said of philosophy, 'she can teach us to hear of the calamities of others with magnanimity; but it is religion only that can teach us to bear our own with resignation.' When Miss Evans offered the book to Appleton in 1859, the publishers declined it, probably feeling that America's optimistic belief in Emersonian reform and progress was still too strong for such a work. But another publisher gambled on its publication that year. As battlefield casualties brought tragedy to America's homes, the public agreed that the times called for religious solace instead of sunny philosophy. By October 1863, 30,000 copies of *Beulah* had been sold and Appleton, with perhaps some regret and embarrassment, ordered as many as a thousand copies at one time for the retail bookselling half of its firm.

As soon as the war was over Miss Evans came to New York again to offer another novel, which was accepted by the first publisher to see it. It was obviously right for the times. The heroine, brilliant and beautiful Edna Earl, was only another Beulah, but innumerable women were eager to listen to her erudite arguments extolling Christian faith as man's greatest consolation. *St. Elmo*, as the book was called after the dazzling first name of its hero, indulged in a series of speciously elegant debates between the devout heroine and the cynical hero. The lust of St. Elmo for his mother's ward, the pious Edna, recalled that of Rochester for Jane Eyre, but it was not this alone that made the book popular. It was the heroine's belief in God's providence that appealed to those in need of faith, and her recondite proof not only convinced the doubting, but dazzled the ladies who sought culture. Edna's conversation was more abstrusely refined than the prose of a gift book, and her ablity to refute male arguments was more genteel and telling than that of an orator for woman's rights. The 'dissipated and unhallowed' St. Elmo Murray might declare:

Nineteen years ago, to satisfy my hunger, I set out to hunt the daintiest food this world could furnish, and like other fools, have learned finally, that life is but a huge, mellow, golden Ösher, that mockingly sifts its bitter dust upon our eager lips.

But Edna just picked up his esoteric allusion and in her elegantly crocheted prose improved upon it:

Mr. Murray, if you insist on your bitter Ösher simile, why shut your eyes to the palpable analogy suggested? Naturalists assert that the Solanum, or apple of Sodom, contains in its normal state neither dust nor ashes, unless it is punctured by an insect (the Tenthredo), which converts the whole inside into dust, leaving nothing but the rind entire, without any loss of color. Human life is as fair and tempting as the fruit of 'Ain Jidy,' till stung and poisoned by the Tenthredo of sin.

This sort of proof evidently convinced not only the reader but St. Elmo, who finally renounced his wayward atheism to become a minister, accepted by Edna with 'implicit faith' as 'my first and my last and my only love.'

The name St. Elmo, associated with virtue and excellence, was bestowed upon subjects as various as girls' schools, a cigar, a blend of punch, hotels, steamboats, and thirteen towns dotting the continent from New York to California. Even little boys, poor fellows, were christened in honor of Edna's reformed lover. The book was adapted with success for the stage, after some of its polysyllables were replaced by melodramatic action; it inspired a full-length parody, *St. Twel'mo;* probably helped the sale of unabridged dictionaries; and by 1884 had, along with her lesser works, earned the author $100,000.

In 1868, the year after Edna Earl's coruscated conversation first appeared in print, it met a serious rival in the words of an equally devout Northern lady, Elizabeth Stuart Phelps. From her mother, the author of *The Sunny Side; or The Country Minister's Wife,* Miss Phelps had inherited her name, her talent as a religious writer, and an optimistic faith. She had written ten books—including a temperance tale—while still in her nonage, and in the last years of the Civil War she began work on a novel whose thesis that heaven is a happy place was meant to assuage the grief she had felt upon the deaths of both her mother and stepmother and that of her fiancé, killed at Antietam. The idea behind *The Gates Ajar* was not new, for as early as 1863 a publisher was advertising the anonymous *Heaven Our Home* as describing 'a Social Heaven in which there will be the most Perfect Recognition, Intercourse, Fellowship, and Bliss.' But Miss Phelps's book, aided by the popularity of *St. Elmo's* theme, and dealing directly with the problems of the bereaved, appeared at the right moment.

Addressed to women, *The Gates Ajar* was in keeping with the period of feminine authorship. Its title derived from an elegy by Fanny Forester; its structure, like that of *St. Elmo,* was in great part conversation; its characters were women; and its subject, a girl's search for solace. Like thousands of real women, the heroine Mary Cabot, upon learning of her brother's death in battle, can find comfort neither in bleak orthodox theology nor in the nebulous transcendencies of newer philosophies and religions. But like the readers she is assuaged by her aunt's descriptions of a domesticated heaven. There, Mrs. Forceythe tells her, we continue a normal life in a home like that on earth, mingling with friends old and new, and, in short, we discover that the ways of heaven are those of earth, purified and purged of mundane irritations. Even little children find the kitchens of these heavenly mansions stocked with cookie jars perpetually overflowing with gingersnaps.

With a pretentious modesty Miss Phelps claimed the book was inspired: 'The angel said unto me "Write!" and I wrote.' Miss Phelps's conception of herself as a stenographer for divinity was much like that of her neighbor Mrs. Stowe, who always insisted that her hand only held the pen while God composed *Uncle Tom's Cabin.* Even if the subject, style, and structure of the novels of both these ladies seem dictated more by prevailing standards than by heavenly criteria, their works were revered in their time. Though theologians attacked Miss Phelps and Mark Twain was moved to write a parody, *Captain Stormfield's Visit to Heaven,* within a few years eager women bought 100,000 copies of *The Gates Ajar.* It called out imitations, such as George Wood's *The Gates Wide Open,* which had been a failure when issued as *Future Life* in 1858, and it received the dubious compliment of having a gentleman's wing collar impiously but appropriately given its title. A flippant newspaperman commenting on her success reported in the first month of 1870: 'Miss Phelps has made $20,000 out of *The Gates Ajar.* She won't be likely to shut them at this rate.' The royalty figures may not have been correct, but there is no denying Miss Phelps's future was estimated with wonderful nicety. She wrote three sequels—*Beyond the Gates, The Gates Between,* and *Within the Gates*—establishing herself as America's foremost authority on the home life of heaven.

The religious novel like the historical novel is always with us, but its postwar popularity did not last long. The works of the Reverend E. P. Roe were the only successful latecomers. His first, *Barriers Burned Away,* published in 1872, was his most widely read novel; it used the dramatic setting of the Chicago fire as an appropriate background for a story of spiritual conversion. Ten years after its first printing, a 'limited' edition of a hundred thousand copies was immediately sold out. Roe's *Opening a Chestnut Burr,* published in 1874, and several others employing a similar formula all had a tremendous following. Over the years, the Reverend Roe's many books brought him an annual royalty of $15,000 in contrast to the $200 that the average book then earned for a run-of-the-mill author. As late as the mid-'eighties Matthew Arnold thought the country was 'nourished and formed' by 'a native author called Roe,' but the accused considered this an odd judgment, since 'no critic has ever been so daft as to call any of my books a classic.'

When memories of the Civil War dimmed, many Americans became aware that the war had made them a powerful people, and subconsciously they found the religious novel and its first cousin, the domestic novel, too provincial for their tastes. Likewise, they were tired of the naïveté with which temperance stories were circulated in the hope that literature would eradicate social evil. Having learned what it took to root out slavery, these people were somewhat cynical and their prosperity made them more interested in worldly affairs. This public, interested in the sophisticated world of England and the Continent, turned to flamboyant foreign writings. Of course, Americans continued to enjoy earlier English favorites, such as Dickens and Thackeray or Trollope, whose Barsetshire series and Parliamentary Novels were issued in this country as soon as they came out in England. Trollope's slow, quiet creation of characters made them great favorites to be followed in book after book, but a new style of English character also came into favor. This was the sensational figure, frequently a criminal, whose adventures, usually in high society, afforded Americans a vicarious, if lurid, view of an extravagant way of life.

Romances dealing with criminals were nothing new—they had been written by Ainsworth and Bulwer and Dickens—and novels about wicked characters like St. Elmo were common enough too, but the sensation novel differed from them in point of view. It was focused on an abnormal or unnatural event intended only to induce a thrill. When its plot of passion was set in opulent surroundings, the thrill was presumably heightened. The techniques of the sensation novel, with its tableaux and hectic dialogue, were those of the popular theater. Its immediate forerunners included Mrs. Henry Wood's lachrymose and melodramatic *East Lynne,* a story of unconventional behavior in English society, popular both as a novel and a play during and directly after the war. Mrs. Wood's theme of crime and infidelity became stock subject matter, though this virtuous English author brought all right at the end when the heroine returns home in disguise to nurse her children and her paramour is found guilty of murder.

Mrs. Wood's sensationalism paled beside that of Mary Elizabeth Braddon, another English novelist, whose *Lady Audley's Secret* was equally indebted to Bulwer-Lytton and Wilkie Collins. Lady Audley's secret was simply that this pretty little governess who had made herself the wife of rich old Sir Michael Audley had another husband still alive. That he was still breathing was not Lady Audley's fault, for she had tried to murder him as well as the inquisitive nephew of her second husband. The novel, whose leading figure ends in an asylum instead of a divorce court, deals with bigamy, murder, arson, and insanity, but its appeal to Americans rested also on lush descriptions of high life in titled society.

The most popular of the English women who wrote sensational novels was Louise de la Ramée, known as Ouida. Her works were as exotic as her pen name. She included no criminals in her books, but they were hardly missed in her ostentatious pictures of life among the sophisticates of English society. Her settings were elegantly bohemian; her characters, effete worldings and rakish guardsmen; her plots, sophisticated intrigues;

and her point of view, cynical and fast paced. Ouida's intention was obvious: *épater les bourgeois*. With the Americans she succeeded admirably. The public found her at one and the same time shocking and fascinating. During the late 'sixties it made *Under Two Flags* a best seller and in grateful return she dedicated *Tricotrin*, the story of an unconventional musical genius and a homeless heroine, to 'the American people, in cordial acknowledgment of their reception of my works.'

Almost any novel with a cosmopolitan setting and a story of life among the aristocracy was likely to have a following during the postwar years. There was, for instance, Disraeli's *Lothair*, a spirited story of a young nobleman's romantic, military, and religious adventures. Since it seemed only remotely related to the sensational school, *Lothair* was cautiously issued in 1870 with a first edition of 2,000 copies. The public evidently found it close enough to its currently favorite type of fiction and orders came pouring in until the sale reached 80,000 copies. There were also Louisa Mühlbach's historical novels, which had been refused by almost every New York publisher. When *Joseph II and His Court* was finally accepted by Appleton in 1865, it proved, according to another publisher, 'a great commercial success,' and for some years every one of the Austrian lady's pictures of glittering court life was eagerly read by the Americans. The appeal of the exotic novel was so wide that not only did it include the fiction of Disraeli and Mühlbach but it created an audience for Wilkie Collins. During the winter of 1873-4 Collins made a tour of the United States, reading from his works, of which the most popular were *The Moonstone*, a terror story about a stolen diamond with a curse on it, and *The Woman in White*, a complicated detective story about the intrigues of an English baronet who places his wife in an insane asylum in order to obtain her fortune.

Perhaps the most successful of all sensational novelists was Charles Reade, whose bulky historical romance, *The Cloister and the Hearth, A Tale of the Middle Ages*, had enjoyed only a moderate popularity when published in 1861. With disappointment Reade declared, 'I write for the public, and the public don't care about the dead.' He decided instead that 'an aristocratic divorce suit, the last great social scandal, a sensational suicide from Waterloo Bridge, a woman murdered in Seven Dials, or a baby found strangled in a bandbox at Piccadilly Circus interests them more.' Accordingly he determined to attract popular attention while at the same time writing novels with a social purpose. *Griffith Gaunt*, a highly colored story of bigamy, murder, and mistaken identity among eighteenth-century gentry, was less significant for its attack upon a worldly clergy than for its almost pathological sensationalism. As soon as it was printed in 1866, a New York journal, *The Round Table*, attacked it as so 'indecent' that 'the lowest sensational weekly papers . . . did not dare to undertake its publication.' Reade sued *The Round Table* and though awarded only six cents in damages, the notoriety of the trial, in which most of the novel was read to the jury, made the work a scandalous success. Pirated immediately in cheap editions, it was soon dramatized by Augustin Daly and made Reade's name so well known that a public was waiting for him when he published *A Terrible Temptation* in 1871. Even if issued anonymously, this novel would have attracted attention quickly enough. Its purpose—an exposé of so-called 'baby farms'—was startling, but its lurid plot of a reformed Don Juan attempting to purchase a legitimate heir was the real cause for interest. The New York *Sun* declared it 'the most indecent book that has lately been issued from the press . . . a mass of brothel garbage' served by a 'narrator of vice.' Reade did not sue this time, but he got his reward in sales just the same. Americans, as one of them observed, were eager 'to satisfy a morbid curiosity . . . as to the evils peculiar to high places.' They bought edition after edition of *A Terrible Temptation*. When the London *Times* refused Reade space to defend himself against attacks he was able to reply contemptuously, 'in the United States three publishers have already sold three hundred and seventy thousand copies of this novel—which, I take it, is about thirty times the circulation of the Times in the United States, and nearly six times its English circulation.' So great was the novel's popularity that, although it had been serialized in *Every Saturday* prior to book publication, *Harper's Weekly* was glad to reprint it and pay Reade for the privilege. Reade's subjects and his point of view were congenial to the ethos of postwar America. *A Terrible Temptation* only remotely resembled anti-slavery or temperance tales in that it too was an example of sensational fiction with a message, yet before the firing on Fort Sumter it was the message in a novel that was admired—after Appomattox, it was the sensation.

Chapter 8

The Spirit of Poetry

Popular poetry in the decades before the Civil War agreed with the favorite fiction of the day in attitude, if not always in theme. The dialectic of the popular mind was by turns sentimental and homely, moral and humanitarian, religious and patriotic, and, finally, at a late date, cosmopolitan. These were the dominant strains, though not the only ones, and they were not all simultaneously favored, but a poem to be popular had to be pitched to one of them. The belief or idea that called out a prose statement just as surely evoked a poetic phrase.

Readers who luxuriated in the sentimental *Reveries of a Bachelor* turned with understanding to the versification of Mrs. Hemans or Mrs. Sigourney. Those who enjoyed the domesticity of feminine novelists were equally at home in Whittier's snowbound New England household. The truisims of Timothy Titcomb were translated into the more portable morality of Martin Tupper. Readers of *The Lamplighter* were prepared for Holmes's injunctions to 'Build thee more stately mansions, O my soul.' The optative mood of the 1840's was perfectly expressed in Longfellow's poem about the boy who bore a banner with the strange device: 'Excelsior!' The motto happened to be that of the state of New York; it might as well have belonged to the nation at large. The humanitarianism that flowered in *Uncle Tom's Cabin* grew from the same seeds that blossomed as *Evangeline* and *The Biglow Papers*. *The Man Without a Country* traveled the same patriotic direction as *Paul Revere's Ride*. The fervid faith of *Beulah* or *St. Elmo* animated Bailey's *Festus*. Finally, the cosmopolitanism of Ouida was complemented by Owen Meredith's *Lucile*. Look where one might, prose and poetry moved in a harmony of ideas and feelings.

Byron and Scott were still widely read, and even earlier poets such as Campbell and Edward Young lingered in old people's memories and young people's schoolbooks, but the times called out their own poets. Unlike the favorites of the past, many of the popular new poets were American. There was a self-conscious interest in native verse that exhibited itself in gift books and anthologies. In 1839, with his own fame established as a poet of America's landscape, Bryant issued his *Selections from the American Poets,* and the same year one Mr. Keese offered a culling of *The Poets of America, Illustrated by One of Her Painters.* Three years later Rufus Griswold, the favorite anthologist of the day, brought out the first edition of his bulky *Poets and Poetry of America.* By 1849 this collection had gone through eleven printings, and hoping to do even better by taking advantage of the current feminism, the editor subdivided his work by sexes. A *Gems from American Poets,* issued in 1844, Thomas Buchanan Read's *Female Poets of America* and Caroline May's *The American Female Poets,* both published in 1848, had sold well. So Griswold in 1849 reworked part of his old anthology into *The Female Poets of America,* avoiding plagiarism of Read's title by a thoughtful addition of the word 'The.' By 1856 his ladies were in their fifth printing and his male poets had meanwhile gone through another six printings.

Fiction, of course, continued more popular than verse because its prosy plots were read with greater ease by most people. Poetry, however, was not really to be compared with the novel, for if its sales were lower its honor stood higher. The prevailing conception was that described by Longfellow in his blank verse 'The Spirit of Poetry':

> Its presence shall uplift thy thoughts from earth,
> As to the sunshine and the pure, bright air.

The poet's commanding eminence removed him from the people, yet allowed him, as Lowell noted, to 'piece together our fragmentary apprehensions of our own life and that larger life whose unconscious instruments we are, making of the jumbled bits of our dissected map of experience a coherent chart.' The novelist might be approached as an equal; to the poet a reader came, hat in hand, awaiting a statement or an interpretation of his own amorphous feelings and ideas. 'The proof of poetry,' Lowell observed for his generation, was tested by an ability to 'reduce to the essence of a single line the vague philosophy which is floating in all men's minds.' He who most successfully met this criterion was the people's poet, the poet to be read, the poet to be revered. For those who entertained this view his name was Henry Wadsworth Longfellow.

Longfellow had an established public even before he issued a line of verse, for he began his literary career as a prose writer of some popularity. His three prose works—*Outre-Mer, Hyperion,* and *Kavanagh* —published between 1833 and 1849, had by 1864 sold over 29,000 copies. 'The surprising fact here,' as William Charvat has pointed out, 'is that the total printings of the prose works was 85% of that of the seven separate volumes of original verse published in the same period.' Prose consistently sold better than poetry, and not even the most popular volume of Longfellow's poetry ever came within hailing distance of Mrs. Stowe's most popular novel. But Longfellow was the first American to make a living from his poetry, and a very good living too. The opportunity to furnish his colonial mansion, Craigie House, with fine plate and vintage wines came, in part from his expression of prevailing poetic beliefs, in part from his shrewd business sense. He knew how to market his poems, apportioning new verses among magazines, newspapers, gift books, and his own volumes in carefully calculated ratios, and doling out a new book or a collected edition at strategic intervals. Except for his drama, *The Spanish Student,* no poetic work by Longfellow sold fewer than 2,000 copies, and his first dozen volumes of new and collected poems sold about 155,000 copies between 1839 and 1864. An indication of Longfellow's growing public is to be found in prices publishers could afford to pay for his works. In 1840 he received $15 for the first printing of 'The Village Blacksmith'; in 1874 'The Hanging of the Crane' brought $3,000. Another judgment of increasing popularity may be made by observing that a volume of his collected poetry issued for less than a dollar in 1846 sold but 6,000 copies, while a two-volume edition issued in 1850 sold 20,000, and the elegant 'Blue and Gold' edition of 1856 sold 40,000. In the early 'forties first printings of Longfellow's books ran into the hundreds of copies; with *Evangeline* in 1847 the publisher made a first edition of 1,000 copies; for *The Golden Legend* in 1851 he increased this to 3,500; he increased it again to 5,000 for *Hiawatha* in 1855, to 10,000 for *The Courtship of Miles Standish* in 1858, and, finally, to 15,000 for *The Tales of a Wayside Inn*, issued in 1863.

The author's business sense enhanced these sales, but his poetic sense created them. His subjects, sentiments, and style were in perfect harmony with what the book-buying public expected of poetry. Whether his mood was one of quiet melancholy or cheery hopefulness (and more commonly—as with the people themselves—it was the latter), the mood found expression in benign didacticism, preaching morals all could endorse. Although Longfellow's poetry exhorted the reader to struggle for a finer life, it banished the real problems of daily existence. It was the poetry described in his own 'The Day is Done':

> Some simple and heartfelt lay,
> That shall soothe this restless feeling,
> And banish the thoughts of day.

It was often poetry of the twilight hour, neither definite enough for day or night, substituting for reality edifying considerations of a romantic past, a distant region, or a generalized ethical concept. Even when his subject was an outrage such as that which provides the frame for *Evangeline,* Longfellow did not arouse deeply disturbing emotions or ideas. Contemplating the calm tone and pastel shades of *Evangeline,* the flintier poet Whittier was puzzled to find 'the tide of the story runs as smoothly as if nothing had occurred.'

Like his subject matter, Longfellow's metrics posed no problems. Whether he employed the common ballad, the well-known sonnet, or with great adroitness handled unusual meters such as the Latin hexameter in *Evangeline* and the trochaic tetrameter in *Hiawatha,* his language flowed easily and the beat of his rhythm was memorable. His words were generally arranged in normal prose order, communicating immediately to an unsophisticated mind. His metaphors, though insistent and obtrusive, were simple in a didactic sense. He thought of sermons, found stones on which to engrave them, and of them shaped blocks with which to

> Make the house, where Gods may dwell,
> Beautiful, entire, and clean.

Longfellow gave his readers more than homely ethics artfully decorated. Desirable as these were to the reading public, he brought them also glimpses of foreign culture not only in extended similes and tags of quotations, but in many of his settings and subjects. And even more, he employed his narrative gifts to tell stirring stories of America's own past. For a nation coming of age he created single-handed a folklore whose heroes and heroines included Paul Revere, Miles Standish, Priscilla, Evangeline, and Hiawatha. All of them were enthusiastically received by a people who, while restlessly moving forward, were searching the past for signs of greatness in their native land.

The Song of Hiawatha was probably the most popular of Longfellow's American narratives, the story carried along by its infectious, tripping meter. Four-fifths of the first printing of more than 5,000 copies were sold before publication in November 1855, and a new printing of 3,000 was immediately ordered. Within a month the publishers were sending the eleven-thousandth copy to press. Booksellers could not keep the simple brown cloth-bound book in stock. During the same year an unknown poet named Walt Whitman could not dispose of the thousand or so copies of a thin quarto he had printed under the title *Leaves of Grass*. Although the title and the fancy filigree binding resembled Fanny Fern's recently popular book of sketches, no one was willing to pay a dollar for Whitman's poems when for the same price he might have Longfellow's. 'The books were put into the stores,' Whitman said, and then he added: 'But nobody bought them.' Although he told the people 'what I assume you shall assume,' Whitman's strange, tuneless 'barbaric yawp' was not for them. His exuberant, erotic affirmations they never read. He might ask readers to

> Loafe with me on the grass . . . loose the stop from your throat,
> Not words, not music or rhyme I want.

But they were not interested. Their ears were attuned to the poet who described them thus:

> Ye who love a nation's legends,
> Love the ballads of a people,
> That like voices from afar off
> Call to us to pause and listen,
> Speak in tones so plain and childlike,
> Scarcely can the ear distinguish
> Whether they are sung or spoken;—
> Listen to this Indian Legend,
> To this Song of Hiawatha!

For the public, 1855 was the year of *Hiawatha*, not of *Leaves of Grass*. And so was 1856. On New Year's Day his publisher told Longfellow the poem was 'going at the rate of three hundred a day.' Currier and Ives, who understood public tastes, turned some of the presses that had recently run temperance lithographs to printing a whole series of Hiawatha pictures. Popular songs told of the love of Hiawatha and Minnehaha; dramatic readings of the poem were presented on the stage; parodies sprouted like weeds in a well-fertilized garden (seven in bound form almost as long as the original, and scores of shorter ones in magazines and newspapers); and a New York theater produced a musical extravaganza based on *Hiawatha*. At first Longfellow objected to this flip reception, but he stopped grumbling when his publisher pointed out that it spurred sales. In five months 30,000 copies were sold and still the poem found new readers. Even five years after publication it sold at the rate of 2,000 copies annually, and, as if to atone for the parodies, an august scholar translated its facile rhythms into Latin.

'It cannot be denied that Henry W. Longfellow is the first of our living American poets,' the *Southern Literary Messenger* declared in 1855, yet he was challenged from overseas by Tennyson, also a great favorite. As the *Democratic Review* pointed out, 'The poets all used to chime in with "The Lay of the Last Minstrel," then they caroled nothing but love ditties like Moore, then imitated Byron; and now they whimper like Tennyson.' For some time Tennyson was a poet's poet, known only to select American readers. His first volume of *Poems*, issued in 1842, had a printing of 2,000 copies, and even *The Princess*, published in 1848, had a first edition of only 1,000 copies, though its equivocal treatment of the militant woman aroused fair enthusiasm among both feminists and anti-feminists, each of whom found in it verses to substantiate their own beliefs. By the 'fifties Tennyson was becoming popular. His songs for *The Princess* appeared in over a hundred American magazines and newspapers and sheet music settings sold widely, though not so widely as adaptations from Mrs. Hemans. *In Memoriam,* if by no means a best seller, stirred up a good deal of controversy upon its publication in 1850. Although Emerson might say privately that 'Tennyson's In Memoriam is the commonplaces of condolence among good Unitarians in the first week of mourning,' many Americans found it obscure and strangely disturbing. To some it appeared irreligious, or at least unorthodox; to others it was an inspiring and comforting work. *Maud* had a mixed reception too when it appeared in the fall of 1855, along with *Hiawatha*. Although four printings were called out by March, they totaled only 8,400 copies against Longfellow's 50,000, and Tennyson was still mainly the poet for intellectuals.

Not until the *Idylls of the King* appeared in 1859 was Tennyson established as a truly popular poet, a position he retained through the years with the publication of further volumes of his spacious Arthurian legendry. Having seriously considered the scientific knowledge of his time, Tennyson had come to hold a hopeful faith consistent with that professed by many Americans. He was for them a great expositor of belief in man's progress, occupied with ethical considerations of the very sort that most of his transatlantic readers wanted to formulate. Not to like Tennyson became a heresy, according to a later American laureate, Bayard Taylor. Even when in his varied verse Tennyson's ideas did not always please, his superb craftsmanship did, to the degree that it obscured what the offensive words were saying. His melodious lines and sensitive descriptions of sea and land won over most of those who were upon occasion critical of his ideas. His sales were tremendous, though surpassed by Longfellow's. For example, the *Idylls* in 1859 sold 11,000 copies within a month, while the year before Longfellow noted that *The Courtship of Miles Standish* deployed 'an army of twenty-five thousand in one week.' But when the simple, homely narrative of *Enoch Arden* sold 40,000 copies in its authorized edition of 1864, Tennyson came close to challenging Longfellow's claim to the title of America's poet laureate.

Tradition has established Browning as the other great English poet of the Victorian period, to be placed beside Tennyson. In his own time he occupied no such position in the minds of American readers. Not until *Men and Women* appeared in 1855 did any of Browning's fourteen volumes of poetry attract public attention in the United States. Until then he was thought obscure or esoteric; the new collection improved matters only to the extent that people said he could be understood but should not: he was immoral. *Dramatis Personae* attracted a wider and more appreciative audience in 1864, but its reception was still slim. Beginning about 1870 Browning's earlier work began to seem more comprehensible and proper, and in that year the timetables of the Chicago and Alton Railroad included a selection of Browning's poems for the entertainment of weary commuters! Yet even after Browning Societies began to spring up in the 'eighties, the poetry did not become popular. It was the property of special cultists. Browning's character analysis and his allusiveness presumed a background of reference wider than most people had. The verse was often too gnomic, the language too condensed to yield quotable lines such as the public liked. It was a poetry of ideas requiring more than one reading for sense, and it was lacking in the obvious music that most people equated with poetry.

In mid-century when Americans thought of English poets other than Tennyson they did not include Browning. But there were British favorites. For a few years serious attention was given to Philip Bailey's turgid epic, *Festus*. The American publisher who issued this Victorian Faustus in 1845 prefaced his edition with an apologetic admission that it had 'extravagances which all will discover.' Some accepted the lengthy dialogues between Lucifer and the young Festus as 'extravagances of deep and eloquent passion,' as the publisher hurried on to explain they were, but after a few years enthusiasm for Bailey simmered away when people discovered that though his sonorous blank verse had occasional moving passages, most of it was 'rant and fustian,' as Rufus Griswold insisted.

An even more interesting example of the Victorian middle-class mind and one even more popular in America was the British poet, Martin Farquhar Tupper. He was the author of thirty-five books, including a five-act drama about Washington and several novels, but he was known almost exclusively for his four series of *Proverbial Philosophy*, published between 1838 and 1842 and collected in 1876. Though he wrote on innumerable subjects he contributed to none either a new idea or a sharper vision. He was the Polonius of Victorian poetry. His very appeal rested on his ability to versify platitudes, embalming them with a pompously antiquated style that he and his readers thought dignified because it often aped the King James version. Guided literally by the 'philosophy' of proverbs, Tupper was able to accept all the cant of the day as serious thought. He declared 'all the world is glad to worship Smooth Respectability,' if it but 'crown every passing day with some good action daily,' either in 'the happy home of Christians' or 'the temple of utility,' feeling that 'by culture man may do all things,' as long as 'the harmony of nature is preserved by each one knowing his place.' So high was America's regard for Tupper that the San Francisco Grand Jury of 1850, unable to locate a Bible for swearing in, used a copy of *Proverbial Philosophy* as an adequate substitute. On Tupper's tour of this country in 1851 not only did John Jacob Astor give a dinner jointly honoring him and Washington Irving, but President Fillmore invited him to dine with the entire Cabinet. Tupper himself was hardly more pleased with these honors than by his discovery that the doctor in charge of an American lunatic asylum had placed in each patient's room a copy of his poem,

'Never Give Up.' By 1858 Oliver Wendell Holmes thought that 80,000 copies of the *Proverbial Philosophy* had been sold, as against only 12,000 in England, and contemporary newspapers lavishly estimated that Tupper's sales ranged from half a million to a million and a half. Even if the newspapers obviously exaggerated the circulation of pirated and unauthorized editions, the *Southern Literary Messenger* rightly declared, 'The "Proverbial Philosophy" has struck with almost miraculous force and effect upon the minds and hearts of a large class of American readers, and has at once rendered its author's name and character famous and familiar in our country.'

Still another popular English author was Mrs. Felicia Hemans, who lingered on from an earlier day. Though she died prematurely in 1835, even in the 'fifties her fame was as bright as it had been when an American publisher offered her a free home and an annual salary of $1,500 to accept the nominal editorship of his magazine, a sinecure for which she had only to loan her name. Her 'Casabianca,' telling how 'The boy stood on the burning deck,' and 'The Landing of the Pilgrim Fathers' were set pieces for elocutionists in and out of school. Though she tortured history and geography in her account of the *Mayflower* landing, she so thoroughly impressed her views upon the American mind that it is hardly possible for later generations to think of the Plymouth coast as anything but 'stern' and 'rock-bound.' Not only did these poems first receive book publication in America, but she led all other poets in her appearances in American gift books and annuals. A count made by Professor Bradford A. Booth shows that seventy-five of her poems appeared in these anthologies between 1825 and 1865, as against a mere seventeen by Tennyson. According to one journalist, Mrs. Hemans was 'endenizen'd' in thousands of American hearts. American critics were great ones at endenizening, but the description was apt enough in this instance.

For one of America's native favorites, Mrs. Lydia Huntley Sigourney, critics could think of no higher tribute than to call her 'the Mrs. Hemans of America'. Beginning with *Moral Pieces in Prose and Verse* in 1815, for half a century books flowed from Mrs. Sigourney's ever-moist pen. Sometimes they came at the rate of seven a year, until there were 65 in all, compounded in part of her 2,000 magazine contributions. A vain, pushing woman, pomaded and rouged, affecting humility to extort encomiums from the writers and civic figures to whom she sent complimentary copies of her books, she had a formula that attracted a public. Her poems all teach generalized ethical lessons, praising sobriety, patience, honesty, submissiveness, and other bourgeois virtues. She purposefully appealed to the class of women who read domestic fiction and was quite properly selected by *The Ladies' Wreath* as a prime example of the fact that 'in the actual world the path of women is very circumscribed, but . . . her imagination may range with the freedom of an angel's wing.' Death was Mrs. Sigourney's favorite theme. Nothing set her rhymes flowing like the passing of a missionary in Burma, the wasting away of an infant, or the demise of a deaf and dumb girl. One of her edifying effusions was entitled 'Monody on the Death of the Principal of the Connecticut Retreat for the Insane.' She struck just the right note, for as one admirer said of her poetry, 'It makes me sad, but not unhappy.' A 'gemmy' poet who overdecorated everything, she considered a straightforward word unpoetic. When she wrote an epic on Pocahontas, Mrs. Sigourney described but did not name Captain John Smith, for, after all, she declared his surname 'would be inadmissable in verse.'

The steady stream of volumes by Mrs. Sigourney and the frequent reprintings of Mrs. Hemans's poems continued through the 'fifties and 'sixties, but in those decades newer authors rose to challenge them in popularity and to be compared, momentarily, with Longfellow and Tennyson, with Tupper and Bailey. One of these new poets was Josiah Gilbert Holland, a journalist of Springfield, Massachusetts, who in 1858 published two best sellers: Titcomb's *Letters,* a collection of platitudinous essays blending morality and manners, and *Bitter-Sweet,* a long narrative poem. By the outbreak of the war the *Letters* had gone through twenty-six editions and the fifteenth edition of the poem was being sold. In course of time *Bitter-Sweet* sold about 90,000 copies, some of them in a special illustrated edition bound in a fabric called 'extra illuminated cloth,' priced at $6, and some 'in Turkey antique . . . put up in a neat box,' priced at $8. Holland, called by his modern biographer 'the major prophet of the unsophisticated, the supreme apostle to the naive,' blended local color and pious arguments in a way that suited the same public that in 1859 was buying Miss Evans's novel *Beulah.* His two hundred pages of blank verse described the Thanksgiving gathering of a New England family, at which each person revealed his private sorrows and wondered why God permitted such grief. Finally all discover satisfactory answers, and, buoyed up by new faith, they determined to improve their lives. Of this animated sermon James Russell

Lowell said in a contemporary review, 'We feel sure that none of the characters ever went to bed in their lives, but always sidled through the more decorous subterfuge of "retiring." ' But the public went on buying the poem and gave an even greater welcome to *Kathrina*, which was issued in 1867, the year of *St. Elmo*. The heroine, Kathrina, was essentially Miss Evans's Edna Earl set to verse. A hundred thousand people soon bought the story of her marriage to an agnostic author whose writings, though technically proficient, lack the spark of greatness until he is converted to Christianity by the dying Kathrina, who leaves him and the reader convinced he will soon be not only a best-selling but also an edifying author.

Whittier had been a well-known, even a popular poet before *Snow-Bound* appeared in 1866. But it was this work that made him truly popular. For almost forty years his contributions of prose and poetry to newspapers and magazines had been collected in successive volumes; his propaganda for the Abolitionist movement was widely known, and his songs, hymns, and rustic ballads had given him a solid reputation. Thousands had memorized 'Maud Muller,' 'Barbara Frietchie,' 'The Barefoot Boy,' and other of his pastoral pictures and local legendry, for they had made of him a minor Longfellow in popular affection. At least twenty-one editions of collected poems had appeared by 1866, but *Snow-Bound* marked the culmination of his slow accretion of fame. The most sustained of his works, its subject and point of view were suited to the moment. Whittier's meticulous though idyllic picture of the spiritual peace of home was like an elegy for a simpler, more wholesome day destroyed by the recent Civil War. Those who longed for what was gone found in Whittier's wistful poem a happy reminiscence of a lost serenity. Its honest simplicity made *Snow-Bound* understandable to the unsophisticated and appealed to the more cultivated who were searching for an integrated way of life. Within six months 18,000 copies of the poem were in print and by the time the year was out 28,000 had been issued. Its fame built up a public eager for his next work, *The Tent on the Beach*, which for a time in 1867 reached a sale of a thousand copies a day. The poet who had never before known commercial success, after the publication of *Snow-Bound*, accumulated an estate of $100,000 from royalties on prose and verse.

The other New England poets did not capture really large followings; they seem to have been more respected than read. Emerson, well known as moralist, lecturer, and essayist, records the sale of only 849 copies of his *Poems* during 1847, their first year of publication. The forty-four-year-old philosopher was not yet regarded as a respectable radical; many years passed before his writings were thought fit for school and library editions and then for such compilations as an *Emerson Calendar* and an *Emerson Treasury*. Of Lowell's works only *The Vision of Sir Launfal,* and, to a lesser extent, *A Fable for Critics* and the two series of *The Biglow Papers,* had any real sale. The timely wit and vigor of *The Biglow Papers* made them a temporary success, quoted and copied widely, but most of Lowell's poetry was not well known until he himself was famous as minister to Spain and to England in the 'seventies and 'eighties. Then his writings began to be enshrined in 'household,' 'illustrated,' 'family,' and 'library' editions. Bryant, too, had no popular following. Only in the 'seventies did he, like Lowell, have some belated success with his translations of the *Iliad* and the *Odyssey* and his collected editions, a sort of living memorial to the culture of which he was considered a representative. Holmes was well known both as poet and prose writer. His *Autocrat of the Breakfast-Table* focused a clear morning light upon the temper of the times more commonly viewed in such twilight sentiment as the *Reveries of a Bachelor.* The humorous treatment of prevailing interests made it a success in 1858 with a sale said to number 20,000 copies, but it was perhaps too astringent, witty, and regional for wider sale. Holmes's verses, with a few exceptions, were also too localized for popular favor. Although a few poems, such as 'Old Ironsides,' stirred public interest, his poetry was mainly *vers de société* about Boston or Cambridge civic and social affairs, too urbane and too special for a general public. His poems were perfectly suited to an occasion, but their grace seemed remote if one was not a participant at the affairs they honored. Besides, they were brief and to read a collection of them was monotonous. Only once did readers turn to the kind of verse of which Holmes was a master, and then it was not one of his poems they selected. It was William Allen Butler's *Nothing to Wear,* a success of the season of 1857. This satire of Flora M'Flimsy, a society lady who claimed she had nothing to wear to parties, captured the popular imagination at a time when social climbers were making themselves strenuously felt. The poem was set in New York, a better stage than Holmes's Boston, for, though the public might still consider Boston the hub of the world's morality, its society was beginning to seem too exclusive and rarefied.

The New Englanders may have won respect in the postwar years, but young Owen Meredith was the poet whose work was immediately sold and read. The son of Bulwer-Lytton, he took a pseudonym to avoid confusion with the author of *Pelham,* though a reading of his poetry showed he had learned a great deal from his father about high society as a theme and graceful writing as a form. In 1853, when his popular poetry was still some years off, he scorned Tom Moore's kind of verse, which stood high on what he called 'the popularity platform (as the Yankees say).' 'I can never admit to myself,' he declared, 'that Poetry is a thing to be with albums on a drawing room table, and be turned over by every stupid chance comer that may enter half an hour too soon for dinner, to be sung by a young lady at a piano, and there end.' But that is just where his poetry tended and ended. With anapests almost as tripping as Moore's he wrote *Lucile,* a novel in verse that not only pleased those who liked the romantic poetry of Moore but also appealed to the middle-class culture he professed to scorn. It was a success from the moment of its publication in 1860.

Meredith effected a remarkable union of diverse strains in the twelve cantos of *Lucile,* the story of an involved love affair in high society. His structure he learned from Mrs. Browning's *Aurora Leigh,* which had aroused some interest when issued in 1857; his plot came from a novel by George Sand, and his worldly characters were imitations of those found in his father's social fiction and Byron's poems. The public that turned to Ouida naturally enough made a best seller of *Lucile* too. Even as late as 1877 it was proclaimed the 'most salable volume of poetry' in the *Publishers' Weekly* poll of bookstores, with Holland's works coming in second and third.

Though the story of *Lucile* was sophisticated and the meter flippantly gay, the poem was liberally sprinkled with edifying aphorisms of an eminently quotable sort. A public attuned to Longfellow was pleased with such lines as:

> Honest love, honest sorrow,
> Honest work for the day, honest hope for the morrow,
> Are these worth nothing more than the hand they make weary,
> The heart they have saddened, the life they leave dreary?

And lady readers were happy to see him place women in a position neither so advanced as that for which feminists argued nor so retired as that approved by old-fashioned moralists. Many an American lady was glad to have a masculine hand copy into her autograph album such lines as Meredith's statement that woman's place was

To uplift,
Purify, and confirm by its own gracious gift,
The world, in despite of the world's dull endeavor
To degrade, and drag down, and oppose it forever.

The comparison might appear odd to a later day, but it is understandable
that Meredith's friend, John Forster, said of *Lucile*, 'It reminds me of
Werter, I don't know why, except that it is the voice of the Age.' The
poem answered a temporary conception of what poetry should be, blending high romance and lofty moral sentiments in easy verse. It sold far
more copies in the United States than in England, for it was pirated by
more than fifty different publishers, whose editions varied from paper-
covered pamphlets to plush bindings. The luxurious printings were generally favored, such as that in the appropriately named 'Ajax Padded
Poets' series, and in these forms *Lucile* came to rest on the parlor tables
of America next to Jean Ingelow's *Poems* in their squat pages and
tawdry bindings, or the elaborately illustrated editions of Tennyson and
Longfellow.

The mid-century was the great era of poetry. Though poetry never
ranked with prose in popularity, it was more widely read in those years
than it has ever been since. New poets came along in time but few found
a great following. Edward FitzGerald's *Rubáiyát of Omar Khayyám*,
which had been quietly issued in Ohio in 1870, eleven years after the first
obscure English printing, was too melancholy for the majority of people
at the time. But eventually, when the flush of mid-century optimism
faded, its brief quatrains, balancing the theme of life's brevity, were
found to express the quintessence of faith in an age of skepticism. As
Arthur C. Benson said,

The sad and wasted form of his philosophy came slowly forwards, dimly smiling, draped in this rich Oriental fabric, and with all the added mystery of a
venerable antiquity. It heightened the charm to readers, living in a season of
outworn faith and restless dissatisfaction, to find that eight hundred years before, far across the centuries, in the dim and remote East, the same problems
had pressed sadly on the mind of an ancient and accomplished sage.

The compression of Omar's Epicurean philosophy in epigrammatic lines
of vivid imagery and the supple repetitive form in which they were cast
made the poem easy to read and therefore a better candidate for popularity than poetic statements of the same ideas that were more diffuse or
symbolic. Its popularity came in the 'nineties, but even then it was a bit
specialized. Omar was a cult rather than an accepted philosopher, and

innumerable parodies indicate that he was not entirely accepted by those people his readers would have called 'philistines.' Just as the first American edition came from outside normal publishing channels, so the later, more popular printings were generally issued by special publishers. Thomas Bird Mosher's 19 artistic editions between 1893 and 1911, which averaged 1,025 copies, were symbolic of his American sponsorship and reading public. The vogue of FitzGerald was esoteric, identified with limited, illustrated, and 'fine' gift editions, until E. Haldeman-Julius in 1919 made *Omar* the first of his Little Blue Book Series, in which it has annually sold an average of 50,000 copies.

As the century moved on into its later decades the people's poets were still those established in the 'forties and 'fifties. By school and by parent they were carried over into the minds of younger generations of readers, who, with rare exceptions, found no new favorites for themselves. New techniques in poetry divorced it from the common reader, who was busy anyway with more 'practical' problems than those considered appropriate to poetry. As Bryant said near the end of his poetic career, 'After all, poetic wares are not for the market of the present day. Poetry may get printed in the newspapers, but no man makes money by it for the simple reason that nobody cares a fig for it. The taste for it is something old-fashioned; the march of the age is in another direction; mankind are occupied with politics, railroads, and steamboats.' Bryant was right. His age, and that of Longfellow and Tennyson, was past. A tougher-minded era more concerned with mechanics than with nature, more interested in politics than religion, had less use for the poet. No longer was the poet the seer and interpreter. He was relegated, as Bryant said, to the newspaper. Although later poets were popular, such as James Whitcomb Riley and Edgar Guest, they were poets of the newspaper, doled out and read in the spirit of a daily editorial.

Chapter 9

Roughing It

The West had always been a subject of interest to the American people. Its dense forests, undulating prairies, wide rivers, and high mountains served both as barrier and beacon. West meant wilderness, but it meant adventure and opportunity too. Byron and other romantic poets made of it a region where man and nature might meet in harmony; Irving clothed it with classic grandeur; Cooper knew it as a place of reality enshrouded in romantic beauty; Mrs. Trollope and Dickens excoriated its crudeness. These were only a few of the popular expositors of the West. Pioneers and politics etched it more deeply in the American mind. Lewis and Clark, Andrew Jackson and Daniel Boone, Abraham Lincoln and Davy Crockett, Marcus Whitman and Frémont—they were among the figures who made it assume heroic but comprehensible shape. The fur trade, the Santa Fé commerce, the Mexican War, the California gold rush, the Donner Party disaster, the Mormon migration, the Gadsden Purchase—these were some of the events that brought the West home to the Easterner. 'Manifest destiny,' 'fifty-four forty or fight,' 'bleeding Kansas,' 'go West, young man'—these were some of the catch phrases that attracted the people. The compass of America pointed West throughout the nineteenth century.

At the opening of the century the center of population was just outside Baltimore. By 1850 it was in the middle of Ohio. The body of America was moving westward, yet its mind remained unsure of the abstraction called West. It was still remote and incomprehensible. Cartographers inscribed 'the great American desert' across vast sections of its uncharted wilderness and most readers could only barely conceive its outlines. Irving and others who had seen something of the nearer West depicted its fertile land, but most people still thought of the plains as a wasteland and the Rockies as one great impenetrable mountain ridge. Voyagers like young Richard Henry Dana, reporters like Bayard Taylor, and explorers from Lewis and Clark to Frémont described the West to interested readers (Senate and Congress alike distributed Frémont's reports by the tens of thousands and more copies were circulated during his unsuccessful presidential campaign), but their public was smaller than that which enjoyed fiction and narrative verse. Neither novelist nor poet could domesticate the West. It was too new, too strange. While the Donners starved in California, the reading public wept at the plight of the Acadians smoothly set forth in Longfellow's *Evangeline*. When the Emigrant Aid Company was founded in 1854, the public read *The Lamplighter*. In 1863 Virginia City attracted thousands to its silver deposits; on the eastern seaboard people read *Lady Audley's Secret* or Mrs. Southworth's romance, *The Fatal Marriage*. As late as 1870 fewer than 3 per cent of America's new books dealt with the West.

The West moved into popular literature slowly. As the land that had once been West—Ohio, Indiana, Illinois—came into the orbit of the East, it served as a background in literature, even though it was not the setting for any best seller of the first half of the nineteenth century. But the Far West remained aloof and remote. Only after the Civil War did the land beyond the Rockies make its way into popular literature as part of the general interest in what was called 'local color.' Then in a reunited nation, people of one region grew curious about those of another, wondering about differences that were fast disappearing as industrialism threatened to shape all into a common mold. In the 'seventies *Scribner's Magazine*, for example, began to replace its serials from English authors with articles, fiction, and poetry by Helen Hunt Jackson, Bret Harte, Joaquin Miller, John Muir, and John Burroughs.

Before its establishment as a subject of general interest, the West entered America's popular literature through the backdoor of humor. Humorous writing had a growing public after the 1820's, and it continued through the century as one of the favorite modes of expression. A touch of humor blended with the kind of moral sentimentality found in *The Lamplighter* helped make Fanny Fern an outstanding favorite. She capitalized on a mood that as early as 1833 caused some thirty newspapers to print Seba Smith's homespun political philosophy in the letters of the Yankee Jack Downing and that during the 'forties brought a public to Frances Whitcher's magazine sketches about the Widow Bedott, a gossiping New England housewife. The public for such writing was large enough to make one collection of Downing letters have 10 printings from 1834 to 1836 and to bring the *Widow Bedott Papers* a sale of 100,000 copies in the 23 printings issued in the decade after 1855. But Down East humor was only a forerunner of local-color stories about regions yet stranger where comedy of a more outlandish type flourished.

The mid-nineteenth century developed its own special brand of humor, which in great part derived its impetus from the frontier. This Western humor, unlike that of Britain or the Eastern seaboard, was not refined from natural speech into a literary idiom wittier or more brilliantly modeled. The written humor of the West purposefully attempted to retain the flavor of the spoken word as it sounded when frontiersmen swapped stories around campfires, at local taverns, and on the flatboats or wagons that carried them ever westward. The stories these pioneers told were as exaggerated as their own lives and as fantastic as the new land surrounding them.

Before the Far West was opened to any but a few trappers and explorers, the Old Southwest was the site of such stories. There, in the region between the Savannah and the Mississippi, in the backwoods land of Alabama, Georgia, Mississippi, and the Great Smokies, were found the conditions soon to be repeated on the outer rim of the continent. From this region first trickled back the tall tales and amusing local-color stories that were tough and earthy and marked by scrutiny of a scene as strange as it was wonderful. Either to conceal their nostalgia or to demonstrate their independence, the backwoodsmen produced a humor forthright and loud, brief and pungent, in which they bragged about the frontier or derided the settled land and its people to the east. Often in the form of a hoax, it was a simple, direct outburst of fun meant to bewilder those not in on the secret—the secret of the life that Westerners led. More sophisticated travelers, hearing these tales in camping grounds and raw new villages or seeing them in local newspapers, brought them a wider audience. From these middlemen came the Davy Crockett almanacs, popular pamphlets attributed to the frontier hero and capitalizing on the picturesque eccentricities of backwoods life. From such purveyors too came works like that of the learned jurist, Augustus B. Longstreet, whose *Georgia Scenes,* first issued in 1835, was by 1860 in a ninth printing. His aim, as the author said, was 'to supply a chasm in history which has always been overlooked—the manners, customs, amusement, wit, and dialect' of a peculiar frontier people. The same purpose motivated Joseph G. Baldwin's *Flush Times of Alabama and Mississippi*, and years later Mark Twain was to follow the same path in his 'Jumping Frog' and *Roughing It*. Mark Twain was a son of the Old Southwest, to which he returned again and again for his subject matter, but his humor matured during his residence in the Far West.

Before Mark Twain's time the new humor of the West tended to break into separate parts. Each of the segments was popular, but only when Mark Twain reassembled them with conscious art did this nineteenth-century humor produce an author who was a long-lived national favorite. First came those humorists who put their emphasis on the parody of Eastern manners and mores. Among them were George Horatio Derby and Prentice Mulford, both sophisticated Easterners who moved to California and took on some of its protective coloring. Over a third of Derby's *Phoenixiana*, published in 1855, burlesqued polite culture, parodying Longfellow and Emerson and laughing at the pretentious program notes written for ladies who attended symphonies to find sentimental stories in the pure music. Mulford, though he lacked Derby's wit, also made a reputation by caricaturing the inflated elegance of Eastern culture as represented in its refined fiction. Such travesties were likewise the forte of Bill Nye, Orpheus C. Kerr, and Artemus Ward. Charles Henry Webb, a San Francisco newspaperman, went so far as to write two full-length parodies of popular novels: Reade's *Griffith Gaunt* becoming *Liffith Lank; or, Lunacy*, and Augusta Evans's ponderous work emerging as *St. Twel'mo; or, The Cuneiform Cyclopedist of Chattanooga*. When Mark Twain's day came, he devoted half of his third book to a parody entitled 'Awful, Terrible Medieval Romance.'

Bret Harte was of this school, for he began his literary career with *Condensed Novels*, parodies of Dickens, Reade, Bulwer-Lytton, T. S. Arthur, Disraeli, and other current favorites. Having started with one aspect of Western humor, the burlesque of Eastern culture, Harte continued with another aspect, the use of local color. Playing both ends against the middle, he next emulated some of the men he had lampooned, using their tested techniques in a new setting. The local-color setting he got from the frontier humorists; the characters and the mood, from Dickens. Dickens died in 1870, but to read *The Luck of Roaring Camp* published that year one might think he had only 'gone west' to California.

The sentimental humor, the eccentric characters, the incongruous contrasts, and the theatrical presentation were the same. Little Nell, Mr. Micawber, Scrooge, and other familiar figures were naturalized as citizens of the Mother Lode under such new names as Piney, Colonel Starbottle, and Dick Bullen. If, on one hand, Harte was the heir of Dickens, on the other, he was in the tradition of the frontier humorist. The pathos and romantic morality of 'How Santa Claus Came to Simpson's Bar' was reminiscent of Boz, while the character Jim Smiley was the typical tall-tale teller, already known by this name in Mark Twain's 'The Celebrated Jumping Frog of Calaveras County.' Within six months Harte's first book of short stories sold only 3,500 copies, but soon his 'Plain Language from Truthful James,' better known as 'The Heathen Chinee,' was everywhere quoted and reprinted, and by 1873 his tales were being published in cheap editions that were said to average a sale of 35,000 copies each. Immediately the University of California invited him to become a Professor of English Literature and the *Atlantic Monthly* offered him $10,000 for a dozen contributions of any sort and of any length. The Western humorists' local color had come of age.

The Westerner's amusement at the polite culture of the East and his interest in his own folkways had furnished more sophisticated writers with attitudes on which to build their own literary reputations, but other aspects of Western humor also attracted a wide reading public when refurbished by professionals. By the 1860's the works of professional funnymen began to swamp bookstores. Aiming to get as many laughs per page as possible, they were more indebted to the robust exaggeration of Western humor than to its localization and parody. Pretending not to be authors at all, they issued their books under the names of their simple characters, so that buyers asked for a work by Artemus Ward, not one by Charles Farrar Browne about Ward, or by Petroleum V. Nasby, not one by David Ross Locke about Nasby. To maintain this guise, such authors ostensibly used the common language and confused logic of simple men, but being professionals they thought the more they exaggerated, the funnier they were. They juxtaposed incongruous parts of speech, mixed metaphors, misquoted Scriptures and classics, and strained to contort spelling and grammar, in part following the Westerner's own delight in crudities and his scorn for Eastern elegance, but most of all making an extravagant use of the Westerner's sense of exaggeration. Some polite arbiters of literature, like the sober E. C. Stedman, were outraged at the 'horrible degeneracy in public taste' when they found 'the whole country . . . flooded, deluged, swamped, beneath a muddy tide of slang, vulgarity, inartistic bathos, impertinence and buffoonery that is not wit.' But most readers reveled in the incongruities and laughed heartily with the humorist who wrote: 'I shall withdraw from public life and start a grocery, and in that humble calling will float peacefully down the stream of time until my weather-beaten bark strikes on the rocks of death, getting my liquor meanwhile (of which I consume many) at wholesale prices.' And readers flocked to buy copies of books that contained such wonderfully illogical logic as Ward's statement: 'I tell you, feller-citizens, it would have been ten dollars in Jeff Davis's pockets if he'd never been born.'

The sales of these humorists' works were almost as fantastic as their humor. There was, for example, Benjamin Penhallow Shillaber's *Life and Sayings of Mrs. Partington,* which sold at least 20,000 copies in its first printing during 1854, creating a wide public for several succeeding books about this small-town Yankee Mrs. Malaprop. Charles Farrar Browne's first collection did even better, *Artemus Ward: His Book* reaching 40,000 buyers within six months of 1862. Henry Wheeler Shaw, previously established through other books, sold 90,000 copies of the first of his *Farmer's Allminax* issued in 1869 under the name of Josh Billings, and during the ten years of their publication the circulation of these annuals sometimes rose as high as 127,000 and never dropped below 50,000. Beginning in 1881, the Wyoming editor Bill Nye probably sold 100,000 copies each of his first three books, reaching a peak of at least half a million with his comic *History of the United States;* and the publisher of George Wilbur Peck contended that within six years he sold 1,290,000 copies of half a dozen books about Peck's bad boy. Even a forgotten humorist like Stanley Huntley is said to have sold 300,000 copies of one of his books about the Spoopendyke family, and a newspaper humorist like Robert Burdette promoted large sales for the text of his *Rise and Fall of the Moustache* as he swung around the lyceum circle delivering this lecture no less than five thousand times. Other humorists with a great following included: James Montgomery Bailey, known from coast to coast as the 'Danbury News Man'; Robert Henry Newell, who called himself 'Orpheus C. Kerr'; Opie Read, editor of the *Arkansas Traveler;* Mortimer Neal Thomson, the parodist who masqueraded as 'Doesticks'; and Charles Henry Smith of *Bill Arp, So-Called.* More than a thin residue of frontier mannerisms made these comedians popular. The cultural appetites of the time grew by what they fed upon;

humor was in vogue and humorous books, Western or otherwise, were in demand.

The parodists, the local-color writers, and the professional funnymen had taken Western humor and broken it into parts. Mark Twain reunited the separated parts. Rising above them as an artist, but employing all their traditional attitudes and devices, he drew on the robust humor of tall tales, the amused burlesque of elegance, the romance of local color, the cracker-barrel wit of homespun philosophers, and the raucous verbal slapstick of professional funnymen. Folk tales that had long floated around the frontier Mark Twain retold as his own, jokes that first belonged to Derby and Artemus Ward he appropriated casually, and in his *Tom Sawyer* readers found Aunt Polly to be a twin sister of Mrs. Partington in appearance, ideas, and language and recognized their respective nephews, Tom and Ike, to be no further removed than first cousins.

The Innocents Abroad was Mark Twain's first full-length book, and the attitude that shaped it was born in the West. Innocents, indeed! This was the West abroad. Written originally for a California newspaper, this account of a Grand Tour of Europe and the Holy Land showed a typical frontier reaction to ancient culture. Mark Twain was more knowing than he would admit, but he gave his readers just what they expected of one who had already established a reputation as 'The Wild Humorist of the Pacific Slope.' Exhibiting typical frontier ignorance and prejudice, he insisted that copies of Old Masters were better looking than the originals and contended that 'Petrarch, the gentleman who loved another man's Laura . . . lavished upon her all through life a love which was a clear waste of the raw material.' He had the Westerner's pride in his home scene, finding Lake Como 'dull' by comparison with Tahoe. Like all Western humorists he took pleasure in frustrating possessors of an older culture: when shown a sample of Columbus's handwriting he merely said, 'Why, I have seen boys in America only fourteen years old that could write better than that. If you have got any specimens of penmanship of real merit, trot them out!—and if you haven't, drive on.' Poker-faced exaggeration, exuberant hoaxes, contorted language, irreverence, irrelevant logic, and raucous iconoclasm—all these devices of the Western humorist were in *The Innocents Abroad*.

The Nation's reviewer found in Mark Twain's book 'all the prominent characteristics of our peculiar school of humorists—their audacity, their extravagance and exaggeration.' Readers found them too, and therefore bought the book. America had traveled a long way from the period that had made a best seller of Washington Irving because he admired the tradition and art of the Old World. Now with a Civil War won, with a nation fully established in the eyes of the world, and with the recognition that this land had its own sense of humor as it had its own sense of importance, the people welcomed another view of foreign culture.

The travesty of Old World culture was a popular theme of the day, as J. Ross Browne's *Yusef,* John Franklin Swift's *Going to Jericho,* and James De Mille's *The Dodge Club* proved. But *The Innocents Abroad* outsold all three of these combined, to become the most popular of all satires upon the Grand Tour. The author's genius and his previous reputation in part accounted for this popularity, but *The Innocents Abroad* also profited by an unusually good publicity campaign. Its setting—the first great conducted tour of the Old World—was already well publicized by the dozen correspondents assigned to the cruise, and Mark Twain's humorous view of the expedition was known through his own newspaper accounts and a lecture tour that took him from New York to Iowa to whet interest in his forthcoming book by reading snippets from its yet unpublished pages. By the end of April 1869, the American Publishing Company of Hartford, previously known for its religious texts, sent *The Innocents Abroad* to press with a print order of 20,000 copies and a contract guaranteeing the author a percentage a fourth larger than was ever paid any author except Horace Greeley. To insure a favorable reception the publishers sent newspapers all over the country five reviews said to be 'copied from leading journals,' so that lazy and gullible editors might reprint these laudatory notices. But the publishers didn't have to resort to such devices to insure good critical attention because Howells, the arbiter of literature, praised it in the *Atlantic.* Mark Twain quipped in reply that he felt like the woman who was so happy to learn her baby had come white. A month after publication 12,000 copies had been sold, within five months 31,000 were in the hands of satisfied purchasers, and by the end of its first year 67,000 copies had been bought at $3.50 each. The Mercantile Library of New York kept its 115 copies in constant circulation, and on the other side of the continent the humorist's old Washoe friends were eagerly reading about what he had been doing since he shook the dust of Nevada from his feet. Continuing at the rate of several thousand monthly, *The Innocents Abroad* rolled up a sale of 85,000 copies within 16 months. According to the best estimates, its second anniversary saw it pass the 100,000 mark. Mark Twain's reputation was established.

For his next book he turned to the West itself. *Roughing It* was written as a man might talk. It has all the formlessness and all the personal zest of a man yarning about his past. 'When I was writing the "Innocents,"' he told his publisher, 'my daily stint was 30 pages of MS and I hardly ever got beyond it; but I have gone over that nearly every day for the last ten. That shows I am writing with red-hot interest.' The book was held together by this interest, which revealed the character of the narrator, and by his exuberant recollection of the Comstock's bonanza days. It was a shapeless, sprawling work which grew as a frontier humorist's tall tales grow. What delighted readers were the isolated character description, the unexpected anecdote, the interpolated tall tale, the outbursts of high good humor—all redolent of the West and presenting its character better than did the basic structure of fact. For *Roughing It* Mark Twain received a royalty equivalent to 50 per cent of the profits on a sale of 100,000 copies, a contract such as no publisher would give to any but an assured best seller. Within three months nearly 40,000 copies were purchased, but then sales began to taper off. The last part of the book, dealing with the Hawaiian Islands, was simply padding, old articles thrown in to round out the required number of pages, and so irrelevant and anticlimactic that the account ran downhill and left the reader disappointed and perhaps unwilling to recommend the work to friends. Ten years passed before 100,000 copies were sold. The book was a success but not in the terms of *The Innocents Abroad*.

A year after *Roughing It* Mark Twain published *The Gilded Age*, a melodramatic and satirical novel of post-Civil War boom times, written in collaboration with Charles Dudley Warner. It is a confused work—the tone of the two authors never fused into one. Mark Twain's own sections, lacking controlled structure, ricochet off into wonderful but rather irrelevant materials. Within a month *The Gilded Age* sold 40,000 copies, the figure that *Roughing It* reached before its sales started to slow down. Forty thousand purchasers seems to have been Mark Twain's steady and immediate market at the time. Nine years passed before the author could say that *The Gilded Age* had sold 60,000 copies, and his figures may have been exaggerated, for he was notoriously openhanded with statistics that concerned his own fortunes.

Tom Sawyer was issued in 1876, three years after the publication of *The Gilded Age*. Although *Tom Sawyer* has become one of Mark Twain's best-loved books, read alike by child and adult, it showed a further dropping off in his immediate audience. Not until 1882, six years after publication, did the author claim that *Tom* had sold 40,000 copies, once again the figure that seems to mark his maximum contemporary public. By 1884 he was expansively insisting that his publisher 'never issued with less than 43,000 orders on hand, except in one instance—& it usually took him 5 or 6 months' canvassing to get them.' Figures from less biased authorities belie Mark Twain's estimates. Having lifted by 3,000 his normal ceiling of 40,000 sales, he strained a little further to claim that his next book, *A Tramp Abroad,* 'issued with 48,000.' Albert Bigelow Paine, Clemens's biographer, thinks 25,000 was the advance sale, far better than that with which the comparable *The Innocents Abroad* had started off, but Paine points out that in its first few years the earlier travel book sold at least twice as many copies as *A Tramp Abroad* did in a like period, which would leave the sales of the latter hovering around the 40,000 mark.

Mark Twain's works had given the American Publishing Company a reputation comparable to that of the older, better-established firms of Boston, New York, and Philadelphia, but he felt that he himself had not profited proportionately. For his next book, *The Prince and the Pauper,* he tried the firm of James Osgood, obtaining from it a contract that essentially made him the publisher. The author furnished the capital for production and paid Osgood a royalty of 7½ per cent to handle the sales. The system was similar to the one Cooper had used in publishing his early and most popular romances, a scheme that only a widely read author could suggest and obtain. But the sales of *The Prince and the Pauper* and Mark Twain's next book, *Life on the Mississippi,* evidently did not satisfy him. In 1883 he broke completely with the American Publishing Company when it would not grant him over 50 per cent of the large profits he expected on his new book, *The Adventures of Huckleberry Finn.* With a great fanfare of publicity he founded his own firm, installed a relative to run it, and in February 1885 began distributing *Huckleberry Finn.*

Forty thousand advance orders were garnered by agents, who sold the work on the house-to-house subscription basis always employed for Mark Twain's books. It was a big advance sale, yet the figure of 40,000 seems only to indicate that Mark Twain quickly tapped his usual public. A few weeks after publication the sales climbed to 50,000, which indicated that something more than conventional publicity was at work. During the fifteen years since *The Innocents Abroad* Mark Twain had found and retained a substantial audience. Now when he gave his readers a work that was the quintessence of his genius, they must have urged his new book even more strongly than usual upon their friends, and these friends, on reading *Huckleberry Finn*, must have urged it upon their friends and their friends' children as well. *Tom Sawyer* had prepared the way for this sequel, which was that rare thing—a continuation better than the original. In a prose as alive as the main character who spoke it, readers found all the wonder and delight of Mark Twain's humor and satire, his realism in a local-color portrait of the Southern frontier's backcountry folkways, and his moving romantic dream of the adventures of youth. The qualities that had exhibited themselves fitfully in every one of his books were now fused with supreme art into a perfect whole.

Some external events helped promote the sale of *Huckleberry Finn* too. Soon after publication, the Library of Concord, Massachusetts, banned the book from its shelves, finding it unfit to rest beside such native authors as Emerson and Thoreau. As Louisa May Alcott said, 'If Mr. Clemens cannot think of something better to tell our pure-minded lads and lasses, he had best stop writing for them.' Clemens commented with pleasure, 'That will sell 25,000 copies for us sure.' Whether that was the cause nobody can say, but the copies were sold. For the first time a Massachusetts banning helped a book to the best-seller list. *Huckleberry Finn* continued to pile up greater and greater profits for the author, even though he was troubled by pirates who issued unauthorized editions at 50 cents a copy and by newspapers unwilling to review a subscription work that bought no advertising space. Lifted above the plateau of sales on which he had stood so long, Mark Twain was now an acknowledged favorite. In the years after *Huckleberry Finn's* publication, many feeble and uneven works such as *The American Claimant* and *Tom Sawyer Abroad* were mingled with such fine books as *A Connecticut Yankee in King Arthur's Court* and *The Tragedy of Pudd'nhead Wilson*, but Mark Twain was finally established as one of the outstanding and most popular figures in the literature of America.

During the humorist's long career as an author almost all of his books were sold by subscription. This system of door-to-door canvassing, bringing books direct from publisher to reader, was long established, but fiction in a lighter vein was not commonly sold in this fashion. Bret Harte felt that the very contrast helped sell Mark Twain's books, for he saw *The Innocents Abroad* as 'an Indian spring in an alkaline literary desert' that stretched all the way back to colonial days when Cotton Mather endorsed book peddlers who disseminated religious tracts. George Washington, Daniel Webster, and Rutherford B. Hayes were among those who had participated in this old system of vending, which took on new life when demobilized Civil War soldiers began to canvass for histories of the conflict in which they had played a subordinate part. For some fifteen years after the war, bookstores had a hard time because writings by such figures as Mark Twain, Horace Greeley, Henry Ward Beecher, and P. T. Barnum appeared in their stock only when obtained by devious means or when their original popularity was exhausted. As one publishing company stated, 'statistics show that, outside of school books and periodicals, more than three-fourths of all the money expended in the United States for books each year passed through the hands of agents.' If many people objected to the annoying persistence of book agents, there were enough buyers to insure at least thirty sales for every thousand inhabitants in a town. Salesmen often paid for board, clothing, and travel by trading at retail value the books they received at wholesale prices; so the business was a good one for those unable to find more stable employment during the hard times of the 'seventies. Although publishers requested their canvassers to memorize a long 'spiel' including passages of the book, most agents found it possible to clear a hundred dollars a month through more active leg work and less mental strain. By such means almost a million copies of *Picturesque America* were sold, and the distribution of this great parlor book of handsome engravings, nominally edited by William Cullen Bryant, must have astounded the venerable New England poet, who half a century earlier had found it took five years for bookstores to sell 270 copies of the *Poems,* which included 'Thanatopsis' and 'To a Waterfowl.'

Subscription agents did best of all with books about the late war. In seven years Greeley's *American Conflict* sold 250,000 copies; Joseph T. Headley's *The Great Rebellion* and T. P. Kettell's *History of the Great Rebellion* respectively sold 150,000 and 120,000 copies in nine years; and one of Albert D. Richardson's books, *The Secret Service,* sold 100,000 copies in six years, while his other, *Beyond the Mississippi,* sold 90,000 copies in four years. These were tremendous sales for a period of poor economic conditions. Southerners would not have wanted these Northern views of the war even could they have afforded them, but it was presumably unreconstructed rebels who in three years spent their money on 62,000 copies of *A Constitutional View of the Late War Between the States,* by the former Confederate Vice President, Alexander H. Stephens. That the subscription system as much as the subject accounted for these great sales was proved when General Sherman insisted his *Memoirs* be distributed only through bookstores. Over the years they slowly sold 60,000 copies, although an eyewitness account of the war by a soldier of great fame should have been more popular than the writings of such men as Kettell and Richardson. As a publisher said, 'I have no doubt the sale would have doubled at least had it been sold by subscription only.'

Sherman's royalties of $25,000 set some other generals to thinking that after all the pen might be mightier than the sword. Grant, the greatest general of them all and a President besides, was an ideal author to add to the list of any subscription publisher, though the old soldier was skeptical of his abilities as an author and even of public interest in an account of his life. Mark Twain, looking for material to keep the presses of his publishing firm busy, argued his neighbor into the writing, encouraged him as it proceeded, and endorsed it enthusiastically when completed. On May 1, 1885, with the agents in the field only two months, 60,000 orders had come in for the bulky two-volume *Memoirs* and Clemens jubilantly figured the work would sell 300,000 sets, so that 'General Grant's royalties will amount to $420,000, and will make up the largest single check ever paid an author in the world's history.' With a schoolboy's enthusiasm for fantastic statistics, Mark Twain noted, 'If I pay the General in silver coin at $12 per pound it will weigh seventeen tons.' His estimates were sound, even though sales might not have been so great had not the work received a lot of free publicity when Grant died suddenly on the eve of publication. Three months after the first books were delivered to subscribers, Clemens wrote a check to Mrs. Grant for $200,000, certainly the largest single royalty payment in America's literary history, and in course of time, when the estimated 300,000 sets were sold, the General's widow received upwards of $420,000 in payment for the *Memoirs*.

The patriotic appeal that made people buy Civil War histories and biographies from disabled, or at least demobilized, soldiers grew thinner as the war receded into the past. As more books cluttered the parlor table and shelves, sales resistance became greater. To break it, book agents became more and more insistent, and their increasingly obnoxious manners completed the circle of reasons why people closed doors against subscription books. The quality of books often dropped too, as Clemens's own list of titles indicates. From Grant's *Memoirs* the firm went down to *McClellan's Own Story*, the apologia of a general removed from his command and beaten for the presidency. Finally Clemens traveled down the scale to issue a book of Hawaiian tales by His Majesty, King Kalakaua, which barely made expenses. But as the subscription book slipped from popularity another type of publication—the dime novel—rose in favor.

The subscription book was often bought for display; the dime novel was bought only for reading. Though described by price rather than content, the dime novel represented a definite literary genre. Addressed to simple-minded people, and therefore soon to become the property of children, it served a dual purpose for adults. The exciting stories were good entertainment and the point of view was inspirational. Almost unconsciously the authors of the dime novels fortified the century's avowed belief in democratic equality and the self-made man, those contradictory doctrines which were equally enticing to an age that produced Abraham Lincoln and Cornelius Vanderbilt as two of its most famous figures. In its simple fashion the dime novel kept the faith. Its subject matter, nearly always American, lauded the plain dignity of human worth on the frontier, or during the trying times of the Revolution and the Civil War, its favorite settings. The characters were guileless men—explorers, trappers, cowboys, or soldiers—who performed heroic deeds. Such activities and achievements were denied to readers who had to conform to anonymous urban life and the confining efficiency of a mechanized age. The dime novel was a glorious substitute for life, fulfilling the promises that reality broke.

As time went on, most so-called dime novels cost a nickel, which was all their juvenile inheritors could or would pay for them, but the earlier examples that really sold for a dime were intended for adults. Both audiences found in them a fresh and exciting restatement of many ideas and beliefs already conventional in the Oliver Optic books distributed as Sunday School prizes, the Peter Parley juveniles which sold some seven million copies between 1825 and the Civil War, and even in the staple McGuffey Readers. Integrity and industry, pluck and patriotism, individualism and energy were recommended as primary virtues in all these works, but what might be only edifying in the 107,000,000 copies of McGuffey's Readers distributed to schools between 1836 and 1890 was exciting when told in novelettes of adventure and romance. The favored setting of the frontier was in part responsible for the popularity of these works among people whose intellect or taste was as thin as their purses.

Erastus Beadle had a shrewd sense of popular taste. His publishing firm had appealed to the new woman with a *Dime Ladies' Letter Writer* and a periodical entitled *The Home Weekly;* he was to capitalize on Western

humor by giving 'The Celebrated Jumping Frog' its first book publication, but he did best of all when in the midsummer of 1860 he issued
Malaeska, or the Indian Wife of the White Hunter, the first dime novel.
Its author, Ann Sophia Stephens, had previously followed fashion by
writing popular historical romances in the vein of Scott, melodramatic
stories typical of the feminine fiction of the 'fifties, and a humorous book
in the Down East tradition. Now she set a new style in novels. Within a
few months 65,000 copies of *Malaeska* were being eagerly read, and it
is said to have sold 300,000 copies in all before its day was done. Beadle
knew he had a good thing in the pocket-size paper-bound novelette
whose 120 pages combined conventional moral attitudes, stereotyped
heroism and villainy, and the romance of the frontier in a simply told
and fast-paced story that could be afforded by any man with a dime to
spare. He saw that the success of Mrs. Stephens' book could be repeated.
Before the summer was out he plastered the country around New York
with newspaper ads, sandwich-board men, and billboards reading 'Who
is Seth Jones?' With the public curiosity intrigued by this new system of
advertising, these placards were shortly replaced by others bearing the
portrait of a typical frontiersman in coonskin cap, buckskin blouse and
leggings, and carrying a long musket. 'I'm Seth Jones,' these posters declared. On the first of October the bookstores were stocked with Edward
S. Ellis's *Seth Jones; or, The Captives of the Frontier*, a story of the
eighteenth-century wilderness of New York, straight out of the Leather-
Stocking Tales and Mrs. Stephens. Sixty thousand copies were sold
almost instantly and the sales continued until half a million copies of this
novelette in its salmon-colored wrappers were in the hands of delighted
readers. The dime novel was established. Though Mrs. Stephens continued to write many more exciting tales and Ellis turned out about 150
similar stories, no single dime novel ever had a success equal to the first
two. The type sold by the millions, but since one example was as good
or as bad as the next, and writers managed to grind out their 25,000- to
30,000-word stories weekly, no one book stood out above another in significance or sales. Nearly every title had a first printing of 60,000 copies,
and most had several reprintings. Paradoxically, this literature of escape
from the machine age was itself an example of that age.

The Civil War stimulated the sales of dime novels. As morale builders
they were shipped to the Northern armies in such vast numbers that a
Beadle book came to be considered equipment almost as standard as a
bayonet. Had they been a bit bulkier and bound more sturdily, there

would undoubtedly have been legends about dime novels that stopped
Minié balls, a fabulous power attributed only to the Bible. Even without
this virtue, the novels seemed more popular than the thousands of copies
of *Come to Jesus* distributed by the Christian Commission. To promote
patriotism many novels dealt with the Revolution as a struggle for democracy, of which the current war was but another battle. There were anti-
slavery dime novels too, in the pattern of *Uncle Tom's Cabin*. *Maum
Guinea and Her Plantation Children* by Mrs. Metta Victoria Victor was
the most successful of these, even receiving praise from President Lincoln. Because of their worthy causes dime novels were endorsed by
Seward, Henry Ward Beecher, and other leaders of public opinion, for
in their early days few people scorned them as descendants of the sensational tales of such romancers as Sylvanus Cobb, Joseph Holt Ingraham,
George Lippard, Emerson Bennett, or Maturin Murray Ballou.

Nobody spoke of the dime novels as serious works of literature but few
saw any reason to object to them. In them morality was as lofty as the
elegant English their characters spoke; good and evil were so sharply
divided that nobody could have been confused for a moment. If heroes
swore, it was 'by the Horns of Gabriel,' for profane oaths never sullied
the lips that knew neither liquor nor tobacco. If a man gambled, one
knew instantly he was a scoundrel, though blood might have to be shed
by the good as well as the bad. Death frequently threatened the heroines,
but never a fate worse than death. Not even a villain had a mind so evil
as that. The setting was nearly always the pure open stretches of God's
country and the heroes were frequently such established American deities
as Daniel Boone, Kit Carson, Buffalo Bill, Davy Crockett, Sam Houston,
Big Foot Wallace, and General Custer.

These novels poured by the thousands from the presses of Beadle and
his many competitors, the wordage calculated by the price—for there
were nickel, dime, and twenty-cent 'libraries'—but the ethic of the paper-
covered novelette was for a long time always the same. Even the titles
varied by no more than a semicolon. The standard treatment demanded
alliteration and the parting of the title smartly in the middle by a punc-
tuation mark, so that one knew what one was getting, no matter whether
the title was *Double Dan, the Dastard; or, The Pirates of the Pecos* or
Roaring Ralph Rockwood, the Reckless Ranger. But the dime novel was
like any other stimulant. As appetites were jaded by what they fed on,
they demanded a heavier dosage of thrills. From heroes who could have
been at home in the stories of James Fenimore Cooper, the dime novel

branched out to adulate more and more lurid figures. Operating on a Gresham's law of fiction, bad heroes drove out good ones, until two-gun men like Wild Bill Hickock or cool-eyed killers like Jesse James and Billy the Kid replaced the old plainsmen and frontier scouts. When the books became almost exclusively the property of boys, parents tried to meet the challenge of dime novels through such watered versions as the tales of Harry Castlemon and Charles Carleton Coffin, but parental endorsement of works that might once have been considered satisfactory dime novels now proved them to be no longer thrilling.

Dime-novel stories of shootings in the Wild West had led to the subject of banditry, and tales of frontier lawlessness in turn led to ones about the more sophisticated crime of Broadway and the Bowery. In 1886 Russell Coryell created the first of the Nick Carter stories and the dime novel plunged into a world of detectives and cardsharps, of opium dens and abductions. The form essentially became a serial, each novel a thrilling episode in a never-completed saga, as 4,000,000 copies of Nick Carter stories were sold to a goggle-eyed public that read the adventures secreted behind geography books or in such hiding places as the family hayloft. The dime novel that began as a short adventurous tale for adults degenerated into a lurid piece of hackwork written for children. The Post Office Department, which has often officially tried to censor literature, accidentally killed the dime novel by so increasing postal rates as to make the old paper-covered pamphlet unprofitable. But the genre did not really die; it was simply transmuted into the pulp magazine, in which form it again became the property of adults as well as adolescents. For the young it left behind another legacy: the stories of Frank Merriwell, the all-time all-American boy, for whose more wholesome adventures, still cast in the dime novel mold, parents were willing to pay the price demanded of books in hard bindings. The death of the dime novel, if it ever really occurred, was accompanied by the birth of the nickelodeon, the motion picture, and the radio, which simply transferred the old stories of cowboys, desperadoes, and Indians to more dynamic forms. Slowly but surely, the passing of the physical frontier had made the once strange and forbidding West into an area psychically congenial to creators of popular art.

Chapter 10

The Gilded Age

The Civil War brought the West into the orbit of the East, as it brought the South under dominion of the North. This meant that to the great seaboard cities of New York, Boston, and Philadelphia went the financial and cultural direction of the nation. The nation was unified, but at terrible cultural expense.

The raw materials of the West fed the manufacturing machinery of the East, as the spirit of the frontier nourished the purposes of the new industrialism. Western individualism, vulgarized and freed of responsibility, was crudely amalgamated with Eastern centralism, organized for acquisition. Earth was scarred by mining pits and railway tracks; air was fouled and darkened by factory soot; water was polluted by industrial wastes or ran unchecked down eroded mountains once covered by forests. Americans became imperialists within their own nation. Not until they had exploited its humans and gutted its natural resources did they search out other lands to conquer—the Philippines, Cuba, Hawaii—where fresh fields and more backward peoples offered new and easy areas of exploitation.

A predatory class of capitalists emerged as ultimate victors of the Civil War and the westering spirit of pioneers. The class that made and owned the machines was the class that set standards. It moved men into cities; it controlled working hours, pay, and living conditions; it dictated what crops could be grown and how they could be marketed; it even established a national code of ethics and new standards of culture. Contemplating the behavior of the railroad builders, the elder Charles Francis

Adams, Ambassador to England and a keeper of the public conscience, ruefully declared, 'The five years which succeeded the late war have witnessed some of the most remarkable examples of organized lawlessness under the forms of law, which mankind has yet had an opportunity to study.' Adams lived to see one of his sons devote his talents to the business of railroads and stockyards, another to ponder what he came to call 'the degradation of the democratic dogma,' and a third to contend his education had unfitted him for his times. The opinion of the times was that the son who became president of Jay Gould's railroad was the only one to achieve success.

To this era Mark Twain gave the lasting name 'The Gilded Age.' Mark Twain's satire was neither very deep nor very wide, for like the public he might be disgusted by the Crédit Mobilier scandals and the corruption of Grant's administration, but to him Grant was still a hero (a general opinion upheld by the sales of his autobiography) and railroad financiers were still barons of impressive stature. Yet in that year of 1873 when *The Gilded Age* was published, the nation was afflicted by its first postwar depression. Though city laborers had known slums and bad working conditions since Appomattox, prosperity was bright as gold for the men of big business. Then in the midsummer calm of 1873 Jay Cooke's great banking house crashed to bankruptcy. It was but a symbol of events to come. On the Western plains prices of wheat and pork fell and their producers were impoverished. In the Eastern cities banks and business houses toppled and the people were driven to panic. In 1874 almost 6,000 busineses failed. As the years went on, more and more dwindled or crashed out of existence. Throughout 1878 about 900 firms were financially broken every month. Long bread lines covered city blocks by day; at night families ferreted out places to sleep. In 1875 New York's jails housed almost 250,000 people, who turned to them for sleeping quarters, booked for no worse crime than poverty. Violence and rioting were common.

Four years of depression were marked by increasing unemployment and lowered wages for those who found jobs. When the leading railroads announced a new 10 per cent wage cut in July 1877, workers tried a protest by strikes, which quickly spread from one end of the nation to another. Poorly organized, their opposition was beaten down, though the President of the United States himself had to lend a hand before transportation could be returned to 'normal.' The labor movement of the day, as its historian, Professor Norman Ware, has observed, 'was not a busi-

ness but . . . a vague, primitive, embryonic sentiment, a religion in the
making.' Balancing the movement among workers were the farmers' organizations. Convinced that the railroads, banks, market agencies, and
even the very currency structure were working against them, the farmers
founded Granges, which began as social units to discuss ways of achieving 'the good life.' As pressure became greater, they developed co-opera-
tive stores and mills and formed the Alliance, which was more purposefully political. Finally they joined with urban labor organizations to
create the militant political party of Populism. While great industrial
trusts rose to power on one side, on the other were established the Populists, the national Socialist Labor Party, the Knights of Labor (numbering 700,000 members shortly after the new Panic of 1884), and an even
more powerful American Federation of Labor.

A new kind of civil war was brought forth upon the nation. One year
saw almost the entire telegraph system paralyzed; another, huge steel
mills closed and picketed. In 1886 the McCormick Harvester plant locked
its employees out when they tried to achieve unionism. At one of the
workers' protest meetings somebody threw a bomb; policemen and
workers began shooting, and the meeting closed with wounded and
dead on both sides. In the ensuing months eight Anarchists were condemned to death or life imprisonment in a trial that linked them to this
Haymarket Riot only because their beliefs supposedly inflamed the bomb
throwers. By 1893 a new financial panic had broken across the nation.
The next year, when poverty was acute, the Pullman Company cut wages
but maintained rents in the company-owned town. Eugene Debs's American Railway Union answered with a strike that provoked sympathetic
echoes. President Cleveland found that the only solution was to call out
troops, as Hayes had done sixteen years earlier. Other, more fundamental
answers neither the government nor the ruling class would consider. The
immigration of Chinese labor was officially suspended, a Civil Service reform act was passed, a Department of Labor was created, and a weak
anti-trust act was legislated—but such moves were of only slight importance. Politics and high finance continued to walk arm in arm. The Supreme Court declared the income tax invalid and Debs was sentenced to
jail. Anger spread through the people, erupting into more strikes, while
even mild-mannered social theorists like Jacob Coxey led 'armies' to press
their grievances and solutions upon the lawmakers at Washington.

The moral standards of the time were as shoddy as its financial practices, but both were hidden behind a specious show of decency. The

great middle class remained genteel in deportment. Stifled by convention and obedient to the seemingly fair dictates of the new capitalist class, they were properly horrified at the unseemly behavior of working people. As Godkin, the editor of *The Nation,* declared, it was a 'chromo civilization,' badly delineated and highly colored. The newly rich, in control of the nation's business and politics, were cynical in their practices and sanctimonious in their defenses. Though the middle class had long and heated discussions about the supposed cleavage between religion and science, the men of big business used arguments from both sides to justify their own behavior. The concept of evolution as a struggle of the fitter for survival was said to be illustrated by individuals in business as much as by species in development. Making a sophistical use of Darwinianism, big-business spokesmen declared, 'the whole process is immutable; there's nothing one can do, it's just nature.' Or, using religious arguments, industrialism's interpreters said, 'God has called us to labor in the vineyard; if we succeed it is obviously a mark of His favor. Wealth comes by diligence and sobriety, and is simply a blessing for moral achievement. Continued poverty is obviously a sign of bad or weak character.' Rich and poor alike honestly believed such divergent and jerry-built theories. Only when the obvious thievery of the Tweed Ring or the Erie Ring, the machinations of Jay Gould and Jay Cooke, or the blatant behavior of Jim Fisk made the theories unpalatable, only then did the rich have to foist the belief on the poor through a controlled press and pulpit.

The sanctity of wealth, championed by educators, preachers, and public leaders, and dinned into children through the McGuffey Readers, was brazenly summed up in the statement of a railroad official, George Baer, who proclaimed, 'The rights and interests of the laboring man will be protected and cared for—not by the labor agitators, but by the Christian men to whom God in His infinite wisdom has given the control of the property interests of the country.' Such sophistries about the divine right of property were given a classic formulation in Andrew Carnegie's *Gospel of Wealth,* issued in 1889, a dozen years after the first great railroad strikes and three years after the Haymarket Riot. At this testament of an immigrant bobbin boy risen to multimillionaire, many people nodded their heads, more often in agreement than in wonder.

A middle-class tendency to sanctify business prepared the way for success stories and formulas. Orison Swett Marden's *Pushing to the Front* was the most popular book of its type. Reminiscent of *Self-Help* by the appropriately named Englishman, Samuel Smiles, Marden's book went through twelve printings in 1894, the year of publication. It prepared an audience for Frank C. Haddock's *Power of Will*, issued in 1907, as well as for many other works by Marden himself. By the end of the century men and women had read 3,000,000 copies of Marden's books and many subscribed to his magazine, simply entitled *Success*, in the hope that it would make Andrew Carnegies of them, or at least of their children. For the children themselves there was still the seemingly endless series of Horatio Alger books, with such titles as *Strive and Succeed* and *Bound to Rise*, which sold millions upon millions of copies to be given to children who generally preferred to think of success in terms of dime-novel heroics.

Russell Conwell's *Acres of Diamonds* was the most successful of all success books for adults, and perhaps the simplest and most striking statement of the doctrine of divine right of property. Conwell, a Philadelphia minister, first contrived this famous piece as a sermon, and as such it was published in his *Gleams of Grace*, issued in 1887 by the Business Man's Association of Grace Baptist Church. The sponsorship was no accident, for the text was just what business men wanted to hear, and soon Conwell took his sermon out of the church to deliver it up and down the country in Chautauqua meetings. With slight changes of text he spoke his piece 6,152 times to audiences estimated at thirteen millions. Conwell was the age's complement to William Jennings Bryan. One voice was as resonant and as persuasive as another. If Bryan was a spokesman of revolt who time and again ran for President, Conwell was the preacher of the *status quo* who in campaign after campaign wrote the official biographies of Republican party candidates. But always he was best known for his *Acres of Diamonds*, a temporal sermon larded with twenty-five anecdotes, each an illustration of his central cliché: opportunity waits in your own backyard. Let no man range the earth in his restless search for wealth, Conwell declared. Let him but dig in his garden, as did the legendary Persian, and he will find it a veritable diamond mine. And what was the use of the wealth one would find through such localized diligence? 'Money is power,' Conwell proclaimed, 'and for a man to say, "I do not want money" is to say, "I do not wish to do any good to my fellow-men.'" Money, saith the preacher of Philadelphia, all is money.

Conwell had once been a subscription book agent and he was always keenly alive to the commerce of publishing. It was told of him that when news of Bayard Taylor's death in Germany reached America, he realized the public would want a good biography of this romantic yet respected figure. Before Taylor's body arrived in his native land, Conwell's biography was complete; before the funeral was held, 5,000 copies had been sold. With gifts and interests of this sort, Conwell overlooked no opportunities for the circulation of *Acres of Diamonds*. The text was issued and reissued in magazines, religious and lay, and following its first separate book publication of 1888 it went into one printing after another. At least eleven different editions were circulated, one of them with more than 150 illustrations and supplementary material, including 'incidents from the lives of great men and women who have succeeded.' Conwell was a success in his own terms and in his backyard of Philadelphia he spent his money establishing Temple College for working men and women.

For all Conwell's sermons, it can hardly be said that he was seriously concerned with religious problems. His was the gospel of wealth and success. Though multitudes were satisfied by Conwell's message, others looked for further guidance in the great struggle between religion and science that marked the closing half of the nineteenth century. Publishers of cheap paper-bound editions had great success with such books as Thomas Hughes's *Manliness of Christ* and G. J. Romanes's *Scientific Evidence of Organic Evolution*. When a revised version of the Bible appeared during the early 'eighties, two Chicago newspapers printed its text in full, and New York bookstores were said to have sold 200,000 copies of the New Testament within one week. For those dissatisfied with orthodox religious teachings there were new forms of belief, the most significant being Christian Science, whose following grew rapidly after the publication of Mary Baker Eddy's *Science and Health*. For those who felt that science had made the faith of their fathers wholly untenable, Robert Ingersoll was the outstanding American leader. Known as 'the great agnostic,' Ingersoll dazzled millions with oratory no less brilliant than Conwell's or Bryan's, and his many books were surreptitiously read in liberal homes or boldly exhibited on the parlor tables of those who dared to be called scientific or agnostic. Even so enlightened a young Midwestern girl as Mary Austin could speak darkly of 'a book which she meant by all means to read on her own account, as soon as she could come by it, a book utterly interdicted, a book which must be read for no other reason than that it would imperil her immortal soul, an experience not to be missed. It was called "bobingersoll."' And 'bobingersoll' was the way his name was hissed by most people, just as an unreconstructed Southerner might think 'damnyankee' one word.

Men as different as Ingersoll and the revivalists Moody and Sankey, as Conwell and the geologist Le Conte, stirred deep feelings in the almost endless discussions of religion versus science. The subject of religion was naturally one of perennial importance in the making of best sellers, but no novel dealing with religious problems had created outstanding interest since the days of *St. Elmo* and *Gates Ajar*. Now, in the 'eighties, with new social problems pressing for new religious considerations, and with the seeming antagonism between orthodox religion and science first brought fully to the attention of a wide public, people were again ready for novels with religious themes.

Ironically, Ingersoll inspired one of the first of these religious novels. Though he drove some people from the church, Ingersoll's arguments caused many to re-examine their faith and embrace it the more strongly; such was the result of his conversation one day with Lew Wallace, the Civil War general. Shocked by Ingersoll's point of view, Wallace set about studying the life and times of Christ and emerged as a devout believer in His divinity, with a desire to transmit this belief to others. Already the author of *The Fair God*, a moderately successful novel of the Spanish conquest of Mexico, Wallace determined that another historical romance would be the proper medium in which to set forth his beliefs. His publishers were skeptical about this new novel, *Ben-Hur*, thinking it too melodramatic. Their fears appeared well grounded when they issued it in 1880, for during the first seven months the sale was only 2,800 copies, half that of *The Fair God* during a like period. The *Century* reviewer considered a historical romance 'rather of an anachronism nowadays,' and the *Atlantic*, irritated at 'descriptions too lavish,' could hardly surmount 'the inertia to be overcome in taking up a historical romance.' Furthermore, it was thought that the Holy Land setting was lacking in glamour since it had been 'debunked' by Mark Twain, and that $1.50 was expensive during a depression period when all kinds of texts were available in cheap 'library' editions. But the publishers kept the book in print, perhaps counting on its religious import and its highly colored, stirring scenes. Almost two years passed before the work caught on. In the beginning of its third year sales were moving at the rate of 750 copies a month; by 1885 they were up to an average of 1,200 copies monthly, and, as late as six years after publication, the book established the phenomenal record of 4,500 copies, month in and month out. By then everybody was talking about *Ben-Hur*. Even General Grant read it as he was slowly grinding out his *Personal Memoirs*. Though the old general had not tackled a novel for a decade, he wanted to see what sort of writing another Union Army leader was up to, and once started he declared he stayed up all night, reading thirty hours straight along, to finish this exciting and moving story of a convert to Christ's beliefs.

Whatever opposition to the novel as a type still lingered in the villages of America was finally broken by *Ben-Hur*, for it combined the historical values of Scott and the moral worth of Mrs. Stowe, the two previous novelists who had battered down almost the last prejudices against fiction. *Ben-Hur* was endorsed on all sides by clergymen and leaders of public opinion. One limited edition bearing words of approval by the martyred President Garfield was bound in silk, priced at $30, and actually sold. No further, it seemed, could popular approval of a novel go. In course of time an edition was issued under the sponsorship of the Holy See and another was put out in a printing of a million copies by Sears, Roebuck. Probably no other American novel has had either of these distinctions; certainly none has had both. If every American did not read the novel, almost everyone was aware of it. The spectacular dramatization, which opened on Broadway in 1899, toured the country for twenty-one years. Sometimes it was seen in a lavish display that included a cast of 400, a 25,000 candle-power light to symbolize Christ, and an assortment of camels, horses, treadmills, fireworks, simulated waves, and gondolas. Sometimes it was seen under canvas or in a small-town 'opera house' performance, with noticeably amateur acting. But eventually 20,000,000 people were thrilled by the great chariot race between Messala and Ben-Hur, the drama's most exciting incident. According to Irving McKee, Wallace's biographer, small towns were named Ben Hur, and there are still men walking the streets of America bearing the hero's last name as their first, a name they may also see emblazoned on commercial products. And, finally, *Ben-Hur* received the most natural but the highest form of flattery; it precipitated a whole school of imitations, which included, among other popular novels, Marie Corelli's *Barabbas* and Florence Kingsley's *Titus, A Comrade of the Cross*, issued respectively fourteen and fifteen years after their prototype.

Those who felt General Wallace's romance too colorfully dramatic in its consideration of religious problems turned to a British novel, Mrs. Humphry Ward's *Robert Elsmere*, though sometimes it was the other way around, as when a friend wrote Mrs. Ward that 'the antidote to you is *Ben-Hur*.' *Robert Elsmere* told of a young minister whose scientific knowledge dissipated his belief in Christian miracles, causing him to leave his church and to express his devout faith through social work among the laboring people of London. Ingersoll thought the book too conservative, but most Americans, admitting that the hero's renunciation of his church was radical, welcomed the novel as an honest attempt to deal with the problems they themselves faced, both in their struggles with orthodoxy and in their concern with the social effects of the machine age.

Appearing in 1888, when the discussion of religious and humanitarian problems was intense, *Robert Elsmere* attracted a wide audience. An American author declared 'that no other book of equal seriousness ever had so quick a hearing' in this country; and a rather optimistic minister, who found the hero essentially a Unitarian in his actions, declared that 'where one person reads Robert Ingersoll, a hundred read *Robert Elsmere.*' The lengthy book, discussed in pulpit and press, was commonly pirated, once even being issued for only four cents, and so widespread was its public that in 1890 the Muncie, Indiana, newspaper jokingly suggested as an additional question for the census taker: 'Have you read *Robert Elsmere?*' The author thought 'it is probable, from the data I have, that about half a million copies were sold in the States within a year of the book's publication,' though an American trade journal put the number closer to 150,000. Whatever the exact statistics may be, the novel's impress was rightly estimated by a contemporary professor who declared that it had affected the intellectual evolution of the nation.

Robert Elsmere was more symptom than cause of the growing relation between problems of religious dogma and social ethics. The period that had recently seen the American establishment of the Salvation Army and the founding of such institutions as Jane Addams's Hull House in Chicago was sincerely concerned with the application of Christian principles to daily life. Capitalizing on this interest, the notorious English journalist William T. Stead in 1894 stirred a good deal of discussion with his sensational book, *If Christ Came to Chicago,* a work answered the following year by the more decorous *If Jesus Came to Boston,* in which Edward Everett Hale found 'the hub of the universe' replete with virtues that could be approved by its Saviour. The year of Stead's book also brought forth a new novel by Elizabeth Stuart Phelps, who interrupted her cozy considerations of Heaven to write *A Singular Life,* in which her hero, attempting to live according to the dictates of Jesus, forsakes his orthodox church in order to achieve his humanitarian purposes.

Of all the watered and shoddy imitations of *Robert Elsmere,* the most popular was *In His Steps*, first issued in 1896. More succinctly and simply than all the novels on the same theme, *In His Steps* asked on its title page and on almost every one of its text pages the question, 'What Would Jesus Do?' The novel's directness, naïveté, consistency of thesis, and succession of melodramatic incidents made it easy reading, combining the flavor of sanctity with the charm of lurid fiction. Its author, Charles M. Sheldon, a Congregational minister of Topeka, had the ingredients and the attitude for a best seller, but he did not know it. All he wanted of this novel, as of *His Brother's Keeper, The Crucifixion of Philip Strong*, and others he had written since 1890, was to fill the pews of his church. This he accomplished by substituting for Sunday-evening services the reading of his exciting yet pious fiction, each reading ending at a dramatically critical incident whose outcome was revealed the next Sunday. The most successful of these serialized sermons was *In His Steps*.

The story was inspired by the minister's socio-religious beliefs, formulated during his early work in the London slums, which were the setting of *Robert Elsmere*, and it was based in part on his experiences wandering through Topeka's streets disguised as a poor man in search of work. In the novel a sick, jobless young man in a Midwestern town much like Topeka rebukes a congregation patterned on Sheldon's own for its hypocritical behavior. The minister and the church members are so impressed by the dying speech of the job-hunter that they determine to conduct their lives for one year on the one principle of asking themselves at each turning: 'What would Jesus do?' The results are: a newspaper editor almost bankrupts his paper when he refuses to print sensational news or liquor advertisements; a debutante becomes a missionary in the town's poorest and most squalid district, giving her wealth—a round million dollars—to the newspaper's campaign; a college president leaves his cloistered life to enter a political fight against the 'liquor interests'; a young musician gives up her chance for success in light opera to sing at revival meetings; and the superintendent of a railroad reveals that his line has violated interstate-commerce laws. The novel ends with the characters depressed in personal fortunes but heightened in spirit, and envisioning the spread of their code throughout the United States.

As Sheldon read this story to his congregation, a religious weekly of Topeka published it serially, gathering the chapters together in a paperbound book in 1897. Within two years *In His Steps* went through five editions, ranging in price from a dime to a dollar and a quarter, all of

them issued by the local Congregational journal. Then, in 1899, ten different publishers, including dealers in the fading dime novel, became
aware of this local best seller and, discovering the copyright to be defective, they quickly stepped in with their own editions. Not stopping to
ask themselves 'What would Jesus do?', none of these publishers paid the
author royalties. Since they naturally did not choose to reveal their sales
or profits, there is no way to estimate how many copies of the book were
sold. Certainly the book was issued in God's plenty by the sixteen known
American publishers, and in the foreign editions, which varied from a
penny pamphlet hawked in London to twenty translations in lands as
remote as Japan and Russia. Sheldon, with his usual naïveté, supposed
the sales were 8,000,000 copies in the United States and 12,000,000 more
in other English-language editions. Frank Luther Mott, who interviewed
the author before his death in 1946, judged the sales in this country
might more safely be estimated in the neighborhood of 2,000,000 copies,
with an additional 6,000,000 copies in all other lands. This seems a
sound judgment. Though it removes the book from the position of being
'runner-up to the Bible,' as one journalist would have it, it leaves *In His
Steps* as one of America's most popular books.

The same year in which *In His Steps* appeared in book form brought
forth another tremendously popular novel with a religious theme. Following in the path of General Wallace rather than that of Charles
Sheldon, *Quo Vadis?* by Henryk Sienkiewicz attracted tens of thousands
of readers, despite the difficulties they had in ordering a book with a
Latin title, written by a Polish author with an almost unpronounceable
name. During the sixteen years after the publication of *Ben-Hur*, the
historical novel was re-established as a favorite type. A new romance set
in the early Christian era, decked with a style as lush and a subject as
dramatic as Wallace's, was likely to prove popular—no matter how difficult the name of the book or the author. There were incidents to appeal to every type of reader. Those of a religious turn of mind could
lament the martyrdom of early Christians, the prurient could appreciate
the woodland Bacchanalia, the seekers of thrilling adventure could
revel in the destruction of Rome, and the sentimental could weep at
the unhappy love story of Vinicius and Lygia. If it had no chariot race,
Quo Vadis? had a garden-party scene at Nero's villa, lit by torches made
of living men. What was more, the book had a defective copyright, that
perennial boon to best sellers if not to their authors. It was issued in
many pirated editions, some selling for as little as seven cents. Even

in the authorized editions, *Quo Vadis?* remained for eighteen months the best of best sellers.

The book with a religious theme continued popular throughout the 'nineties. The year of *Quo Vadis?* and *In His Steps* also brought out Ralph Waldo Trine's *In Tune with the Infinite*, a tract representative of 'The New Thought' movement. Although it sold well for nonfiction, sixteen years passed before it reached 135,000 copies. The work, which has never been issued in a cheap reprint, has kept on as a steady inspiration, reaching a record of over a million and a quarter copies in its first fifty years. Akin to Trine's book were other slim religious pamphlets of the 'nineties that have long survived the day of their first publication. There are, for example, Henry Van Dyke's *The Other Wise Man*, a sentimental essay originally delivered as a sermon, and the Englishman Henry Drummond's *The Greatest Thing in the World*; a little later came William Allen Knight's *Song of Our Syrian Guest*, not a best seller when issued in 1903, but which in less than half a century has piled up sales of almost 2,000,000 copies.

In their time the religious books that were shaped as fiction were most popular. Almost every year saw at least one new best seller concerned with religious themes. One year—1896—it was Harold Frederic's *The Damnation of Theron Ware*, the story of a simple Methodist minister damned by his recognition of the mean emotionalism of his church and the inability to enter a wider life. Another year—1897—it was Hall Caine's *The Christian*, one of his rugged novels set on the Isle of Man. Still another year—1898—it was *Black Rock*, the tale of a minister's temperance crusade among the Canadian Northwest miners. Written by the Reverend Charles W. Gordon, a Canadian who used the pseudonym of Ralph Connor, *Black Rock*, like its popular successor of 1899, *The Sky Pilot*, coupled the point of view of Sheldon with the muscular attitude of Jack London to attract an audience of some half a million book buyers in its dozen or more pirated editions.

All of these religious novels, except for the two historical romances—*Ben-Hur* and *Quo Vadis?*—had another theme besides religion. In one way or another, they dealt with the proper relation between Christianity and the social issues of the day, for there was great interest in sociological problems. Yet a people concerned with the inequities of society did not have their eyes focused exclusively on current events, for, paradoxically, Scott, Bulwer-Lytton, Dickens, and Thackeray remained established favorites, and a survey of booksellers in 1876 revealed that the

most widely bought fiction included such tested works as *Jane Eyre*,
St. Elmo, *The Scarlet Letter*, *Uncle Tom's Cabin*, *Barriers Burned
Away*, *Griffith Gaunt*, *Under Two Flags*, and *The Wide, Wide World*.
As at all times, people still read the books that were their parents' and
grandparents' favorites, for in popular reading there is always a cultural
lag.

Rising among these older books in the 'eighties and 'nineties were
novels of social inquiry. An early example was John Hay's *The Bread-
Winners*, published in 1884. Much upset by the railway strikes he had
witnessed and sympathetic to the opinions of his father-in-law, a Cleveland capitalist, Hay defended the theory of economic individualism and
class distinction in his novel about murderous and thieving labor or-
ganizers, and his point of view was evidently congenial to a large part
of the book-buying public. The social problems of the day also called
out novels on the other side: some, like Hamlin Garland's *Jason Edwards*
and *A Spoil of Office*, proposed specific remedies (in these instances,
respectively the single tax and the Populist party); some, like Joaquin
Miller's *The Destruction of Gotham*, were flamboyant melodrama
capitalizing on a current interest (Miller pictured the Bowery at war
with Fifth Avenue); and some, like Joseph Kirkland's *Zury*, showed the
unrelieved ugliness of life on a frontier that had closed in on its people,
a view of the Midwestern farm scene quite different from Eggleston's
The Hoosier Schoolmaster, popular in the 'seventies. But none of these
books was widely read. What the public evidently wanted was neither
brooding nor melodrama, nor even, if Garland's work is sufficient indication, any one isolated program. With social problems confronting them
at every turn, the people who read novels seemed to want complete
escape into romance, a combination of romance and serious consideration of religious beliefs, or the treatment of one embracing solution to
all problems. Coincidentally the people's ideal novel of social protest
appeared in the same year as Conwell's simple *Acres of Diamonds*.

Edward Bellamy's *Looking Backward*, which was a long look forward
in 1888, seemed at last to prove that Utopia was really workable. Although nominally concerned with the United States in the year 2000, the
author 'tells almost as much about his present as about the future he
sought to prophesy,' as Lewis Mumford points out. Bellamy's basic opposition to individual competition, his optimistic faith in science and
mechanics, his belief in the essential goodness of man, his distress over
such secondary matters as vulgar advertising, his naive trust in one

simple, over-all cure, and his confident endorsement of a benevolent totalitarianism, all smack of his period.

Conceived as 'a fairy tale of social felicity,' *Looking Backward* describes a future social and economic order through the narrative of Julian West, a young Bostonian who enters a hypnotic sleep in 1887 and revives 113 years later in the changed city. He finds the Boston of the future free of economic inequality, rid of social injustice, without crime and disease, and positively blessed by a high cultural and scientific level because private enterprise with its business monopolies has given way to 'The Great Trust,' a democratic form of state capitalism. With each citizen both a member and an employee of the state, an evil system of artificial conflicts has been transformed to one in which the innate virtues of people create an ideal social intelligence and a lofty concept of ethics. The belief that social change can be effected without revolution or unpleasantness, that society can molt its outer covering and become new in shape and spirit, was particularly appealing to large numbers of oppressed and dissatisfied people.

The story and the characters of *Looking Backward* were as thin and contrived as those of *In His Steps,* and the attitudes of both authors were optimistic, but Bellamy's treatment of a problem larger than Sheldon's was even more delightful because his simple solution involved almost no personal tribulations. Proposing no action inimical to established social and economic patterns, and placing its happy day in a far distant period, *Looking Backward* opened up a dreamland, beautiful at least to the American mind. To the more aesthetic William Morris it was 'a horrible Cockney dream,' requiring the answer of his pre-Raphaelite *News from Nowhere,* depicting a gardenlike Utopia, free of the machinery that Bellamy worshiped as a good American.

Basing his belief on the assumption that machinery, like the system of trusts, is essentially the harbinger rather than the opponent of the good life, Bellamy saw no need for the kind of opposition his contemporaries were expressing through unions, strikes, and socialist parties. His concern was not so much with reforming the society in which he lived as with replacing it by a new one. Though Henry George, for one, called *Looking Backward* 'a castle in the air with clouds for its foundation,' a more ingenuous reading public preferred an achieved solution to difficult or dangerous means. During its first year only 10,000 copies were sold, but in 1889 people began to hear about *Looking Backward.* Then 200,000 copies were demanded and by December 1889 it was selling weekly as many copies as had been sold in its entire first 12 months. It continued to attract sympathetic readers, so that within a decade nearly a million copies were sold in the United States and England, and even fifty years after publication it was still selling some 5,000 copies a year in America alone.

The military regimentation of Bellamy's ideal society quickly interested some retired Army officers in Boston, who founded The Boston Bellamy Club. By 1889 some theosophists in California were impressed by *Looking Backward's* theme of brotherhood and also formed a Bellamy club. Beginning with such scattered and dissimilar groups the country began to be spotted with Nationalist Clubs, as the organized followers of Bellamy called them. The movement soon outgrew its original reactionary custodians, but it never quite got a firm hold in the nation's farms or factories. Its 150 clubs and its 350 newspapers and magazines mostly represented middle-class cultists who knew very little about the practical use of power. The Nationalists drew up platforms endorsing public ownership of business and other programs leading to such a state as Bellamy envisioned, and they entered politics, sometimes affiliating with the Populists, sometimes with the Socialists, but the movement had no great political cohesion and soon faded away. Its potential power was in great part dissipated by the success of Bryan's campaign of 1896, which sucked the psychic energy of reform by directing it toward the question of free silver and other issues outside the interests of the Bellamy followers.

Looking Backward left the nation an important legacy in creating a new picture of the good life, in dramatizing the benefits of mechanization, and in showing that a new deal for the individual rests on a collectivist program. Its immediate effect was to arouse many people untouched by other social theories, creating a greater interest in reform through political economy, and setting the idea of Utopia dancing in many American minds. Bellamy's own sequel, *Equality,* did not attract a wide public, because it was more an economic treatise than a fictional picture of a new social order, but *Looking Backward* did provoke an outpouring of utopian fiction. Nationalist Club members naturally turned to the novel as a means of elaborating their ideas, while persons opposed to Bellamy frequently countered with their own novels, so that, on one side, the 'nineties offered such titles as *Looking Further Backward* and *Young West,* and, on the other, *Mr. East's Experiences in Mr. Bellamy's World* and *Looking Within.* About fifty such novels were published in the years following *Looking Backward,* and even established and distinguished authors like William Dean Howells turned to stories of Utopia.

The most popular utopian novel after *Looking Backward* was Ignatius Donnelly's *Caesar's Column,* published in 1891. Donnelly, a radical Minnesota congressman for six years, and a founder of the Populist party, had an iconoclastic mind. He had already shown it in his *Great Cryptogram,* attributing the authorship of Shakespeare's plays to Bacon, and in his *Atlantis: The Antediluvian World,* a ponderous consideration of Plato's lost and idyllic civilization, a work that created quite a stir when issued in 1882 and eventually went through 50 printings. Donnelly was a fighting man, the founder of a farming community with Fourierist overtones, and a militant politician. His approach to the sociological novel was a long way removed from that of the professional Massachusetts writer Bellamy, who saw in it the material for a smooth and pleasing story of an achieved Utopia. Although Donnelly also often visualized the future in terms of scientific achievements, the inventions he conceived included poison gas, while Bellamy predicted the radio that delighted its listeners with classical music. Donnelly's was a hard and dynamic novel, showing the proletariat's bloody war with an entrenched plutocracy before it came to a period of peace and plenty. *Caesar's Column* was a call to revolt that provoked enough attention to sell some 60,000 copies in its first year, but its views were too radical to attract many followers and it died away after the first sensation, while Bellamy's book continued to allure new readers.

One other popular sociological novel appeared in the 'nineties, though it was not a utopian work. *The Honorable Peter Stirling,* by the sober historical scholar, Paul Leicester Ford, was rather an anticipation of the muckraking movement. A publisher, but a very skeptical publisher, was found for the book, his contract calling for the author to deposit money as a guarantee that a thousand copies would be sold within three years. The novel came out in 1894 and at first the reception seemed to justify the publisher's hesitancy. The public was not interested in this romantic tale of a political crusader's fight against tenements and adulterated milk, or by the battle in which he led the militia against strikers. Then a San Francisco bookseller identified the hero with President Cleveland and the novel's one scandalous event with charges leveled at the President during his first campaign against Blaine. That sent people hurrying to the San Francisco bookstore and to bookstores all over the country. In addition to a subject for gossip they found a good novel, and so they kept on buying it. For five years it continued to sell at the original price of $1.50, and then a cheap reprint was issued with the remarkable notice, 'limited to 100,000 copies.' The public bought that out too, as they bought out every issue that came along. By 1945, fifty years after first publication, *The Honorable Peter Stirling* was in a seventy-sixth printing and had sold half a million copies; 60 per cent of the New York Public Library branches still found at least one copy in active circulation.

During the last two decades of the century there was an audience for a variety of foreign novels dealing with contemporary social problems. The interest was broad enough to include Tolstoy's *Anna Karenina* and *War and Peace* (in editions as cheap as 60 cents, they had a big following for years after their original publication in 1886), and *The Heavenly Twins*, by the British suffragette, Mrs. Frances McFall, who published under the pseudonym Sarah Grand. Mrs. McFall's flamboyant style was an anticipation of Elinor Glyn's, but her subject was right for 1893, the year that it appeared in America. *The Heavenly Twins* told the story of a beautiful young girl who was made to marry a debauched man, and though it hinted at venereal disease, the American public accepted the book the same year that Stephen Crane's *Maggie*, the story of a New York prostitute, could be issued only by the author in a small and sleazy printing that sold but a hundred copies. *Maggie* was reissued after the success of *The Red Badge of Courage*, the best of the current rash of historical novels, which was serialized by some thirty or forty newspapers and had fourteen printings between October 1895 and October 1896; yet even then Crane's story of 'a girl of the streets' interested only a very few people. But Mrs. McFall's novel was a polite plea for women's rights swathed in a style that was romantic and enacted by characters who were glamorous, and so it was received as a piquant rather than a drab expression of the prevailing interest in social issues.

Subjects of social significance were in demand, but, on the whole, their treatment could not be too realistic, too revolutionary, or too analytical if they were to find big audiences. Henry Blake Fuller's *Cliff-Dwellers*, for example, did not warrant a second printing; readers objected primarily to its minute realism in the examination of the ways of big business. Even the interesting story of *The Rise of Silas Lapham* was, perhaps, too scrupulously detailed for a wide public. Henry Adams's two novels, *Democracy*, dealing with current political ethics, and *Esther*, a study of religious faith, were probably too attenuated in their analysis. Much the same difficulty kept people from following Henry James's concern with fine moral distinctions between American and European codes of values.

By the end of the nineteenth century the novel was acceptable to almost everybody in the country, and yet many still felt strongly that fiction could not provide the proper insight into serious problems. A wide audience for expository tracts was conditioned in great part by the Chautauqua, a kind of lay church for those who no longer took their guidance solely from religious doctrines, and by political speakers touring the country to reach the 'grass roots,' quite unconsciously stimulating interest in wider reading about current issues. Though the new novel nearly always outsold the new tract, increasing numbers of people, educated in the rapidly expanded high school system of the country, were taking advantage of the nonfiction as well as the fiction available in the well-distributed series of cheap reprints known as 'libraries.' For as little as two cents, never for more than fifty cents, one could buy the works of Emerson and Thoreau, of Macaulay and Carlyle, to be read by the easy illumination of the incandescent bulbs that were beginning to replace gas and kerosene. So good were the selections that the University of California senior class in 1887 found that its list of the world's fifty best books could be bought for a total of $9.22. With such a background, the tract, or even the tome, that seemed to offer a solution to current problems was assured of an increased public.

Of all the current documents of social analysis the one that found the widest audience was Henry George's *Progress and Poverty*. Written during the depression and labor troubles of 1877, *Progress and Poverty* was conditioned by its times and by the author's own experiences. As a resident of California, George watched the rich new frontier come under the control of a few land-hungry speculators. As a visitor to New York he saw the effects of an industrial age in creating what he called 'the shocking contrast between monstrous wealth and debasing want.' For these problems he had one simple solution: 'charge the expenses of government upon our land.' Though he restated this idea in many ways, modifying and expanding it, he always returned to his one thesis with an almost religious fervor. Pointing out that individual poverty increases as the nation becomes more prosperous, George contended that private land ownership confines interest and wages to marginal gains, while non-producing landlords reap the benefits of social advance. To return this value to the community, *Progress and Poverty* advocated a 'Single Tax,' amounting to the whole or almost the whole of economic rent. By this means, George said, all other taxes could be abolished and, with production unpenalized, the conditions of both labor and capital would be improved.

Progress and Poverty, allying economic theory with current political reality, was simple enough to understand and had the wonderful power of posing only one direct solution to a myriad of problems. The idea of a 'Single Tax' had an appeal for almost everybody but the constantly berated landlord. Since George's book sanctioned unrestrained individualism in every aspect but that of land ownership, it could be welcomed by businessmen, for, as one reviewer declared, 'so far from being a work of communistic tendencies, the reader will find in it arguments to overthrow nearly all the communist theories of the present day.' Accordingly, many manufacturers looked with sympathy upon this treatise that proposed to do away with their labor troubles and, at the same time, abolish the taxes on their goods and their incomes. Workingmen, on the other hand, were taken by the argument that they would be better paid if landholders no longer received rewards for increases in production. To thousands it seemed that if George were followed, the world of Bellamy might be created as painlessly as Bellamy supposed, and a lot sooner. It is natural that many children grew up, as Mary Austin did, to suppose that *Progress and Poverty* 'was something like the Bible, only more important.'

Like a few other best sellers of the period, *Progress and Poverty* got off to a slow start; its sales gradually increased by word-of-mouth advertising. The manuscript having been rejected by three New York publishers, in 1879 George arranged for the first printing of 500 copies in an 'Author's Edition,' to be sold by subscription at $3 a copy. The small edition moved slowly until it was taken over by one of the publishers who originally refused the work. The price was cut to $2; the edition sold out, and a new one was printed to sell at a dollar a copy. By December 1880 the book was beginning to attract attention and was in its fifth printing. The next year this lively treatise on economics passed the sales records of textbooks on the same subject, and a thousand copies were bought by a Boston philanthropist for distribution to public libraries around the country. To this benefactor George wrote in October 1881, 'from all I hear its circulation is between 75,000 and 100,000,' referring to the American and foreign editions. In 1882 a twenty-cent edition was on sale and the book was established as a sure and steady favorite. By 1905 it was estimated to have sold 2,000,000 copies in the American and foreign editions, and another 3,000,000 copies of related books and pamphlets by George had been distributed throughout the world by Single Tax clubs and regular bookstores.

Protection and Free Trade, another book by George, may be said to have reached the circulation of a best seller. In the 1890's, six congressmen arranged each day to introduce a chapter of it into the section of the *Congressional Record* devoted to 'Extension of Remarks.' Gathering these sections together, the congressmen distributed the pamphlet under their franking privileges to more than 1,200,000 voters concerned with the current tariff debates. In this way an enormous reading public was created artificially, but as the public neither sought out the book nor bought it, its significance is slight when placed beside that of *Progress and Poverty,* a favorite created by the ultimate judges, the readers themselves.

Economic issues created another best seller in the 'nineties. Newspapers and magazines, popular lecturers and politicians debated the subject of currency reform vigorously, but the one book that attracted wide attention was the work of a crusader who had drifted from a law practice in Chicago to mining in Colorado. He was William Hope Harvey, a zealous reformer, always known as 'Coin' Harvey after his *Coin's Financial School* was published in 1894. This propagandist pamphlet of 150 pages, a cross between a novel and a treatise in economic theory, attracted a fanatical following among farmers and other depressed followers of Bryan who attributed the current financial collapse to the use of gold as a standard for currency. Contending that not only was gold too slim a base for a large nation, but that it was open to manipulation by a small group of Eastern financiers, they fought the moneyed interests, who said silver inflation was the root of all evil, since the government, under pressure of a Western mining bloc, had to purchase silver useless in foreign exchange and often refused even by American businessmen.

Coin's Financial School was the story of an academy of economics run by a diminutive financial wizard, who looked like a Kewpie doll, had the brain of a radical Adam Smith, and dressed in the top hat, evening coat, knee breeches, and black silk stockings of an old-fashioned ambassador to the Court of St. James's. To the school of Professor Coin came conservative leaders of the day, names in the world of finance, education, journalism, industry, and society, well known to readers of the daily paper. They came for education or to refute the bimetallist heresy of Professor Coin, but none of them was smart enough for the little fellow.

In vivid caricature and lively text these august figures were represented
as arguing difficult dialectics in favor of the gold standard or as asking
rhetorical questions of their teacher. No matter how abstruse the argument or how involved the question, Professor Coin shot back a simple
and satisfactory answer instantly, a reply that immediately clarified the
issue. There was no escaping the clear logic of this pixy professor, and
thousands were intrigued by his dramatic ability to refute the spokesmen that the daily press had taught them to consider sacrosanct.

The single-minded drive, the elementary arguments, the fictional technique, the pert style of both drawings and text, the naive iconoclasm in
exposing the names of real persons—all these appealed to the credulous
minds of people in search of arguments favoring free silver. Nothing but
Bryan's oratorical speeches could compete with *Coin's Financial School*
as an appeal to a large, dissatisfied, and fanatical populace. Harvey's
book appeared the same year as Ford's *Honorable Peter Stirling,* and
though both found large publics, they were almost entirely separate
ones. Harvey's public was, to a great extent, made up of reformers shad-
ing off into the lunatic fringe. Thousands apparently believed there was
a real Professor Coin, who conducted a school in Chicago at which the
events narrated had actually occurred. Many sent congratulations to the
professor, or wrote for his advice and asked how they might be enrolled
as students for the coming semester. Even the less guileless made him
a new folk hero and Harvey's twenty-five-cent pamphlets reached out
into a public generally unaccustomed to reading books. By May 1895
Coin's Financial School was said to have reached a circulation of 300,000
copies. The *Review of Reviews* querulously observed that the work
seemed to 'sway public opinion from the Alleghenies to the Pacific, and
from the Great Lakes to the Gulf of Mexico.' As Bryan's 1896 campaign
against McKinley made the issue of free silver the leading subject of the
day, Harvey's work drew even wider attention, with a whole school of
contra-Coin pamphlets spreading in its wake across the nation. *Coin's
Financial School* brought in more and more tuition fees, and Harvey contributed all his profits—gold as well as silver—to the Bryan campaign
upon which the book fed. Not until the issue of the 'Cross of Gold'
dropped away with Bryan's defeat did Harvey's book also dwindle into
the literature of lost and forgotten causes.

While the stirring and radical beliefs of Populists and Socialists, of
labor unions and agrarians, were changing the mind of the nation, many
people still attempted to cling to the outworn ethics professed at the

dawning of the Gilded Age. The middle class, always less radical than the workers and less emancipated than the wealthy, still subscribed, by and large, to the beliefs propounded years earlier by such apologists of the *status quo* as Henry Ward Beecher and Russell Conwell. Henry Seidel Canby, who grew up in this middle-class 'age of confidence,' recalls that 'boys and girls . . . were told daily in school and home that to be busy was to be virtuous, that work meant happiness, and that he who produced wealth was the saviour of his country.'

Horatio Alger died in 1899 but his spirit lived on. The year of his passing saw the publication of Elbert Hubbard's *A Message to Garcia*, a story for adults in a vein typical of Alger, with a moral he would have endorsed. This little essay, which Hubbard sometimes called 'a small homily,' sometimes 'a preachment,' told how, during the Spanish-American War, Lieutenant Rowan was sent by McKinley to find General Garcia, head of the Cuban insurgent forces, and discover what aid he needed against the Spanish. The story was no more than an anecdote leading into a lengthy exposition of the moral. As Hubbard said,

The point I wish to make is this: McKinley gave Rowan a letter to be delivered to Garcia; Rowan took the letter and did not ask, 'Where is he at?' By the Eternal! there is a man whose form should be cast in deathless bronze and the statue placed in every college of the land. It is not book-learning young men need, nor instruction about this and that, but a stiffening of the vertebrae which will cause them to be loyal to a trust, to act promptly, concentrate their energies: do the thing—'Carry a message to Garcia!'

Hubbard, a retired soap manufacturer, printed the essay in the arty *Philistine*, a magazine founded to promote his self-conscious bohemian interests. There it was seen by the General Passenger Agent of the New York Central Railroad, who found it just what he wanted to promote the 'efficiency' of his workers. He ordered a hundred thousand copies, but Hubbard could furnish only 3,000. The railroad accepted them and, with the author's permission, printed half a million more copies within three months, to be sold at half a cent each in hundred-copy lots or given away free by the copy. By October 1899, the railroad and Hubbard's own publishing house had printed 981,000 copies. On the first of the new year there were more than a million copies in print. The railroad and Hubbard went on in this way, issuing editions that varied from flimsy pamphlets distributed without charge to ostentatiously illuminated and signed copies, printed on Japan vellum, bound in three-quarters levant, and sold for $15. Translation followed upon translation, and foreign militarists, considering the work as inspirational for soldiers as for railway employees, made it regulation equipment on both sides of the Russo-Japanese War. By December 1913, Elbert Hubbard estimated that 40,000,000 copies had been distributed. The figure may be high, but certainly in its day *A Message to Garcia* was one of America's best-known pieces of writing.

Had *A Message to Garcia* not been sponsored and distributed without cost by great corporations, Hubbard's essay might never have approached its wide circulation, yet the work was the sort demanded by an age of turmoil in search of easy panaceas. A sober economic treatise like Thorstein Veblen's *Theory of the Leisure Class,* also issued in 1899, was not for a wide public, even though its vitriol provoked a fair amount of discussion. Readers of a radical turn of mind wanted books to guide them, but generally the text had to propose simple and direct solutions, such as those of *In His Steps, Looking Backward, Progress and Poverty,* or *Coin's Financial School.* Readers who wanted assurance that the system of financial aristocracy was sound, that if a man but played the game diligently and efficiently he too might become president of a corporation, delighted in *A Message to Garcia.* Many readers from both sides, either too little or too much affected by the stresses of the day, demanded complete escape literature, romances of a wonderful never-never land. The reading publics were varied, the desires of any one were diverse, but all of them were shaped by the times, and the times were out of joint.

Chapter 11

When Knighthood Was in Flower

The Gilded Age glittered brightly for many years after the novel by Mark Twain and Warner gave it a name. Its self-made men continued to fight with the men it had unmade and neither side won a clear victory, though it was evident enough who held the spoils. By 1896 seven-eighths of the nation's wealth was in the hands of one-eighth of its people, of whom 1 per cent owned more than the other 99. Behind such statistics lay the reasons for movements as diverse as the American Railway Union, the Single Tax organization, the Populists, and the Nationalists. Behind these figures lay also the reasons for rigid economic and social controls imposed by a ruling class. 'To Have and to Hold' was more than the name of a costume romance popular in 1900; it was a way of life between the Civil War and the First World War for those who belonged to or could struggle into the ruling fraction of the nation. The once optimistic Whitman might denounce the 'scrofulous wealth' of the times, but Mark Twain, who had satirized its incubus, gave way in *A Connecticut Yankee in King Arthur's Court* to a glorification of the go-getting, machine-loving, money-creating spirit of the times. Andrew Carnegie, the pauper immigrant boy who now had a castle in his native Scotland, spoke for his side of the United States when he declared, 'The sixty-five million Americans of today could buy up the one hundred and forty millions of Russians, Austrians, and Spaniards; or, after purchasing wealthy France, would have pocket money to acquire Denmark, Norway, Switzerland, and Greece.' By 65,000,000 Carnegie

180

really meant the 8,000,000 who controlled this nation's wealth, and though his statement celebrated nationalism it also betrayed the typical inferiority complex of the *nouveaux riches:* the desire to possess foreign culture through wealth. Once, it was said, admission to society depended on two questions, 'Who was your grandfather?' and 'How much do you know?' Now both were replaced by 'How much are you worth?' With money enough one might buy an improved version of one's grandfather through the so-called 'Mug Books,' or local Who's Whos of the times, and one might even set out on an inevitably successful search for ancestors even more remote and therefore even more patrician.

In the post-Civil War period, many Americans of the lower financial levels banded together for political and economic gains, while thousands on the higher levels organized for claims to caste and heredity. In part, of course, such associations filled the void left by the receding church and answered the nostalgic desires for neighborliness that existed in towns now grown to impersonal cities. But most of all the new social groups of the wealthy and the upper middle classes seemed to satisfy a yearning for distinction and aristocracy. In a brief decade men now moved from shirt-sleeves to coats of arms, aided by societies ostensibly called forth by the series of patriotic centennials that began in 1875. In 1890 alone, there came into being The Sons of the American Revolution, The Daughters of the American Revolution, and The Colonial Dames of America, all products of ancestor worship. That year also saw the creation of a Colonial Order of the Crown for descendants of Charlemagne, and there was soon an Order of the Crown of America for those ostensibly related to other royalty. Any unfortunates who could find kinship neither to William the Conqueror nor to George Washington might join other flamboyant organizations that had as compensation an even greater mumbo jumbo. Making much of exact hierarchy and loose history, these societies delighted their followers with such trappings as ostrich plumes, costume-makers' swords, gold braid, and wondrously elegant titles.

Better even than buying an improved version of a grandfather was the purchase of somebody else's noble ancestry for the children. A great many of the weathiest families saw to it that their daughters married authentic foreign titles, for which, it was estimated, during the century's last three decades the proud fathers paid out doweries amounting to some $200,000,000. The year 1895 marked the high point, with the weddings of Consuelo Vanderbilt to the Duke of Marlborough, of Anna Gould to Count Boni de Castellane, of Mary Leiter to the Marquess

Curzon of Kedleston, and of Pauline Whitney to Sir Almeric Paget, Baron Queenborough. Every year from the 'seventies through the 'nineties saw similar alliances, climaxed in 1899 by the marriage of Prince Michael Cantacuzene of Russia to Julia Grant, the daughter of the President whose *Memoirs* had left his family such a handsome estate.

Those of the wealthy class who had neither the daughters nor the money to marry into nobility could at least make the Grand Tour of the Continent and enjoy the triumph of American capital over European aristocracy. By 1893 over 90,000 Americans visited Europe each year. Having made money at home, wealthy Americans found it bought 'culture' abroad, culture that might be exported to their native land in the shape of a mansion built of borrowed architectural styles and furnished with the ornamental bric-a-brac of lands old and far remote. From Fifth Avenue to Nob Hill the silhouettes of cities were altered by the building of vast residences incorporating in a single fantastic design the turrets of French châteaux, the spires and crenelations of Rhenish castles, and the gables of English manor houses, all encrusted with cast-iron ornamentation and florid jigsaw ruching. The wealthiest people set the style; others followed. Even those who lived in row houses delighted in what Mark Twain called Queen Anne fronts and Maryanne behinds.

In the row houses as in the mansions, the new books that were read were those answering the desires that brought forth the architecture itself. Most of the people who lived in the better row houses still hoped to get ahead within the frame of America's social and economic organization, possibly to have mansions of their own some day. People who lived in mansions, or modest approximations, were secure to indulge their desire to escape contemporary problems and dream of foreign conquests matching their triumphs at home. All these householders, shuddering at Bryan, could hardly be expected to read *Coin's Financial School*. Though they might bow politely in the direction of the noble sentiments of *In His Steps* or feel that *Looking Backward* presented a very pretty Utopia, they had no need for radical solutions and surely wanted no part of *Caesar's Column*. Books certainly crossed social and economic lines, but distinct reading publics existed side by side. Readers allied socially and economically with the world of Professor Coin often voyaged into the world celebrated by the romantic novelist, but few traveled the other way. The direction was natural, for the romance offered something for everybody, and the reform book offered something only for those who had nothing else. For all readers the romance was an escape, an antidote to this world through an excursion to another where what was seen was ordered better and what was not seen did not exist.

Toward the end of the century the romance became almost synonymous with the novel in the public mind and was the most popular form of reading matter. It attracted readers in even greater numbers than before. In 1894 some 700 new works of fiction were issued; in 1901 the number had snowballed to over 2,200. By the latter date fiction accounted for more than 27 per cent of the nation's publishing output, with biography and history a poor second and theology third. Just after the turn of the century Frank Norris, who had begun as a versifier of medieval romance and developed into a writer of realistic novels, could complain that the public had not grown with him because it insisted that fiction provide escape rather than reality. About that he was right, but he was wrong when he contended that the only reason was that 'the people who buy novels are the well-to-do people. They belong to a class whose whole scheme of life is concerned solely with an aim to avoid the unpleasant.' There were plenty of people besides the well-to-do who wanted to avoid the unpleasant, enough to allow at least six novels during 1901 to achieve sales of 150,000 copies each and another nine to sell 100,000 copies apiece. A novel-reading public numbering into the hundreds of thousands obviously was not entirely a wealthy public, even though it was in large part a public anxious to emulate the taste of the wealthy or share vicariously through fiction in the pleasures presumably granted to those with ample funds.

The novel was increasingly popular because more people were being educated to the level where they might read for pleasure, though not for knowledge and considered thought. Public school pupils increased from 9,500,000 in 1878 to 15,000,000 in 1898, with higher education becoming fairly common, for the period began with fewer than 800 and ended with some 5,500 high schools. Public libraries also increased greatly; by 1900 there were over 1,700, each having a collection of more than 5,000 volumes. In 1893 a survey of their loans revealed the novel to be the most popular type of reading. Scott, Dickens, Thackeray, Hawthorne, Cooper, Bulwer-Lytton, and George Eliot were most in demand, and with the passing of instruction in Greek and Latin literature, these novelists were, ironically, called 'classics.' Only three contemporary novels were reported by 50 per cent or more of the libraries, but they all ranked high: *Ben-Hur* (83 per cent), *Little Lord Fauntleroy* (72 per cent), and *Ramona* (68 per cent). New fiction reached the public mainly through bookstores, which were increasing in number and size throughout the land. Bookselling had become a sound business enterprise as improved distribution from publisher to jobber to retailer, fixed discounts, and traveling salesmen replaced semiannual auctions at which New York publishers disposed of all but their newest books to department stores. Though price cutting continued, the new novel was generally marked at a dollar to a dollar and a half, and the public learned to accept literature as branded and clearly priced merchandise that readers could afford.

Bookselling having become a big business, the term 'best seller' entered the American language. Seemingly coined for the lists that *The Bookman* began publishing in 1895, it did not achieve general currency for some years. Neither the *Oxford English Dictionary* nor the *Dictionary of American English* noted its use prior to 1905, when *The Athenaeum* observed, with the disparaging tone generally associated with the word, 'Fortunately the "best sellers" are the worst survivors.' But this connotation is as ill-suited (consider Scott, Byron, Cooper, Dickens, Thackeray, Clemens) as the term is to the subject itself. Yet the expression lingered on, suiting the commercialism of the century that adopted it. Redolent of publicity and advertising men, the term is untrustworthy by its very nature: it indicates a superlative; it is used as a comparative. 'Best seller' means only a book that sells better than the general run of books in a given place during a given time. As measurement of either quantity or duration, it is open to question.

Ever since its introduction by *The Bookman,* a list of best sellers has conventionally been compiled from reports of bookdealers all over the country, so that if ten small stores report Book A and two large stores report Book B, A tops the list and B sinks to the bottom, though in numbers of copies sold the reverse might be expected. Such discrimination against numbers of sales might seem to work in favor of national coverage, yet books often appear on best-seller lists though they are not among the current favorites of cities that have no stores represented in the tabulation. Indeed, whole states are neglected, though that can hardly be helped in view of the fact that as late as 1935 Mississippi, for example, had no bookstores available for 77 per cent of its population. The lists are further suspect because it is not unknown for a dealer holding a large stock of a book to list it as his best seller, hoping to attract the trade of people bent on following fashion. In terms of duration the measurement is also open to question. The book ranking highest in any calendar year may not be the most widely sold book issued that year, a distinction often belonging to a work whose sales continue from publication in the fall of one year to the fall of the next. There is, of course, no relation between the order in two successive best-seller lists, because the number of copies needed to win first place in one year may be only a small fraction of that needed in the next. Because accurate statistics are often not revealed by publishers, the lists remain a primary source for students of sales as for buyers themselves. Certainly, the whole concept of best sellers accords with the increase in the book-buying public to the point where it represents a mass culture hesitant of its own taste and dependent upon the endorsement of the greatest numbers.

More authors came to public attention with the growth of interest in the novel, many of them Americans after the International Copyright Law of 1891 for the first time made their works no more expensive to issue than those by foreigners. After 1894 more novels, though not always more popular novels, came from Americans than from Europeans, but the *Publishers' Weekly* brooded on 'how many of our novelists seek material outside of their native land.' In their choice of subject and their attitude toward it the novelists, like the reading public, were turning to foreign scenes and distant times because they afforded glamorous escape from contemporary problems. Furthermore, the manners of European nobility fascinated Americans who, having the dollars, felt they should buy continental culture and station. Though only a few Americans could afford the grand marital alliance, the Grand Tour, or the grand house, greater numbers could afford the pinchbeck splendor of organizations like the Colonial Order of the Crown, and even more could attempt to satisfy their desires through the medium of romantic fiction. Paradoxically, for many Americans to be American meant to turn one's eyes to Europe. In various ways the United States was proving itself the inheritor and conqueror of Europe, and merely by reading a romantic novel many people identified themselves with this aspect of the nation's success; they felt that they too were sharing the spirit of the times in which our industrial might whipped the power of Spain in a romantic galloping and sailing war.

The social and economic cleavage of the times demanded that fiction either face the issues realistically and purposefully or ignore them in favor of a romantic escape. All through the last decades of the century and well into the opening of the new one it was not supposed that a reader could endorse both a realistic novel and a romantic one. Only an occasional hardheaded reviewer, like one writing in *The Critic* of 1888, could ask, 'Must we because we confess a liking for Mr. James or Mr. Howells, by that confession declare ourselves at war with Dumas or Stevenson?' Most people said 'Yes,' since they identified realism with an inartistic presentation of facts that somehow made for degradation, pessimism, and radicalism, alien to the finer spirit of romance. Even a critic as cultured as Richard Watson Gilder could be much exercised at the enemy's taking over such a fine word as realism to cover his black art. Gilder insisted he did not object to realism: 'The more reality the better! But let it be reality all the way through; reality of the spirit as well as of the flesh, not a grovelling reality which ignores the "romantic spirit."' So realism was satisfactory to the inheritors of the genteel tradition just so long as it was romantic. No wonder that Theodore Dreiser, a struggling young New York journalist, could find no relation between life and popular literature: 'the discrepancy existing between my own observations and those displayed' in the novels that 'seemed to deal with phases of sweetness and beauty and success and goodness such as I rarely encountered.' But such disparity was just what most readers enjoyed. Divergent publics occasionally welcomed the same books, such as *Ben-Hur* or *Quo Vadis?*, one relishing the social message, the other the gaudy romance of history; but that was the accidental or perhaps the designed good fortune of the authors, for by and large readers were split and the majority favored romance and romance alone.

The romance grew more popular during the 'eighties, though the next two decades were to make it supreme. The most popular type presented American ways succeeding in a foreign culture. Sometimes the heroes and heroines were really Americans accepted by or triumphing over Europeans, sometimes they were foreigners possessed of those democratic, go-getting qualities that Americans thought peculiarly their own, but always explicitly or tacitly readers in the United States were afforded glimpses of an aristocratic way of life that they could vicariously share or master in the myopic eyes of their imaginations.

The desire for approbation from aristocratic Europe and the hunger to possess its culture quickly caused Americans to make a best seller out of a most unlikely French novel, a thin little idyll entitled *L'Abbé Constantin*, the first timorous venture of Ludovic Halévy into the world of prose fiction. The story, based on the life of Mrs. John Mackay, wife of the Irish day laborer who made a fortune in Nevada's Comstock Lode, told of an American woman buying the château of a French marchioness and establishing herself as a *grande dame*. The Abbé of the village church, who feared his new patron would be soulless and moneyloving because she is American, is delighted to discover her a cultivated, sympathetic Lady Bountiful, whose sister makes a most eligible bride for the old man's nephew. Published in France in 1882 as a *feuilleton*, *L'Abbé Constantin* was immediately translated and issued in America, where it became a great success in innumerable pirated editions, ranging in price from a dime for a pamphlet to $17.50 for a heavily padded edition. It was soon standard reading in schools, as a model of behavior for children who, having learned to succeed with Horatio Alger, now needed to know how to use wealth to command European approval. Of all French novels, Halévy's was the most suited to America, its popularity probably surpassing even Zola's *Nana* and Maupassant's short stories, which, though kept out of the hands of children, attracted many adults through their depiction of the voluptuous life of Europeans.

Remotely related in theme but close in spirit to *L'Abbé Constantin* was *Little Lord Fauntleroy*, a children's tale read by young and old alike. Written by Frances Hodgson Burnett, an Englishwoman who had married an American, the novel told about an angelic, blond-haired, lacecollared, and velvet-pantalooned lad reared in New York by his American mother, the widow of a British nobleman's younger son. When little Cedric becomes Lord Fauntleroy and goes to live on his ancestral estate he guides his grandfather, the Earl of Dorincourt, in the ways of *noblesse oblige* by changing this haughty curmudgeon into a kindly philanthropist concerned with better living conditions for his tenants, while the little Lord himself practices democracy as he makes friends with workingmen and nobles alike. Starting life as a serial in the juvenile magazine, *St. Nicholas*, *Little Lord Fauntleroy* moved into adult circles as a book published in 1896 and as a play, which ran on Broadway for four years and toured the nation with road companies almost as numerous as those that produced *Uncle Tom's Cabin* or *Ben-Hur*. The seven-year-old titular character became the darling of Anglophile grownups, but he plagued little boys, who were taught to address their mothers as 'Dearest' and were forced to walk the streets of Des Moines or Detroit garbed in the fussy costume that little Cedric Errol wore at the castle of Dorincourt.

The year that brought *L'Abbé Constantin* to American readers saw also the first publication of a novel by Francis Marion Crawford, soon to become a leading purveyor of elegant romance to the same public.

Crawford, nephew of Julia Ward Howe, was less concerned with trampling out the vintage of the grapes of wrath than with describing the glory of European lords he had seen. An elegant expatriate in a luxurious, artistic palazzo whose foundations rose from the Mediterranean, whence he sailed his yacht to America every few years, Crawford created characters as romantic as himself. Ouida, whose spiritual heir he was, declared that to read his books was to feel in the company of a well-bred man of superior gifts. Nearly every year the American public had a new chance for such contact as novels came tumbling from his pen. His advance royalties were frequently $10,000, which his publishers could well afford to pay a novelist who in fourteen years sold more than half a million copies of his books in America and still found an eager audience as he turned out historical romances and charming pictures of cosmopolitan life, sophisticated and aesthetic. No one work stood out above another; all had the sense of giving stay-at-home Americans an intimate understanding of genteel or exotic people in various foreign lands, and almost all were equally welcomed. Their very titles indicated what one might expect of Crawford, and for some twenty-five years an avid public read his more than forty novels, which included: *A Roman Singer* (1884), *Saracinesca* (1887), *A Cigarette-Maker's Romance* (1890), *The Children of the King* (1892), *Don Orsino* (1892), *Love in Idleness* (1894), *Casa Braccio* (1895), *In the Palace of the King* (1900), *Cecilia, a Story of Modern Rome* (1902), and *A Lady of Rome* (1906).

Crawford's success with a long line of romances was soon challenged by the thirty-nine novels of Archibald Clavering Gunter, which, if neither so polished in composition nor so understanding of the characters' social milieu, were more direct in relating American standards to European. A retired stockbroker of California, Gunter could find no publisher willing to handle his awkwardly written *Mr. Barnes of New York* and so issued it himself in 1887 as the first of his long line of yellow-backed novels, soon to be seen in innumerable hammocks, summer resorts, excursion boats, Pullman Palace Cars, or wherever else Americans moved for dreams and escape. Its hero, Mr. Barnes, was a wealthy yet typical American whose adventures in Europe included a romance with an English belle (considered above his station until his finances made him satisfactory to her and her chaperone) and involvement in a Corsican vendetta concerning his future brother-in-law. Though readers found the Corsicans dark, fascinating people, they also found Corsican standards

antiquated and superstitious, easily overcome by such modern, enlightened Americans as the Mr. Barneses with whom they associated
themselves. Even if *Mr. Barnes of New York* may not have sold a million copies as Gunter's biographer alleges, and if his books were not
'the most successful novels ever published' as the author-publisher contended, there is no doubt that his first romance and such successors as
*Mr. Potter of Texas, Baron Montez of Panama and Paris, The King's
Stockbroker,* and *A Princess of Paris* had a great vogue that probably
carried all of Gunter's novels to more than a million readers.

While Crawford and Gunter were attracting the public, two better-
remembered novelists—William Dean Howells and Henry James—were
being paid respect but no royalties. Both were realists and both were
too subtle to suit public taste, even when they dealt with the relation of
American to European standards. Howells was probably voicing his own
opinion when one of the characters of *The Rise of Silas Lapham* declared, 'The novelists might be the greatest possible help to us if they
painted life as it is, and human feelings in their true proportion and relation, but for the most part they have been and are altogether noxious.'
Henry James declared that his novels were all under tombstones as soon
as published, for even though he showed American girls capturing
Europe or rising above its decadent ethics in such works as *Daisy
Miller* and *The Portrait of a Lady,* of the former he admitted sadly to
Howells, 'I have made $200 by the whole American career of D. M.'

Among the distinguished men of letters, only Mark Twain could flavor
a realistic analysis of society with such romance as the people wanted.
With his usual ambivalence he excoriated the morality of the Gilded
Age and yet was fascinated by some of its surface trappings. During the
'eighties he produced two books that could be read with pleasure even
by the public that fed on Crawford and Gunter. In *The Prince and the
Pauper* he showed that, given the title and the raiment, any boy might
pass for a king, and in *A Connecticut Yankee in King Arthur's Court*
he delighted in the idea of American big-business efficiency triumphing
over feudalism. The books held within them realistic and satirical strains
and argued for a better democracy than most of the reading public was
concerned with, but they could be read, and undoubtedly often were
read, for very different reasons.

Despite the passage of the International Copyright Law, which
brought increased opportunities for Americans to find publishers, foreign
authors continued popular because their mere foreignness gave them a

cachet. One who was accepted by the American public at her own pretentious value was Marie Corelli. In a strange way she combined the appeals of Ouida and Mrs. Humphry Ward, though if indebted to either it could only have been to the garish, sweet vulgarity of the former lady. *Thelma,* her second book, was the first to be issued in America, and with its publication in 1887 she quickly became a favorite novelist. The lurid, ill-plotted romance tells of the love of a young English baronet for a Norwegian girl, whose ethics, true to the faith and honor of her Viking ancestors, make her unhappy in the immoral, irreligious high society of Britain. So widely was this dramatic tale read that American publishers were quick to snatch Miss Corelli's first book, *A Romance of Two Worlds,* before the copyright law could force them to pay royalties to the author. Even more fanciful than *Thelma, A Romance of Two Worlds* dealt not with two worlds of moral values in a mortal society, but with the contrast between the corruption of the present and the glory of the hereafter as revealed to the heroine by a strange sage who expounded something called 'The Electrical Principle of Christianity.' The denunciation of corruption in high British society may have titillated some readers but its pseudo-scientific social criticism also attracted others who were seeking salvation through media as diverse as Christian Science, *In His Steps,* and *Looking Backward.* Marie Corelli continued to be an outstanding success as she poured forth her steady stream of florid romances tinctured with social criticism of worldly society and its infidelity. When her melodramatic *Sorrows of Satan* was published in 1895 she still commanded a great many readers even though they were not told of this new book by reviewers; for she refused copies to reviewers because they had so long derided her purple settings, lush prose, obvious characterization, naive preaching, and tawdry sentiments. Literary critics might scorn her fiction, but Queen Victoria endorsed it as though she were appointing a royal purveyor of light romances to the court, and the general American reading public found that what was to the Queen's taste was also to theirs.

A far better but equally popular English romancer was Robert Louis Stevenson. When he disembarked from an emigrant ship in 1879 he found few people in New York who knew his works and no editor willing to give him an assignment. Eight years later his *Treasure Island, The Strange Case of Dr. Jekyll and Mr. Hyde,* and *Kidnapped* had made him a famous author. Children and adults alike were delighted by his fanciful adventure stories, which had been cheaply reprinted in pirated editions and more widely read in America than England. Upon his return to the United States in 1887 he found adaptations of *Dr. Jekyll and Mr. Hyde* playing on two New York stages and his future writing in tremendous demand among publishers and editors. The *New York World* offered him £2,000 a year for weekly articles on any subjects he chose; *Scribner's* with equal freedom offered £700 for twelve monthly articles; and Samuel S. McClure was delighted to buy the serial rights of his next book for £1,600. Only thirty-seven years old, Stevenson had already established himself as a model for other authors who played the sedulous ape to his style and subjects. His imitators had their moment, and some of the writers inspired by him had temporary successes perhaps even greater than his own. *Treasure Island* suggested to H. Rider Haggard the idea of trying his hand at an adventurous romance for boys, and adults too. The result, after but six weeks of writing, was *King Solomon's Mines*, which, in England at least, for a while outsold the book that inspired it. Haggard's next novel in the same vein, *She*, was aimed at an adult public, which in England bought copies at the rate of a thousand a week, while in America, according to the author, it 'was pirated by the hundred thousand.' As quickly as Haggard could turn out a new romance, and that was quick indeed, American publishers reprinted cheap, unauthorized editions, sponsored imitations, and gained publicity as dramatists adapted these works for the New York stage.

Stevenson's *Prince Otto* was not an especially popular book, either in America or abroad, when issued in 1885, and yet its theme and its manner anticipated the tastes of the romance-reading public. Set in the independent principality of Grünewald, a never-never land, and given no actual date for its mythical events, the romance established but the one fact that the season was spring, and in a vernal mood it told of the intrigues, the adventures, and the loves encountered by Prince Otto as he traveled incognito through his charming land. Weaker than Dumas's work, the slim romance was a kind of daydreaming melodrama, an easy fantasia flavored with allegory, posturing in its style, and imparting to its story a pseudomedieval flavor for an unreal modern world. At the moment the combination did not take, but these ingredients, when faster paced in plot and less discursive in moral commentary, became the materials of the romancers popular during the 'nineties and the first years of the new century.

Nine years after *Prince Otto* was published, Stevenson died on a far-distant South Sea island, but that same year of 1894 his hero gained

a new life when his person was split between Rudolf Rassendyl and
Rupert of Hentzau and his principality was rediscovered as the kingdom of Ruritania. The new novelist Anthony Hope may never have read
Prince Otto, but his *Prisoner of Zenda* was made of similar materials,
more ingeniously blended. It was a rollicking, swashbuckling romance,
this tale of the Englishman Rudolf who resembled the Ruritanian King
Rupert so closely that he could successfully impersonate him when the
monarch was imprisoned in the castle at Zenda by his treacherous
brother, Black Michael. The rococo romancing about a tinsel aristocracy
and its salvation by a man who, though English, was a commoner, delighted the public that was building its homes with jigsaw turrets, join-
ing societies glorifying lineage, and gaping at newspaper accounts of
weddings between wealthy Americans and European nobility. Ruritania
soon became a place on the mind's map more real to most Americans
than Poland or any of its Balkan neighbors. Within the year of publication, *The Prisoner of Zenda* went through 26 printings, all without bene-
fit of cheap, unauthorized editions, for the days of pirating were past. A
dramatization of the novel, with the glamorous Sothern playing the part
of Rudolf, and a sequel by Hope increased book sales, which kept on
year after year. The original publishers have never let the book go out
of print, and even half a century after it was first issued, 48 of the New
York Public Library's 54 branches find it necessary to stock copies of
The Prisoner of Zenda.

Anthony Hope started a fad that lasted for more than a decade, for
nearly every year saw the publication of romances about an imaginary
kingdom, costume pieces filled with flashing swords, swishing cloaks, daring intrigue, and beautiful highborn heroines. In 1895 Richard Harding
Davis, as romantic himself as Rudolf Rassendyl, tried his hand at a
variation of the Ruritanian theme in *The Princess Aline;* in 1898 Agnes and
Egerton Castle gave the material a historical flavor by setting *The Pride
of Jennico* in a Bohemian kingdom during the eighteenth century; while
1899 was marked by the use of Hope's pattern in three tales: Richard Harding Davis's new work, *The King's Jackal,* H. B. M. Davis's romance, *Princess Xenia,* and Harold MacGrath's *Arms and the Woman,* which further
developed the idea by introducing an American in the plot. In 1900 Mac-
Grath tried the formula once again in *The Puppet Crown,* and so it went
year after year. Dozens of Danubian principalities, relics of feudal days,
were discovered to lie in the general area of Europe vaguely described
as two days distant from London or Paris. Often they were ruled by a

beautiful princess—a Gibson girl with a crown—whose sovereignty was threatened by some villainous nobleman. To her rescue came a foreigner, catapulted by some peculiar chance right into the midst of an intrigue that we are given to understand was shaking the courts of Austria, Russia, and Germany, and even keeping the lights burning late in Downing Street. But in the isolated principality—always set high in scenic mountains with passes and gorges whose topography is peculiarly fitted for horseback chases—only the foreigner and a few retainers loyal to the princess are present to fight the plotters with courage and wit. Through masked balls and moats, through dungeon keeps and quaint Alpine inns, they pursue one another, now one in the lead, now the other, until finally the villain is killed or perhaps flees to the neigboring kingdom that was assisting him, and the rightful ruler is firmly established upon the centuries-old throne.

Though no one of the Ruritanian romances of the 'nineties had a great success, the type itself was enormously popular as it dwindled into bargain-basement baroque. The public appetite never seemed to be cloyed by so much fiction, sweet and soft as a marshmallow. As pretty but as flat in their high coloring as the Maxfield Parrish paintings that illustrated some of them, it was hard to tell one romance from another, or at least to tell how one was better or poorer. Not until 1901 did a distinctive successor to *The Prisoner of Zenda* come along. Then, George Barr McCutcheon, an Indiana farm boy turned newspaper editor, sold his *Graustark* outright for $500 and soon found it earning hundreds of thousands of dollars for publishers and dramatic adaptors. The romance was awkwardly written and naively conceived in character and incident, but it attracted a wide public, in part because more sophisticated readers had begun to tire of the mythical kingdom theme, and the level of McCutcheon's writing was appropriate to the readers who had inherited the subject. But more significant than this paradoxical cause of success was McCutcheon's new twist to the old theme, a development he belabored most energetically. The hero of his novel, who rescues the Princess Yetive from Prince Gabriel's kidnapping attempt, is an American, just, as readers could say, 'like me.' McCutcheon glorified the clean, fresh young American man, the believer in democracy, the real 'go-getter,' whose active modern ways triumph over the decadent plots of feudal-minded Europeans. To underline the point, the objections of Graustark's nobility to a marriage between princess and commoner are answered by the hero's declaration that there is no reason to consider the alliance ill-suited, for is he not an American and is not every American boy a potential ruler, a future President of the world's greatest nation? And so not only does the hero marry the Princess, but his friend Harry is wed to her lady-in-waiting. With such a thesis McCutcheon reinvigorated the old Ruritanian romance, gave to it a new name, the Graustarkian romance, and wrote a best seller. During the first nine months of publication the book sold 150,000 copies; the profits soon became so great that publishers voluntarily paid royalties, and bewildered readers paid the highest tribute of all by writing the author in all sincerity for directions to the wonderful realm of Graustark, where they too might meet or marry a princess or her lady-in-waiting.

The year 1894, which saw the beginning of the craze for romances about mythical principalities, also introduced a new fad with *Trilby*. George Du Maurier had already published *Peter Ibbetson*, a strange dream fantasy, which, while more popular here than in England, had had no great success, and there was no reason for him to expect that he would do much better with his second novel. Accordingly, Du Maurier sold the manuscript outright to Harper's, and it was only the phenomenal success of the book and the publishers' decency or desire for his next novel that nevertheless caused them to pay him a flat 15 per cent royalty. The charming picture of bohemian life in the Latin Quarter, the tender romance of Trilby, the artist's model, and the painter, Little Billee, the lurid melodrama of Svengali's hypnotic power over the poor girl—all these combined the sophisticated foreign subject and the sentimental attitude in a way that delighted a large public. Du Maurier's view of Parisian life was readily received in homes where Zola's *Nana* was not welcome, although mention of models posing in the 'altogether' scandalized some people and augmented sales on that score alone. But in general the work sold for other reasons and was accounted tender and pure, much admired by young girls, who made Trilby their model in all but a few of the more questionable aspects of her behavior. Girls by the thousands yearned for feet as graceful as hers, spoke of their own as 'Trilbies,' wore Trilby slippers, cultivated a so-called 'Trilby-type' of beauty, and dressed themselves in Trilby hats and coats (decorated with costume jewelry shaped like Trilby's own foot); they nibbled Trilby chocolates, played Trilby waltzes, and during many a summer evening of 1894 and 1895 lifted their voices to the sad strains of 'Ben Bolt,' the fifty-year-old lyric revived by its introduction into Du Maurier's novel. An enterprising real-estate man named a Florida town Trilby and expected self-respecting but sentimental folk to live on Svengali Street or Little Billee Street, and though it was perhaps too much to assume that this would last, a suburb of Columbus, Ohio, still bears the name of Trilby.

Throughout the country *Trilby* was in tremendous demand. Chicago, a city of a million people, had 26 copies in its public library and the librarian contended 'we could use 260 and never find a copy on the shelves.' The St. Louis library, with either a larger budget or a more sentimental librarian, accumulated no fewer than 400 copies, all battered by good use. Sales were comparable, even though the novel was issued at the then extravagant price of $1.75. Within a few months 100,000 copies were sold and the popularity kept up through 1895, when the work, in its second year, was second in the list of best sellers. In that year the author collected almost £5,000 in royalties, indicative of sales better than 100,000 copies, and he received another £4,500 for the dramatic adaptation by Paul Potter. The drama toured the nation, playing to audiences almost as mesmerized as Trilby herself at the sight of the leading lady's bare feet and the sound of her beautiful voice. Whistler's lawsuit, charging that he had been libeled in the novel, two parodies entitled *Biltry* and *Drilby,* and a burlesque operetta called *Thrilby* all helped to keep up public interest. *Trilby* was an enormous success, but neither Du Maurier's next and last novel nor any imitator achieved a similar following. The work was but one great, isolated contribution to the period's desire for romance.

Rudyard Kipling was another author who set his own style of romance and found no successful imitator except himself. Enjoying a far longer period of popularity than Du Maurier, all through the 'nineties Kipling attracted readers who were more faithful and had more varied tastes because he offered so many things to so many different people. His stories conjuring up the richness and the excitement of India delighted a public that had first found Francis Marion Crawford through his *Mr. Isaacs, A Tale of Modern India.* But instead of Crawford's preciosity, Kipling presented a freshly mannered technique and an imaginative realization of the code of public-school Englishmen for which many Americans subconsciously yearned. Kipling's fables and simple allegories made his points clearly enough, though sometimes he pounded the table too hard—but this was not surprising for a man who felt himself a colonial outsider in his own land, and it pleased a people who bragged and blustered but felt themselves outsiders in the world of nations. His poetry, often but another medium for voicing the ideas found in his prose, attracted a public that had long been without a popular poet. These poems were as simple to understand as Longfellow's and as tuneful as Tennyson's; and they offered a different vision peculiarly well suited to a new generation. The readers of this generation delighted in Kipling for, though still in search of inspiration, they were more intrigued by the glamour of ancient culture and alien ways, even while flexing their muscles for empire building. Gunga Din, who didn't know fear because he had his job to do, was in harmony with the man who carried the message to Garcia; from another poem Americans picked up the catchword of imperialism—'the white man's burden'—and smugly applied it to the Spanish-American War. Though 'Recessional' and 'If' came late, their ideas had already been foreshadowed in earlier poems, loved by the American public for their righteous, uplifting tone, and as well suited to this land as to that for which they were written.

Never granted the title in his own nation, Kipling was America's unofficial poet laureate as well as one of her most popular prose writers. Where Du Maurier had two towns named for his book, Kipling had a full six—from Louisiana to Montana—honoring the author himself; three communities chose his first name and three his last. Though he himself retained the distinction that came early in the 'nineties, Kipling's later works had a smaller following, partly because he was outgrown by the younger generation, which was his primary public. But in greater part the falling off of sales was simply a matter of publishing commerce; the early works appeared before the copyright law and could be pirated in many cheap editions but the later books were more expensive and less available. *The Light that Failed,* appealing because of its stirring Indian battle scenes and the pathos of bohemian art life that anticipated *Trilby,* was a thin novel by comparison with *Captains Courageous,* the only Kipling book set in this country; but of the two, *The Light that Failed* had a far greater sale. It came at a time when Kipling was a new and exciting discovery and it was made available in numerous editions reasonably priced. The reason for the difference in reception is in part paralleled by S. S. McClure's point about other Kipling works; McClure observed that where once he could pick up a *Jungle Book* story for $125, 'five years later I paid $25,000 for the serial rights of *Kim.*' McClure was a shrewd editor and he paid such a high price because Kipling's works were in demand, yet to some extent, Kipling's popularity waned as his books were priced out of the widest market.

The romancers, so varied in themselves, occasionally found competition from more realistic English novelists, but no American realist could contend against the general drift toward romance. Thomas Hardy was a quiet but persistent favorite, American magazines printing some of his fiction almost every year after 1873. Frequently two serials were running concurrently in different magazines, and they were soon transformed into books so that at least one full work by Hardy was presented to America in all but two of the years between 1873 and 1899. If the many undated editions could be properly placed, it might be found that every year brought forth a book by Hardy, usually in a pirated edition, sometimes priced as cheap as three cents a copy, but more generally sold for twenty or twenty-five cents. Hardy's growing public, which had made *Far from the Madding Crowd* a competitor of Blackmore's *Lorna Doone* in 1874, called for six editions of *The Mayor of Casterbridge* in 1886, and by 1891 required eight editions within the year for *Tess,* a more romantic novel.

James Barrie was closer to the romantic tenor of the times but he stressed the honest, humble ways of his native Scotland, and it was this in part that made him popular in America. He possessed the sentiment, the pathos, and the whimsical turn of mind that delighted readers in those years, but he was also a man acting like a little boy in recollecting through his mother's eyes the quaint charm of a simpler life in his native region. Though many Americans demanded that their fiction take them away to romantic and unreal lands, others, equally intent upon escape, preferred the settings of their novels to have the semblance of realism, so long as that realism conveyed an essentially romantic picture of an earlier, purer life when men and women lived closer to nature and still saw ways to find success in homely achievements. This Barrie presented in the sketches gathered in *Auld Licht Idylls,* the sequel *A Window in Thrums,* and his novel *The Little Minister,* all of which were frequently and cheaply reprinted because the copyright law did not apply to these works issued before its passage in 1891.

Perhaps even more popular than Barrie was Ian Maclaren, whose *Beside the Bonnie Briar Bush* appeared in America in 1895, three years after its obvious model, *Auld Licht Idylls.* These quietly humorous sketches of rural Scottish life were in the year of their publication more widely sold than the year-old *Trilby,* or *The Prisoner of Zenda.* Before 1895 was out Maclaren's work was successfully dramatized and the publishers quickly brought out a companion work, *Days of Auld Lang Syne.*

The new book, though not so popular as the first, was still on the best-seller list the next year when the author, whose real name was the Reverend Dr. John Watson, traveled around America delivering sermons, giving lectures, and reading his own stories so successfully that in two and a half months his tour netted over $35,000.

Arthur Conan Doyle was another Englishman whose literary fame brought him to America for a successful lecture tour. He arrived in 1894, four years after *A Study in Scarlet*, the first of his detective stories, appeared in this country. His popularity grew through three editions of this book, *The Sign of the Four, The Adventures of Sherlock Holmes*, and *The Memoirs of Sherlock Holmes*. Doyle had begun as a conventional historical romancer, but later he applied the techniques of the romance to a new type of fiction. The American public came to know him only as the creator of two characters permanently enshrined in this nation's literary mythology—Sherlock Holmes the master detective and his friend Watson, who could grasp only the most elementary clue.

Though the Holmes stories emphasized mystery and crime, which had won a public for *The Woman in White* and *Lady Audley's Secret*, they offered more than that to readers. They created simple, clear characters whose personalities remained constant but whose thrilling adventures were ever changing—ingredients typical of the romance, which emphasizes the excitements of plot involving characters clearly representative of good and evil. If Baker Street was not so elegant an address as the palace in Ruritania, it was a place quite as strange and glamorous, and the contest between the hawk-nosed detective and various criminals intent upon the persons or the fortunes of highborn Britishers and foreigners was just a new twist to the Ruritanian kind of intrigue. Omitting the ingredient of love and the idea of the mythical principality, it still gave readers an amateur hero pitted against professional villains in combat, chase, and rescue. Lacking copyright protection, the first two Holmes books circulated widely, and though only *The Hound of the Baskervilles* reached best-seller lists in an authorized edition, almost every literate American became aware of the great detective not only through the cheap pamphlet reprints but through media as diverse as William Gillette's melodramatic stage adaptation, newspaper allusions, and a comic-strip parody.

As the century ran out and another came in, the vogue for romance continued. Despite, or perhaps because of, financial depressions and strikes, romantic tales of far-off times and places attracted great audi-

Chapter 12

Their Yesterdays

America toward the end of the century was a paradox: confused by internal class struggle, secure as it turned a bold front upon the world. Sure of its industrial might, elated by its mechanical contrivances, boastful of its national wealth, proud of its form of government (whose various centennials were celebrated in a series of jubilees stretching from 1875 to 1890), and lordly in welcoming hundreds of thousands of immigrants, America was yet torn by economic and political dissension. While Carnegie declared that God was in His heaven and all was right with the U.S.A., almost 10 per cent of the electorate in 1892 turned against two former Presidents—Republican and Democratic candidates, Harrison and Cleveland—to cast a million votes for the Populist ticket. Another financial crisis occurred in 1893. In 1896 the Populist hero Bryan captured the Democratic party and very nearly won the election too. McKinley's administration brought good business, better returns to farmers, and national unity in the Spanish-American War, but problems still remained. The nation might be prosperous but prices were high and many individuals found it hard to keep up with such prosperity. If they could not succeed in the settled East, they found fewer opportunities to try the old American solution of turning westward. The frontier was gone, or at least the government had no choice farming land to give away. The country began to be fenced in by barbed wire, and mechanization came to the farm. Capitalist economy, controlled by the cities, moved on to the farms in the shape of mortgages or such expensive implements as reapers and harvesters, putting the farmers into big business or in the grip of it.

During these years and under these conditions, some readers searched for panaceas in fiction and tracts, some escaped vicariously to older, settled cultures or envisioned themselves consorting with Graustarkian princesses, and still others turned to the vigorous past of America itself, searching for roots or pining for the large, free land that was gone. Chauvinist pride, brought to a peak by the centennials of this country's founding and the display of power in the Spanish-American War, created a demand for historical romances of America. The present of economic turmoil, of entrenched monopolies, predatory trusts, and octopus railroads faded with the reading of these pretty tales about America's past. Nationalistic nostalgia, fed by these diverse impulses, created a vogue for costume pieces about the federal and frontier periods, this demand lasting well into the first decade of the new century, when it began to be replaced by its offspring: the novel of simple, decent country life, a picture of the old folks at home in the back-country eddies of contemporary America, or the clean open spaces to the west.

The Old South, conceived as a land of courtly colonels, chivalrous dandies, beautiful belles, happy-go-lucky Negroes, and large plantations, was one of the first subjects to be seen through the hazy retrospect of historical romancing. Joel Chandler Harris's *Uncle Remus* collections, published between 1881 and 1906, and F. Hopkinson Smith's novelette, *Colonel Carter of Cartersville,* published in 1891, though not orthodox romances, helped set the tone for later fiction, and their leading characters became prototypes of a new conception of slave and master to replace Uncle Tom and Simon Legree. When the bloody-shirt politics of Reconstruction faded away, a more sympathetic view of the South was welcomed along with nationalistic Romeo-and-Juliet tales about lovers separated by sectional warfare. As William Dean Howells remarked, 'The wrecks of slavery are fast growing a fungus crop of sentiment,' a growth that not only fastened onto fiction but crept over the stage in Bronson Howard's *Shenandoah* (1888), Augustus Thomas's *Alabama* (1891) and his dramatization of *Colonel Carter of Cartersville* (1892), and Belasco's *The Heart of Maryland* (1895). From the middle of the 'nineties on, the stage was for many years indebted to the historical romance for its most popular productions. One best-selling novel after another was dramatized to play to standing room; and even such successes as Clyde Fitch's *Nathan*

Hale (1899) and *Barbara Frietchie* (1899), although specially written for the stage, were cut in the same pattern.

The myth-making historical romance conjured up grandiose Southern plantations worked by happy Negroes on one end of the continent and on the other created a comparable arcadia of splendid, idle Spanish ranchos tended by simple, pious Indians. The latter achievement was the product of Helen Hunt Jackson's *Ramona,* whose publication in 1884 preceded the general historical outburst. Though early, it foreshadowed a pattern in sentimentalizing a simpler America closer to the soil. Picture postcards showing the Ramona country, the site of her wedding, and even 'the original Ramona' were sent east by chambers of commerce and real-estate dealers, enticing visitors to see the originals and the beautiful Spanish missions, restored in a wave of local pride and antiquarianism that followed hard upon the publication of Mrs. Jackson's romance. *Ramona* was a steady rather than big seller, its popularity mainly concentrated in the locality it celebrated. More than sixty years were needed to sell 600,000 copies, the Los Angeles Public Library alone purchasing a thousand of them, for *Ramona* was more a symptom than a realization of the popularity of the native historical romance.

The new style in fiction really hit its stride in the late 'nineties. The year 1896 was marked by the widespread reading of Frederic J. Stimson's *King Noanett,* a story of seventeenth-century England and America, and Sir Gilbert Parker's *The Seats of the Mighty,* about Wolfe's capture of Quebec; but 1897 set the historical romance in America proper and made it the new vogue in American reading matter. First of the new type was James Lane Allen's *The Choir Invisible,* which only *Quo Vadis?* nosed out for top place on *The Bookman's* new best-seller list. Allen's romance of eighteenth-century Kentucky was only a slightly altered reissue of his *John Gray* unsuccessfully published in 1893, but the public taste had now caught up with the author. This idealistic tale of a frontier schoolmaster, a 'Galahad in buckskins' hopelessly in love with an older married woman, captivated sentimental readers who also found a special appeal in the hardy nobility attributed to earlier Americans. Within three years 250,000 copies of *The Choir Invisible* were sold and the public was ready to receive more stories of early America. These soon came pouring off the presses. Second among the ten best sellers of 1898 was S. Weir Mitchell's *Hugh Wynne,* the story of a Free or fighting Quaker, whose adventures during the Revolution brought him in contact with Washington, Lafayette, Arnold, and André, thus introducing real figures as the final element to make a complete historical romance. Winston Churchill's *Richard Carvel*, published the following year, had a similar setting and tone; his adventurous young hero from Maryland came to know not only such British leaders as Walpole and Fox but to serve on the *Bonnehomme Richard* under John Paul Jones. *Richard Carvel* sold 420,000 copies within two years, establishing Churchill as one of the leading historical romancers of his period. Competing with it was *Janice Meredith* by Paul Leicester Ford, already well known for his *Honorable Peter Stirling*. This frilly tale described a Tory heiress coquetting her way through the Revolution, incidentally encountering Washington, Hamilton, and other patriot leaders, as well as some 275,000 book buyers during the years from 1899 to 1902.

Observing these successes, Talcott Williams, a leading journalist, in 1900 declared that 'subject has become the decisive factor' in attracting a public to historical romances and since the country was 'in for a new series of centennials which mark the post-Revolutionary epoch, I predict that in the next decade the success of a popular novel will be made on that narrower selvage of history which began with the Western march.' The prophecy was a good one, confirmed that very year by Maurice Thompson's *Alice of Old Vincennes*, a novel dealing with George Rogers Clark's campaign in the Old Northwest. In 1901 Winston Churchill again turned up with a popular romance, *The Crisis*, featuring the descendants of Richard Carvel in St. Louis during the Civil War, the hero fighting for the Union, the heroine an ardent rebel. For four months *The Crisis* led all books in sales. By late summer 320,000 copies were in readers' hands; the book still appeared on the best-seller lists a year later, and eventually more than a million copies were sold. In 1902 came Emerson Hough's *The Mississippi Bubble*, about John Law's adventures among the Iroquois in New France and his fantastic speculation in the lands of the Louisiana Territory. The year 1903 was a quiet one for the historical novel but in 1904 George Rogers Clark was on the march again, this time turning up in Winston Churchill's *The Crossing*, a romance about the settling of Kentucky. Not so popular as his earlier works, *The Crossing* was Churchill's last full-blown historical romance, though his later books still had a great following and for a few more years other tales of earlier America had plenty of readers. There was, for example, Thomas Dixon's flamboyant *The Clansman*, which is said to have sold 40,000 copies during ten days in 1905, for despite inept writing its sympathetic picture of the Ku Klux Klan stirred great discussion. Even as late as 1909 Emerson Hough reappeared on the best-seller list with 54-40 *or Fight!*, a romantic tale of the Oregon boundary dispute. But the vogue for James Lane Allen's type of fiction was almost over, and in the year of Hough's last success the humorous magazine *Life* published this epitaph:

> Mix Metaphors, and while the sun still shines
> Make hay with highly sentimental dames;
> The public favor suffers quick declines;
> 'Tis a long lane that has no turning, James.

If James Lane Allen's day was done, his sentimentalism, high idealism, enthusiasm for the noble simplicity of homely characters, and backwoods setting continued popular when taken out of costume and moved to isolated districts of the present day. From Graustark there had been no more distant or enchanted principality to go to, but from Churchill's or Allen's eighteenth-century Kentucky it was an easy trip to the backwoods or small towns of contemporary America, a pleasant reassurance that pioneer values still survived in out-of-the-way regions.

Novels about simple country folk vicariously satisfied many Americans yearning for the rural ways they had left in searching out a living in the big cities. Such fiction also pleased urban-bred people who shared the common American belief that the country somehow created purer, happier lives. For a few hours, the standardized anonymity of New York, Chicago, and other metropolitan centers could be put out of one's mind by reading about the wholesome friendliness of small-town life. The drab constrictions of housekeeping in a flat could be forgotten through pages describing the spaciousness of farm homes with their husking bees and quilting parties. Homesickness for a neighborly world where people used first names not only made the rural novel a best seller but in 1905 was coupled with big city salesmanship to establish the first Rotary Club in Chicago. Though 1905 was also the founding year of the I.W.W. and the publication date of Jack London's *War of the Classes* and Daniel De Leon's *Socialist Reconstruction of Society,* it was Rotary and the rural novel that attracted most people. The socially conscious Americans who planned to improve the cities were far fewer than the gently discontent who dreamed of a better life close to nature and the folksy ways of the country. Muckrakers might startle people with their exposés of corruption in politics and big business, but a book like Lincoln Steffens's *The Shame of the Cities,* published in 1904, could not compete with such fiction as that year's best sellers, *The Little Shepherd of Kingdom Come* and *Rebecca of Sunnybrook Farm.*

The most popular of the country novels was Edward N. Westcott's *David Harum,* published toward the end of 1898. Though its rural setting was anticipated by *The Jucklins,* Opie Read's story of the Carolina back country, which was widely sold on trains and newsstands in cheap paperbound editions, Westcott was the primary inspiration for later stories of country life. He established the pattern others were to follow: the generally romantic atmosphere was tempered by a realism of the b'gosh sort, the leading character was a quaint eccentric possessed of a simple ingenuity expressed in homely philosophy, and the kindly though shrewd country folk, unlearned and commonsensical, were capable of solving problems that beset the more sophisticated city people.

Properly subtitled 'A Story of American Life,' *David Harum* radiated a warm optimism expressed in pithy statements that people were soon quoting everywhere, like 'A reasonable amount of fleas is good for a dog—they keep him f'm broodin' on bein' a dog.' For some while it was hardly possible to hold a civil conversation without using one of the salty apothegms of the Yankee horse trader, although some people preferred the rich brogue and skeptical comments on the current scene derived from Finley Peter Dunne's Irish saloon keeper, Mr. Dooley, whose shrewd humor appeared in a series of books that began coming out in 1898. The urban and therefore more caustic Dooley was sometimes issued in first editions of 30,000 copies, but not one of the books in which he appeared could rival the rustic *David Harum.* Six publishers had refused Westcott's novel, one contending that 'it's vulgar and smells of the stables,' but the public loved it and made the horse-trading David into a folk hero, a kind of latter-day Benjamin Franklin of upstate New York. *David Harum* established one popularity record after another: by 1899 it was in its sixth printing and it stayed on top of the best-seller list for eight consecutive months, occupying lower places for at least another year. By February 1901 over 400,000 copies had been sold (some in a de luxe edition priced at $10) and three years later the number of sales was up to nearly three quarters of a million.

Westcott died just before *David Harum,* his only novel, was published, but there were plenty of authors ready to cultivate the general field he had opened. In 1900 came Irving Bacheller's *Eben Holden,* a favorite of that year and the next, which within nine months reached a circulation of 250,000 copies. Though set in the time of the Civil War and introducing Lincoln and Horace Greeley in the established fashion of historical fiction, the book centered on the resourceful New England hired man Eben, celebrated for his pointed anecdotes and his shrewdness in conducting the affairs of his employers. While *Eben Holden* was slacking off from its sale of 9,000 copies a week, Bacheller's *D'ri and I* came out in 1901 with an advance sale of 65,000, its purchasers presumably pleased because this story also dealt with a character noted for his backwoods wit. The years after Bacheller's successes were marked by the popularity of two very different novels, each distantly related to the Westcott type. The first was Owen Wister's *The Virginian*, published in 1902. Set in the western cattle country that was being made romantically popular by the author's friend President Roosevelt, the locale precluded the humorously shrewd comments of *David Harum* or *Eben Holden*, but allowed for another kind of quotable colloquial expression, of which the most famous was 'When you call me that, *smile!*' The novel was also in the prevailing vogue to the extent that it featured a single eccentric character, the cowboy known only as 'The Virginian,' who though illiterate is pure in heart; it had the basic appeal of removing the city-bred reader to the open country, the land of the 'strenuous life' currently being celebrated by the President. *The Virginian* topped the best-seller list during its year of publication and for five months in 1903, by which time it had sold more than 300,000 copies. In the latter year John Fox's *The Little Shepherd of Kingdom Come* was published, immediately appearing on the best-seller list and staying there well into 1904. Its events take place during the Civil War, but the novel is less historical than regional, concentrating upon the unusual though simple life of a Cumberland Mountains settlement and the close family feelings that extend even to the orphan boy who is the novel's hero.

Booth Tarkington was another writer who dealt with the life of the small town. Though he wrote many novels, Tarkington attracted a following mainly through such works as *The Conquest of Canaan*, the story of a prodigal son in a small Indiana town, and a trilogy about the coming of industrialism to the Midwest—*The Turmoil, The Magnificent Ambersons,* and *The Midlander*. With well-observed details he evoked a way of life already faded, concerning himself with the problems of modern standards impinging on the old. Explaining Tarkington's popularity, Grant Overton found he 'believes in all those things which make up the creed of the average, sane, wholesome person in this country.' His first novel about political corruption was quickly followed by historical romances—*Monsieur Beaucaire,* set in eighteenth-century England, and *The Two Vanrevels,* dealing with nineteenth-century America. Tarkington then proceeded to the novel of small-town life, continuing to help the public escape into the past through his later popular successes, *Penrod* and *Seventeen,* charming studies of childhood days.

Somewhat nearer to the classic formula of *David Harum* was Joseph C. Lincoln's *Cap'n Eri,* whose following in 1904 was, however, not comparable to that of *The Little Shepherd of Kingdom Come* or *The Virginian.* This loosely contrived novel was essentially a presentation of its main character, a wise old Down East seadog marked by a salty humor and a wholesome, hearty attitude toward life. Like other popular portrayals of Yankees, *Cap'n Eri* showed none of the repressions that marked Edith Wharton's *Ethan Frome,* a study of New England character that had but a small following when issued in 1911. Howells wrote to Mrs. Wharton, 'What the American public always wants is a tragedy with a happy ending'; if she did not furnish the proper ending and Lincoln did not present enough story or sufficient pathos, his book came far closer to satisfying the general taste. Declaring he had no interest in 'the sex problem, the divorce question, and all that sort of thing,' which he felt might better be left to the 'specialist in nervous diseases,' Lincoln's credo was approximately that of the widest reading public: 'There's enough sorrow in this world without finding it in books.'

The cheery view of life animating these novels of rural life became soggy with happiness when women began to try their hands at the new genre. Women have always been the great readers of fiction in America and nearly every novel has had to appeal to them to be successful, but in only a few periods have the popular novels been written mainly by women and for women. Syrupy pathos, sentiment, and optimism then flourish until the reader is drowned in tears or scorched in the sunshine of gladness. The writers and readers of the new happiness novels were often the women who, as little girls twenty years before, were steeped in the long series of *Elsie Dinsmore* books, Harriet Lothrop's *Five Little Peppers,* and the seventy-five books of Isabella Alden's 'Pansy' series, which according to Mary Austin reveal more of the culture of the 'eighties than could otherwise be described. Mid-nineteenth-century morality hung over these new books and into them seeped the attitude of mind of such domestic novels of the 'fifties as *The Wide, Wide World,* still circulating in libraries and cheap reprints. Though the readers were young in mind (often rightly so, because these new books were as popular with teen-agers as with adults), the frame of reference was as old as Queen Victoria.

The first of these feminine novels to show how happiness grows out of adversity was Alice Hegan Rice's *Mrs. Wiggs of the Cabbage Patch,* published in 1901. Despite its bucolic title, the story was set in the suburban slums of Louisville's factory district. The book compensated for its lack of the rural touch so popular in those days by an unfailing emphasis on optimism, The very first words of the novel, 'My but it's nice and cold this morning! The thermometer's done fell up to zero,' was a statement that Mrs. Wiggs made cheerfully, for in her life the thermometer always fell upwards. Further along the first page, the reader learned that 'the substance of her philosophy lay in keeping the dust off her rose-colored spectacles,' a job that might have been difficult for any other widow trying to rear a family of five children amid hardships and dire poverty. But Mrs. Wiggs, a gay and courageous women who talked in phrases at once tender and shrewd, had such buoyant enthusiasm that she solved not only her own problems but those of the wealthy benefactors who interested themselves in her case. In the end she could conclude, 'Looks like ever' thing in the world comes right, if we jes' wait long enough,' a point of view that heartened innumerable readers faced by difficulties less arduous than hers.

Although published quietly in an edition of 2,000, *Mrs. Wiggs,* really no more than a novelette, soon attracted a following that had the Century Company's presses turning out 40,000 copies a month. The book was on the best-seller lists for two years, and in its dramatized form ran for seven seasons, sometimes with three road companies playing simultaneously. Finally even the residents of the real Cabbage Patch found good luck coming their way: the original site of Mrs. Rice's tenement town enjoyed a real-estate boom when some enterprising publicists of Louisville built new cottages and arranged stop-over privileges for trains carrying tourists who wanted to gawk at the original of Mrs. Wiggs herself.

While *Mrs. Wiggs* was still on the best-seller list she was joined in 1903 by *Rebecca of Sunnybrook Farm,* a novel by Kate Douglas Wiggin. The poor but precocious young heroine carried on her conversations without the homely adages common to David Harum and Mrs. Wiggs, but she was quite as much an individual in her own right, and almost as beloved by readers, young and old. Schoolgirls liked her better than Mrs. Wiggs, because the tone was more juvenile, as was appropriate to a work by a kindergarten teacher already known for *The Birds' Christmas Carol*, a perennial favorite of the Christmas season. Not a child of the slums as Mrs. Wiggs's offspring were, Rebecca met all the other requirements of the prevailing vogue: she knew quite as much adversity as could be expected of one so young; her mother was widowed and poor (a necessity in fictional parenthood of the day); and Rebecca herself lived on a farm, moving among quaint village neighbors with unending good humor. Though readers confused this novel by a Mrs. Wiggin with Mrs. Rice's novel about a Mrs. Wiggs, neither was crowded out of sales, for the public heart was big enough to welcome two such happy books and on top of them to take another by Mrs. Rice, *Lovey Mary*, a short-lived but great success in 1903, which the author contended had 'the largest advance sale of any book of the year.'

The year that *Rebecca of Sunnybrook Farm* and *Lovey Mary* were published, and while *Mrs. Wiggs* was still on the best-seller list, another sentimental novel appeared by a woman whose fiction was to outsell that of any of her sister novelists and perhaps to outsell all of them combined. This was Gene Stratton-Porter's *The Song of the Cardinal*. Though the spirit and the title recalled James Lane Allen's *A Kentucky Cardinal*, issued almost a decade earlier, this story of a farmer who loved nature and of the life of a pair of birds was completely original, a result of the author's intense love of the outdoors and the amateur naturalism that led her to constant prowling after haunts of birds, moths, and bees. Mrs. Porter wrote fiction based on her own interest in collecting what she called 'specimens' of nature—such as eggs, feathers, herbs, and wildflowers—thereby extending the popularity of the novel with a rural setting by bringing to it the interest in nature lore growing up under President Roosevelt's publicity about conservation, and the nonfictional studies of wild life written by such men as John Muir, John Burroughs, Dan Beard, and Ernest Thompson Seton. Even more sentimental, idealistic, and cheery-minded than the women novelists who preceded her, Mrs. Porter combined the qualities for which a large part of the reading public was searching. Her second book, *Freckles*, issued in 1904, brought her that public and she kept it for twenty years as she went on writing best seller after best seller, accumulating some $2,000,000 in royalties.

Freckles, the story of a young boy who believes himself to be an orphan but is eventually found by his wealthy father, was set in the Limberlost Swamp of Indiana, where the waif grows up close to nature, drawing inspiration from the ways of insects, birds, and animals, and enjoying the beauty of flowers and trees. The book was not a great success immediately but began to attract readers when reissued in 1910 after the publication of its companion piece, *A Girl of the Limberlost,* the story of Freckles' friend, Eleonora, who hunts the swamps for moths, which she sells to obtain money for an education. Both novels found their public mainly through fifty-cent reprints, indicating that Mrs. Porter was the favorite of people who did not patronize new-book stores, read reviews, or come of the economic level that tends to make for sophistication.

Judging by the fan mail that her daughter published, a great part of Mrs. Porter's public was on the fringe of poverty, composed of men and women who had encountered troubles, who could not keep jobs, or who appeared to be congenitally created to attract difficulty. The Gene Stratton-Porter books seemed to lift up the downcast, giving a passing sense of courage to go on after the readers should get out of the sanitariums, the reform schools, the hospitals, and the prisons from which they often wrote. Through the Limberlost novels these people were taken out of the ways of man, where they had found grief, into the world of nature, which was made to seem arcadian; and they were carried back to childhood, which appeared peculiarly idyllic by comparison with their maturity. Children read these books too, but mainly they were the printed daydreams of people mature in age if not in taste and sentiment. Wherever they came from, Mrs. Porter's public had plenty of fifty-cent pieces; in five years the reprint edition of *Freckles* sold almost 700,000 copies and *A Girl of the Limberlost* did nearly as well.

As the years passed, Gene Stratton-Porter was more than merely another novelist; she was an American phenomenon, 'a public institution, like Yellowstone Park,' as William Lyon Phelps said. Though she complained of her bad critical reception and declared that she was writing with maturity 'a more deeply searching and a more highly polished brand of English,' and that for her natural history 'in Norway or Sweden I would have earned a Nobel prize,' she could not object to the popular reception of her novels. *The Harvester,* published in 1911, was the first of her works to deal with adults and the first to sell many copies at the regular price of a standard novel; two years later came *Laddie,* a fictionized version of her own childhood in the Limberlost country; in 1915 she published *Michael O'Halloran,* about a little newsboy whose pluck she described with conventional moralizing; and several other novels later appeared on best-seller lists of the year of their publication. These, with her first two books about children in the Limberlost, were her most popular works, the ones that helped compensate for the criticism directed at her. When a reader called *Laddie* 'molasses fiction,' Mrs. Porter could joyfully answer

What a wonderful compliment! All the world loves sweets. Afield, bears as well as flies would drown in it. Molasses is more necessary to the happiness of human and beast than vinegar . . . So I shall keep straight on writing of the love and joy of life . . . God gave me a taste for sweets and the sales of the books I write prove that a few other people are similar to me in this.

She was quite right in her affected understatement about a 'few' other people. The viscous flow of her prose could not cloy a public that feasted on its bright sweetness until she became one of the all-time best sellers of America. By the end of 1946 nearly 2,000,000 copies of *Freckles* had been sold, *A Girl of the Limberlost* was just behind with 1,822,100 copies, and the other popular works all topped a million copies—*The Harvester* with 1,584,000, *Laddie* with 1,530,000, and *Michael O'Halloran* with 1,168,000. All told, her five most popular books sold over 8,000,000 copies, for the most part during her own lifetime, a record not surpassed up to that date by any American novelist whose works were not used in schools.

At this same time, another Mrs. Porter captured an enormous public, though it was largely a juvenile audience that read Eleanor Hodgman Porter's novels about Pollyanna, the girl whose generosity, affection, and almost masochistic cheerfulness gave the dictionaries a new name for 'a blindly optimistic person.' *Pollyanna*, published in 1913 along with Gene Stratton-Porter's *Laddie* and remaining on the best-seller lists with it for two years, was the story of a young orphan sent to live with a prim aunt whose affection she finally won through a constant pretense at gladness. Before the public had even finished with the first book, Mrs. Porter had a sequel on the market. In the year that Van Wyck Brooks was proclaiming *America's Coming-of-Age*, the public was making a best seller of *Pollyanna Grows Up*. That was 1915, when the *Lusitania* was sunk and poison gas was first used in warfare, but a large number of book buyers were busily following the attempts of a mature, or at least older, Pollyanna to bring happiness to a world-weary Boston lady and a poor crippled boy, and finally, best of all, to gladden hearts overseas during a residence in Germany. Evidently a segment of the public still wants to hear about the girl with the 'glad game,' because since Mrs. Porter's death in 1920 her publishers have hired no less than five other women to write sequels, which along with the two original Pollyanna books have accounted for a sale of over 2,000,000 copies.

The two Mrs. Porters were the most popular purveyors of their type of fiction, but they had no monopoly on it. Plenty of other women added to the cheery cycle of stories simpering with delight and mawkish with pathos. Concerned with children or at least young people, the subjects, like the point of view, made them as suitable for girls as for grown women, thereby attracting two publics with a single book. Following the pattern of *Mrs. Wiggs,* the novels were generally short and filled with simple action and easy language—no strain upon either adult or youthful reader. The birth rate of orphan girls was alarmingly high in the popular fiction of this school, for somehow orphans were considered purer in heart and nobler in spirit than children still burdened with parents. They comforted the sick, gladdened the lonely, or patched the romances of others, and as an incidental result generally found love from their elders or perhaps from a boy of their own age. If a parent were left in these novels, it was usually the mother, inevitably poor, self-sacrificing, and intent upon making a happy home. The books that in one way or another fitted into these patterns and achieved great popularity included: Lucy M. Montgomery's *Anne of Green Gables,* almost exclusively a story for girls; Eleanor Abbott's *Molly Make-Believe,* a best seller of 1910 and 1911, telling of a young girl shyly befriending a sick man and winning his love; Kathleen Norris's *Mother,* the story of a girl's realization that her mother endows their simple home with more character and happiness than is found in the luxurious house of the society woman she serves as secretary; and Jean Webster's *Daddy-Long-Legs* and *Dear Enemy,* whimsical stories of orphan girls. A variant upon these themes and the only competitor from overseas was *The Rosary,* by the British novelist, Florence Barclay, a foreign and somewhat more cultivated Laura Jean Libbey. The story of a plain young woman with a marvelous voice who sings Rogers and Nevins's sentimental song to inspire faith in her blind lover, *The Rosary* was the top best seller of 1910, its year of publication, continued popular in 1911, and in reprint after reprint has by now sold well over a million copies. Finally, there was the perennial favorite, Grace Livingston Hill, whose eighty-nine volumes of wholesome romance sold 3,000,000 copies, forming a link between the work of her aunt, Isabella 'Pansy' Alden, and that of Kathleen Norris and Temple Bailey. Such contemporary standards for fiction about girls indicate why the booksellers' wallflowers included only females like *Sister Carrie, Jennie Gerhardt,* and *Susan Lenox,* who were abandoned, but not through orphanage.

While the women were reading such fiction, men had to have novels too. More rugged in setting and subject, but no less sentimental in attitude, the fiction that attracted men was as innocent as that patronized by women. Both were essentially an escape from the complexities of modern life, the women's novels idealizing the far-away time of youth, the men's turning to the distant places of America where people breathed the clean air of plains and mountains under wide skies. Both equated the beauties of nature with purity and the behavior of animals with innocence. The two types sometimes met, as in the stories by Gene Stratton-Porter, but in a literature that avoided sex there was an ironic division of books into those popular with fathers and sons and those favored by mothers and daughters. Possessed of a similar Sunday School morality and employing almost as many clichés of pathos and sentiment as the women's books, the novels written by, and mostly for, men stressed the primitive virtues of vigor and courage and were filled with fighting, adventure, and sport. Early examples of novels more popular among men than women included Ralph Connor's *Black Rock* and *The Sky Pilot,* stories of the Christian influence working among rough western men; Owen Wister's cowboy tale, *The Virginian;* and even such stories of animals as Alfred Ollivant's *Bob, Son of Battle,* which had a success in America unknown in England, where it was first issued. Even novels not specifically addressed to men profited from their interests. John Fox's *The Trail of the Lonesome Pine,* a best seller of 1908 and 1909, like his earlier *Little Shepherd of Kingdom Come,* dealt with the Kentucky mountaineers, but it derived part of its popularity, as did Hough's historical *54-40 or Fight!,* from its appeal to men yearning for freedom and the rugged life.

No single formula emerged for the masculine novel, but Jack London, one of its first popular authors, gave a great impetus to the so-called red-blooded romance. Men and boys who admired President Roosevelt found in London's writing a literary example of Teddy's strenuous life, ingenuously combining, as the President himself did, a zest for reform with an appreciation of the virile use of the Big Stick. When London sent the manuscript of *The Call of the Wild* to his publishers in 1903, they feared 'it is too true to nature and too good work to be really popular with the sentimental public which swallows Seton-Thompson with delight,' but they were quickly proved wrong. The story of a dog throwing off its past as a children's pet and responding to the call of nature as the leader of a wolf pack was not only a *tour de force* in the study of animal psychology, but a perfect symbol of masculine yearning for the primitive. Despite his professed socialism, London's great power lay in pictures of the wild life where human or beast triumphed by rising above the ordinary run. It was this that delighted readers who translated his Nietzschean doctrine into terms of their own lives, dreaming of rugged-individualistic successes that reality did not allow them. It was for such readers that bookstores bought 40,000 copies of London's next novel, *The Sea-Wolf,* before its publication in 1904. Though Wolf Larsen, the superman of this book, went down to defeat, it was more in terms of plot than emotion, and readers came away satisfied, remembering the philosophy of the will to power that was the strong core of the novel. Year after year London turned out stories and novels, the most popular celebrating brute strength in primitive settings; and if he exaggerated when he said he was the world's best-known and highest-paid author, London nevertheless remained a favorite of the school of fiction by and for men.

Other men also wrote novels largely for their own sex and came to the forefront of popularity with fiction about the rough outdoor life, set mainly in the Yukon popularized by London, or on the last frontiers of the Northwestern United States and Canada. Among the most popular authors of this school were Stewart Edward White, Rex Beach, and James Oliver Curwood, all of whom came to prominence just after the opening of the century and made the best-seller lists off and on into the 1920's with new novels, or stayed in high popularity through reprints. The very titles of their works indicate the nature of the books: *The Blazed Trail, The Silent Places, The Rules of the Game* by Stewart Edward White; *The Spoilers, The Barrier,* and *The Silver Horde* by Rex Beach; and *The Courage of Captain Plum, River's End,* and *The Valley of Silent Men* by James Oliver Curwood. By 1926 Rex Beach's publishers were able to advertise that over 3,250,000 copies of his books had been sold, a record probably almost matched by White and Curwood.

The most widely admired of all male novelists was Harold Bell Wright, whose long outpouring of fiction in time surpassed that of Gene Stratton-Porter, not only in number of books but in readers, attracting women as well as men. Wright, a former minister of the Church of the Disciples of Christ, introduced a new note into fiction about the outdoors by bringing to it a simple, muscular Christianity. With a religious doctrine reminiscent of Sheldon's *In His Steps* and Connor's *Black Rock,* an Ozarks setting like that of James Lane Allen and John Fox, or western locales like those of dime novels and frontier fiction, and a style of writing, if it can be so designated, as direct and simple as Gene Stratton-Porter's, Harold Bell Wright unconsciously combined divergent appeals to become a novelist surpassing any of these predecessors in popularity.

Assisted by a mail-order bookseller who became his publisher, Wright's novels were printed in editions larger and more flamboyantly advertised than the works of his competitors who issued from more conventional firms. After two fairly successful novels, *That Printer of Udell's* and *The Shepherd of the Hills,* Wright's third work, *The Calling of Dan Matthews,* was brought out in 1909 in an unprecedented first printing of 100,000 copies. The grandiose publication was warranted, for this story of a minister who finds himself more open to religion living among the plain people of the Ozarks than with his hypocritical city congregation was an enormous success. By the spring of 1910 another 100,000 copies went to press, and they in turn attracted buyers to the earlier novels, which reached sales of more than half a million copies during this period. Having found his market, Wright's publisher issued his next book, *The Winning of Barbara Worth,* in a first printing of 175,000 copies. It was set in the new scene of Colorado and criticized Eastern financiers, showed the difficulties of farming, insisted that a man should be judged by his actions rather than his ancestors, and considered the matter of land reclamation recently popularized by Theodore Roosevelt. The book had as much plot as theme. Melodramatic action and sentimental description carried readers along from the opening-scene discovery of a four-year-old foundling during a sandstorm, through her maturity as a beautiful and noble young woman, her engagement to a member of a rich, aristocratic New York family, and her final acceptance into its elite society when proof is found that she comes from a similar background. More than half a million copies were quickly called for and the book became a best seller of 1911 and 1912.

While *The Winning of Barbara Worth* was still moving into and out of bookstores at an unprecedented rate, Wright published his next book, *Their Yesterdays.* As much tract as novel, *Their Yesterdays* has as hero and heroine two nameless characters, who were childhood playmates in the country and, though later separated in the maelstrom of city life, are ever guided by similar ideals and youthful memories. Having experienced what the author calls the Thirteen Truly Great Things of Life—Dreams,

Occupation, Knowledge, Ignorance, Religion, Tradition, Temptation, Life, Death, Failure, Success, Love, Memories—the man and the woman meet again, finding in one another the realization of their desires. The opening page of this lay sermon is worth notice, not only as a sample of Harold Bell Wright's style but as an illustration of the contemporary quest for a happy past. Only a people unable to let bygones be bygones could make a success of a book that began:

There was a man.
And it happened—as such things often so happen—that this man went back into his days that were gone. Again and again and again he went back. Even as every man, even as you and I, so this man went back into his Yesterdays.
Then—why then there was a woman.
And it happened—as such things sometimes so happen—that this woman also went back into her days that were gone. Again and again and again she went back. Even as every woman, even as you and I, so this woman went back into her Yesterdays.
So it happened—as such things do happen—that the Yesterdays of this man and the Yesterdays of this woman became Their Yesterdays, and that they went back, then, no more alone but always together.
Even as one, they, forever after, went back.

Issued in 1912, *Their Yesterdays* pushed *Barbara Worth* down to sixth place on the year's best-seller list, achieved third place itself, and hung on into 1913. Over the years it sold some 700,000 copies, according to a statement the author furnished to Frank L. Mott. The success of one Harold Bell Wright novel after another is said to have made Doubleday, Page wonder if it could not create a competitor out of Ellen Glasgow, whose *The Deliverance, The Wheel of Life,* and *Life and Gabriella* had been moderately popular. 'Why don't you write an optimistic novel about the West?' a publisher's representative asked Miss Glasgow. Her reply, 'If there is anything I know less about than the West, it is optimism,' left the field still securely in the hands of Harold Bell Wright.

Since a novel by Wright inevitably became a best seller and generally remained on the lists for two years, his publication dates were carefully spaced so that a new book would appear just as the old one was falling off in popularity. This publishing control continued until 1934, and the same sort of stereotyped characters, melodramatic plots, wooden dialogue, and platitudinous preaching about such matters as clean living and hard work appeared in *The Eyes of the World, When a Man's a Man, The Re-Creation of Brian Kent,* and other books generally issued with a first printing of half a million copies. Although declaring he never looked 'toward a place in literature,' Wright firmly established himself in the sociology of belles-lettres, for his first twelve novels averaged a sale of nearly three quarters of a million copies, and the entire nineteen are said to have sold somewhat more than 10,000,000 over a period of forty years.

During the vogue for historical romances, a young New York dentist named Zane Grey tried his hand at a first novel, *Betty Zane*, based on the accounts of an ancestor from frontier Ohio and dealing with the siege of Fort Henry in 1782. Unable to find a publisher, the perservering author printed the work himself and then went on to write about Simon Girty in *The Spirit of the Border*, successfully issued by a large publishing house in 1906. After that, Zane Grey's books were printed as fast as he could write them, a rapid process since he moved from historical research to action-crammed stories of an Old West that existed mainly in his own mind. Fiction varying from the dime novel to *The Virginian* had already dealt with scouts, desperadoes, and cowboys, but Zane Grey made the subject peculiarly his own. In the minds of millions he shaped a myth of the western range involving a stereotyped struggle between ruthless villains and noble heroes unyieldingly faithful to a frontier code of justice in the protection of friends and homespun heroines. Zane Grey's fourth book, *Riders of the Purple Sage*, published in 1912 at the height of the sales of *The Winning of Barbara Worth* and *Their Yesterdays*, was the first of a long series to compete with Harold Bell Wright. Its story of a struggle between Mormons and Gentiles, of a hideaway behind a waterfall, of fast riding and shooting was neither history nor reality, but it was exciting escape literature, a printed daydream for the Walter Mittys of the pre-motion-picture era. When Burton Rascoe asked querulously, 'Do Mr. Grey's readers believe in the existence of such people as Mr. Grey depicts; do they accept the code of conduct implicit in Mr. Grey's novels?', another literary critic, T. K. Whipple, could point out that the questions were irrelevant. 'I no more believe in the existence of such people as Mr. Grey's,' Whipple replied, 'than I believe in the existence of the shepherds of Theocritus; I no more accept the code of conduct implicit in Mr. Grey's novels than I do the code of conduct implicit in Congreve's comedies.' What Whipple found in Zane Grey, and what he suspected others found too, was not only escape but a quick substitute for heroic strength: 'We turn to him not for insight into human nature and human problems nor for refinements of art, but simply for crude epic stories, as we might to an old Norse skald, maker of the sagas of the folk.'

After *Riders of the Purple Sage,* Zane Grey was thoroughly established. Though he had previously made the best-seller lists, beginning with 1917 he was never off them until 1925 (an unequaled record), and even after that his books continued to pile up sales in popular reprints. Most of these novels had the same themes and settings, but occasionally Grey took advantage of topical issues, such as when in *The Desert of Wheat,* published during World War I, he depicted a character killed in a fire set by the German-inspired I.W.W. intent on ruining America's crops. Even though his publishers generally brought out a book a year, they had to ration Grey's tremendous output; the result was that he left reams of manuscripts when he died in 1939, and his novels still appeared year by year. By late 1947 sixty-three novels had been published with a total sale above 19,000,000. This is an all-time record for the sales of a writer of adult fiction not rated as a 'classic' or worthy of school editions, but it works out to an average for each novel far below that of Gene Stratton-Porter and Harold Bell Wright.

The novel of masculine escape reached a new extreme in the search for primitive freedom with the publication in 1914 of Edgar Rice Burroughs's *Tarzan of the Apes.* Almost forty years old, the author had a well-established career of failure in assorted businesses and four years' experience in writing for pulp magazines before his first novel was issued. The fantastic story of a sprig of British nobility orphaned in the wilds of Africa and reared by a race of apes bigger and smarter than gorillas, *Tarzan* seemed indebted to Kipling and H. Rider Haggard, but Burroughs insisted his only inspiration was the story of Romulus and Remus. If his child of nature has founded no culture comparable to Rome, he has surely influenced the minds of countless American boys and men. Not a great success immediately, *Tarzan of the Apes* failed to make the 1914 best-seller list dominated by Harold Bell Wright and Eleanor Porter, but in time the hero has become more famous than Wright's foundling, Barbara Worth, and, though his name is copyright like a patent medicine, it has given the language a new word for brute strength to compete with the weaker Pollyanna.

With the passage of years and many sequels, Tarzan's African adventures (including the finding of a suitable American girl as mate and the birth of his child and grandchild) have become part of modern mythology. In the eyes of contemporary man, huddled in large cities and frustrated by a restrictive civilization, Tarzan was a joyous symbol of primitivism, an affirmation of life, endowing the reader with a Promethean sense of power. As in a folk saga, no one Tarzan story stood out above another, and for this reason no Burroughs book has made any startling publishing record or achieved placement on an annual list of best sellers. It is estimated, however, that about 25,000,000 copies of *Tarzan of the Apes* and its more than thirty sequels have been printed and sold in fifty-six languages. The total published in America may be no greater than that of the work of Harold Bell Wright or Zane Grey, but all these forests of paper (along with their translations into motion pictures, radio programs, and comic strips) have been devoted to the one character Tarzan, a feat unachieved by the hero of any other American novel.

In contrast to novels concerning the free, open life and fiction about the simple ways of farm and ranch, the new century's first decade produced many stories showing the other side of the coin: the American who left the country to make his way in the big city. Novels dealing with the rise of a self-made man through rapacity and questionable business deals were for a limited public, the greater number of people still paradoxically believing in the prevailing ethic of big business while wanting to escape from its results. One novel of the realistic school that had a wide reading was Frank Norris's *The Pit*. It was among the best sellers of 1903 in spite of its iconoclasm, perhaps because Norris's capitalist repents his single-minded pursuit of power and is willing, upon the loss of his money, to face a simple life of hard work in the West. Another popular study of life in the big city of Chicago was Upton Sinclair's *The Jungle*, issued in 1906, but less widely sold than Winston Churchill's *Coniston*, a mild novel of reform published the same year. More discussed than read, *The Jungle* gained notoriety for its shocking incidents disclosing the filthy conditions of meat packing, which prompted an investigation culminating in pure-food legislation. Its depiction of a man falling into a vat of lard to be boiled alive was better known than its description of the way in which an immigrant worker arrives at a belief in socialism. Though Sinclair wanted to change the public mind, he succeeded mainly in turning its stomach. *The Jungle* was one of the few muckraking novels to attract a public that, when it read about the city, usually preferred O. Henry's charming vignettes. William Sydney Porter, as O. Henry was properly named, could not compete with the two Mrs. Porters, but he was nearly as sentimental in endowing the anonymous little people of New York with an air of romance. Turning from the subject of Mrs. Astor's 'Four Hundred' to the larger population memorialized in his collection, *The Four Million,* he told with quiet humor of the pathos, the struggle, the whirligig of fortune encountered by the simple men and women who made up *The Voice of the City.*

As is generally true, the popular poetry of the times employed some of the themes and attitudes of the fiction that was most widely read. Not all the leading subjects of novel writers attracted poets, for there was no popular narrative verse on historical subjects or set in mythical lands such as Ruritania and Graustark. The poem of social protest was also little known, with the startling exception of Edwin Markham's 'The Man with the Hoe,' a rhetorical depiction of workers 'bowed by the weight of centuries,' which was first printed in the San Francisco *Examiner* during 1899 and then swept across the country to be widely quoted for a short time. But the subjects of simple country life, the homely virtues, and the recollections of childhood were popular in verse as well as in prose, even if the favorite poems of the time hardly surpassed in sentiment or technique the lyrics of such popular songs as 'In the Good Old Summer Time' (1902), 'In the Shade of the Old Apple Tree' (1905), 'School Days' (1907), and 'Little Gray Home in the West' (1911). No collection of poems came anywhere near competing with a really successful novel, and even the most popular poets rated far down when included on best-seller lists; for as Don Marquis once said, 'Publishing a volume of verse is like dropping a rose petal down the Grand Canyon and waiting for an echo,' an analogy satisfactorily measuring the decibels of applause for all but a few poets since the days of Longfellow.

The romantic, unctuous verse of Ella Wheeler Wilcox was still widely read around the end of the century, but it was her contemporary, Will Carleton, who anticipated the themes of the period. Carleton, a Middle Westerner, was best known for 'Over the Hills to the Poorhouse,' published as long ago as 1873 in his *Farm Ballads,* but a succession of books and readings kept him before the public well into the twentieth century, and his publisher could boast that ten volumes had sold a total of more than half a million copies. The rural subject matter of Carleton found its most popular versifier in James Whitcomb Riley, an Indiana journalist known for his genial poems in rustic dialect. Beginning in 1883 with *The Old Swimmin'-Hole and 'Leven More Poems,* Riley continued until his death in 1916 to attract a large public through wistful poetry about youth and life on the farm. A quaint, whimsical kindliness and a cheerful attitude of mind, blended frequently with an obtrusive pathos, marked Riley's poetry, a perfect counterpart to much of the fiction of his day. In

1906, Edgar A. Guest, still another Midwesterner combining poetry and journalism, began writing a daily verse for a Detroit newspaper. Collecting the most appealing of these contributions in *Home Rhymes, A Heap o' Livin'* and other books, his works were extremely popular with the people he calls 'folks.' Established as the bard of the breakfast table by his widely syndicated stanzas, even as late as the 1920's Guest's books often sold 300,000 copies in a single year. While Guest was just coming to be known to readers of the Detroit *Free Press,* Robert W. Service was attracting a following with his vigorous poetry about life in the Klondike. *Songs of a Sourdough,* published in 1907 (reissued that year as *The Spell of the Yukon*), and followed in 1909 by the *Ballads of a Cheechako,* delighted a public searching for rollicking tales of the frontier popularized by Jack London, and for a long time it was hard to avoid a rendition in parlor or playhouse of 'The Shooting of Dan McGrew.' The years when Guest and Service were widely read were those that introduced the first volumes of the so-called Chicago School, including Edgar Lee Masters's *Spoon River Anthology* and Carl Sandburg's *Chicago Poems.* As resolutely Midwestern as the popular versifiers, the Chicago poets had no public, for they used the common American idiom without sentiment and were opposed to the meretricious idealism generally equated with poetry; and their free verse lacked the rhyming tags that the public required as distinguishing marks of verse.

In poetry as in prose, the largest reading public of the years between the Spanish-American War and the First World War insisted upon romance. Romance has always been an important element of America's popular literature, for close adherence to fact or the exactitude of a reasoning mind set standards too demanding for a wide, democratic audience. But popular acceptance in this era embraced a romanticism peculiarly anaemic, lacking the spontaneity and humanitarian impulses that characterized the reading matter of some earlier periods. There was, however, no one public admiring only one type of literature. As the number of Americans increased from some 63,000,000 in 1890 to 100,000,000 at the time of our entrance into World War I, it was not uncommon for novels with different subject matter each to have a sale of a million copies. Upton Sinclair, attacking 'Our Bourgeois Literature' in 1904, observed that the contemporary novelist could achieve a following with any subject from 'the olden time, with noble dames and gallant gentlemen dallying with graceful sentiment,' to 'the ways of Mrs. Wiggs, her patient frugality and beautiful contentment in that state of life to which it has pleased God to call her.' The only requisite was that the writer possess a romantic view conforming to the prevailing genteel standards. Confronted by a complex culture, depressed, confused, or yearning for a life happier than sober actuality, the people needed myths and symbols to endow them with strength and joy, and these they often found in the idyls of the printed page.

Chapter 13

The Plastic Age

The shot that was fired at Sarajevo took some time to be heard around the world. In America it sounded like only the beginning of another Balkan squabble. The New York Stock Exchange, forced to close on August 1, 1914, when Germany declared war on Russia, was a more delicate seismograph than the best-seller list, which in 1915 listed as leading authors Booth Tarkington, Winston Churchill, Gene Stratton-Porter, Eleanor Porter, and Zane Grey. Americans in general shrugged their shoulders at what the newspapers liked to call 'saber-rattling.' Even after two years of foreign war and sinkings of American vessels, the public that wanted to go its own way elected a President on the slogan, 'He kept us out of war.' In time, the Zeppelin raids on England, the fiercely militaristic behavior of the Kaiser, and the atrocity stories about Belgian children with hands cut off made an impression on the public mind. As the United States finally moved close to battle, books about the war came into greater circulation; they prepared the public for war and a war-conscious people wanted them.

The first widely read war book was *Mr. Britling Sees It Through* by H. G. Wells. Published in 1916, it found fewer readers that year than the current Harold Bell Wright novel, but by 1917 it led all other books in sales. Wells's novel was a perfect indoctrination for Americans because it showed the ability of an ordinary Englishman to measure up to the times even though he must change his values. The heroic pertinacity of the British contrasted to the barbarity of the Germans was made more immediate by the fact that an American character, observing Mr. Britling's behavior, is no longer able to remain neutral and joins the Canadian Army.

An American who actually did join the British Army provided the next popular book about the war. Arthur Guy Empey's *Over the Top* brought the life of a machine gunner in trench warfare home to the Americans. Advertised as the personal story of 'an American who *WENT*,' the book appeared at the psychological moment of June 1917. Using the slang of the soldier so freely that a thirty-five-page dictionary had to be appended, *Over the Top* vividly describes the drama of fighting and thus had a particular appeal to men of draft age. As the publisher contended, it told 'prospective soldiers pretty nearly what is awaiting them.' The lecture tour of Empey, invalided home but still amply dynamic, also helped attract a public that by January 1, 1918, had bought 350,000 copies. As the advertisements said, *Over the Top* sold 250 copies every working hour over a period of seven months.

The year of America's entrance into the war brought a demand for other war books. *The First Hundred Thousand* by the Highlander Captain Ian Hay was a volume of reminiscences 'straight from the trenches,' which competed with Empey's work among men who wanted to know what battle was really like. May Sinclair's *Tree of Heaven* brought courage and understanding to American women through its story of an English mother who watches the secure lives of her four children interrupted by the war. Both men and women could find amused respite from the horror of battle in Edward Streeter's *Dere Mable*, outrageously misspelled love letters of a rookie who stumbles through all the petty irritations of Army life. Published in April 1918, as millions of men were learning to roll puttees and execute 'Squads Right,' the book found over half a million buyers eager for comic relief. Its sequels, *'Same Old Bill, eh Mable!'* and *As You Were, Bill!* had nearly half as many customers. Robert Service returned to popularity with his *Rhymes of a Red Cross Man*, and there was a temporary demand for verse of high idealism and nobility, particularly 'I Have a Rendezvous with Death' by the American aviator Alan Seeger and 'In Flanders Fields' by the Canadian Captain John McCrae, which became the generation's best-known poems, along with the earlier 'Trees' by Joyce Kilmer, who died in the Second Battle of the Marne.

There were other popular war books too, such as the *Adventures* of the dashing correspondent Richard Harding Davis, Donald Hankey's

A Student in Arms, the several inspirational books by Coningsby Dawson about the glory of a great crusade, and the propagandist *My Four Years in Germany* by former ambassador James W. Gerard, which sold 90,000 copies during one week of October 1917, and eventually reached a sale of 500,000 copies. But, considering how fundamentally the war changed the world, it was a subject of less interest to the American reading public than might be expected. Neither 1914 nor 1915 found a book about or shaped by the war on the over-all best-seller list. In 1916 *Mr. Britling Sees It Through* made the list, but the enemy that most people read about was Jean Webster's *Dear Enemy,* a story of a young girl supervising an orphan asylum. The year 1917 brought books varying from *Over the Top* to *The Plattsburg Manual,* though Wells's story was still the only popular example of the creative imagination touched by the bloody events of the time. The final year of fighting produced a few more novels inspired by the war, none of them selling as well as Zane Grey's *The U.P. Trail.*

A month after the Armistice there appeared the last book whose popularity was shaped by the animosities of the war. This was *The Four Horsemen of the Apocalypse* by V. Blasco Ibáñez, who oddly but ingeniously combined exotic romance with hatred of the Germans. Despite the difficulty of the author's name and his title, the novel was in demand at all bookstores for its picturesque account of the life of wealthy ranchers in the Argentine and in the art studios of Paris, as well as for its vivid descriptions of German atrocities endorsed by an intellectual Prussian distantly related to the alluring Argentinian hero. Competing with novels by Eleanor Porter, Gene Stratton-Porter, and Ralph Connor, *The Four Horsemen of the Apocalypse* was a best seller until March 1920, holding first place over all other books for nine of those fifteen months. In 1921 a motion-picture version swept a new actor, Rudolph Valentino, to stardom. By that time the subjects of battle and the enemy had retreated from the best-seller list to remain away until the very end of the decade. Then in 1929, as the world trembled on the edge of a great postwar depression, the American reading public turned to a bitter novel, *All Quiet on the Western Front,* by Erich Maria Remarque, a former German soldier who provided the last disenchanting statement to a people tired of abstractions like glory and honor.

The first years of peace began to show the effect of the war upon public taste. The 'twenties did not produce many popular books about the combat itself, but one work after another was stamped by the change in interests and values that could be attributed to the war. In 1920 two of the most popular books were Philip Gibbs's *Now It Can Be Told* and John M. Keynes's *The Economic Consequences of the Peace,* interesting to a people surfeited with high ideals and disillusioned by results. The lofty morality and noble international ethics of Wilson were repudiated. Soon it was found that he had not made the world safe for democracy: by 1922 Russia was a Communist state, Italy a Fascist kingdom. Skepticism was growing in America, and the iconoclastic attitude toward former leaders was fed by exposés such as the anonymous *Mirrors of Downing Street, Mirrors of Washington,* and *Painted Windows.* Ugly post-mortems and uglier prophecies were followed by complete revulsion against the war. As F. Scott Fitzgerald said, a new generation found 'all Gods dead, all wars fought, all faiths in man shaken.' The American people wanted to forget the past; if they did not want to make a brighter future, they wanted to enjoy the present.

Ideas that had circulated for some time among limited groups of so-called advanced or intellectual persons suddenly found widespread acceptance in the 'twenties. Their reception was hastened and intensified by the dislocation of the war, but they were not all war born. New standards of conduct, new conventions, new loyalties, new prejudices, and new social relations were fostered by matters only indirectly related to the war. The automobile probably affected the rhythm of America more than the machine gun. In 1906 Woodrow Wilson could declare that automobiles were 'the picture of arrogance of wealth, with all its independence and carelessness.' By 1920 Henry Ford's precise signature was known and admired throughout the country, carried by cars as spindly and practical as their manufacturer. A magazine and newspaper poll of 1923 showed Ford the national favorite for President at the next election. Calvin Coolidge succeeded to the presidency, but the policies of this reasonably accurate facsimile of Ford (minus mechanical aptitude) probably did not shape the nation as much as did the products of the automobile manufacturer.

By the outbreak of war in 1914, Ford had built half a million cars; by 1931 his twenty-millionth car had left the assembly line. In that year there were about a quarter as many automobiles on the highways as there were books in the nation's public libraries. When Robert and Helen Lynd went to Muncie, Indiana, to make a sociological survey of the average American's changing ways, a shrewd resident simply remarked: 'Why on earth do you need to study what's changing this country? I can tell you what's happening in just four letters: A-U-T-O.' The automobile, the Lynds found, had helped do away with such old dicta as 'Rain or shine, I never miss a Sunday morning at church'; 'I don't need exercise, walking to the office keeps me fit'; 'I wouldn't think of moving out of town and being so far from my friends'; 'A high-school boy does not need much spending money'; and 'Parents ought to know where their children are.' For adults the lure of the automobile was so great that it upset the old habit of careful saving, of never buying what cannot be paid for in cash. For children the automobile created new urges for motion and speed, destroying the unity of Sundays and evenings at home. Significantly, the Lynds found that of thirty girls brought into 'Middletown's' juvenile court charged with 'sex crimes,' nineteen were listed as having committed the offense in an automobile.

The automobile was the most dislocating of the new inventions, but others helped change the American mind. By 1920 the motion picture had passed from a curiosity and a cheap form of entertainment at makeshift theaters to a leading national industry. Muncie, Indiana, the Lynds' average town, with a population of 30,000 in 1924, had nine motion picture houses operating from 1 to 11 P.M. every day, all year round. Throughout the nation about 100,000,000 people weekly paid admission to the more than 20,000 theaters showing the latest films. Those who stayed home found entertainment in the phonograph, dancing to the new recordings of jazz, which Paul Whiteman called 'the folk music of the machine age.' Soon the phonograph met competition from the radio, which grew from the earphone and crystal gadgets that boys tinkered with in 1919 to the Queen-Anne-style mahogany-encased superheterodyne sets from whose loudspeakers there poured noise that no family member could escape. The first commercial radio broadcast was made in 1920; by 1930 about 40 per cent of America's families owned at least one radio receiver.

With such inventions and 'improvements,' the idea of an evening of reading, aloud or singly, in the family parlor began to disappear. But if new ways disrupted old reading habits, they brought a demand for books that would explain a new generation. Likewise, the trend toward living in apartments too small for family book collections helped create the modern lending library, a far cry from Franklin's Library Company, for the twentieth-century institution was founded on lack of home space and a recognition that many books were meant for the moment only. The loss of reading time to new forms of entertainment was in great part offset by the creation of a larger public capable of reading. In 1890 less than

6 per cent of the fourteen-to-seventeen-year-olders attended high school; by 1928 the number had jumped to over 41 per cent. This educational preparation was in great part responsible for Chicago's public-library circulation increasing five times as rapidly as its population between 1880 and 1920. The spread of schooling was also reflected in the national production of new books, which was 60 per cent larger in 1929 than in 1920. If economic prosperity affected these figures, the level of education alone was indicated by other statistics: the annual output of new fiction doubled during the 'twenties, and almost half the books withdrawn in 1923 from the Chicago Public Library were novels. Plenty of persons read no more than before (even in Pennsylvania almost four and a half million people had no convenient public libraries, and in Louisiana only two cities had bookstores), but it was estimated that the fictitious average American of the 'twenties bought two books a year, withdrew two from public libraries, rented two from circulating libraries, and borrowed one from a friend, a total of seven volumes annually read by each mature individual.

The books most widely read by Americans during the 'twenties were generally those explaining the times or reflecting postwar dislocations. The psychological effect of 4,000,000 men under arms, half of them abroad, had changed the American mind, as had the failure of those men to find the ideals for which they ostensibly went to battle. The generation had learned that there was no gallantry about trench warfare. It had discovered the product of war was further wrangling, and it had heard former allies call us Uncle Shylock. It had seen familiar forms of government disappear while alien 'isms' arose. In uprisings such as the Seattle general strike, the Boston Police strike, the bombing of J. P. Morgan and Company, and the murders charged to two anarchists named Sacco and Vanzetti, the generation thought it found a Communist menace; Congress passed isolationist laws to limit foreign immigration, and old heroes like Guy Empey proclaimed, 'My motto for the Reds is S O S—ship or shoot.'

The generation saw changes in the social structure, for the war had made a new rich class, a new poor class, and given labor a new status. The times were prosperous, but many who suffered from the high cost of living laughed wryly at the joke about the man without a dollar who was fifty cents better off than before the inflation. The generation also found the status of women altered. Obtaining the jobs from which men had gone marching off to war, women had increased economic independence, which made for increased moral independence. Their escape from home into the anonymity of city life allowed more freedom without fear of social ostracism. Even dress changed as women asserted their independence in clothes not only more comfortable and practical, but as free as their wearers' lives. As the 'twenties advanced, skirts shrank until the knee was bared. In 1913 more than nineteen yards of material were needed for a lady's complete costume; in 1928 no one wanted to be a lady, and seven yards were ample to cover the average woman.

Faced by abnormal conditions, the people swept into office a man who promised a return to 'normalcy,' found him a simpleton surrounded by rascals, but kept his party in power. During a business slump, almost 5,000,000 persons voted for the socialistic LaFollette in 1924, but a nation burning with problems preferred to 'keep cool with Coolidge,' the man who profoundly declared 'the business of America is business.' Contemptuous of their elders, who were held responsible for a world that had gone to war and emerged without peace, the new generation was disillusioned about the past and cynical about the present with its commercial Coolidge. In tones of weariness urgent with vitality, the younger generation shunned the corruption of politics, was disdainful of religion, and sneered at the bleakness of American culture, said to be mass-produced and enslaved by the machine. In vigorously affirmative statements of disillusion, this younger generation defied past ethics as bourgeois, Puritan, or Victorian, terms often considered exact synonyms, all meaning hypocritical. Prohibition was flouted—not only the Eighteenth Amendment but all suppressions sanctioned by genteel tradition, orthodox religion, and conventional morality. Books expressing this new way of life were in demand by those people who wished to share it and by those who tried to understand what had happened to their sons and daughters.

Old books once scorned as indecent or dangerous helped lead the way to the generation's own new books. When in 1918 a popular series of reprints was established with the appropriate name, 'The Modern Library,' its first selection was *The Picture of Dorian Gray*, 'quite naturally' Malcolm Cowley thought. While plainer Americans were enjoying the simple, clean ways of Zane Grey, those who were soon to call themselves 'sophisticated' were hankering toward Dorian Gray's aesthetic life. The paradoxes of Shaw also seeped down to a new public. Though his plays were never widely popular in printed or dramatic form, his iconoclastic satire was the spirit of the age. Books like *Leaves of Grass* and *The Rubáiyát*, formerly enjoyed mainly by advanced coteries, now began to affect the

general mind; and Darwin, never a best seller, was partly understood
by great numbers who bandied his name around in cant phrases jibing
at the Tennessee law against instruction in biology. 'Psychology' and
'Behaviorism' were new terms freely used as people heard of John B.
Watson's theory that humans are governed by certain physiological re-
actions. The theories, or at least the language, of the eminent Viennese
Doctor Freud descended from the clinical sphere to the world of chit-
chat as people learned to pepper and salt their conversation with references to 'libido,' 'neurosis,' 'Oedipus complex,' and 'inferiority complex.'
In the opinion of many young people Freud seemed to make sexual freedom almost essential, for did he not show repressions to be unhealthy and
inhibitions evil? With the blessings of psychology, the sense of sin was
washed clean.

During the first postwar years, established novelists as dissimilar as
H. G. Wells and Mary Roberts Rinehart gave the public stories about
the breaking of old standards, the failure of old beliefs, and the coming
of new mores. In 1918 and 1919 Wells attracted a large public with *Joan
and Peter*, his story of two young people who learn that their guardian's
conventional ideas about education are fatuous and fail to ward off war.
Galsworthy's *The Saint's Progress*, published in 1919, was similarly iconoclastic in portraying a clergyman too spiritual for modern life: as his
standards become more Christian his daughters find them less useful
than their own pragmatic discoveries. In 1919 too, when readers were
presented with John Reed's account of the recent *Ten Days That Shook
the World*, they preferred Mrs. Rinehart's version of *Dangerous Days*,
attracted not only by her story about a spy and a munitions plant but
by the revelation of fast life as led by newly rich Midwesterners. Ethel
Dell's *The Lamp in the Desert*, widely read the following year, compounded the romance of British Army life in Egypt with a flamboyant
story of modern morals, and even Edith Wharton's *The Age of Innocence*
interested a large public in 1920. Though dealing with New York society
of the 1870's, its ironic attitude toward earlier moral standards was an
oblique comment on the contemporary world, which the *Boston Transcript* felt was handled with the same 'yellow pages of fiction' that marked
newer novelists.

The new generation came into its own in 1920 with twenty-four-year-
old F. Scott Fitzgerald's *This Side of Paradise*. This novel was 'a nine
days' wonder with the critics,' as Sidney Howard declared, and its influence was more widespread than its immediate public of 52,000 book

buyers. Capturing the bittersweet mood of jazz-age youth, Fitzgerald's story of world-weariness, cynicism, and sophistication among Princeton-bred youths became not only a model for other writers but for great parts of a public that had never read about the antics of his hero, Amory Blaine. A rash of college novels broke out on publishers' lists, the authors usually indebted to Fitzgerald, sometimes coming to his point of view because they experienced the same ethos. With an almost desperate eagerness youthful readers wanted to be at one with the beautiful and damned, with all the sad young men of F. Scott Fitzgerald. As Aldous Huxley observed, 'Sin, like art, is subject to the vagaries of fashion and the fluctuations of taste,' and Fitzgerald helped new conceptions of good and evil make their way into popular fiction. Where novelists formerly equated nobility with a hero and chastity with a heroine, frank sincerity and honest enjoyment of the moment were now considered the most desirable attributes of young men and women, at least in fiction.

Fitzgerald's new conceptions of hero and heroine were in keeping with the prevailing mood of youth, whose desires were also satisfied through still other types of characters created by an Englishwoman, Edith M. Hull. Her novel, *The Sheik*, on the best-seller lists of 1921 and 1922, portrayed an inexperienced English girl who, during an unchaperoned tour of the desert, is abducted by an Arab chieftan from whom she at first attempts to escape but with whom she later falls passionately in love. Stirred by this exotic romance, girls hid the book under their mattresses, and young matrons peered skeptically over its pages at their husbands listening to the radio. Rudolph Valentino was firmly established as a hero when the motion-picture version provided him with his second starring role, and the book's title added a new word to the language: 'sheik' no longer meant the chief of a tribe or religious body but 'a masterful man of irresistible romantic charm.'

All kinds of books, mostly novels, depicted the new moral standards. Their popularity was generally occasioned by the same urge that on a lower literacy level raised the circulation of Bernarr McFadden's *True Story* magazine from 300,000 in 1923 to 1,500,000 in 1925, and that in 1923 brought financial success to movie versions of O'Neill's *Anna Christie* and *Salomé* starring Nazimova, while Charles Ray's production of *The Courtship of Miles Standish* was a failure at the box office. Among the widely read new books was Robert Keable's *Simon Called Peter*, whose sales were undoubtedly augmented by the ban that Boston put upon it, a stricture that also interested readers in books as varied as

Cabell's *Jurgen*, Lawrence's *Women in Love*, Marks's *The Plastic Age*, Warner Fabian's *Flaming Youth*, and even Joyce's *Ulysses*. *Simon Called Peter* was the story of an Army chaplain who found he could not get the confidence of soldiers until he made himself one with them through disguise, learning thoroughly the life his beliefs would formerly have branded as sinful. Keable's novel had its moment in the sun, to be crowded out by Gertrude Atherton's *Black Oxen*, the most widely read book of 1923, the year that *Babbitt* was published. Mrs. Atherton, herself sixty-six years old, undoubtedly titillated a great many of her contemporaries with the story of a woman of fifty-eight who resumes her youthful appearance and personality through a glandular operation and is so rejuvenated that she attracts proposals from a young journalist and an Austrian prince.

In 1924, as some million young men and women enrolled in colleges and universities, the reading public was shocked to learn of their goings-on through Percy Marks's *The Plastic Age*. Marks, twelve years out of the University of California and then an instructor at Brown, revealed to parents by the hundreds of thousands the campus world that F. Scott Fitzgerald had already exhibited for a more limited public. Marks's own alma mater put *The Plastic Age* in a locked case lest the undergraduates be corrupted by what the author contended was an accurate portrayal of their mores; Boston attempted to keep the book from its stores. From the novel one learned that the so-called 'cream' of American youth was as perplexed and dissipated as any member of Gertrude Stein's 'lost generation,' conversing in language exactly like that of the soldiers who were shocking theater-goers in the current stage hit, *What Price Glory*. The average student, it appeared, came to college 'chock-full of ideals and illusions,' and the beginning of wisdom was to knock these 'plumb to hell'; he was taught by professors that 'every intelligent man with ideals eventually becomes a cynic'; he 'was tortured by doubt and indecision'; 'learned more in the bull sessions than he did in the classroom'; 'often felt older and wiser than his father'; read Omar and Havelock Ellis; declared 'Christianity is just a name, there isn't any such thing'; drank bootleg gin to 'jazz me up'; spent a great deal of time petting, sometimes contracting venereal disease, unless he was merely 'sublimating his sex instincts.' Telling things that the novel's hero contended the students themselves couldn't write home about, *The Plastic Age* was a sensational portrait of the American as a young man, a subject for discussions and recriminations between young people and their elders, a work to be cited in editorials and sermons.

All through the decade there continued to appear novels depicting the new moral codes of a rising generation. In 1924 along with *The Plastic Age* people were reading Michael Arlen's *The Green Hat,* dealing with a worldly society like that of the author's previous *These Charming People,* but having a nymphomaniac's tragic life as its central subject. The next year, Arlen's story of Iris March was forced down the list of popular books, even beneath Gene Stratton-Porter's *Keeper of the Bees,* as 100,000 people began buying A. Hamilton Gibbs's *Soundings,* telling of the frank search for love by a girl reared by her father, an unconventional artist. In 1926 the most popular novel was John Erskine's *Helen of Troy,* the witty story of what happened to this classical problem girl after her return home. In 1927 a respectable Western judge, Ben Lindsey, hit the headlines with his book *Companionate Marriage.* Though Lindsey suggested only that birth control be legalized and that childless marriages be dissolved by mutual agreement, the idea got around that he advocated unions without sanction by clergy, which could be broken any time the partners tired of them. As a term his title was bandied about in drawing-room conversation more than in bookstores. The year 1927 also revived Elinor Glyn's notoriety when she introduced the meaning of sex appeal into the simple article 'It,' the title of a successful movie featuring Clara Bow. In 1928 Viña Delmar's novel *Bad Girl* was a temporary sensation because of its flat reportage of a casual romance that led to marriage and a fully described pregnancy. The last year of the decade brought the publication of Katharine Brush's *Young Man of Manhattan,* a portrait of New York considered far more interesting than the one presented in Dos Passos's *42nd Parallel.* First a *Saturday Evening Post* serial, later a motion picture, her fast-paced novel about the turbulent married life of a sports writer and a movie columnist with its insight into the glamour surrounding newspaper reporters, nightclubs, and studio apartments, delighted a wide public.

Throughout the period a large public found one book after another to give it a sensational acquaintance with the doctrines and attitudes that shaped the less widely read and more serious treatments of contemporary life by Sherwood Anderson, Hemingway, Dreiser, Fitzgerald, and Dos Passos. As Mark Sullivan dolefully remarked, 'Many a father had to tolerate a conversation overheard in the sitting room between eighteen-year-old Nelly and her beau, a conversation which shocked the old gentleman—because a man he never heard of named Hemingway wrote a book he never heard of called "The Sun Also Rises." ' Sullivan might have added that Nelly herself probably had not heard of the author's book, or at least had not read it. Whether the Nellies of the day read *The Sun Also Rises,* learned its values second hand through Hemingway's imitators, or absorbed them by contacts with the life normal to their generation, they assumed an attitude and called it sophistication. James Branch Cabell grumbled that 'oncoming antiquaries, I suspect, will not ever give us sophisticated writers of the 'twenties our due credit for the pains with which we learned to converse in drawing-rooms about brothels and privies and homosexuality and syphilis and all other affairs which in our first youth were taboo,' but without question due credit in the form of sales was given to the sophisticated writers. Of course, the eighteen-year-old Nellies did not read the most 'daring' or most thoughtful books, nor did their parlor conversation extend so far as the discussions in Cabell's drawing-room. But their parents, either curious and troubled or attempting to keep up with the children, included in their own reading diverse writings whose only common denominator was a supposed sophistication. Not only was this worldliness attributed to the novels of such college professors as Percy Marks and John Erskine, but it was also found in humor varying from the pert *Gentlemen Prefer Blondes,* which the author Anita Loos subtitled the 'Illuminating Diary of a Professional Lady,' through the ribald fantasy of Thorne Smith's *Topper* to the crude scatology of Chic Sale's *The Specialist.*

With the revolution in morals accompanied by a contempt for all tradition, so-called sophisticates found it smart to ignore accepted etiquette and enjoyed displaying bad manners ranging from 'gate crashing' to practiced rudeness toward their elders. But at the same time more ingenuous persons who had got rich quickly wanted to become polite with equal speed and found manuals of behavior an efficient shortcut. Lilian Eichler's *The Book of Etiquette,* published in 1921, was one accepted work; but *Etiquette: The Blue Book of Social Usage,* issued the following year in a timorous edition of 5,000 copies, in 1923 attracted more readers than Papini's *Life of Christ* and soon made the name of its author, Emily Post, synonymous with proper manners. Mrs. Post made concessions to changed standards, but in part her appeal undoubtedly derived from the scenes of fiction involving such characters as Mrs. Toplofty, Lucy Wellborn, and Mr. Oldname, who displayed breeding and wealth with a vulgar blatancy that must at once have terrified and titillated eager newcomers to society.

The younger generation's ethic was only part of the subject matter of the times, for the generation against which it revolted was also opened to scrutiny. The very year after the war ended, the most popular book of nonfiction was *The Education of Henry Adams*, a serious and difficult consideration of America's changing culture. It shocked older people and made younger ones reflective when they found a member of the nation's outstanding family, a grandson and a great-grandson of Presidents, declaring that a nineteenth-century education was as useless or misleading to the modern American as his eighteenth-century education had been to the man born in 1838. In Adams the thoughtful reader found both a theory of history and the story of a personality frustrated by the practical temper of America. Men and women disillusioned by the teachings of the past in a world that had just ended a futile war read Adams that year as they read Wells's denunciation in *Joan and Peter* of outworn codes of education, and they queried the values handed down to them. In an era of moral failure and monetary success it was becoming an accepted belief among younger and more liberal-minded readers that the more of financial wealth, the less of cultural. Growing up in an environment of practicality, they questioned whether it was possible to fulfil oneself in a modern America worshiping efficiency and the salesman's success, yet drugged by a rigid code of morality whose values were negative, if not insincere.

Influential as Adams's autobiography was, more people read the novels of Sinclair Lewis because they were simpler in form and idea, were concerned entirely with familiar contemporary scenes, and were boyishly vigorous in their obvious satire. Published in 1920, *Main Street* became the most popular book of the year in which Harding was inaugurated, bringing to all the Main Streets of the nation Lewis's view of the 'village virus': the smug, intolerant, unimaginatively standardized belief that whatsoever the town banker does not know and sanction is heresy, not only worthless to know but wicked to consider. Because Lewis had a remarkable ability to mimic the village idiom and depict the furnishings of a small town, readers accepted his fiction as a sociological survey exposing parochial folly. In its first year the book sold just under 300,000 copies, and it won another 100,000 buyers before going into a cheaper edition. Then Lewis presented his public another satirical novel, *Babbitt*. That was in 1922, while President Harding was declaring, 'If I could plant a Rotary club in every city and hamlet in this country I would then rest assured that our ideals of freedom would be safe and civilization would progress.'

Lewis's portrait of the typical Midwestern real-estate broker, George Folansbee Babbitt, was an ironic answer to the President's desires. This character was a perfect follower of Harding's credo, and though stultified by concepts and values that the President praised, Babbitt's frustrated conformance stamped him forever as a conventional representative of the middle class. Accordingly, though Harding added the word 'normalcy' to the American language, Lewis made an even greater contribution, his hero's surname becoming a new word of scorn in the sophisticated vocabulary of the time, eventually to be enshrined in dictionaries. Lewis continued his attack through the 'twenties in such popular novels as *Arrowsmith, Elmer Gantry,* and *Dodsworth,* the circulation of each of these works surpassing that of an issue of *The American Mercury,* edited by H. L. Mencken, his more boisterous rival for the position of the nation's most popular iconoclast. Finally crowned with America's first Nobel Prize for literature, Lewis was the most solidly established of all the new authors. A survey in 1933 showed that there were 472 copies of his books in the St. Louis Public Library, 310 in the Newark Public Library, and 290 in the Boston Public Library, while at this date the same libraries had respectively only 30, 101, and 3 copies of the works of Hemingway, who had so disturbed Mark Sullivan's Nelly and her father.

Realistic and satirical reappraisal extended behind contemporary America to the lives and times of those formerly accepted as models for behavior or belief. Henry Adams's dispassionate skepticism about his own career may have influenced those who re-examined the past, but it was Lytton Strachey's *Queen Victoria,* published in 1921, which formulated the new style. The urbane irony of Strachey's biography marked the end of Victorianism in writings about famous people, and readers rushed to buy what a critic called 'a grand, gossipy book telling about the domestic life of Queen Victoria,' for they enjoyed seeing her as a human being removed from her pedestal. Issued with a run-of-the-mill printing of 6,500 copies, the book had by the end of its first year sold 50,000 copies and in reprints found 150,000 buyers by 1927. Such success inevitably produced followers, some of them enlarging on Strachey's delicate use of the imagination either by psychoanalyzing their subjects or filling out known actions with fictional assumptions about unrecorded days and nights. Among the best sellers thus created were André Maurois's *Ariel* about Shelley, and E. Barrington's *Glorious Apollo* about Byron, the former listed as nonfiction, the latter as fiction, though there seemed little reason for such division. In this favorable climate, Gamaliel Bradford, long a practitioner of what he called 'psychography,' at last achieved a popular audience in 1923 with *Damaged Souls,* studies of Americans as diverse as P. T. Barnum and Aaron Burr. Strachey's attitude toward a respected historical figure and his new techniques were soon debased by a school of so-called debunking biographers, more invidious and less graceful than their master. Throughout the decade writers made a reputation on their ability to beard dead lions, some even giving a further twist to the tale by friendly treatment of figures like Lucrezia Borgia, Henry the Eighth, or even Al Capone.

The novel and the new biography (only a shade removed from fiction) reflected and sometimes abetted or even initiated the decade's reversal of values. Accustomed to think of books as sources of knowledge, Americans seemingly felt that if some volumes disturbed the mind, others could put it at ease. Accordingly, to balance the interest in books revealing changed attitudes and beliefs, there was a demand for solid studies of the causes of the change. The war had interested people in books about history and current events, preparing the way for works that related the present to the past. As a world power the United States was trying to find its place in the stream of history, and as a national problem one generation was trying to find its relation to another. In an era of flux many people thought they might find their bearings by reading the two fat volumes of Wells's *Outline of History.* Already respected for his surveys of modern life in *Mr. Britling Sees It Through, Joan and Peter,* and *God the Invisible King,* the name of H. G. Wells and the sight of his bulky volumes seemed to promise explanation. For two years—1921 and 1922—his new book led all nonfiction in sales, its price declining from $10.50 to $5.00 as its popularity mounted. Although plenty of Americans agreed with Ford that 'History is bunk,' they bought Wells's book as though mere ownership would impart knowledge, even if they got mired somewhere around page 118 with the flooding of the Mediterranean valley. But *The Outline of History* was not enough to sate people's desire to understand the past in order to cope with the present, and the public went on in 1922 to make a best seller of Van Loon's syncopated *Story of Mankind* and in 1923 of James Harvey Robinson's *The Mind in the Making.* Throughout the decade histories continued to flourish, until at its end, while the intellectuals were gloomily reading Spengler's *Decline of the West,* a hopeful public was turning to the Beards' *Rise of American Civilization.*

Paralleling the interest in history was a national concern with science, an all-embracing word for a mysterious subject. Science had not only helped win the war and combat disease as in the recent influenza epidemic, but it had brought into daily use such wonders and comforts as automobiles, radios, and electric irons, and it had made agnostics or atheists of a new generation. 'Is it scientific?' was a new national criterion. To understand the background of history and the bases of modern science would presumably explain the reasons behind recent change. So people bought books about science, some from an earnest desire to find what the new world was all about, some to reinforce their smattering of classroom knowledge, and some merely to appear enlightened or to take comfort in possessing a book of modern faith. The four volumes of J. Arthur Thomson's *Outline of Science* averaged a sale of 10,000 sets a year; Albert Wiggam's *New Decalogue of Science* was widely purchased (even though many buyers must have had the experience of the lady from 'Middletown' who admitted, 'I have tried three times to get into *The New Decalogue of Science,* but I never have time to give to it'); and Lewis's *Arrowsmith* and his collaborator De Kruif's *Microbe Hunters* attracted a following from those awed by science.

Many people who did not find ultimate answers in books about science and who could no longer have faith in religion turned to popularizations of philosophy. Will Durant's smooth synopses written for Haldemann-Julius's Little Blue Books were collected in a single volume priced at $5 and entitled *The Story of Philosophy.* At a price that promised edification and with a title that assured fictional treatment, the book was a great success, selling some 100,000 copies within a year and paving the way for a sequel, *The Mansions of Philosophy.* Some readers in search of a modern philosophy bought Walter Lippmann's *Preface to Morals,* but more looked upon the well-publicized Abbé Dimnet as a modern sage, for his *Art of Thinking* held out not only solace but the promise of success. Oldsters, still trusting to the family physician, turned to the several books of Dr. Joseph Collins bearing such titles as *The Doctor Looks at Love and Life.*

An era troubled in ethics but secure in the pocketbook failed to make a best seller of any popularization of economics, a science too dismal even for the newly enfranchised women who purchased Shaw's *Intelligent Woman's Guide to Socialism and Capitalism,* possibly more flattered by the title's adjective than interested in the subjects described by its two concluding nouns. Women were responsible for a great part of the sales of books on philosophy, and they were an even greater aid to authors who wrote about psychology or new theories concerning the subconscious. With Josephine Jackson and Helen Salisbury, women readers in 1922 learned how to go about *Outwitting Our Nerves*, meanwhile entrusting their bodies to Lulu Hunt Peters's *Diet and Health*, a perennial best seller guaranteed to provide both euphoria and a fashionably slender waistline. At the Mah Jong tables women spoke as glibly of complexes as of calories. For a moment in 1923 psychic and physical disorders were considered equally curable by the new theory of a wizened French doctor named Emile Coué who opened a clinic in New York, gave a series of well-publicized lectures, and saw his book on *Self-Mastery Through Conscious Auto-suggestion* become a feminine fad as ladies throughout the nation solemnly reiterated 'Every day in every way I am getting better and better.' The next year they had got well enough to forget Coué, but the fad for diluted Freud still continued. In the typical Midwestern settlement of 30,000 people that the Lynds called Middletown, the sociologists in 1924 found 250 women thronging lectures on 'How We Reach Our Sub-Conscious Minds,' 30 of them willing to pay $25 extra for a course of 'definite psychological instruction for gaining and maintaining bodily fitness and mental poise and for building personality.' It is not surprising that in 1926 a good many readers, including men, were making a best seller of George A. Dorsey's *Why We Behave Like Human Beings*.

Neither science nor psychology satisfied the demands of all the people. Freed by mechanical devices—autos, radios, motion pictures, and airplanes—many persons discovered that these contrivances but confined them the more to materialism, and they looked for spiritual liberation. During the war many bereaved families had found solace in spiritualism, some turning in all seriousness to ouija boards, and some accepting the beliefs of the well-known scientist, Sir Oliver Lodge, whose *Raymond* recorded spirit messages received from a son killed in battle. While Douglas Fairbanks was cheering folks with his *Laugh and Live*, readers were flocking with the same enthusiasm to Wells's *God the Invisible King*, describing what the author called 'a heartening God but not a palliating God.' Though both of these works were unorthodox, their essence was spiritual. This war-born heritage, aggravated by the new generation's revolutionary morals and hostile endorsement of science, led many older people to search for a way of salvation that would give greater meaning to life. In great part it was this yearning that

brought popularity to A. S. M. Hutchinson's novel *If Winter Comes,*
portraying a whimsically idealistic Englishman before and during the
war, his character chastened to a Christ-like degree as he meets current
social problems. William Lyon Phelps, the great book booster, declared
Hutchinson's tale 'a spiritual force,' and by merely saying so he helped
make it that for the many Americans who in 1922 bought more copies
of it than of any other new novel, including *The Sheik.* More definitely
spiritual was the new *Life of Christ* by Giovanni Papini, which dec-
orously but informally presented Jesus as a human, drawing a tacit
parallel between His world and the present day from the birth in
the manger ('What is the world but an immense stable where men
produce filth and wallow in it?') to the agony in the garden and the
crucifixion. Listed among the 10 most popular books of nonfiction for
three years beginning with 1923, Papini's work eventually sold 250,000
copies. An even more widely read but far less reverent treatment of
Christ's life was Bruce Barton's *The Man Nobody Knows,* which reconciled religion and modern morality by reducing the former to the
latter, creating a Gospel according to the times of Coolidge, and a
Saviour for supersalesmen. Barton's Jesus was a rugged outdoor man,
a go-getter dedicated to service, a creator of slogans, a great ad-
ministrator, in short, the best businessman ever, who 'picked up twelve
men from the bottom ranks' and with them built up a sweet-running
'organization that conquered the world.' *Ecce* Efficiency!

Barton's conception of Jesus was liked because it was as contemporary
as the bull market in stocks, as evangelical as an advertising agent, and
in accord with the tastes and standards satirized in *Babbitt.* But in
this pliable era when values that were newest were generally accounted
best, many people still yearned for old-fashioned decorum and dignity.
Shocked by the prevailing cynicism of the jazz age, rebuffed by the
bleakness and incomprehensibility of science, disturbed by man's loss
of nobility to probing biologists and psychologists, there was still a
large public that was proud to purse its lips and declare it was of another
school of thought. Its readers kept Harold Bell Wright, Gene Stratton-
Porter, and James Oliver Curwood on the best-seller lists year after year,
cherishing the simple but tried values of heroism and honesty, of idealism and decency, of manliness and morality. It was this public that
made Irving Bacheller's *The Light in the Clearing* the most popular
novel of 1917 next to *Mr. Britling Sees It Through,* for this study of
an early New York governor's sturdy principles had, as Bacheller's biog-

rapher said, 'light in the story—the light of character.' In 1920 this
public made Bacheller's tale of Lincoln's youth, *A Man for the Ages*,
rank just below novels by Zane Grey, Peter B. Kyne, Harold Bell
Wright, and James Oliver Curwood, and it soon pushed a reprint edition to almost 130,000 copies. In the same year, people in quest of
simple values were buying Cornelia Stratton Parker's *An American
Idyll*, telling of the author's comradely marriage to a professor with
high ideals; and from 1922 through 1924 they likewise kept on the best-
seller lists *The Americanization of Edward Bok*, a story of an immigrant's achievements in this land, which was awarded the Pulitzer
Prize as the biography best 'teaching patriotic and unselfish services.'
Edna Ferber's *So Big*, the most widely read novel of 1924, appealed
to those who were shocked or grieved by *The Plastic Age*, its nearest
contender. Marks's story of a boy who disgraces his mother when
expelled from college for contracting syphilis was offset by Miss Ferber's
tale of a boy whose achievements as an architect justify his mother's
sacrifices to educate him.

Most of the novels celebrating traditional values had an American
setting, but the stout character of Britons and Canadians was also held
up as a model and, through snob appeal, sometimes considered worthy
of emulation because they were British. In 1926 and 1927, when *The
Private Life of Helen of Troy* and *Elmer Gantry* were respectively the
most widely sold books, many Americans were reading Warwick Deep-
ing's *Sorrell and Son*, in which an Englishman impoverished by the war
accepts a menial job that his son may have money for the education
which makes him a gentleman and a doctor. This story of the warm
sympathy between two generations and the respect each pays the other's
beliefs heartened many Americans whose headlines those years related
young and old only through such events as the scandalous marriage of
'Peaches' and 'Daddy' Browning or the news of a San Francisco girl
who killed her mother for denying her the chance to go dancing. There
was assurance to be found too in Galsworthy's *Forsyte Saga*, depicting
England's conservative gentry in a time of reversal of beliefs; in Mazo
de la Roche's *Jalna*, about three generations of a Canadian family
ruled by a strong-willed matriarch; and in Louis Hémon's popular idyl,
Maria Chapdelaine, telling of the simple French-Canadian farm girl
who marries a neighbor instead of the American who offers 'all sorts
of contrivances you never heard of to save you labour.'

The desire of the older generation for a young people with the fundamental virtues attributed to earlier America found its answer one May evening of 1927 as Lindbergh landed his plane at Le Bourget airfield. In this clean-cut, simple, modest Midwestern boy, who hailed from the very town that served as the model of *Main Street,* all America suddenly discovered a hero in the much-rebuked younger generation. Here was a young man who was courageous instead of commercial, dignified instead of defiant or degenerate, and yet who obviously understood his generation's god of science. Moreover, his transatlantic flight seemed to symbolize mechanization as a means of bringing people closer together. In quick response to public sentiment, President Coolidge sent a cruiser to bring Lindbergh home, commissioned him a colonel, and awarded him the Congressional Medal of Honor, and the rest of the nation in its various ways attempted to heap its most cherished honors upon him. When later in 1927 he published his autobiographical account, entitled *We* with suitable modesty, it naturally appeared immediately among the best sellers, where it stayed throughout 1928. Well over half a million copies of the book were sold, earning the aviator-turned-author some $100,000 in royalties, far less than the sums he had refused for many undignified schemes to capitalize on his dramatic flight.

Pre-eminently Lindbergh represented the achievement of wholesome youth, but for many he was also the god of romance lifted rather than crushed by the machine. Throughout the postwar years, Americans felt themselves stultified by the efficient mechanized uniformity of the prevailing culture. Many escaped through the ways they had learned from a younger generation, which often consisted of a mixture of two parts bootleg gin to a dash of pure and applied science. But others still turned to the traditional refuge of daydreaming about exotic lands and the days of derring-do when swords flashed in rescue of beautiful highborn maidens. Though the era's great motion-picture actors were such lovers as Valentino and John Gilbert, Douglas Fairbanks had an enormous following too, and such films as *Foolish Wives* and *Our Dancing Daughters* were balanced by *The Black Pirate* and *The Gaucho.* Readers of books likewise turned sometimes to romantic adventure stories for vicarious release.

Joseph Conrad for the first and only time appeared on the lists of American best sellers in 1919 with his *Arrow of Gold,* the lush romance of a sailing captain who aids a Bourbon pretender to the Spanish throne, and though the *Boston Transcript* found the novel 'rather shoddy stuff for a writer of Conrad's caliber,' there were plenty of readers who wanted such stories. The next year they formed a public for Frederick O'Brien's *White Shadows in the South Seas,* a picturesque travel account preparing an audience for Somerset Maugham's *The Moon and Sixpence,* which sold close to 100,000 copies within six months. Thanks to Maugham, young men could vicariously dally with Gauguin maids under the shade of banyan trees, as girls were dreaming of Edith Hull's Sheik. While many serious novels were showing man shaped by his social and cultural environment, the men themselves preferred light fiction through which they could escape to a world in which heroes shaped their own circumstances. This was the world of Rafael Sabatini, whose first romances—*Scaramouche* and *Captain Blood*—started him on the road that led to a new best seller every year from 1923 through 1925, when his work began to be replaced in popular favor by P. C. Wren's *Beau Geste* and *Beau Sabreur,* the latter telling of an American girl rescued by a gallant French officer from Arabs somewhat less savory than Miss Hull's. Only slightly more credible but equally colorful were the autobiographical accounts of Richard Halliburton, *The Royal Road to Romance* and *The Glorious Adventure,* both best sellers of 1927 competing with *We,* though their author was an artificial Lindbergh, a publicity agent's hero. Not too distantly related to Halliburton and popular for similar reasons were Count Luckner, styled the *Sea Devil* in Lowell Thomas's biography; Richard Byrd, the North Pole explorer and author of *Skyward;* Trader Horn, the garrulous oldster who in six months of 1927 told 125,000 book buyers his story of ivory trading in Africa; and the fraudulent Joan Lowell who claimed she had been rocked in *The Cradle of the Deep.*

A very different and far quieter kind of escape was provided by Thornton Wilder's *Bridge of San Luis Rey.* An ironic story of a Franciscan who wished to prove that the destruction of a bridge in eighteenth-century Peru was an act of divine providence, this pseudo-antiquarian work recounted the biographies of the five disparate persons who were plunged to their deaths. The slim book had the urbane manner, gracious gentility, and arch tone associated by devotees of Cabell with sophistication, and yet, as a book reviewer wrote, 'a belief in the miracle of love runs through it all.' Wilder was vehemently attacked by Communists as a leisure-class writer, longing for 'the security, material and intellectual, of a Christian aristocracy,' but in defense Sinclair Lewis observed that the book answered popular needs because its author 'in an age of realism dreams the old and lovely dreams of the eternal romantics.' Within ninety days Wilder's thin novella had sold 100,000 copies, to become the most popular book of 1928, the last full year of an era of extravagance; and the Pulitzer Prize was for the first time awarded to a work of fiction not set in North America.

More conventional escape through fiction was offered in the mystery, intrigue, and spy stories that flourished throughout the decade. E. Phillips Oppenheim and Mary Roberts Rinehart, two popular purveyors, had a new book every twelve months or so, one author or the other being on the best-seller list for half the years of the decade. Mrs. Rinehart alone continued to average an annual sale of 300,000 copies. The desire for a world of easily solved enigmas also helped create another form of diversion in the sudden fad of puzzle books. Combining an appeal to *ersatz* erudition with an evasion of the period's real problems, the *Cross-Word-Puzzle Book* in 1924 entranced a public only recently graduated from Coué. People with only the most nebulous ideas about LaFollette's Progressive Party or the Dawes Plan busied themselves identifying a Greek coin as a drachma or the Roman goddess of war as Bellona. This mental doodling spread over the nation like a nervous disease as cross-word-puzzle collections, both general and specific, found competition from other so-called brain tests like the *Ask Me Another* series, and finally made a kind of folk hero of Robert Ripley, whose collection of esoteric tidbits, *Believe It or Not*, gave a pat phrase to a whole generation.

What could one believe, if anything, in an era marked by disillusion, frustration, cynicism, iconoclasm, and novel panaceas? This was indeed the great question in a plastic age whose elasticity, stretched to a limit, snapped at the end of 1929 as the financial structure was split wide. Symptomatic of what happened to the nation, the popular song of 1928 was 'Making Whoopee,' a tune suddenly changed in the last months of the next year to 'Brother, Can You Spare a Dime?'

Chapter 14

Little Man, What Now?

The spirit of the 'twenties died in the final months of the decade's last year, as though the calendar determined a state of mind and the money that upheld it. In late October 1929, the stock market crashed; before the year ran out, some forty billion dollars in paper profits and real money were lost by people who, a short time before, had called themselves investors. On Wall Street the market registered the severity of the shock; reports from outlying provinces described the widely extended damage. As working capital was destroyed, income thinned out; in a vicious circle unemployed men caused those still employed to lose their jobs. Without salary, the man who was once on a Buick assembly line could buy no new radio, and the man on the RCA work bench lost his job. The nation's income was cut in half between 1929 and 1932. Within six months of the stock market collapse, Milwaukee was operating a municipal soup kitchen; within a year every fourth factory worker in the average town of Muncie, Indiana, was out of work. Soon the unemployed were numbered by millions. For ten long years the number of people dependent on some sort of relief was thought to fluctuate somewhere between 8 and 25 millions. Impoverished families were so common that nobody could provide an accurate count.

Behind the uncertain statistics were human beings haunting employment agencies, saving pennies to buy newspapers for their want ads, making the futile rounds of offices and factories, pawning and selling possessions, cashing in life-insurance policies, and finally retreating to relief agencies provided by a new administration. All along the line, every family felt the pinch of the Depression. Everybody gave up something. Many didn't 'give up'—they simply had things taken from them. At this lowest level were the jobless crowded into makeshift colonies of shacks called Hoovervilles. Above them in economic status came those who, at the rate of a thousand a day in 1933, lost their own homes by foreclosure but could still move in with friends or family to set up a double household. Further up came the middle class that could retain a hold on its house, though to do so might mean surrendering the telephone, foregoing a summer vacation, doing without a maid-of-all-work who used to 'come in' once a week, and abandoning the pleasant habit of dining out once in a while. This was the economic group that had once bought new books; now it found little money for such luxuries.

The pathological loss of confidence in self and society that marked the victims of disaster began to be relieved by the advent of the new President. In Roosevelt the public found a man whose personal conquest of disease symbolically promised triumph over the Depression. His inaugural statement, 'The only thing we have to fear is fear itself,' radiated strength and cheer. National apathy under Hoover gave way to hope as the vibrantly assured Roosevelt moved into action, breaking tradition as he went. For the moment, the Depression seemed to recede in a welter of NRA Blue Eagle parades. While Pecora's investigating committee exposed the malpractices of big bankers during Hoover's days, everybody in 1933 began to hum 'Who's Afraid of the Big Bad Wolf?' Mere action began to look like progress: banks were closed and reopened with greater security, the gold standard was abandoned, farm prices were bolstered by an Agricultural Adjustment Administration, the Federal Reserve system was overhauled, the Reconstruction Finance Corporation was extended, and relief was undertaken by a kaleidoscopic series of agencies. Action, experimentation, and change were the prescriptions of the day, affording psychological or economic tonic. Liquor and *Ulysses* were legalized in November 1933, bringing into the open two forbidden fruits of the Jazz Age; and the next month Communist Russia was recognized as an official entity.

Affected by this dynamic spirit of the New Deal, reformers sprang up like dandelions in a reseeded lawn, advancing schemes ranging from Technocracy to Communism. Huey Long, Father Coughlin, and Dr. Townsend became minority messiahs. The President, wooing their votes, seeing virtue in some of their ideas, or sensing a national need to placate their extravagance, turned more and more to legislation directed toward social reform, giving the nation in 1935 a labor-relations act, a social-security law, a bill regulating public utilities, and a new tax structure.

The National Resources Committee surveying consumer spending during this turbulent winter of 1935-6 discovered that of the total national income of fifty billion dollars, better than thirty-nine were spent on food, shelter, clothing, and personal care, leaving three and three-quarter billions for automobiles and a billion and a half for tobacco, but only somewhat more than half a billion for all sorts of reading matter. The spare time afforded by joblessness or the newly legislated five-day week sent many people to the movies, where they hoped to win at Bank Night or come home with some free china, but it also helped to increase the reading of books, particularly in public libraries.

In addition to affording amusement or an escape during enforced idleness, books seemed a possible source for knowledge of how America had got into the Depression and how it might get out. So anxious were people to learn from the printed word that in course of time they even made a best seller of Mortimer Adler's heavy study, brightly entitled *How to Read a Book*. The Depression naturally brought a severe slump in book buying, and production decreased from the 214,334,000 copies of new books printed in 1929 to the 110,790,000 of 1933, many millions of which were to languish unbound in warehouses. But the book business (aided by schools and libraries) stood up well compared with the drop in paid admissions to motion pictures—from 177,000,000 to 60,000,000 during the same period. Books evidently had certain values that were recognized in the trying times. The values sought are indicated by the fact that in those same years the sale of fiction dropped 9 per cent below the general market, while the sales totals of books on economics and sociology almost doubled, though not enough people agreed on any one work about these subjects to make it a best seller. Many people could not afford to pay for what they wanted from books, but they did obtain reading matter from public libraries, which between 1929 and 1933 added some 4,000,000 new card holders to their rolls; the new and old patrons together increased withdrawals by nearly 40 per cent. These borrowings included old books, available and remembered for their tested worth; but new publications offering answers or escape simultaneously attracted a wide public, which read now one, now the other in a schizophrenic desire to cope with the rapidly altering times. The two authors most widely read were Zane Grey and Kathleen Norris. Public library budgets, insufficient to buy enough books for increased membership or to provide ample reading-room space, caused many potential borrowers to turn elsewhere, bringing about a great rise of rental libraries during the 1930's.

Even during Roosevelt's administration of reform and recovery, the external facts of the Depression remained visible to all in stock-market statistics, boarded-up factories, apple vendors, and breadlines. The causes and deeper effects were hard to understand. The nation had known plenty of financial panics and periods of 'bad times,' but this was different. The events euphemistically called a Depression seemed to wipe away all traditional values, social as well as economic, leaving readers to wonder along with the hero of Hans Fallada's best-selling novel, *Little Man, What Now?* Like the simple people in Fallada's tender story of postwar Germany, many Americans found the present bleak and the future bearable only if they buoyed up their courage with wistful hope. Trapped between an uncertain future and an alien past, young people particularly began to suspect America as a land of broken promise, a nation whose beliefs were geared to a decrepit economic and social system in need of thorough overhauling. While old folks generally clung to ideas of rugged individualism but flirted at the same time with Dr. Townsend's theory of state support, the younger minds tended toward new beliefs. Even the editor of the *Christian Century* could declare, 'It is either on to Moscow or back to sin!'

The battles of the 'twenties for freedom in language and sex relations were taken for granted, and liquor was available to those who would drink; the fight now was not against conservative social ethics but against capitalist economics. Marx replaced Freud as a guide; youthful faces turned left from Montparnasse to Moscow. Although young people and so-called intellectuals constituted the majority of those who toyed with Marxism, the nation at large became aware of class consciousness. Even of the relatively homogeneous society of 50,000 people in Muncie, Indiana, a businessman could say, 'Classes are certainly drawing apart here.' The cynical debunking of the 'twenties now turned upon big business and politics, making a best seller of Drew Pearson and Robert Allen's *Washington Merry-Go-Round;* a Pulitzer Prize winner of the musical travesty, *Of Thee I Sing;* and an unprecedented newsstand success of *Ballyhoo,* a magazine dedicated to satirizing advertising and commercialism. Such flip sniping at once-respected institutions and people was part of the general tendency to blame bankers or brokers or politicians for the crisis, an attitude nevertheless accompanied by a growing feeling that the system, not its representatives, was at fault. Lincoln Steffens's statement, 'I have seen the future and it works,' was an opinion of Russia's communism as contrasted to America's capitalism that trickled down to many people who never read his *Autobiography*, for in the year of its publication more Americans, entranced by vanished glamour, bought the Grand Duchess Marie's *Education of a Princess*. But if this representative of Russia's past headed the nonfiction best sellers of 1931, that year also found M. Ilin's *New Russia's Primer* on the list, and many persons were buying Maurice Hindus's *Red Bread*. By 1933 John Strachey's *The Coming Struggle for Power* had given a cant phrase to a large number of the younger generation.

Fiction too felt the impact of Marxism, though the new proletarian novel appealed almost exclusively to the coterie of intellectuals already convinced of Marxist verities. Not until the publication of Steinbeck's *Grapes of Wrath* in 1939 was a so-called proletarian novel widely enough read for the working class to be aware of it. Steinbeck was an author of the decade. His first novel was published in 1929 on the eve of the Depression, but this and two more novels together had not sold 3,000 copies. Then slowly he came to public notice with his appealing story of paisano life, *Tortilla Flat;* a proletarian novel, *In Dubious Battle,* which seemed too doctrinaire for wide circulation; his sentimental novella, *Of Mice and Men,* also a stage success; and, finally, *The Grapes of Wrath,* the epic of the contemporary dispossessed. This panoramic saga of migratory laborers harried across the continent created a strong sense of identity, its action centered on the warm portrayal of simple but fully developed people, its thesis realized in homely, natural dialogue, so that readers could obtain a direct emotional apprehension of the dislocation of the times and find meaning in its affirmative philosophy: 'We ain't gonna die out. People is goin' on—changin' a little, maybe, but goin' right on.' A work of propaganda almost as stirring in its time as *Uncle Tom's Cabin* was in the 1850's, *The Grapes of Wrath* became the subject of impassioned discussion as the period's most popular novel representing the search for answers in terms of social values.

American discontent with the prevailing economic system varied from serious curiosity about Communism to idle hopefulness that tomorrow's mail would bring a flood of dimes from the recipients of last month's chain letter. Meanwhile, many readers began to feel that concern with worldly matters was the root of all evil. An editorial in the Muncie, Indiana, newspaper voiced a common belief: 'Great spiritual values have come out of the depression; many a family that has lost its car has found its soul.' Social consciousness became a new religion for many so-called intellectuals, but most members of the dispossessed middle class felt uncomfortable with ideas whose radicalism exceeded those of the New Deal. Science, an agreeable substitute for religion during the 'twenties, appeared less satisfactory under the stress of hard times and suffered discredit as men became aware of a relation between its applied use in mechanization and the breakdown of the productive system. In theory too, science seemed less dependable as it went into realms so far beyond the layman that it became almost mystical. The orthodox religion of organized churches failed to attract many new-comers, but there was a definite increase in the numbers searching for new sources of faith. Roosevelt's tinkering with the social system had accustomed uncertain, restless Americans to rapid change, the spirit of his New Deal creating an atmosphere favorable to novel beliefs that appeared to promise a millennium here and now. In such a climate religious systems flourished as well as social schemes. All kinds of sects and cults sprang into being, ranging from the so-called Oxford Group of Dr. Frank Buchman, attracting the upper class through mildly con-fessional house parties, to the Jehovah's Witnesses of Judge Rutherford, appealing to militantly fanatic members of the lower class yearning for righteousness and martyrdom. The most flamboyant of the new messiahs was Father Divine, who relieved many Negroes of their worldly possessions, in return furnishing free meals and rooms at his branch 'heavens.' All afforded a sense of immediate salvation, or at least escape, to people weary of established systems.

This renewed interest in religion was noticeable in the books that people chose to read. Throughout the 'twenties hardly a volume of religious import, other than the biographies of Christ by Papini and Barton, was to be found among the best sellers; but for fifteen years after 1931 each annual list included at least one religious book, for the need of faith intensified as the problems of the Depression mounted and then turned into the greater problems of war. In 1931 Willa Cather's *Shadows on the Rock,* a novel of Catholic values, sold even better than had her *Death Comes for the Archbishop* four years earlier. Her later work was neither more moving nor more dramatic, but it had behind it not only her increased reputation but the temper of the times. In 1932 Lloyd Douglas's *Magnificent Obsession* came to the best-seller lists, for though issued by an obscure firm, it set forth an attitude of mind for whose expression people were evidently searching. His novel was the first in a long series of fictionized homilies which expounded the gospel that the good life for an individual could be achieved through altruism and amity based on the principles of the New Testament. Douglas, a Congregational clergyman, was the spiritual heir of Harold Bell Wright and continued his more rugged predecessor's success with one tremendously popular novel after another: *Forgive Us Our Trespasses* in 1932, *Green Light* in 1935, *White Banners* in 1936, and *Disputed Passage* in 1939. The year that first found the public turning to Douglas also returned the Abbé Dimnet to favor with his spiritual advice imparted in *What We Live By*. Other popular religious books of the 'thirties included such diverse works as the first publication of Dickens's *The Life of Our Lord*, written originally for his children; Alexis Carrel's *Man the Unknown*, a scientist's acceptance of miracles and personal immortality; Henry C. Link's *Return to Religion*, allying modern psychology with the Christian faith; and Sholem Asch's *The Nazarene*, an unorthodox but inspiring novel about Christ. In the war-torn 'forties, when the demand for Bibles was greater than bookstore supply, the popular novels included A. J. Cronin's *The Keys of the Kingdom*, Franz Werfel's *The Song of Bernadette*, and Douglas's *The Robe*, the most widely sold books of 1941, 1942, and 1943 respectively, as well as Gladys Schmitt's *David the King* and Russell Janney's *The Miracle of the Bells*. Varied as these books were, significantly none of them had either the flintiness of Jehovah's Witnesses nor the flamboyance of Father Divine, their tone generally being closer to that of the Oxford Group, for such was the tenor of the new religion embraced by those who could afford to purchase new books and who could find faith through the printed word instead of in active service and deed.

Closely akin to the religious novels of the 'thirties and rising to popularity from the same psychological need that brought them a public was Pearl Buck's *The Good Earth*, the most widely read new book of 1932. If this story of a Chinese family offered no explicit pattern for Americans, it did have allegorical significance in dramatizing the belief that honest toil may bring happiness but that wealth and luxury may destroy the spiritual meaning of life. Miss Buck's style, reminiscent of the rhythms of the King James version, gave her novel an almost Biblical assurance in its championing of the old American belief in hard work, thrift, ceaseless enterprise, and the value of living close to the land. Whether by coincidence or the nature of Pearl Buck's appeal, her novels in Chicago's public libraries during 1933 and 1934 enjoyed exactly the same rate of circulation as those by Gene Stratton-Porter.

In 1932, second only to *The Good Earth* was Charles Morgan's *The Fountain*. Set in the more familiar surroundings of the European Continent during the First World War and having Britishers, Dutch, and Germans as characters, this novel, like Miss Buck's, combined a story of human passion with a theme of spiritual aspiration. The thesis, perhaps better called a 'message,' served as nostrum, and the fairly conventional romantic story was a palatable coating that made Depression-ridden readers willing to accept a hero who, in the midst of a turbulent love affair, desires to withdraw from the world in search of meditation and inner peace. Skepticism about worldly values that had proved disappointing also prepared a public for James Hilton's sentimental novelette, *Good-Bye, Mr. Chips,* about a kindly schoolmaster, and his *Lost Horizon,* depicting an idyllic land of eternal youth and charming Buddhist mysticism. Issued in October 1933, *Lost Horizon* had an advance sale of just 1,100 copies and did not exhaust its first printing of 2,500 copies until the following spring. The publishers then risked a second printing, which sold 800 copies to bookstores. A full year after the book was issued it came to popular attention through the recommendation of Alexander Woollcott, who went 'quietly mad' over it during one of his broadcasts on a program appropriately sponsored by Cream of Wheat, a manufacturer of mush. By Christmas, Hilton's novel was traveling out of bookstores at the rate of 6,000 copies a week, and a large public was becoming aware of a new word, Shangri-la, now embedded in the dictionary as the name of an earthly paradise, at least for those who have found the world too much with them. In course of time a motion-picture version and a quip by President Roosevelt carried knowledge of the book to still more people, many of whom bought the work when it was issued as the first of the new 25-cent Pocket Books series. With a final stroke of unconscious irony, the name of Hilton's placid lamasery was given to a great American aircraft carrier constructed during the Second World War.

Pearl Buck and James Hilton prepared the public to see in Oriental philosophy a possible corrective to western civilization's undue emphasis upon mechanics. When Miss Buck's husband, who was also her publisher, introduced the United States to Lin Yutang's graceful but simple exposition, *The Importance of Living*, he found enough readers skeptical about machine-age culture and the philosophy of go-getting to make this the most popular work of nonfiction published during 1938. Americans of that year discovered a western counterpart to the philosophy of Pearl Buck and Lin Yutang in A. J. Cronin's *The Citadel*. This story of an idealistic Scottish doctor corrupted by a large and lucrative city practice had a wide following among Depression-worn people who compensated for loss of money through books showing that wealth drives out integrity and the spiritual life.

During the years of 1934 and 1935, when *Good-Bye, Mr. Chips* and *Lost Horizon* were on the best-seller lists, Alexander Woollcott, who had assisted Hilton to popularity, was challenging them with his own *While Rome Burns*. Having succeeded William Lyon Phelps as America's favorite book endorser, Woollcott became a legend in his own right, creating a fad for the delicately crocheted prose in which he made his adventures among great and near-great people of society and the arts as delightfully whimsical as any fictional Mr. Chips. If he offered no philosophy or any sense of higher idealism, this atrabilious sentimentalist did furnish a pretty piece of fiddling during a depression in his aptly titled *While Rome Burns*, an escape to a world of charming and eccentric characters which attracted some 125,000 book buyers.

Escapes of other sorts were furnished by various popular books. In 1931 an odd compilation called *Boners* rated higher in sales than James Truslow Adams's *Epic of America* or Stuart Chase's *Mexico*, which was an inquiry into the social and economic structure of our neighbor. *Boners*, a collection of children's incorrect answers to school quizzes, afforded the reader, during those particularly trying times, the age-old pleasure of laughing at someone else's errors and the concomitant opportunity to forget his own. A generation being scolded by its youngsters for failing to know the right answers undoubtedly was happy to see that it had no monopoly on fallibility. Directly behind *Boners* in sales were two manuals by Ely Culbertson, the newly enshrined arbiter of contract bridge. Neither so faddish nor so esoteric as Mah Jong, this new game arose in a favorable social environment when men and women had more time on their hands and less money to spend on afternoon shopping or evening outings. People who could no longer afford expensive entertainment asked friends over to play bridge after dinner, while those still in the dinner-giving economic bracket found bridge a good substitute for strained conversation about bad times or sad stories of lost fortunes. While most businesses were going into red ink, the playing-card manufacturer used the substance only for printing heart and diamond suits. Ely Culbertson, who had good reason to know, estimated that in 1931 alone some $100,000,000 were spent for bridge lessons and playing cards.

The desire to escape from reality led not only to such adult pleasures as bridge playing but even to a yearning for childhood as expressed in the happy magic of childish stories. Thus it was that Walt Disney's animated cartoon *Snow White* became one of the great box office successes of the Depression and a mature public bought Munro Leaf's *Ferdinand,* a juvenile story about an indolent flower-loving bull, into which was read all kinds of symbolism. Narcotics of one sort or another flourished as they always do during a troubled period; the most popular of those expressed through the medium of the printed word were generally addressed to a public searching for mysticism, idealism, and romance removed from material values and a mechanistic society.

For people whose ideas of the good life were less spiritual, there were plenty of books telling readers how to live at ease on a limited budget or recoup a lost fortune. Those members of the generation who had accumulated paper profits in the Bull Market only to have the crash and middle age arrive simultaneously were eager buyers of Walter B. Pitkin's *Life Begins at Forty.* This thin volume holding out hopes of a fresh start and a fine finish convinced many a paunchy person that it was earlier than he thought. Published in 1932 with an advance sale of 3,500 copies, *Life Begins at Forty* found an increasing number of readers as the years carried people deeper into the Depression and middle age, until by 1938 the book's sales were hovering around the 200,000 mark. Eager for practical advice or panaceas, Americans of the 'thirties welcomed a great number of other manuals, even though their counsel varied from Edmund Jacobson's *You Must Relax* and Pitkin's *Take It Easy!* to Dorothea Brande's *Wake Up and Live!* In a period when uncertain finances sent many a woman to office work while she waited for a young man to accumulate enough money for marriage, Marjorie Hillis found a ready-made public for her *Live Alone and Like It.* This work, originally given the more querulous title of *The Problem of a Single Woman,* was the forerunner of her even more affirmative and optimistic *Orchids on Your Budget.*

The year of 1936, which brought forth Miss Hillis's first manual, produced the most popular of all the success books, written by Dale Carnegie, already widely known as a salesman of popular psychology through lecture tours and his grandiloquently named Carnegie Institute of Effective Speaking and Human Relations. As with his school, Carnegie yoked two goals together in the title of his book, promising twin successes to all readers of his *How to Win Friends and Influence People.* In a breezy style Carnegie set forth truisms with such mechanical simplicity that people were charmed to find they could codify their human relations by mastering the six infallible rules of friendship, the nine ways of convincing opponents without arousing resentment, and the sevenfold formula for a happy home life. Carnegie left the reader with no tenuous subleties, for his regulations were set forth in homely language, illustrated with simple examples, and endorsed by the confirming words of acknowledged leaders of modern and ancient times. The hearty vigor of his style seemed to imply for his readers a success as immediate as that which he himself came to enjoy through his book. Printed at the end of 1936 with a prepublication sale of only 1,500 copies, *How to Win Friends and Influence People* was congenially received by *The Reader's Digest,* to whose policy of terse, simply stated optimism it conformed. From the summary in the January 1937 issue of that popular Depression-born magazine, the book went on to win buyers and influence readers, for condensation, like serialization, was becoming an important incentive to sales. By the end of its first year, well over 750,000 copies had been sold of both the original edition (temptingly priced as a bargain at $1.96) and of the 25-cent reprint. All through the ensuing years of depression and recession, of arguments about Aid to Britain and America First, of war and peace and rearmament, people kept right on buying Dale Carnegie's manual in the hope of finding ways to a more secure life and means to convince others of the rightness of their own opinions. By the opening of 1948 *How to Win Friends and Influence People* had sold 1,229,000 copies of the regular trade edition and an additional 2,100,000 in the Pocket Books reprint, a grand total of almost three and a third million copies. This was enough to put a copy into the hands of about one family out of every ten in America. Throughout 1948 the book was still selling at the corner drugstores and newsstands of the nation, though by this time

Mr. Carnegie gave himself competition with a new work, *How to Stop Worrying*, addressed to those harassed people who had not yet found serenity a natural product of gregariousness.

The mere act of perusing a 'How to' book seemed emblematic of success for many discomfited persons, just as women sometimes believe that the reading of recipes in a new cook book automatically insures better dinners. While studying Mr. Carnegie's or Miss Hillis's recipes, the readers found the ingredients so readily available and the preparation so simple that their mouths watered at the thought of the success soon to be served. Even if they slipped back into old ways or never tried the new ones, they received temporarily a sense of attainment, as though the fulfilment was inherent in the wish.

Readers who wanted books for relaxation without aspiring to better either their commercial or spiritual life began to discover mystery stories during the Depression. This type of fiction, which was almost a century old, had been enshrined in its own special niche of classics by admirers of Poe and Conan Doyle and had enjoyed sporadic popular success in such long-separated examples as Anna Katharine Green's *The Leavenworth Case* of 1878; Bram Stoker's fantastically eerie *Dracula*, published in 1897; Meredith Nicholson's *The House of a Thousand Candles*, issued in 1905; the works of Mary Roberts Rinehart and E. Phillips Oppenheim; and the Dr. Fu-Manchu stories of Sax Rohmer, which began to appear in 1913 along with Earl Derr Biggers's *Seven Keys to Baldpate*. Although all these novels could be loosely grouped as mysteries, their emphases varied, some focusing on the deductive problem, some on espionage and diplomatic intrigue, some on pseudo science, and some on the psychology of the criminal mind. They had in common the offering of mental relaxation or even escape; but they were no more an evasion of reality than many other popular novels. The two years after Miss Green's book was issued were those in which a novel entitled *Airy, Fairy Lilian* and a story by Ouida were among the best sellers; Bram Stoker's horror story competed for readers with *Quo Vadis?* and *The Choir Invisible;* the publication date of Nicholson's novel coincided with the popularity of Hichens's *Garden of Allah;* and the first of Sax Rohmer's tales appeared simultaneously with *Pollyanna*.

Obviously, to say that the mystery story reached popular success as a genre in the 'thirties because readers were searching for escape is not to get at the essential matter. Mystery stories merely afforded another kind of escape, successful in part because they had been made 'respectable' both by the polished and seemingly sophisticated works of S. S. Van Dine, and by the writings of E. C. Bentley, Agatha Christie, J. S. Fletcher, and Dorothy Sayers, whose prior publication in England gave them a cachet of foreign approval. Lifted from the area of shabby sensationalism to that of ingenious ratiocination, the mystery story turned into the detective story, a trimly tailored, credible narrative, affording readers the relaxation of concentrating on a problem removed from their daily lives. Though enjoyed by all kinds of people for a variety of reasons, the opportunity for a man baffled in business or a woman frustrated by a reduced budget to inflate the ego through exhibiting greater intelligence than the conventional Watson of these tales may have been a subconscious reason why many turned to the detective story. The growth of rental libraries, fostering cheap access to new books that did not warrant the expense of purchase, perhaps also helped popularize a genre good for one reading only.

Achieving social decency (the rationalization of respectability usually included a myth about professors endorsing them), detective stories afforded a new type of literature for readers who wanted the excitement of novels without the usual fuller values of fiction. Here they could get action and suspense that discarded or subordinated setting, mood, descriptive passages, or the humanity of characters as these elements got in the way of the plot. Having in part gained repute because they employed the refinement or erudition of an S. S. Van Dine or an Agatha Christie, detective stories ironically went their own way, leaving the diatonic tuning of carillons, the aesthetics of Oriental vases, and the intricacies of chess to shift for themselves. In general, they became puzzles masquerading as fiction, for few readers cared about the artistic abilities or the scholarship of the author any more than they really cared about the substance of the quotation in a Double-crostic. According to Raymond Chandler, one of the masters of the new form, the tendency was 'to get murder away from the upper-classes, the weekend house party and the vicar's rose-garden.' Dashiell Hammett, a kind of poor-man's Hemingway, brought to the common reader the tough code and curt dialogue of *The Sun Also Rises* in his *Maltese Falcon, The Glass Key,* and *The Thin Man,* issued respectively in the first three years of the Depression. 'Hammett,' Chandler observed, 'gave murder back to the kind of people that commit it for reasons, not just to provide a corpse; and with the means at hand, not with hand-wrought duelling pistols, curare, and tropical fish.' The amateur detective often continued to have personal crotchets and a fund of quaint lore, and the story itself developed new subleties impinging on the psychlogical thriller as knowledge of mental disorders spread during the Second World War and as the times grew more neurotic. But, in general, the detective story of the 'thirties and 'forties turned away from the world of S. S. Van Dine and his immediate British forebears to become a brisk genre of its own under the handling of such popular writers as Ellery Queen, Ngaio Marsh, Rex Stout, Craig Rice, Mignon Eberhart, Leslie Ford, and Erle Stanley Gardner.

The flourishing of the detective story is documented by Howard Haycraft's discovery that whereas the *Book Review Digest* listed only 12 books of this type in 1914 (extended to 97 in 1925), in the last year of the 'thirties it recorded 217, not counting innumerable reprints. Nearly a quarter of the new novels of the 'thirties were detective-mystery stories, though no single example in this or the next decade was on a best-seller list, unless the type is stretched to include Daphne du Maurier's *Rebecca* or Rachel Field's *All This, and Heaven Too*. This was true partly because no one detective story stands far above another (readers enjoy the type rather than the particular example), but mainly because a story of this nature is quickly read and not interesting to reread. Accordingly, the detective story may be sold to individuals in cheap reprints, but in its original edition the sales (averaging 2,000 copies) are chiefly to rental libraries, which frequently report a circulation of a single copy to fifty readers. Howard Haycraft figures that almost any detective story, therefore, is read by 15,000 persons, and that taken together the new mysteries published in any single year reach some 5,000,000 readings, though, of course, the number of different readers is far less than that. The steady following that turns to rental libraries for its new detective fiction creates both a ceiling and a basement for sales, making this type of story a safe piece of merchandise, as the usual novel is not. Only rarely does a detective story stay in print more than a few months, first in its original format, then later in a cheap reprint.

Paradoxically, this type of fiction, which has failed in twenty years to get an example on the approved best-seller lists, has nevertheless contributed to America its most widely read modern author. Beginning in 1933 with *The Case of the Velvet Claws*, Erle Stanley Gardner, a retired trial lawyer, has in fifteen years sold more than 28,000,000 copies of his books. At the usual rate of five readers to a copy, this is enough for every American—man, woman, child, and infant—to have read at least one of his detective stories. Since there are still illiterates and non-book-readers in the 140,000,000 population, along with youngsters not yet aware of A-B-C, it can only be assumed that Gardner has a large and faithful following waiting for any work he turns out.

Gardner's major books, issued under his own name, have maintained a consistency in quality as they have in character and situation, so that he has built up a steady reading public that knows what to expect of each new book bearing his signature and the rhythmic title that has become a kind of trademark. The restrictions of his genre and the continuing use of the same characters afford a double surety of brand quality usually found only in such juveniles as the Bobbsey Twins series. Gardner's slickly contrived plotting and fast pace, representative of the detective-story type currently most popular, are handled with great adroitness, yet without the subtlety that might detract or deter the simpler reader. His only sophistication resides in the legal knowledge of Perry Mason, who handles the curious complexities and loopholes of the law as ingeniously as Arthur Train's Mr. Tutt, to the delighted surprise of laymen. Thus Gardner takes advantage of the drama inherent in trials and appeals to an apparently basic American awe of professional knowledge coupled with a skepticism about the essential logic underlying its mumbo-jumbo.

Gardner's novels are spoken into a dictating machine with such speed that not only does he keep three full-time secretaries occupied, but he manages to keep his readers busy too His first novel was produced in three and a half days, though part of each twenty-four hours was devoted to legal work; and since then he has addressed hundreds of millions of words of plotted stories to his dictating machines at a rate once reaching a quarter of a million words in a month. The resulting sixty-odd books are sold at many prices, ranging from $2 to 25 cents; but the greatest American sale is in the latter category, one publisher alone having sold a million copies of each of eleven Erle Stanley Gardner novels at that price. Since reprints go uncounted on the records of best sellers, Gardner's work has often been officially topped by a novel that had a sale of but a scant hundred thousand. But if he has not won a top place in book-review sections, either on the critical pages or in the tabulation of circulation figures, Erle Stanley Gardner does not need to worry. For five consecutive years his novels have sold more than 4,000,000 copies annually, a high point being reached in 1945 with a turnover of 6,104,000 Gardner books—better than one copy for every eight persons who had voted in the previous presidential election.

Rivaling, even surpassing, the cult of the detective story was the reborn enthusiasm for historical novels. This type of fiction has never died out entirely since the time of Scott and Cooper, but various periods have brought it special popularity. The 'thirties and 'forties formed one such era. The 'twenties had placed some historical novels among the annual top ten, including such disparate works as Bacheller's *A Man for the Ages* and Wilder's *Bridge of San Luis Rey*, but every year from 1930 to 1948 brought forth a new and extremely popular romance of the past, each one cut in the same pattern. Not only buyers but borrowers seemed to prefer these books to all others. Miss Jeanette Foster's check of 15,000 public-library users during 1933 and 1934 revealed that more than 18 per cent of their reading was in adventure stories as against 12 per cent in detective stories. Except for love stories (borrowed about as often as detective stories), no other type of fiction came near these two; but it must be recognized that though all adventure and love stories are not historical novels, all historical novels fall into one or both of these categories. A period of stress and turmoil, leading people to books both for escape and explanation, favored the revival of historical novels. In a time when to face the present or the future was unpleasant, looking backward was a comparative pleasure, affording surcease from contemporary problems and an understanding that people of other ages had weathered worse times. Furthermore, as Bernard De Voto has pointed out, 'The historical novel is a pure form of social myth. It projects into the past reasons why we have become what we are. Our guilt will rest less heavily on us in the dark if we could not become other than we are, if we have done as well with our dust as the components of the dust allowed.' Such were the reasons that led readers to historical novels, though perhaps the success in 1930 of Edna Ferber's *Cimarron* needs no such rationalization in light of the popularity of her *Show Boat*, and the appeal of many a successor to *Anthony Adverse* was but a secondary reaction to Hervey Allen's pacesetter.

In mid-June 1933, when most Americans were tormented by debt and by doubt, they were presented with a lusty yarn about a character named Anthony Adverse, who rollicked through the turbulent Napoleonic era, obtaining women and wealth with equal ease. Issued with great publicity just in time to catch the summer reader, *Anthony Adverse* provided him (or, more usually, her) with three books for the price of one, 1,224 pages of reading all for $3. Prepublication advertising had placed nearly 20,000 copies in bookstores by the date of issue, and favorable reactions of the first readers helped the novel to sell the rest of the summer at the rate of 10,000 copies a week. The holiday trade boosted sales above 15,000 copies a week, so that by Christmas Eve 178,828 copies had gone out to bookstore buyers and subscribers to the Book-of-the-Month Club. Still the demand for *Anthony Adverse* did not slacken as 175,000 more copies were sold during 1934, and large stores learned to push it like branded merchandise, until R. H. Macy was credited with 60,000 of its first 320,000 sales. During 1935 and 1936 *Anthony Adverse* at last began to taper off to 65,000 and 63,000 copies respectively as late-comers trickled in, many attracted by the cheap reprint issued at the time of the motion-picture version, others really believing this to be an American classic worth owning in its two-volume illustrated library edition. By the end of its third year, *Anthony Adverse* was pushing toward a sale of three quarters of a million copies, and it has never died out entirely, for even thirteen years after publication it was selling a steady 10,000 copies a year. Those who did not buy it rented the work from circulating libraries, often at fees almost as fat as the sales price, or waited patiently to withdraw it from their public library, making Hervey Allen, on the strength of this one work, the sixth most widely read author during 1933 and 1934 in the Chicago public libraries—far above Edgar Wallace, who rated tenth despite his forty-four detective stories.

The success of *Anthony Adverse* led publishers to search out more historical novels, much as motion-picture producers create a cycle of a certain type of film after one example has become popular. The novels ranged in subject from Stark Young's *So Red the Rose,* a conventional costume piece about the Old South, through Caroline Miller's Pulitzer-Prize-winning *Lamb in His Bosom,* a study of pioneer life in back-country Georgia during the Civil War, to Franz Werfel's *Forty Days of Musa Dagh,* about besieged Armenians of the First World War. Different as their settings were, all had some of the qualities that had led to the success of *Anthony Adverse.* They usually dealt with eras of great turmoil, which made for dramatic action and perhaps appeared to cast light on current events, and most of them were longer than the conventional novel. In a period of depression a simple shortcut to factual information and a sudden uplift made successes of *The Reader's Digest* and *Life;* but, paradoxically, readers wanted their entertainment to last, whether in a double-bill motion picture or a long novel.

The perfect successor to *Anthony Adverse* came in June 1936, almost three years to the day after Hervey Allen's book was issued. Margaret Mitchell's *Gone with the Wind* would probably have found a large audience even had the current of taste not swept a way open for it, but the times were just right. Most of those who were going to read *Anthony Adverse* had presumably done so and they were primed for a historical romance conforming to it in heft and hue. *Gone with the Wind* was another example of a big summer book good for all seasons, its size comparable to that of *Anthony Adverse,* a feature emphasized by Miss Mitchell's publishers, who in paraphrasing the advertisements for Allen's book called hers 'Three novels in one—1,057 pages—a complete vacation's reading.' By Christmas, the sales were a round million, over five times as great as Allen's in a like period. An increased Book-of-the-Month Club membership accounted for more sales than the selection of *Anthony Adverse* had enjoyed, but the novel was more popular at stores too, causing the Macmillan Company to ship out 50,000 copies in one day, an all-time record on reorders. The end of 1937 saw a million and a half copies in print and in demand, as *Gone with the Wind* swept through bookstores as fast as a hurricane. Not only did it for a short time become America's speediest-selling novel, but over the long haul it became the nation's largest-selling novel. Within four years it was issued in several different editions (one was priced at $7.50 and another, illustrated by scenes from the motion picture, cost 69 cents), but most of the sales—by 1949 nearly 4,000,000 copies in this country alone—were at the original $3, 50 per cent more than the cost of the popular edition of *Anthony Adverse.*

Although *Gone with the Wind* was in great part popular because it was a particularly dramatic historical novel, it was a novel first of all. Some of its appeal derived from the usual romantic aspects of historical fiction: the portrayal of a lost cause, an unattainable ideal, and a charming way of life that was gone. The action, crowding exciting event upon exciting event, was also representative of the usual historical novel, but *Gone with the Wind* placed its emphasis as much on the private individual as on the panorama. More than *Anthony Adverse* it represented the shift from the tradition of *When Knighthood Was in Flower* to that of accepted realism in contemporary fiction. Scarlett O'Hara and Rhett Butler, the two strong figures, and Melanie Hamilton and Ashley Wilkes, the two weak ones, were products of external characterization rather than psychological motivation, yet they gave the appearance of reality in manners and dialogue, seeming to be shaped by inner stresses and social forces rather than by prefabricated temperaments. The discussion of character, therefore, was as great as that of action, making a dual appeal. Readers, when they come by the millions, are less tutored and less demanding than those who have read much fiction, and to them it seemed that Miss Mitchell's characters were as accurately portrayed as her authentic Atlanta topography. Scarlett, being a heroine unusually wilful, mean, and selfish for popular fiction, was credited with being peculiarly real; and Rhett Butler was thought as real as Clark Gable, as indeed he was.

With the success of *Gone with the Wind* the historical novel was even more firmly established as a popular genre. The year after its publication, four of the five best-selling works of fiction were historical novels. In addition to Miss Mitchell's book—again topping the list—were Kenneth Roberts's *Northwest Passage,* Vaughan Wilkins's *And So—Victoria,* and Walter D. Edmonds's *Drums Along the Mohawk.* Year in and year out after that at least one new historical novel established some kind of sales record, a good many of them in the established Scott-to-*Scaramouche* tradition, but adding more seductive strumpets than the old-fashioned historical romance had allowed.

The fictionizing of history continued to attract established novelists such as Kenneth Roberts, whose *Oliver Wiswell* in 1940 made a 'lost cause' of the Tory side of the American Revolution; Daphne du Maurier, whose *The King's General* in 1946 was accepted by three book clubs and reached a million copies in print within six weeks; and such well-known women writers as Frances Parkinson Keyes and Elizabeth Goudge. But the successful precedents of Hervey Allen and Margaret Mitchell brought new novelists flocking into the field, very nearly making it their own. Among them were Marguerite Steen with *The Sun is My Undoing;* Thomas B. Costain, whose *Black Rose* sold about a million and a third copies, including those of the dollar reprint 'limited' to 250,000 copies; Samuel Shellabarger, whose *Captain from Castile* was so popular that 775,000 copies of his next work, *The Prince of Foxes,* were put to press before publication; F. Van Wyck Mason with his *Stars on the Sea* and *Eagle in the Sky;* and Frank Yerby, whose *Foxes of Harrow* sold 1,200,000 copies. The most sensational, if not the most successful, of all the new historical novelists was Kathleen Winsor. Her full-bodied narrative of the Restoration period, *Forever Amber,* was presumably considered a bit too broad for the book clubs that had helped the other novels, but its reputation for frankness attracted independent readers as well as the attention of the Superior Court of Massachusetts. Justice Donahue's decision that the romance 'while conducive to sleep is not conducive to a desire to sleep with a member of the opposite sex' did not seem to harm the notorious reputation of the work, which in less than three years attracted over a million and a half buyers to its original-priced edition.

In some part the historical romance was in demand because many of its most widely read examples dealt with an earlier America, more serene or more triumphant, appealing to the nostalgic urge of people living through a period of distress. This attraction was strong enough to popularize a literary genre called Americana, concerned with the exploration of salient national characteristics, past and present. A product of hard times, the interest in Americana smacked of psychological regression among a people frustrated by the present and hoping to find comfort in the happier, younger days of their land. The New Deal, upsetting established relations between citizen and government, paradoxically helped to focus attention upon tradition, and, as a subsidiary part of its relief program, Roosevelt's administration further aroused interest in Americana by sponsoring the American Guide Series of some seven hundred local histories, by assisting in the revival of various folk arts, and by commissioning paintings on regional subjects for post offices and court houses. As the years of the New Deal shifted to those of the war, Americana continued to interest a people driven to test national values against the alien ways of Fascism and Communism. Even on a simpler basis, Americana was attractive when older Americans were forced to stay at home physically and spiritually while younger men sent abroad by the Army and Navy yearned for the land they knew and the ways that were customary. Propaganda, governmental and commercial, reinforced the mood of evangelical patriotism until one powerful journalist proclaimed that the natural and desirable result of the war was to make this the American century.

The interest in Americana began as early as 1929, when, for the first time since Longfellow's day, a long verse narrative elbowed its way into the best-seller class as Stephen Vincent Benét's *John Brown's Body* was accepted by a book club. With that surprise beginning, the antiquarian rummaging in the attic of our past continued year after year. Fiction's use of the American heritage ranged from Edna Ferber's *Cimarron,* a near-relative of the historical novel and the most widely read book of 1930, to Thomas Wolfe's *Of Time and the River,* a poetic evocation of youth nourished by a patriotic, mystical belief that the greatness of America haunts and kindles the imaginations of its young men. At one geographic extreme, the scene of these popular novels was the New England of Mary Ellen Chase's *Mary Peters* and *Windswept*, its Puritan tradition probed in J. P. Marquand's works beginning with *The Late George Apley* and Santayana's *The Last Puritan;* at the other pole was Marjorie Kinnan Rawlings's *The Yearling*, set in Florida's hummock country. The land between these geographic borders and extending ever westward to the Pacific was all used too, the past of upstate New York appearing in Taylor Caldwell's *This Side of Innocence*, the iron towns of Pennsylvania in Marcia Davenport's *Valley of Decision*, and even the Brooklyn slums yielding their tender recollections of things past in Betty Smith's story of sensitive childhood, *A Tree Grows in Brooklyn*. Far to the southwest, the cattle-raising country during the 'eighties formed the setting of Niven Busch's *Duel in the Sun*. A strange blend of Zane Grey and James M. Cain, this full-blown Wild West story attracted little attention upon first publication in 1944. When reissued in a 25-cent edition in 1947, as an adjunct of a motion-picture version, *Duel in the Sun* found 2,300,000 buyers in little more than a year.

Varied as were its settings, Americana was measured less by the longitude or latitude of space than by its distance in time from the meridian of the present. Generally it did not travel far back to a distant past, preferring to linger on the middle distance of a recent but stable period or an era of growth whose travail was deadened by the opaque qualities imparted by time and a tender vision. A soft mood of longing and a happy sentimental subject seemed to fit the regressive desires of the 'thirties and 'forties, a feeling summed up in the title *Our Hearts Were Young and Gay* by Cornelia Otis Skinner and Emily Kimbrough, but exemplified almost equally well by Frederick Lewis Allen's *Only Yesterday* and the many testaments of filial affection, including Clarence Day's *Life with Father* and *Life with Mother*, Arthur E. Hertzler's *Horse and Buggy Doctor*, and Bellamy Partridge's *Country Lawyer*. True, the popular nonfiction of Americana included Ludwig's *Lincoln*, James Truslow Adams's *Epic of America* and *The March of Democracy*, Douglas Southall Freeman's *R. E. Lee*, Carl Van Doren's *Benjamin Franklin*, Margaret Leech's *Reveille in Washington*, Catherine Bowen's *Yankee from Olympus*, Irving Stone's *Immortal Wife*, and John Gunther's monumentally detailed *Inside U.S.A.*, but subjects less sweeping and dramatic were most generally in demand. The serene charm of the past captured even our more formal historians. Van Wyck Brooks, once an astringent critic of

American culture, now emerged as a popular writer with his *Flowering of New England* and its several sequels presenting winsome tableaux of old-fashioned literary days and ways.

The mellow pilgrimage to the past made for a revaluation of the 'twenties' standards. The 'booboisie' of the Bible Belt once excoriated by Mencken was now discovered to have a folk culture affectionately revealed in Carl Carmer's *Stars Fell on Alabama*. Even Queen Victoria was resuscitated as the ironic scrutiny of Lytton Strachey gave way to the sympathetic portrayal of Laurence Housman's *Victoria Regina*, a great theatrical success as interpreted by Helen Hayes. The lyrical approach to earlier or simpler ways formed a new cycle of motion pictures, and the stage blossomed with operettas and ballets set in America's hinterland of the past. Lynn Riggs's severe *Green Grow the Lilacs* was turned into the gay sentiment of *Oklahoma!; Liliom* was given a free ride on a New England merry-go-round in *Carousel;* and even Amelia Bloomer was treated with respectful good humor in *Bloomer Girl*. As the cult of Americana flourished, publishers began to issue series about various aspects of the nation: the rivers, the mountains, the highways, the pioneer trails, the cities, the national parks, the folk regions, the blue-blooded society groups, and even the murders. For those people accustomed by the movies, by *Life*, and by *Look* to pictures instead of text, there were innumerable volumes collecting photographs and paintings of America by region, by era, or by any other scheme that would make a neatly packaged pictorial bundle—often a collection of facts and statements whose mere assemblage was thought to convey understanding, as though the means automatically created the end. Placed on the coffee table, these mechanical depictions of America served as this generation's heir to the Victorian gift book.

So general was the area and the appeal of Americana that it could be said to encompass even Betty MacDonald's *The Egg and I*, whose frank, simple, humorous account of an experience close to the earth appealed to a troubled generation of urban Americans. The tone of the book was implied by shrewd advertisements featuring the author's open, smiling face, just as another publisher indicated the nature of *Forever Amber* with photographs emphasizing the seductive sophistication of Kathleen Winsor. *The Egg and I* was a delightfully reassuring work for those who were spiritually ill at ease among the physical comforts of steam-heated, electric-driven apartments and houses, for through this story of life on a Western chicken ranch they found that a return to nature could be even more irksome than an escape from it. As a New York book reviewer declared, 'To city people sitting snug and dry, Mrs. MacDonald's life in the woods comes as unadulterated fun.' Its purchasers were not those who bought *Duel in the Sun* for 25 cents, but the wealthier, more sophisticated class of book buyers who could make a best seller out of a small work costing $2.75. At this price they bought 15,000 copies a week even a year after publication, and within two years they had purchased nearly a million and a third copies, all at the original price.

Another type of reading matter that came to popularity during the Depression was the anthology. Of course there had always been collections that, like Quiller-Couch's *Oxford Book of English Verse* or Louis Untermeyer's samplings of modern poetry, had slowly achieved large sales as an informed individual's selection of materials, specialized and scattered. Now, in a period when readers wanted to get a lot of book for their money, the anthologies had a new appeal. Not only did they seem a good economy, insuring an approved choice from many established authors for the price of a book by one new unknown writer, but they also suited the speedy tempo of the times, like *The Reader's Digest*, America's most widely circulated magazine. One evening with a *Treasury of Thought*, an *Omnibus of Opera*, or a *Cavalcade of Cat Stories* saved a lot of time reading through philosophy, attending opera, or searching for stories about your favorite domestic animal.

Like so many other literary fads, the popularity of the anthology was in part attributable to Alexander Woollcott, whose *Woollcott Reader* issued in 1935 soon sold 105,000 copies to people who admired his taste and expected his bittersweet personality to be adumbrated in the prose and poetry he selected. Publishers soon began to follow Woollcott's lead, seeing a quick way to issue a book at little cost, since authors generally get small pay for such reprints and many usable pieces are not in copyright. In a short time the making of anthologies was put on a mechanized basis as collections were pasted up on every conceivable subject, not forgetting Americana, crime, popular psychology, or the romance of history. Book clubs found them ideal dividends, one, for example, distributing half a million copies of a *Treasury of the World's Great Letters;* book buyers saw in them wonderful solutions to the problem of selecting a gift, for they were conveniently labeled as a *Christmas Companion,* or arranged according to personal interests as *Stories for Sportsmen* or *Bedside Book of Best Love Stories;*

and readers found them good for whiling away time on train or plane. As Russell Maloney remarked, the word 'anthology' degenerated in exactly the same way as the word 'hostess.'

Once a lady with whom one had a pleasant and rewarding personal relationship, a hostess is now an anonymous female who acts as headwaiter in a tearoom, hands paper bags to the airsick, or dances with strangers in a public dance hall. An anthology used to be the enterprise of a man who just couldn't resist the temptation to compile an anthology; it was often exciting and always interesting. These days, however, an anthology is likely to be a weary commercial enterprise with no more individuality than a can of baked beans.

Mr. Maloney might have added that anthologies, as snippets from longer works, began to assume the uniformity not only of cans of beans, but of cans of dehydrated beans.

      ＊   ＊   ＊   ＊

As the nation crept out of the shambles of depression, the popularity of anthologies, Americana, mystery stories, and historical romances did not slacken, but books about warring ideologies also attracted attention. Walt Disney in 1938 called the people's tune with 'Whistle While You Work,' yet the gaiety was somewhat forced; the whistling was that of the small boy passing a graveyard at night, for as the United States left the Depression behind, it moved into production mainly because it was helping the world to rearm for war. Although the Nye investigation of war profiteers provided a circus featuring international bankers and munitions makers as the only begetters of battle, many people began to wonder if war could not come even without this impetus—if, indeed, it could not come right to America despite the succession of Neutrality Acts that Congress wrote into law. In 1936 Mussolini was completing his conquest of Ethiopia, Hitler was marching into the Rhineland, and both dictators were blatantly employing their military power in the so-called Civil War of Spain. At home America's reading public bought more copies of John Gunther's *Inside Europe* than of Marjorie Hillis's *Live Alone and Like It,* perhaps fearing that if they did not learn what was going on abroad, they would indeed be isolated and would not like it at all. That was the year too when Sinclair Lewis's *It Can't Happen Here* became one of the most popular current novels, 'It' now connoting dread Fascism instead of the glamorous sex appeal that Elinor Glyn's novel had invoked but nine years before.

During these foreboding years some Americans turned their faces

away from the threat, but very few any longer found solace by searching for a better way of life in Russia. As we made economic recovery
and Moscow's millennium failed to dawn despite successive Five-Year
Plans, skepticism replaced Communism, and antipathy finally overcame
idealism with the strange trials of former Russian leaders, the in-
vasion of Finland, and the treaty between Stalin and Hitler. Ap-
prehensively curious about the future, Americans in 1939 made a best
seller of Hitler's *Mein Kampf*, bought by the thousands St. Exupéry's
Wind, Sand and Stars, which gave an insight into the brave new world
of flight; explored the militarism *Inside Asia* with John Gunther; reflected with Pierre van Paassen on the chaotic *Days of Our Years;* and
accepted Vincent Sheean's dictum, *Not Peace But a Sword.*

By 1940 a peacetime draft had been enacted and America was making itself into the arsenal of democracy. Soon after, President Roosevelt
declared, 'Books are weapons in the war of ideas,' and, as if in response,
the public turned more and more to accounts about the battle of beliefs
and the actual warfare of armies. Although every American war produced
books about the struggle, never before were there so many popular
works on a war, written by professional novelists and poets, by journalists and foreign correspondents, by leading statesmen and historians,
by amateur tacticians and strategists, by commanding generals and
ordinary soldiers. In 1940 and 1941, before we were suddenly thrust into
a shooting war, our reading on current events was mostly concerned
with warnings, such as Douglas Miller's *You Can't Do Business with
Hitler;* with quasi-official statements of policy, like Alsop and Kintner's
American White Paper; with conditions in enemy-occupied country,
such as Dirk van der Heide's story of refugees, *My Sister and I;* with
the strange land of Russia, once friendly to the enemy, as represented in
Jan Valtin's sensational *Out of the Night;* and with brave pronounce-
ments of an allied leader, such as Churchill's *Blood, Sweat and Tears.*

Most of the books dealing with the war took their momentary place
in the spotlight as the newest interpretation, the most sensational exposé,
or the most affecting portrayal, soon superseded by others pushing the
superlative even higher. The only war novel to stay on the best-seller
lists for two years was Hemingway's *For Whom the Bell Tolls.* Though
none of his eleven previous books had sold widely, they had established Hemingway in the popular mind as an author of significance
whose tale of World War I was a box-office success in its motion-picture
version. The ground thus prepared, Hemingway reaped a crop of

readers when he brought out a novel that not only offered swift, power-ful action and romantic characters but the timely theme that if free-dom is defeated in one place it is diminished for all humanity. Presenting with firsthand knowledge the experiences of an American in the Spanish Civil War, *For Whom the Bell Tolls* gave readers a direct emotional understanding of the pattern of modern warfare. It brought home the meaning of battle involving civilians as well as the military, and through concrete actions dramatized the conflicting ideologies of Fascism, Communism, and Democracy. Published in 1940, Hemingway's novel attracted readers all through the war, whose essential theories and tactics were foreshadowed in its pages, and by 1946 *For Whom the Bell Tolls* had sold almost a million copies.

Among the other books popular prior to America's entrance into the war were those offering insight into the daily lives of ordinary people either of Germany or Great Britain, the major nations on either side of the conflict. On the former score, William L. Shirer's meticulously observant *Berlin Diary* appealed to enough readers to pile up a sale of nearly half a million copies in 1941. On the latter, Jan Struther's *Mrs. Miniver* became the third most widely read novel of 1940. Dur-ing the isolationist debates of 1938, Margaret Halsey's *With Malice Toward Some* was popular because of its flip derision of the English people; by the time of the Dunkirk evacuation and the aerial battle over Britain, American respect for the bulldog tenacity of the British in their island fortress led us to relish not only the sentiment of *Mrs. Miniver,* but even the sentimentalism of Alice Duer Miller's *The White Cliffs,* a long poem assisted to the best-seller lists by Lynn Fontanne's dramatic reading on a national broadcast.

After our actual entry into the war, books reflecting every aspect of it became even more popular. Most titles then focused on this nation's part in the struggle or on the individual American men and women who by the millions were directly involved in the hostilities. At one end of the scale was the large view portrayed in different ways by Ambassador Joseph Davies's *Mission to Moscow,* Wendell Willkie's *One World,* Walter Lippmann's *U. S. Foreign Policy,* Sumner Welles's *The Time for Decision,* Ambassador Grew's *Ten Years in Japan,* and, finally, the official *Report* of General Marshall. At the other extreme was the in-timate view. First there was the problem of the civilian-turned-soldier, amusingly set forth in Marion Hargrove's *See Here, Private Hargrove,* the *Dere Mable* of World War II which sold some 2,800,000 copies.

Then came the accounts of specific groups in battle, such as William
L. White's *They Were Expendable;* Richard Tregaskis's *Guadalcanal
Diary,* describing details of our first victory to a million and a half book
buyers; Lieut. Col. Gordon Seagrave's *Burma Surgeon;* Ernie Pyle's
personal *Here Is Your War* and *Brave Men;* Eve Curie's *Journey Among
Warriors;* Bob Hope's *I Never Left Home;* and Bill Mauldin's *Up
Front,* the bitterly humorous account of a G.I.'s life. Aside from these
two major types of war books, each year brought forth some popular
work concerned with a special view. In 1941 and 1942, when the Capital
became the hub of the war, the popular nonfiction included respectively
Margaret Leech's *Reveille in Washington,* describing the District of
Columbia during the Civil War in a lively and implicit parallel, and W.
M. Kiplinger's informative *Washington Is Like That.* After France fell
to the enemy, many readers turned for sad reminiscence to Elliot Paul's
The Last Time I Saw Paris, whose title gave a refrain to a nostalgic
popular song. Interest in the strategic use of new weapons led readers
to Alexander DeSeversky's *Victory Through Air Power,* and a fear of
spies drew 600,000 buyers to the original edition of John Carlson's
sensational exposé, *Under Cover.*

Whatever their scope or subject, the war books included few novels.
Writers had little time for the artistic reflection and ordering essential
to fiction, and readers generally preferred knowledge of events and
blueprints for a better world. During all the years of American fighting,
only two novels dealing with the war made the best-seller lists. The
first, issued in 1942, was John Steinbeck's *The Moon Is Down,* a stylized
sentimental tale whose thesis—that social decency will always defeat
inhuman barbarity—had a setting reminiscent of Norway under German
dominion. Given a large circulation by one of the book clubs, *The
Moon Is Down* also had big bookstore sales to the readers who remembered *The Grapes of Wrath* as a powerful saga of harried migratory laborers and expected an equally perceptive study of people oppressed by war. In 1944 came John Hersey's *A Bell for Adano,* the first
novel of a correspondent already well known for his *Men on Bataan*
and *Into the Valley.* With a lyrical sociology akin to Steinbeck's, this
story had a theme of topical interest in its depiction of American soldiers
as military governers in Sicily, and it obtained further word-of-mouth
publicity by the rumor that a major character was based on General
Patton, at the moment under discussion for his ostensibly arbitrary
command.

Book sales kept pace with the new prosperity created by war-born manufacturing. With money jingling in their pockets, people discovered books as other goods disappeared from store shelves; and they found time for reading when they were kept home because of gas rationing and dim-outs. In 1933 only 110,790,000 books were printed in this country; in 1943 over 250,000,000 books were printed. Eighty million were trade books of general interest (excluding texts, juveniles, technical works, and Bibles and religious works) intended for a population over the age of fifteen that numbered about 100,000,000 people, many of them under arms and removed from normal book suppliers. Of course, more people borrowed or rented books than bought them, but the general trend was toward reading new books. The public library of Montclair, New Jersey, in a test of books loaned during May 1943, discovered that 65 per cent had been printed after January 1940, and only 13 per cent before 1930. Increased interest in books and a predilection for new ones also marked the reading of men in service. To these ends they were assisted by the military, naval, and U.S.O. libraries and most of all by the Armed Services Editions. This series of reprints, issued without charge to Army and Navy personnel, in three years distributed 119,000,000 volumes which emphasized contemporary works. As Lieut. Col. Ray L. Trautman observed, 'any book selected automatically becomes a "best-reader" if not precisely a "best-seller."'

In determining the troops' choice of reading matter through its offerings, the Armed Services Editions was only extending to service men the effect of book clubs on civilians, for any selection of the two major clubs was almost certain to become a best seller. As the war filled memberships in book clubs, they became increasingly important, making a few books tremendously popular but shortening the lives of all as replacements came along every thirty days. The Book-of-the-Month Club founded in 1926, and The Literary Guild, established the following year, remained the largest organizations, accounting for a sizable part of America's new book business. Before they were founded, only a million people bought books regularly. By 1946 the various clubs had a membership of 3,000,000, the average monthly Literary Guild selection being accepted by half of its 1,250,000 members, and the Book-of-the-Month Club annually distributing almost 11,500,000 books, approximately one and a half times the contents of The Library of Congress. The turnover of readers was nearly as great as that of books, for almost half of the members dropped out every year; but there always seemed to be more where they came from and new clubs for them to go to. In 1946 there were fifty clubs suited to all tastes and interests, their specialties indicated by such titles as Labor Book Club, Scientific Book Club, One World Book Club, Catholic Children's Book Club, Aero and Marine Book Club, Negro Book Club, Executive Book Club, History Book Club, Non-Fiction Book Club, and even a Surprise Package Book Club for youngsters. Although book clubs account for only 22 per cent of all book sales, their percentage in relation to best sellers is far, far higher. Few books now reach top sales without the accolade of the book clubs, and many books would almost certainly not become best sellers without their initial orders, often running to half a million or more copies, which makes for a great deal of word-of-mouth advertising to influence bookstore buyers.

The rise of the book clubs has caused a long and bitter debate about their effect on American reading habits. Many critics, like Q. D. Leavis, contend that they are 'instruments not for improving taste but for standardising it at the middlebrow level.' Others feel that they make a monopoly of literature, harming readers by imposing on them a certain few books (often not so good as the selections that independent buyers might make), and hurting authors by encouraging the writing of certain types of books likely to bring in great royalties through club acceptance. On the other side are many who agree with the bookseller who declared in *The New York Times* that though 'they threaten to inflict on American writing the terrible sameness of taste from which the movies and radio suffer, they have taught a lot of people how to read.' Certainly it must be admitted that many persons without convenient access to bookstores and libraries would not read so much as they do now were there no book clubs, and these readers may graduate from clubs to the selection of their own books. Though some clubs tend to seek the lowest common denominator in taste, particularly in the historical romances they have helped popularize, a great many of the best sellers that other clubs have selected in the years since 1926 seem better as literature than the books popular before 1926, when the first club was established. Good or bad, book clubs are products of the culture of the times and are not likely to pass from the scene until the culture itself changes.

Another great factor increasing book sales during and after the war was the establishment in 1939 of the first successfully manufactured series of cheap paper-bound reprints. Before that date only 4,000 retail stores stocked books (less than a thousand of them large enough to warrant personal calls from publishers' representatives), but the new 25-cent books were soon being distributed to upwards of 70,000 cigar stores, newsstands, and other outlets where books had never before been sold. Reprints, though always popular, had usually been moderately high-priced reissues of recent successes, special 'screen editions' illustrated by photographs from a motion picture, or cheap publications concentrating on the two extremes of literature: the classics of Dickens, Scott, Shakespeare, et cetera, at one end, the substrata writers like Grace Livingston Hill at the other. The new reprints differed in purpose as they did in format, seeking less a special market than an extension of existing ones. Some excellent books were issued in these series, including fiction by such sophisticated writers as Virginia Woolf and Henry James and learned works by little-known anthropologists and scientists; but the large sellers tended to be flamboyant fiction—Wild West tales, detective stories, and novels employing tough language or affording frank discussion of sex. Many of the reprints merely continued the sales histories of books popular in their original printings, like Dale Carnegie's *How to Win Friends and Influence People,* but the 25-cent series also established its own group of best sellers. Most sensational was the popularity of Erskine Caldwell, whose *Tobacco Road* sold 4,000,000 copies in two years; several other works brought his grand total of sales up to 8,000,000 in the same period. Equally indicative of the fact that the 25-cent series had a public different from the regular bookstore customers was the response to James T. Farrell. His *Young Lonigan* sold only 517 copies in the year after its original publication; but within a month after reissue as a pocket-size book, 350,000 copies were sold. Between 40,000,000 and 50,000,000 of these pocket-size reprints are sold annually, one firm alone advertising that in eight years it distributed 200,000,000 copies, 'more books than the combined sales of all best sellers published since 1880.' Almost any book selected for reprinting is a best seller by comparison with its original publication, since the average first printing of a 25-cent publication runs to 300,000 copies.

Although some 35,000,000 Americans had no accessible public library service at the end of the war, it was then estimated that about 49,-000,000 people over the age of 15 read at least one book a month. They were using as many dollars for books alone as they had spent during a Depression year on newspapers, magazines, and books together. The reading of new books was becoming such an accepted part of normal life that a Superior Court judge of California in 1945 granted a divorce to a woman whose husband would not allow her to read enough to 'keep up with the current best sellers.' True, almost 30 per cent of the public remained what might be called non-readers, so infrequently did they pick up a book, yet increased educational opportunities, along with distribution of books through reprints, book clubs, rental libraries, and other means, made for a reading public larger than this nation had ever known.

This public faced an altered world after the war, but one in which, as ever, books could be of service. The war, meant to end threats to the traditional values of western culture, seemed only to reveal new dangers. Outright hostilities simmered down to an ugly armistice as victorious but divided allies challenged one another from behind chauvinistic barriers. What life portended, what new embroilments might be like—these were problems terrifying to contemplate. Every man stood under a mushroom-shaped cloud once the atom bomb was dropped on Hiroshima.

In these days of physical fear and spiritual malaise, when science itself symbolized unknown terrors, readers turned for knowledge to *Atomic Energy for Military Purposes*, the semiofficial report of Henry DeWolf Smyth. Though an elementary knowledge of physics was needed to understand the work, it was soon bought by more than 100,000 people seeking to comprehend the force that had shaped a new world. But in an age of anxiety, a larger number of readers preferred solace to understanding, considering knowledge of one subject less helpful than a generalized nostrum to restore confidence. This they found in Joshua L. Liebman's *Peace of Mind*, a work with a title as appealing to its day as those of Dimnet and Carnegie had been to theirs. Blending religious faith and the techniques of modern psychology, Rabbi Liebman's slim book was a wonderfully persuasive antidote for people who no longer trusted science or believed in man's progress. Issued in March 1946, soon after the end of the war, it appeared at a time when the psychic energy of Americans had lost the direction given by the battle itself. Faced by dislocation and disaster that could not now appear to be resolved daily through military advances, disillusioned by unsuccessful attempts at international co-operation, people were seeking ideas that would bring certainty. In terms of modern psychology, *Peace of Mind* presented age-old religious beliefs acceptable to all faiths, appealing to people who had forgotten God and never knew Freud, as well as to those who found each bleak without the other. Quickly pushed into the class of best sellers (in 1947 it outsold even the year's most popular novel, *The Miracle of the Bells*), for three years *Peace of Mind* rarely fell far from the top in nonfiction sales, so that by March 1949 it had sold over three quarters of a million copies, all at the original price, and another 125,000 copies had been distributed as a book-club dividend.

Competing with *Peace of Mind* but never so popular, were several other works of the same general nature. Lecomte du Noüy inquired into *Human Destiny* by showing that science appeared to prove the existence of God, Norman Vincent Peale presented a *Guide to Confident Living,* and Dale Carnegie set forth formulas to teach men *How to Stop Worrying and Start Living.* The most surprising best seller was a large one-volume abridgment by Professor D. C. Somervell of Arnold J. Toynbee's massive *A Study of History.* With a richly informed perspective, this distinguished British scholar presented a theory of history as suitable to the 'forties as Wells's was to the 'twenties. In Toynbee's view, history passes over into theology; and in showing that civilizations collapse when morals fail, he allowed readers to hope that they might be delivered from disaster through religious belief. The result, the publishers declared, was 'a best seller that is a way of salvation.' In a short time almost 200,000 copies were sold through a book club and stores, many probably never thoroughly read but held by their owners in a kind of estimation that for the twentieth century was akin to the Puritan's regard for *The Practice of Piety.*

The quest for faith infected popular fiction too. There was, for example, Somerset Maugham's *The Razor's Edge,* a novel sharp in its irony but dealing with the mysticism of the Orient as discovered by a disillusioned aviator of the First World War. Helped to popularity by the theme, the book also attracted readers because its author over the years had built up a great public with a long succession of tales adroitly told and conforming to current interests. His early novel, *Of Human Bondage,* had sold but 250 copies in the two years following its publication in 1915; but in only four years during the 'forties *The Razor's Edge* sold about 10,000 times as well, assisted by two book-club selections and a 25-cent reprint.

Just as tense concern over the imperfections of modern life led readers to search for religion, so it caused them to inquire into the

failures of their own society. Antipathy to Russia ruled out popular
success for a Marxist interpretation of the class struggle, leaving attention to focus on books concerned with racial cleavages. The horrors
of Nazi oppression of the Jews brought many Americans an increased
awareness of their own prejudices, interesting them in such dramatic
treatments of anti-Semitism as Gwethalyn Graham's *Earth and High
Heaven* and Laura Z. Hobson's *Gentleman's Agreement*. Likewise, discussion about such practices as segregation of Negroes in the armed
services and a wartime Fair Employment Practice Law brought additional attention to the position of the colored race, preparing a
widespread response to Richard Wright's autobiographical *Black Boy*
and such novels about discrimination against Negroes as Lillian Smith's
Strange Fruit and Sinclair Lewis's *Kingsblood Royal*. Like Somerset
Maugham, Lewis profited not only from a timely subject but from
an established reputation, for he too had a larger public in the 'forties
than ever before. Assisted by book-club distribution, *Kingsblood Royal*
appeared on publication day with more copies in print than *Main Street*
managed to sell over a period of twenty-six years.

If the interest in these books about race relations was sociologically
motivated, they nevertheless derived an added fillip from their sensationalism. A people accustomed by radios, newspapers, popular magazines, and newsreels to a reality of almost unbelievable violence often
demanded fiction whose shock value was at least as great as that of
current events. Habituated to a world of wholesale slaughter, of hor-
rifying torture in concentration camps, and of criminal maladjustment
closer home, readers frequently needed an excess of emotion in novels
if the stories were not to appear pallid beside real life. As a result,
there were popular novels concerned with such matters as the lost
week end of a dipsomaniac, the lubricous life of a Restoration harlot,
the homosexual tendencies both of older, married men and young
boys, and the confinement of a psychotic female in a madhouse. Some
novels with such subjects were serious, well-written works sincerely
attempting to portray the disordered times by analyzing psychoneurotic
characters. In others, however, the aim was for excitement even if it
obscured the essential situation from which it rose, so that a magazine
for retail bookdealers could advise stocking a new novel that 'has
everything in it that made its predecessor sell: horror, sex, madness and
depravity.' It was such an attitude, more than sociological or moral

concern, that made a great best seller of a sober and statistical scientific inquiry entitled *Sexual Behavior in the Human Male;* and perhaps it was this as well as the author's reputation that attracted readers to Steinbeck's *The Wayward Bus,* a murky parable overshadowed by an emphasis on sexual satisfactions.

In an era when changes in values occurred with such speed and cata-strophic effect—during the Depression, the New Deal, the war, and the unsettled peace—facts often seemed the only reality. This uncertainty about values helped explain the tendency of novelists to discern mean-ing by interpreting and reinterpreting a limited area of data, and it helped account for the growing popularity of nonfiction. There was a wide interest in analyses of the situation in which we found ourselves (such as Emery Reves's *Anatomy of Peace*), in exposés of war policy (such as Ralph Ingersoll's *Top Secret*), in panoramic views of the times through which we had just passed (including Upton Sinclair's series of novels about Lanny Budd), in memoirs of statesmen and commanders (the most popular was by the favorite General, Eisen-hower), in realistic novels about the war (such as Norman Mailer's *The Naked and the Dead* and Irwin Shaw's *The Young Lions*), and in studies of the men who had guided our policies. Since the human ele-ment was most readily grasped and since Roosevelt was the one American at the center of all the events that shaped a generation, he became the major figure to be examined by the many books concerned with current history. Reminiscences and recriminations flowed from publishing houses, almost all of them capturing attention, at least for a moment. Roosevelt's juvenilia and ephemera were collected, and people not only read books about him by such distinguished public figures as Secretary of Labor Perkins, Secretary of State Byrnes, Postmaster General Farley, and Robert Sherwood, and by such intimates as his wife and his son Elliott, but they turned even to the recollections of a secret-service agent assigned to guard him and a housekeeper who viewed him through the half-opened kitchen door. A subject of intense affection and bitter hatred during his lifetime, Roosevelt seemed di-rectly after his death to be on the way toward becoming a subject of national mythology. In course of time his character and his actions, like Washington's or Lincoln's, will be interpreted and reinterpreted according to prevailing ideas and beliefs.

Meanwhile there will be new people to write about, figures of history,

American and foreign, and figures of the fictional imagination. The
delight men take in books will continue, their ever-changing tastes
dictating popularity for some, neglect for others. What a new year or
a new era will select is not to be foretold, either by what has been or
by what is, for like the muffled forces of history, the shape of taste
is various and changing, conditioned by events and conditioning them,
never the same and never to be plotted in advance.

❋   ❋   ❋   ❋

Almost three and a half centuries have passed since Captain John
Smith and his comrades landed on these naked shores carrying with
them their timeless book of books, the Bible. Now, in an age of speed
and multiplicity, this great nation has each month its new best seller,
a book of the moment. The Bible still continues to be more widely read
than any other text, even though new works have promised shortcuts
to a peace of mind, a way to influence people, a path that follows in
His steps, or any of the other comforts and pleasures found in the
Bible. Just as each age turns to the Bible in different moods or discovers new interpretations of its words, so each age has its special
texts. Belief does not remain static and taste is ever fluid. For knowledge
and for faith, for surcease and for sensation, each period needs its own
books, books often trivial but written out of the demands of the day. The
timeliness may be in the subject, as in Paine's *Common Sense* or *Parson
Brownlow's Book,* or it may reside in a manner or mood redolent of
a prevailing atmosphere, as in *Pamela* or *Pollyanna.*

Though there is no such thing as a single spirit of an age, but rather
a number of spirits often dwelling together most inharmoniously, the
books popular in a given time, like the customs or the costumes, must
suit the most accepted principles and moods. Shifts in literary tastes are
but segments of men's changing attitudes or beliefs, so that the en-
joyments of past generations may seem to us as fantastic or meretricious
as their opinions. We wonder how the Puritans could find value and
pleasure in a book informing them that to wear a wig was to be irreligious, just as we fail to sympathize with the eighteenth-century
reader who found instruction and palpitation in a sentimental story
of seduction. Each period has its own standards and its own tastes;
like theater tickets, they are good only for this day and this place.

The books a people choose to read somehow reflect their psyche at the moment they select them. This state of mind may not be the only prevalent one, and it may not be the one most common to the larger non-book-reading public. In an election only a small percentage votes to determine 'the people's choice,' and in a measurement of taste through book reading a comparatively few persons create the best sellers of the day. Neither electorate represents a perfect cross section, yet each is an index of the times, even though its choice is frequently shaped by the external pressures of publishers or political parties. The great candidate, whether in politics or in publishing, often does not even get into the race, for he may be too distant from the public. Great thinkers and writers may partake of a temporal ethos, yet their greatness resides in universality, in the ability to reach beyond time and place to ideas and emotions fundamental to all mankind. From them we will usually learn more of man but less of men of the day.

If a student of taste wants to know the thoughts and feelings of the majority who lived during Franklin Pierce's administration, he may find more positive value in Maria Cummins's *The Lamplighter* or T. S. Arthur's *Ten Nights in a Bar-Room* than he will in Thoreau's *Walden*— all books published in 1854. The mores and the manners prevailing in the year of the Teapot Dome scandal can better be extrapolated from Gertrude Atherton's *Black Oxen* than from Wallace Stevens's *Harmonium*. The book that time judges to be great is occasionally also the book popular in its own period; but, by and large, the longer-lived work reflects the demands of the moment only in the most general sense. Usually the book that is popular pleases the reader because it is shaped by the same forces that mold his non-reading hours, so that its dispositions and convictions, its language and subject, re-create the sense of the present, to die away as soon as that present becomes the past. Books of that sort generally are unreadable for succeeding ages; but like other fragments of the past, they help form the present. The volumes themselves may gather dust on library shelves, but they have left lasting impressions on the American mind, etched deeply into a national consciousness. Everybody knows about Crusoe's discovery of Friday's footprint, George Washington chopping the cherry tree, Eliza crossing the ice, and Tom Sawyer whitewashing (or not whitewashing) the fence. These are the images of the popular book. Its persons and places are also embedded in our very vocabulary, so that a man who is unaware of Swift or Hilton, of Mrs. Porter or Miss Hull, of Sinclair

Lewis or Edgar Rice Burroughs can speak of Lilliputian and Shangri-la, of Pollyanna and Sheik, of Babbitt and Tarzan. As seventeenth-century Puritanism, eighteenth-century rationalism, and nineteenth-century romanticism are all dead yet live in the ways they have made us what we are today, so the books that belonged only to an age have paradoxically come to belong to the ages, sometimes as fossil remains, often as invisible but unyielding forces.

Postscript

How to Win Friends and Influence People

Despite the proverb, there is some accounting for tastes. This study, bounded by 'perhaps' and 'although,' examines the tastes that have guided Americans in selecting their popular reading over the past three centuries. Dealing with taste in relation to social compulsions, this inquiry is concerned with the connection between popular books read for pleasure by adult Americans and the times in which those books were read. The readers' pleasure is varied and extensive, including both the Bible and *Forever Amber;* but flexible as the criterion may be, it would be stretched beyond the breaking point should it include dictionaries, school texts, cookbooks, government reports, or manuals on specialized subjects. Such works are sometimes mentioned in this study, but only to illuminate the social background or the general temper of a particular period. The Bible and some specialized doctrinal works are considered in relation to the periods when they were read on the level of general popular literature; but the continued reading of the Bible is taken for granted, while the works of Mary Baker Eddy, the *Book of Mormon,* and other widely distributed sectarian treatises are restricted to special groups of Americans. Shakespeare, Scott, Dickens, and other so-called classic authors are, like the Bible, considered only in relation to their original American audience, unless a striking new wave of popularity occurs at a later date. Some of these works are kept alive by school requirements, some have a continuous and quiet public, but only the nature of their original popularity and the reasons for it are the primary concern of this study. Notice is upon occasion drawn to the continued interest in these established favorites; but the work proceeds in a general chronological sequence, interrupted only by shifting during any given period from one level of the reading public to another, or from one field of public interest to another. Indicative of these fields are the chapter headings, representing not the most widely read books but only a recollection of those whose titles best convey the spirit of prevailing taste.

Concerned with individual books as part of a species, not as isolated best sellers, this investigation neither attempts to isolate the most widely read books from their times, nor to extract into a vacuum certain qualities supposedly inherent in all the books most widely read in America from colonial days to the present. To find such qualities is to discover generalizations so spacious that they apply perfectly to no popular book, but may, indeed, fit equally well the sum of America's less widely read books. If, then, on the one hand, this book does not try to deal with popular books as some have dealt with the question 'What is an American?'—by isolating an abnormal average American who has, say, one and three-eighths children and four fifths of an automobile—neither does it attempt definition in terms of democracy, religion, materialism, or other vague words.

The nature of popular books, like the attitudes of the people who make them popular, is always changing. One might say that the subject of religion has always had a wide appeal (wider, it is true, at some times than others), or that humor or adventure have been components of many popular books. But concepts of religion change as do senses of humor or the ideas of what is adventurous. When history appears to repeat itself by making the doctrinaire poem *The Day of Doom* a popular book in 1662 and the pious novel *The Big Fisherman* a popular book in 1948, there is more difference than repetition. To find relations between these two widely read religious books and the many popular religious books that come between their dates is to look for the lowest common denominator rather than to work out the problem in terms of its own figures. Often there is no lowest common denominator. Only a few years ago there was a demand for biographies of Lincoln, for reminiscences of doctors, and for stories about dogs, so that George Stevens could contemplate a 'super-best-seller' entitled *Lincoln's Doctor's Dog*. These are subjects that have evoked perennial interest. Tomorrow—who knows? Foresight is impossible; even hindsight needs to consider many imponderables that refuse to remain clearly visible.

Literary taste is not an isolated phenomenon. The taste of the largest number of readers is shaped by contemporary pressures more than is the taste of the highly cultivated reader, who has a deeper background of aesthetic experience and knowledge to guide him. Books flourish when they answer a need and die when they do not. The needs of the greatest reading public are various: they include clarification of ideas already in circulation; emotional statement of feelings that people are prepared to accept; popularization of desirable information heretofore obscure; satisfying appeal to forms of entertainment currently considered amusing or exciting. Ranged in this order, one might list as American examples Tom Paine's *The American Crisis;* Mrs. Stowe's *Uncle Tom's Cabin;* Will Durant's *The Story of Philosophy;* and Erle Stanley Gardner's *The Case of the Curious Bride.* But none of these books was popular only because it answered the need with which it is here matched, and there are many books whose popularity relates to a most subtle blending of appeals to all these and other needs of the public. Yet, in some way or another, the popular author is always the one who expresses the people's minds and paraphrases what they consider their private feelings. This combination of social history, cultural history, and literary taste tacitly involves itself in the question, Which came first, the chicken or the egg?—the popular book that shaped public interest or the public interest that shaped the book's popularity? Sometimes one can say clearly it is the first, sometimes the second; most often one can answer only in terms of a dynamic interplay of reader, writer, and the times in which both lived.

At any event, here are investigations that enter into the areas of the literary historian, the sociologist, and the psychologist. The materials studied are like the seven eighths of the iceberg beneath the ocean, not the fragment that rears up so brilliantly into the air serene. The materials are the books taken for granted by the readers of their day, what Isaac D'Israeli called 'the household stuff of literature.' The public that reads them is varied and grows more varied as literacy, public libraries, and bookstores increase. At one end this public shades off into students, teachers, and other serious and constant readers; at the other end it shades off into the people whose reading matter is usually restricted to newspapers and magazines. If a book sells 100,000 copies in 1949, it is tremendously successful; it may even be listed at or near the top of the official twenty best sellers, but the public that bought it represents less than .07 per cent of the whole American population, a population that weekly consumes some 25,000,000 'comic books' and about 10,000,000 pulp magazines. 'Remember this,' said Frank Norris dolefully, 'that for every one person who buys a book there will be six who will talk about it.' The public with which this study is concerned is only the public possessed of enough wealth, education, and leisure to obtain and to read new books as they appear.

This public may be ready to accept a book simply as a popular response, but generally that response has to be stimulated by publicity or the economics of publishing that make for cheap and wide dispersion. The ways in which books can be pushed are many, but pushing of some sort is nearly always needed before the book gets into the public orbit, where it will pull readers by natural attraction. Thus book-club selections often make bookstore buyers. In large part, demand for certain books follows their supply: that is, those most available are the ones most widely purchased by people who want to read and do not know what else to read. But this is not always true, for there are books that almost make their own way, varying from *In His Steps* to *Sexual Behavior in the Human Male*.

Theoretically, any book published in any country at any date (so long as it is available in English and is not too specialized) can become popular in America. Actually, books that are old are often as popular as new ones, proved by a constant demand for the Bible, Shakespeare, Scott, and Dickens, and by the fact that the St. Louis Public Library in 1935 kept 1,897 copies of Mark Twain's works in circulation as against only 30 of Hemingway's. But over and above this demand for 'classics' is that for certain new books, greatly wanted in their own day, hardly at all a short while later. There were, for example, the works of Mrs. E. D. E. N. Southworth, who said she had never met anybody who had not read at least one of her books; and Mrs. Southworth was no recluse. Even today there are readers for those of her books still available in public libraries and in the few cheap issues kept in print, but the appeal of Mrs. Southworth was primarily to her own time. There is an essential difference between the reception of a book that sells a million copies in a year and then may or may not continue to sell slowly, and that of a book with small sales in its year of publication, but which over half a century sells a million copies to a large and late audience composed of students or of adults who feel they should buy it for their shelves if not for their selves. In the house of popularity there are many mansions; the difference between the two types is that which separates *Uncle Tom's Cabin* from *The House of the Seven Gables,* published within a year of one another. Likewise, Scott nowadays surely has as many readers as the 'triumphant twelve or fourteen thousand' who made him a popular success in his own time, but he does not have the audience of such a latter-day Scott as Kenneth Roberts. For even in his selection of historical romances, the average reader prefers the one written in his own period as being closer to him in point of view, in vocabulary, and in artistic design.

In retrospect we can often see reasons why a certain type of book won a wide public, but we cannot always see why the particular representative had the greatest success. Sometimes it is the first and is therefore novel; sometimes it is the last, for which others have prepared a potential audience. Nor can we always see even why an author whose books are compounded of similar elements is now popular, now relatively neglected. Some writers, like Scott or Dickens, make a reputation early, amass a loyal following and continue adding to it those persons who 'missed' the first books and want to read the later ones to enter the discussion that follows publication of a new work. On the other hand, there are authors, like Pearl Buck, whose first book sells enormously and whose subsequent ones do less well, perhaps because the novelty of subject, point of view, or style wears off, and, if necessary, the later books can be discussed in terms of the first. With book clubs now presenting a new book that 'must' be read each month, the life of any book is relatively limited, yesterday's required reading forgotten in favor of today's. Many of these books represent fads of the moment, not even long enough lived to create a cycle or a type. Each new book is but a Roman candle, brilliant against the sky, which darkens again before another and wholly different set piece illumines the heavens for its own brief moment.

What makes America select as its all-time most popular books (of course excluding the Bible and Shakespeare's plays) works as diverse as *How to Win Friends and Influence People, Uncle Tom's Cabin, In His Steps, Ben-Hur,* and *Gone with the Wind* is a question not lightly answered. *How to Win Friends and Influence People* appeals to the American's utilitarian strain, his constant search for success in this world; *In His Steps* appeals to a pietistic strain, a continuing quest for success in terms of the other world; *Uncle Tom's Cabin* is humanitarian in its condemnation of the South; *Gone with the Wind* is romantic in depicting the charms of the South; *Ben-Hur* combines elements that may be discovered in the three other novels but has nothing to satisfy the interest that made a public for Dale Carnegie's work; and surely each of these books has more than one neatly labeled appeal. Were such justifiable companions as *See Here, Private Hargrove* or *Freckles* added to this list of superlatively popular books, the issue would only be further confused. The reasons for the popularity of each book can be seen with some clarity through its relation to certain drives of the period in which it found an audience, but to say what made these and a few others the most widely read of all American books is not to find the sum of America's major ideas and interests, for these diverse texts, popular at one moment, were neglected in the next.

In their time, many men have considered the question what makes one book sell more than another and none have found a definitive answer. Samuel Butler, an author tremendously influential on a limited public but never widely popular, reconciled himself to this quandary by writing:

There are some things which it is madness not to try to know but which it is almost as much madness to try to know. Sometimes publishers, hoping to buy the Holy Ghost with a price, fee a man to read for them and advise them. This is but as the vain tossing of insomnia. God will not have any human being know what will sell.

Robert Southey, who wrote thousands of pages of prose and verse, of which today only his story of 'The Three Bears' is remembered, and remembered without attribution to its author, also pondered the problem, only to come up with this summary: 'The Public and Transubstantiation I hold to be the two greatest mysteries in or out of nature.'

Bibliographical Checklist

Information about the books considered in this study derives from many sources, some as specialized as the inventories of seventeenth-century estates or the bills of lading of seventeenth-century English exporters, both listing books by title. In general, however, data has come from autobiographies, letters, and biographies of authors, editors, and publishers; from diaries, letters, and autobiographies of people who followed or took notice of popular fashions; from newspaper and magazine articles dealing with literary information; from book reviews; from bibliographies and registers of publication like those by Sabin, Evans, Roorbach, Kelly, and Wright; from standard reference books such as the *Dictionary of American Biography* and the Duyckincks' *Cyclopaedia of American Literature;* from publishing trade journals; from booksellers' catalogues; from bookdealers' statistics; from publishers' advertisements and announcements; and, of course, from the popular books described in the text.

Particularly, I should like to express my appreciation for the kind aid of the only other author who has dealt in general with this subject. Professor Frank Luther Mott sent me the galley proofs of his *Golden Multitudes* when my work was half written and urged me to complete it because his interest was in 'the story of best sellers in the United States' and mine in popular reading tastes related to social pressures. His research frequently confirmed my own findings, although we differ on interpretations of popularity, for his depend on the criterion that a best seller is a book that over the years since its publication has had a sale equal to 1 per cent of the population of the continental United States at the time it was first issued. Even leaving aside the disinterest

in relative literacy, transportation and merchandising facilities, value
of currency, and other qualifications, this standard leads to conclusions
different from mine. Using population statistics of one period and sales
statistics of another, Professor Mott finds that Mark Twain's *Life on
the Mississippi* is one of the best sellers rising from the 1880-89 decade
(when population was about 50,000,000) because in 1946 it reached
a sale of half a million copies as the first of a series of 25-cent, pocket-
size reprints. Thus Professor Mott includes as best sellers *Leaves of
Grass,* Poe's *Poems, Moby-Dick,* and other works that when related
to the periods of their first publication are found to have interested
only a very small public.

The following list of sources is selective, merely a notation of those
most serviceable in this work, and is meant neither as a full listing of
the works consulted for this study nor as a complete bibliography for
students interested in any particular topic dealt with in the text.

CHAPTER 1

Much of the information on books available to New Englanders was derived from inventories of estates, bills of lading, and other primary documents
published in compilations of historical societies and learned journals as well as
in local histories and family records. Diaries, particularly Samuel Sewall's, and
memoirs, such as John Dunton's, have proved valuable, as have letters reprinted
in historical and antiquarian journals. Some of these I later discovered to have
been used by Evan A. Evans in his unpublished Harvard University doctoral
thesis, 'Literary References in New England Diaries.'

Important studies of New England intellectual history include Samuel
Eliot Morison's *The Puritan Pronaos* and Thomas Goddard Wright's *Literary
Culture in Early New England.* Intimately allied to their subject and mine are
George E. Littlefield's *Early Boston Booksellers* and his *Early Schools and
School-Books of New England,* Worthington Chauncey Ford's *The Boston Book
Market* 1679-1700, and Lawrence C. Wroth's *The Colonial Printer.*

Useful books on the social background include: Perry Miller's *The New
England Mind—Seventeenth Century,* Miller and Thomas Johnson's *The Puri-
tans,* George Williamson's *Saints and Sinners,* George Francis Dow's *Everyday
Life in the Massachusetts Bay Colony,* William B. Weeden's *Economic and
Social History of New England,* Evarts B. Greene and Virginia Harrington's
American Population Before the Federal Census of 1790, and Edward Eggles-
ton's *Transit of Civilization to New England in the Seventeenth Century.*

For the study of popular reading in the South, I found particular value
in Philip A. Bruce's three great works: *The Institutional History of Virginia,
The Social History of Virginia,* and *The Economic History of Virginia.* George
K. Smart's 'Private Libraries in Colonial Virginia,' *American Literature,* x
(March 1938), contains useful source material. Louis B. Wright's *The First
Gentlemen of Virginia* is in part concerned with a problem similar to that here
investigated, although the interest is in a higher level of culture. Equally impor-

tant in its suggestiveness is Wright's *Middle-Class Culture in Elizabethan England*, a most illuminating study in part concerned with the common Englishman's reading during this period.

CHAPTER 2

Valuable data on the social and intellectual background was obtained from many memoirs and diaries, including Franklin's *Autobiography*; F. B. Dexter, *The Literary Diary of Ezra Stiles*; Ezra Stiles, *Itineraries and Correspondence*; William Bentley, *Diary*; Dr. Alexander Hamilton, *Itinerarium*; Thomas Green, *Diary of a Lover of Literature*; P. L. Ford, *Journal of Hugh Gaine*; Isaiah Thomas, *Diary*; and Samuel Miller, *Brief Retrospect of the Eighteenth Century*. Important secondary sources on the culture of the period include: Merle Curti, *The Growth of American Culture*; Michael Kraus, *Intercolonial Aspects of American Culture*; Thomas J. Wertenbaker, *The Founding of American Civilization* and *The Golden Age in Colonial Culture*; James Truslow Adams, *Provincial Society*; Carl Bridenbaugh, *Cities in the Wilderness*; and Harry B. Parkes, 'New England in the 1730's,' *New England Quarterly*, III (July 1930).

Material on circulating libraries and reading interests derives in part not only from these sources but also from such studies as: C. K. Bolton, 'Circulating Libraries in Boston,' *Colonial Society of Massachusetts Proceedings*, XI; S. B. Weeks, 'Libraries and Literature in North Carolina in the Eighteenth Century,' *Annual Report* of the American Historical Association, 1895; A. Goodhue, Jr., 'The Reading Interests of Harvard Students, 1770-1781,' *Essex Institute Historical Collections*, LXXII (April 1937); Carl Bridenbaugh, 'Press and Book in Eighteenth-Century Philadelphia,' *Pennsylvania Magazine of History and Biography*, LXV (January 1941); G. M. Abbey, *A Short History of the Library Company of Philadelphia*; A. B. Keep, *History of the New York Society Library*; G. S. Eddy, 'Dr. Benjamin Franklin's Library,' *American Antiquarian Society Proceedings*, N.S., XXXIV (October 1924); Elizabeth G. Cook, *Literary Influences in Colonial Newspapers*; Leon Howard, 'Early American Copies of Milton,' *Huntington Library Bulletin*, No. 7 (1935), and 'Influence of Milton on Colonial Poetry,' *Huntington Library Bulletin*, No. 9 (1936); Edwin Elliott Willoughby, 'The Reading of Shakespeare in Colonial America,' *Papers of the Bibliographical Society of America*, XXXI, Part 1 (1937); Agnes Marie Sibley, *Alexander Pope's Prestige in America*; Dale Warren, 'John West, Bookseller,' *New England Quarterly*, VI (September 1933); R. W. Higgins, 'Memoirs of Jonathan Plummer,' *New England Quarterly*, VIII (March 1935); Harry Hayden Clark, 'Influence of Science on American Ideas,' *Transactions of the Wisconsin Academy of Science, Arts, and Letters*, XXXV (1944); Harriet S. Tapley, *Salem Imprints: 1768-1825*; various articles on colonial libraries by Joseph T. Wheeler published in volumes XXXIV-XXXVIII of the *Maryland Historical Magazine*; John T. Winterich, *Early American Books and Printing*; Esther C. Dunn, *Shakespeare in America*; Lawrence Wroth, *An American Bookshelf: 1755*; and Moncure D. Conway, *The Writings of Thomas Paine*.

On the influences of foreign ideas, particularly suggestive and informative are Howard Mumford Jones's *America and French Culture* and his articles, 'Importation of French Books in Philadelphia,' *Modern Philology*, XXXII (November 1934) and 'Importation of French Literature in New York City 1750-

1800,' *Studies in Philology*, XXVIII (October 1931), as well as E. R. White's *American Opinion of France*.

Two leading studies of deism in the American colonies are: G. Adolph Koch, *Republican Religion* and Herbert W. Morais, *Deism in Eighteenth-Century America*.

CHAPTER 3

Many of the sources used in Chapter 2 were also employed for Chapter 3. In addition, one might note the following valuable treatments of the social and intellectual background: Carl Becker, *Eve of the Revolution;* Evarts B. Greene, *The Revolutionary Generation;* and John A. Krout and Dixon R. Fox, *The Completion of Independence*.

Works particularly relevant to special subjects treated in this chapter include: Philip G. Davidson, *Propaganda and the American Revolution;* Merle Curti, 'The Great Mr. Locke, America's Philosopher,' *Huntington Library Bulletin*, No. 11 (1937); Griffith J. McKee, *Life and Correspondence of James Iredell;* Joseph T. Buckingham, *Personal Memoirs;* and John Quincy Adams, *Life in a New England Town*.

Leading sources on almanacs include: George L. Kittredge, *The Old Farmer and His Almanac;* Chester Greenough, 'New England Almanacs, 1766-1775, and the American Revolution,' *American Antiquarian Society Proceedings*, N.S., XLV (October 1935); and Samuel Briggs, *The Essays, Humor, and Poems of Nathaniel Ames, Father and Son*.

Valuable material on Indian Captivities is to be found in Roy Harvey Pearce's 'The Significance of the Captivity Narrative,' *American Literature*, XIX, 1 (March 1947), and in Jason A. Russell's 'The Narratives of the Indian Captivities,' *Education*, LI (1930).

On Parson Weems the three main sources are: Emily Ellsworth Skeel's monumental *Mason Locke Weems*, Lawrence C. Wroth's *Parson Weems*, and W. A. Bryan, 'Three Unpublished Letters of Parson Weems,' *William and Mary College Quarterly*, XXII (July 1943).

CHAPTER 4

The most thorough study of sentimentalism in fiction is Herbert Ross Brown's *The Sentimental Novel in America*, 1789-1860, but other valuable studies include: Edith Birkhead's 'Sentiment and Sensibility in the Eighteenth-Century Novel,' *Essays and Studies of the English Association*, Volume XI; Mildred D. Doyle's *Sentimentalism in American Periodicals*, 1741-1800; A. D. McKillop's *Samuel Richardson;* W. G. Vail's 'Susanna Haswell Rowson,' *American Antiquarian Society Proceedings*, N.S., XLII (1932); Frank G. Black's *The Epistolary Novel;* George G. Raddin's *An Early New York Library of Fiction;* and G. M. S. Tompkins's *The Popular Novel in England*.

Sensibility in fiction is considered in some of the works above and is specifically treated in Walter F. Wright's 'Sensibility in English Prose Fiction 1760-1814,' *Illinois Studies in Language and Literature*, 3 & 4 (1937); and Tremaine McDowell's 'Sensibility in the Eighteenth-Century American Novel,' *Studies in Philology*, XXIV (July 1927).

Gothic fiction is discussed in Sister Mary M. Redden's *Gothic Fiction in the American Magazine*, 1765-1800; O. W. Long's 'Werther in America,' *Studies in Honor of John Albrecht Walz;* and Oral Sumner Coad's 'The Gothic Element in American Literature,' *Journal of English and Germanic Philology*, XXIV, 1 (1925).

The attitude toward fiction may be garnered from many diaries of the time and from contemporary magazines. It is also treated in such special studies as John T. Taylor's *Early Opposition to the English Novel;* G. Harrison Orians's 'Censure of Fiction in American Romances and Magazines, 1789-1810,' *PMLA*, LII (March 1937); Bertha M. Stearns's 'Early New England Magazines for Ladies,' *New England Quarterly*, II, 3 (June 1929); and sections of Frank Luther Mott's *History of American Magazines*, 1741-1850.

Valuable bibliographical studies include Lyle H. Wright's *American Fiction, 1774-1850* and 'A Statistical Study of American Fiction, 1774-1850,' *Huntington Library Quarterly*, II (1939).

CHAPTER 5

Major studies of Scott's popularity include the articles by G. Harrison Orians: 'The Romance Ferment After Waverley,' in *American Literature*, III, 4 (January 1932); 'The Origin of the Ring Tournament in the United States,' *Maryland Historical Magazine*, XXXVI (September 1941); and 'Walter Scott, Mark Twain, and the Civil War,' *South Atlantic Quarterly*, XL (1941); and his unpublished doctoral dissertation, 'The Influence of Scott Before 1860,' (Urbana, 1929). Other studies include: Grace Landrum's 'Sir Walter Scott and His Literary Rivals in the Old South,' *American Literature*, II (November 1930); and her 'Notes on Reading in the Old South,' *American Literature*, III, 1 (March 1931); Henry Adalbert White's *Sir Walter Scott's Novels on the Stage;* James T. Hillhouse's *The Waverley Novels and their Critics;* David Randall's 'Waverley in America,' *Colophon*, N.S., I (Summer 1935); Earl Bradsher, *Matthew Carey;* H. F. Bogner, 'Sir Walter Scott in New Orleans 1818-1832,' *Louisiana Historical Quarterly*, XXI (April 1939); W. Forbes Gray, *Scott in Sunshine and Shadow;* R.V., 'Scott and the Southern States,' *Notes and Queries*, CLXIX (9 November 1935); H. J. Eckinrode, 'Sir Walter Scott and the South,' *North American Review*, CCVI (1917); Henry White, 'Scott's Novels on the Stage,' *Yale Studies in English*, 76 (1927); and an unpublished University of California doctoral dissertation, Paul M. Roberts, 'Sir Walter Scott's Contributions to the English Language' (Berkeley, 1948).

On Byron's reading public in this country the leading study is William Ellery Leonard's *Byron and Byronism in America*. Charles Duffy's 'Thomas Campbell and America,' *American Literature*, XIII (January 1942), furnished most of the data on Campbell. S. M. Ellis's *The Solitary Horseman* yielded much of the information on G. P. R. James. Stanley T. Williams's monumental *Life of Washington Irving*, Henry W. Boynton's biography of Cooper, and Robert E. Spiller's *Fenimore Cooper: Critic of His Times* were major sources for material on these two authors. As indicated in the text, the most useful study of Tom Moore is Howard Mumford Jones's *The Harp That Once—*, although W. F. Trench's *Tom Moore* and B. J. Lossing's 'Tom Moore in America,' *Harper's New Monthly Magazine*, LV (September 1877), were also employed. Material on Wordsworth derived primarily from Annabel Newton's

Wordsworth in Early American Literature; Norman Foerster's 'Wordsworth in America,' *Studies in Philology,* xxvi (January 1929); and Lewis Leary's 'Wordsworth in America,' *Modern Language Notes,* lviii (May 1943).

English travelers, American journalists, reviewers, public figures who wrote autobiographies, and other contemporary authors furnished much of the evidence about even the figures who have been the subjects of modern scholarly studies. Occasional valuable pieces of information were found in modern books not specifically devoted to the subjects here under consideration, and indebtedness to them is indicated in the text.

CHAPTER 6

Among the significant sources for information on the spirit of the times are many published diaries, letters, volumes of recollections, and reports of travelers. These include: Thomas L. Nichols, *Forty Years of American Life;* Samuel G. Goodrich, *Recollections of a Lifetime;* Francis J. Grund, *The Americans in their Moral, Social, and Political Relations;* James C. Derby, *Fifty Years Among Authors;* Clifton Furness's collection, *The Genteel Female; The Diary of Philip Hone,* edited by Allan Nevins; and Nevins's collection, *American Social History as Recorded by British Travellers.*

Valuable secondary sources include: E. Douglas Branch, *The Sentimental Years;* Meade Minnigerode, *The Fabulous Forties;* George Boas (editor), *Romanticism in America;* F. L. Pattee, *The Feminine Fifties;* Arthur M. Schlesinger, *Learning to Behave;* Carl R. Fish, *The Rise of the Common Man.*

These general works contributed information on the gift books, poetry, and fiction of the day, but more specific sources include: Herbert Ross Brown, *The Sentimental Novel in America;* Alexander Cowie, 'The Vogue of the Domestic Novel, 1850-1870,' *South Atlantic Quarterly,* xli (October 1942); Ralph Thompson, *Literary Annuals and Gift Books;* Regis L. Boyle, *Mrs. E. D. E. N. Southworth;* Anna B. Warner, *Susan Warner;* Robert P. Eckert, 'Friendly, Fragrant Fanny Ferns,' *Colophon,* Part 18 (September 1934); Luke M. White, Jr., *Henry William Herbert;* Gordon S. Haight, *Mrs. Sigourney;* Caroline Ticknor, *Hawthorne and His Publisher;* Bertha Faust, *Hawthorne's Contemporaneous Reputation;* Warren S. Tryon and William Charvat (editors), *The Cost Books of Ticknor and Fields;* and, of course, the novels, poems, and gift books themselves, as well as contemporary criticism in newspapers and magazines.

Information on the reading of French books came not only from these general sources and from Howard Mumford Jones's *America and French Culture,* but from Elizabeth B. White's *American Opinion of France;* Albert L. Rabinovitz, 'Criticism of French Novels in Boston Magazines, 1820-1860,' *New England Quarterly,* xiv (September 1941); Grace B. Sherrer's 'French Culture as Presented to Middle-Class America by *Godey's Lady's Book,' American Literature,* iii (November 1931); and Howard Mumford Jones's 'American Comment on George Sand,' *American Literature,* iii (January 1932).

Information about Dickens and Thackeray in America is to be found in W. Glyde Wilkins, *Charles Dickens in America;* E. F. Payne, *Dickens Days in Boston;* Eyre Crow, *With Thackeray in America;* and James Grant Wilson, *Thackeray in the United States.*

CHAPTER 7

Magazines of the period furnished much of the background about book sales and contemporary interests, the most valuable of these being *The American Literary Gazette and Publishers' Circular*. The memoirs of the publisher, J. C. Derby, *Fifty Years Among Authors*, also provided many statements on sales and reading fashions. Modern scholarly studies of the general period that proved particularly useful included Emerson David Fite's *Social and Industrial Conditions in the North During the Civil War*; Arthur C. Cole's *The Irrepressible Conflict*; and Alice Felt Tyler's *Freedom's Ferment*.

The subject of the temperance novel is treated with great detail in Herbert Ross Brown's *The Sentimental Novel in America*, and somewhat more lightly in Edmund Pearson's *Queer Books*.

Modern studies of specific authors that proved specially useful include: Forrest Wilson, *Crusader in Crinoline*, on Harriet Beecher Stowe; Hugh Talmage Lefler, *Hinton Rowan Helper*; E. Merton Coulter, *William G. Brownlow*; Harry Hayden Clark, 'The Vogue of Macaulay,' *Transactions of the Wisconsin Academy of Science, Arts, and Letters*, XXXIV (1943); Mary A. Bennett, *Elizabeth Stuart Phelps*; Ernest Elmo Calkins, 'St. Elmo, or, Named for a Best Seller,' *Saturday Review of Literature* (16 December 1939); Yvonne ffrench, *Ouida*; Walter C. Philipps, *Dickens, Reade, and Collins*; and Malcolm Elwin, *Charles Reade*. Autobiographical statements by all the authors concerned were also useful.

CHAPTER 8

Much of the material for this chapter comes from the letters and the verse of the poets themselves, but bibliographies, biographies, and special studies by modern scholars have also proved most useful. Information about Longfellow's popularity and the sales of his books comes from several sources, including *The Cost Books of Ticknor and Fields* edited by Warren S. Tryon and William Charvat, the *Bibliography* by J. C. Chamberlain and Luther S. Livingston, and from William Charvat's 'Longfellow's Income from His Writings, 1840-1852,' *Papers of the Bibliographical Society of America*, XXXVIII (First quarter, 1944). Two books about Tennyson study him from the same point of view as that with which this work is concerned and inevitably I owe a great debt to John O. Eidson's *Tennyson in America* and Cornelius Weygandt's *The Time of Tennyson*. The abstract of T. P. McCormick's 'Browning's Reputation in America,' printed in *Summaries of Northwestern University Doctoral Dissertations*, Volume 5, furnished some facts concerning Browning's American audience. Tupper's autobiography, *My Life as an Author*, proved a useful source when supplemented by Ralf Buchmann's *Martin F. Tupper*, and one item about Tupper's sales in America was found in Holmes's *Autocrat of the Breakfast-Table*. References to Mrs. Sigourney's popularity pepper the magazines and autobiographies of her time, but more consistent consideration is to be found in Gordon S. Haight's *Mrs. Sigourney*. The only modern treatment of J. G. Holland is the biography by Harry Houston Peckham from which some of the information about him was obtained. Thomas Franklin Currier's *Bibliography of John Greenleaf Whittier* is the work most closely concerned with the problems treated in my study but the biographies by Whitman Bennett and Albert Mordell also yielded information. The main source for information about Owen Meredith is Aurelia Brooks Harlan's biography. The circulation of FitzGerald's work is considered in John T. Winterich's *Books and the Man* and Ambrose G. Potter's *Bibliography of the Rubáiyát*.

CHAPTER 9

The two studies of humor used most in this chapter are both by Walter Blair. The first is his full critical anthology, *Native American Humor*, the second his article, 'The Popularity of Nineteenth-Century American Humorists,' *American Literature*, III (May 1931). Contemporary sources such as J. C. Derby's *Fifty Years Among Authors* were also drawn upon, as was Franklin Walker's fine study, *San Francisco's Literary Frontier*.

Many sources contributed to the information on Twain, beginning with his letters, his *Autobiography*, and the authorized biography by Albert Bigelow Paine. Special studies of particular value included: Bernard De Voto's *Mark Twain's America*; Samuel Charles Webster's *Mark Twain, Business Man*; Edward Wagenknecht's *Mark Twain: The Man and His Work*; A. L. Vogelback's 'The Publication and Reception of *Huckleberry Finn* in America,' *American Literature*, XI (November 1939); Leon T. Dickinson's 'Marketing a Best Seller: Mark Twain's *Innocents Abroad*,' *Papers of the Bibliographical Society of America*, XLI (1947); Frank C. Willson's 'That "Gilded Age" Again,' *Papers of the Bibliographical Society of America*, XXXVII (1943); and several contemporary articles, including particularly George T. Ferris's 'Mark Twain,' *Appleton's Journal* (4 July 1874).

On the subject of subscription publication I found F. E. Compton's monograph, *Subscription Books*, useful, but most information came from documents of the time, such as Henry Bill, *Bill's Confidential Directions to his Agents*; J. H. Mortimer, *Confessions of a Book Agent*, and, best of all, the anonymous *How to Introduce the Memoirs of Ulysses S. Grant*.

On the dime novel I found particularly valuable Merle Curti's illuminating 'Dime Novels and the American Tradition,' *Yale Review*, XXVI (June 1937); E. L. Pearson's *Dime Novels*; Dixon Wecter's chapter on Buffalo Bill in *The Hero in America*; Henry Robinson's 'Mr. Beadle's Books,' *Bookman*, LIX (1929); and the *Bibliography* and catalogues of Charles Bragin, the leading bookdealer in dime novels.

CHAPTER 10

Much of the information on the general social and economic movements of the time may be found in Dennis Tilden Lynch, *The Wild Seventies*; Lewis Mumford, *The Brown Decades*; Ralph Henry Gabriel, *The Course of American Democratic Thought*; Allan Nevins, *The Emergence of Modern America*; Ida Tarbell, *The Nationalizing of Business*; Merle Curti, *The Growth of American Thought*; and Vernon L. Parrington, *The Beginnings of Critical Realism in America*.

The primary information about the authors comes, as usual, in great part from their own works and from contemporary newspaper and magazine comments about them.

Special studies that have proved particularly useful include: Maurice F. Tauber, *Russell Herman Conwell;* Irving McKee, *Ben-Hur Wallace;* Dorothy C. Hockey, 'The Good and the Beautiful,' an unpublished Western Reserve University doctoral dissertation on popular fiction; Arthur E. Morgan, *Edward Bellamy;* Elizabeth Sadler, 'One Book's Influence: *Looking Backward,*' *New England Quarterly,* XVIII (December 1944); Stewart Holbrook, 'A Congress-man Rediscovers Atlantis,' *New York Times Book Review* (30 July 1944), his 'Professor Coin: Financial Wizard,' *New York Times Book Review* (15 October, 1944), and his 'Ignatius Donnelly,' *New Republic* (22 December 1947); Mary Austin, *Earth Horizon;* Henry George, Jr., *The Life of Henry George;* Henry Seidel Canby, *The Age of Confidence;* and R. W. G. Vail, 'A *Message to Garcia*' A Bibliographical Puzzle.

CHAPTER 11

In addition to the books on social background used for Chapter 10, gen-eral information was derived from Arthur M. Schlesinger, *Rise of the City;* Dixon Wecter, *The Saga of American Society;* Mark Sullivan, *Our Times;* Lloyd Morris, *Postscript to Yesterday;* Harold U. Faulkner, *The Quest for Social Justice;* Charles W. Fergusson, *Fifty Million Brothers;* and Amelie Neville, *The Fantastic City.*

Studies of the fiction of the time are to be found in the files of *The Pub-lishers' Weekly* and *The Bookman* for the years concerned, as well as in cer-tain other contemporary articles, including: Paul Shorey, 'Present Conditions of Literary Production,' *Atlantic Monthly* (August 1896); Richard Watson Gilder, 'Certain Tendencies in Current Literature,' *New Princeton Review* (July 1887); Hamilton Wright Mabie, 'The Most Popular Novels in America,' *Forum* (De-cember 1893); and Talcott Williams, 'The Change in Current Fiction,' *Ameri-can Review of Reviews* (December 1900).

More recent studies include: Sidney Kramer, *A History of Stone and Kim-ball;* Grant C. Knight, 'The "Pastry" Period in Literature,' *Saturday Review of Literature* (16 December 1944); Irving H. Hart, 'Fiction Fashions: 1895-1925,' *Publishers' Weekly* (5 February 1927); Arthur Hobson Quinn, *American Fic-tion;* Alfred Kazin, *On Native Grounds;* Raymond H. Shove, *Cheap Book Pro-duction in the United States,* 1870-1891; John T. Winterich, *Books and the Man;* Roger Burlingame, *Of Making Many Books;* Dorothy C. Hockey's dis-sertation, 'The Good and the Beautiful'; Grant Overton, *American Nights Entertainment;* F. W. Halsey, *Our Literary Deluge;* and Herbert R. Brown, 'The Great American Novel,' *American Literature,* VII (March 1935).

Autobiographies of editors, publishers, and authors were also valuable sources, including: James L. Ford, *Forty-Odd Years in the Literary Shop;* George H. Putnam, *Memoirs of a Publisher;* S. S. McClure, *My Autobiography;* Frank L. Tooker, *Joys and Tribulations of an Editor;* J. H. Harper, *The House of Harper;* Henry Holt, *Garrulities of an Octagenarian Editor;* George H. Doran, *Chronicles of Barabbas;* and Theodore Dreiser, *A Book About Myself.*

Valuable statistics about best sellers are collected in Alice Payne Hackett, *Fifty Years of Best Sellers.*

Information about specific authors derived not only from these works and from the authors' own writings but also from special studies, including: Grant C. Knight, *James Lane Allen;* Maude Howe Elliott, *My Cousin, F. Marion*

Crawford; F. O. Matthiessen, *The James Family;* Gerald Bullock, *Marie Corelli;* Michael Elwin, *Old Gods Falling;* Louis N. Feipel, 'The American Issues of "Trilby," ' *Colophon,* N.S., II (Autumn 1937); C. C. Hoyle Miller, *George Du Maurier and Others;* the files of *The Kipling Journal;* Carl J. Weber, *Hardy in America;* Edward Wagenknecht, 'The World and Mary Johnston,' *Sewanee Review,* XLIV (April-June 1936); Theodore G. Ersham, *Bibliographies of Twelve Victorian Authors;* and various entries in the *Dictionary of American Biography.*

CHAPTER 12

Concerned with a period almost the same as that dealt with in Chapters 10 and 11, this chapter had as sources on the social background and the literary scene many of the works previously noted. Special studies of authors considered in this chapter include: Carey McWilliams's consideration of *Ramona* in his *Southern California Country;* Alice Hegan Rice's *The Inky Way;* Edward Noyes Westcott's *The Teller,* including Forbes Heerman's 'An Account of His Life'; Jeanette Porter Meehan's *Lady of the Limberlost;* Frank Norris, *Responsibilities of the Novelist;* Irving Stone's *Sailor on Horseback;* T. K. Whipple's 'Jack London—Wonder Boy' and other sections of his *Study Out the Land;* Edith Wharton's *A Backward Glance;* Alva Johnston's article on Edgar Rice Burroughs, 'How to Become a Great Writer,' *Saturday Evening Post* (29 July 1939); E. H. Lacon Watson's ' "Tarzan" and Literature,' *Fortnightly Review* (June 1923); Paul Leicester Ford's 'The American Historical Novel,' *Atlantic Monthly* (December 1897); Frederic Taber Cooper's 'The Popularity of Harold Bell Wright,' *The Bookman* (January 1915); Irving Bacheller's *From Stores of Memory;* A. J. Hanna's *A Bibliography of the Writings of Irving Bacheller;* William Lyon Phelps's 'Why of the Best Seller,' *The Bookman* (December 1921); and newspaper obituaries of several of the authors under consideration.

CHAPTER 13

Much of the information about the more informal aspects of the society was provided by Frederick Lewis Allen, *Only Yesterday;* Mark Sullivan, *Our Times* (Volumes 4, 5, 6); and Preston W. Slosson, *The Great Crusade and After.* The most used sociological study was Robert and Helen Lynd, *Middletown.*

Sales statistics and other information about publishing and reading trends during the 'twenties were found in books and magazines cited for previous chapters. New sources include: Charles H. Compton, *Who Reads What?;* Archibald Ogden, 'The Book Trade in Wartime,' *Publishers' Weekly* (8 July 1939); Orion H. Cheney, *Economic Survey of the Book Industry, 1930-1931;* Walter Hines Page, *A Publisher's Confession;* E. Haldemann-Julius, *The First Hundred Million;* Frederick A. Stokes, *A Publisher's Random Notes;* Robert L. Duffus, *Books, Their Place in a Democracy;* William S. Gray and Ruth Munroe, *Reading Interests and Habits of Adults;* Walter B. Pitkin, 'A New Survey of the Best Seller,' *Publishers' Weekly* (15 and 22 June 1929); 'Religious Books as Best Sellers,' *Publishers' Weekly* (19 February 1921); Leon Whipple, 'Miracle Books,' *Survey* (1 May 1927); Irving H. Hart, 'The Most Popular Authors of Fiction in the Post-War Period,' *Publishers' Weekly* (12 March

1927); Irving H. Hart, 'Best Sellers in Non-Fiction Since 1921,' *Publishers'*
Weekly (4 February 1933); Herbert F. Jenkins, 'The Nation's Appetite for
Fiction,' *Publishers' Weekly* (24 September 1921); Frederick Lewis Allen,
'Best Sellers: 1900-1935,' *Saturday Review of Literature* (7 December 1935);
and John Bakeless, 'William Lyon Phelps: Book Booster,' *American Mercury*
(November 1935).

More general studies of the literary scene include: Irene and Allen
Cleaton, *Books and Battles;* Malcolm Cowley (editor), *After the Genteel Tra-
dition;* Katharine Fullerton Gerould, 'This Hard-Boiled Era,' *Harper's* (Feb-
ruary 1929); Mark Longaker, *Contemporary Biography;* Alexander Cowie,
'The New Heroine's Code of Virtue,' *American Scholar*, IV (Spring 1935); and
Florin Lee McDonald, *Book Reviewing in the American Newspaper.*

CHAPTER 14

Suggestions about the social background and occasional statistics or other
data were drawn from some of the sources noted for preceding chapters as well
as from Dixon Wecter, *The Age of the Great Depression;* Leo Gurko, *The
Angry Decade;* Frederick Lewis Allen, *Since Yesterday;* William Fielding
Ogburn, *American Society in Wartime;* and Robert and Helen Lynd, *Middletown in Transition.*

Information about general reading trends and the reception of specific
books is partly based on my own recollection. Trade journals and book reviews
were more useful in writing this chapter than others since comparatively fewer
studies of contemporary literary interests have yet been published. Among
those that have appeared, the following were particularly valuable: Douglas
Waples, *Reading in the Depression;* George Stevens, *Lincoln's Doctor's Dog;*
Louis R. Wilson, *The Geography of Reading;* Jeanette H. Foster, 'An Experiment in Classifying Fiction Based on the Characteristics of its Readers,' unpublished doctoral dissertation, University of Chicago Graduate Library School,
1935; Douglas Waples, *People and Print;* Q. D. Leavis, *Fiction and the Reading Public;* Douglas Waples and Ralph Taylor, *What People Want to Read
About;* Howard Haycraft, *Murder for Pleasure;* Howard Haycraft, *Art of the
Mystery Story;* Pierce Butler, *Books and Libraries in Wartime;* Henry C.
Link and Henry Arthur Hopf, *People and Books;* and Alva Johnston, *The Case
of Erle Stanley Gardner.*

Articles of particular interest include: Groff Conklin, 'Pullman Reading,'
Publishers' Weekly (6 July 1935); Leon Carnovsky, 'A Study of the Relation-
ship Between Reading Interests and Actual Reading,' *Library Quarterly*
(January 1934); Bennett Cerf, 'Books that Shook the World,' *Saturday Eve-
ning Post* (3 April 1943); Philip Van Doren Stern, 'Books and Best Sellers,'
Virginia Quarterly Review (January 1942); Margaret C. Banning, 'Changing
Moral Standards in Fiction,' *Saturday Review of Literature* (1 July 1939);
Bernard De Voto, 'Fiction and the Everlasting If,' *Harper's* (June 1938); Bernard De Voto, 'Fiction Fights the Civil War,' *Saturday Review of Literature*
(18 December 1937); John Chamberlain, 'Readers and Writers in Wartime,'
Yale Review (September 1943); Dorothy Canfield Fisher, 'American Readers
and Books,' *American Scholar* (Spring 1944); Louis Adamic, 'What the Proletariat Reads,' *Saturday Review of Literature* (1 December 1934); Edward
Weeks, 'What Makes a Book a Best Seller?, *New York Times Book Review*

(20 December 1936); Harry Hansen, 'Fashions in Fiction,' *Forum* (March 1933); Robert Cantwell, 'What the Working Class Reads,' *New Republic* (17 July 1935); Harvey Breit, 'The Literary Market Place Today,' *New York Times Book Review* (18 May 1947); B. Rosenbaum, 'Why Do They Read It?,' *Scribner's* (August 1937); William Perry, 'What Do You Read, My Lord?,' *American Scholar* (Summer 1937); Harvey Breit, 'The Anthologies,' *New York Times Book Review* (22 December 1946); Russell Maloney, review of a *Treasury of Laughter, New York Times Book Review* (29 December 1946); John K. Hutchins, 'For Better or Worse, The Book Clubs,' *New York Times Book Review* (31 March 1946); and Richard H. Rovere, 'Inside,' *The New Yorker* (23 August 1947).

Chronological Index
of
Books Discussed in the Text

This list of the books most widely read in America in the years immediately following publication places each title under the date of its first printing in English. Those works of the sixteenth, seventeenth, and eighteenth centuries first issued or widely known in foreign editions are marked with an asterisk and listed under the dates of their first British printing, followed by the dates of their first American publication. Foreign books of the nineteenth and twentieth centuries are listed under the dates of their first publication in English and without notation of their first American printings, since, if printed abroad, they were generally soon known here through rapid importations or reprintings.

1792°	Volney, Constantin, *Ruins* (Les Ruines) (1st American printing, 1796)
1794°	Franklin, Benjamin, *Autobiography* (1st American printing, 1818)
1794-5	Paine, Thomas, *The Age of Reason*
1794°	Radcliffe, Mrs. Ann, *Mysteries of Udolpho* (1st American printing, 1794)
1796°	Lewis, Matthew Gregory, *The Monk* (1st American printing, 1799)
1797	Foster, Mrs. Hannah, *The Coquette*
1799°	Campbell, Thomas, *Pleasures of Hope* (1st American printing, 1810)
c.1800	Weems, Mason Locke, *The Life and Memorable Actions of George Washington*
1803	Porter, Jane, *Thaddeus of Warsaw*
1805	Scott, Sir Walter, *The Lay of the Last Minstrel*
1807	Byron, George Gordon, *Hours of Idleness*
1808	Scott, Sir Walter, *Marmion*
1809	Campbell, Thomas, *Gertrude of Wyoming*
1809	Irving, Washington, *History of New York*
1810	Porter, Jane, *The Scottish Chiefs*
1810	Scott, Sir Walter, *The Lady of the Lake*
1811	Mitchell, Isaac, *The Asylum, or Alonzo and Melissa*
1812-18	Byron, George Gordon, *Childe Harold*
1813	Byron, George Gordon, *Bride of Abydos*
1813	Byron, George Gordon, *Giaour*
1814	Scott, Sir Walter, *Waverley*
1815	Scott, Sir Walter, *Guy Mannering*
1815	Sigourney, Lydia Huntley, *Moral Pieces in Prose and Verse*
1816, 1818, 1819, 1832	Scott, Sir Walter, *Tales of My Landlord*
1817	Byron, George Gordon, *Manfred*
1817	Moore, Thomas, *Lalla Rookh*
1817	Scott, Sir Walter, *Rob Roy*
1818	Scott, Sir Walter, *The Heart of Midlothian*
1819-24	Byron, George Gordon, *Don Juan*
1819-20	Irving, Washington, *The Sketch Book*
1819	Scott, Sir Walter, *Ivanhoe*
1820	Scott, Sir Walter, *The Abbott*
1820	Scott, Sir Walter, *The Monastery*
1821	Cooper, James Fenimore, *The Spy*
1821	Scott, Sir Walter, *Kenilworth*
1821	Scott, Sir Walter, *The Pirate*
1822	Irving, Washington, *Bracebridge Hall*
1822	Scott, Sir Walter, *The Fortunes of Nigel*
1823	Cooper, James Fenimore, *The Pilot*

1864	Tennyson, Alfred, *Enoch Arden*
1864	Trowbridge, John T., *Cudjo's Cave*
1864	Whittier, John Greenleaf, *In War Time and Other Poems*, containing 'Barbara Frietchie'
1865	Dickens, Charles, *Our Mutual Friend*
1865	Hale, Edward Everett, *The Man Without a Country*
1865	Mühlbach, Louisa, *Joseph II and His Court*
1865	Richardson, Albert D., *The Secret Service*
1866	Reade, Charles, *Griffith Gaunt*
1866	Whittier, John Greenleaf, *Snow-Bound*
1867ff.	Alger, Horatio, Ragged Dick series
1867	Evans, Augusta Jane, *St. Elmo*
1867	Holland, Josiah Gilbert, *Kathrina*
1867	Ouida, *Under Two Flags*
1867	Richardson, Albert D., *Beyond the Mississippi*
1867	Whittier, John Greenleaf, *The Tent on the Beach*
1868	Collins, William Wilkie, *The Moonstone*
1868	Phelps, Elizabeth Stuart (Ward), *The Gates Ajar*
1868-9	Alcott, Louisa May, *Little Women*
1869ff.	Alger, Horatio, Luck and Pluck series
1869-80	Billings, Josh, *Farmer's Allminax*
1869	Blackmore, Richard Doddridge, *Lorna Doone*
1869	Twain, Mark, *Innocents Abroad*
1870	Dickens, Charles, *The Mystery of Edwin Drood*
1870	Disraeli, Benjamin, *Lothair*
1870	FitzGerald, Edward, *Rubáiyát of Omar Khayyám* (1st American printing)
1870	Harte, Bret, 'The Heathen Chinee' ('Plain Language from Truthful James')
1871ff.	Alger, Horatio, Tattered Tom Series
1871	Eggleston, Edward, *The Hoosier Schoolmaster*
1871	Reade, Charles, *A Terrible Temptation*
1872	Roe, Edward Payson, *Barriers Burned Away*
1872	Twain, Mark, *Roughing It*
1873	Carleton, Will, *Farm Ballads*
1873	Twain, Mark and Warner, Charles Dudley, *The Gilded Age*
1874	Hardy, Thomas, *Far from the Madding Crowd*
1874	Roe, Edward Payson, *Opening a Chestnut Burr*
1876	Southworth, Mrs. E. D. E. N., *Self-Raised*
1876	Twain, Mark, *Tom Sawyer*
1878	Green, Anna Katharine, *The Leavenworth Case*
1879	George, Henry, *Progress and Poverty*
1880	Hughes, Thomas, *Manliness of Christ*
1880	Twain, Mark, *A Tramp Abroad*
1880	Wallace, Lew, *Ben-Hur*

Index

Abbotsford and Newstead Abbey
(Irving), 76
Abbott, Eleanor, Molly Make-Believe,
213
'Abingdon, Alexander,' Boners, 254
Academy of Compliments, The, 14
Acres of Diamonds (Conwell), 161, 162,
169
Adam Bede (Eliot), 97
Adams, Charles Francis, 158
Adams, Henry, 236, 237; Democracy,
173; The Education of Henry
Adams, 236; Esther, 173
Adams, James Truslow, Epic of America,
254, 266; March of Democracy,
266
Adams, John, 34, 35, 38, 45, 48
Adams, John Quincy, 53, 71
Adams, W. T., see Oliver Optic
Addams, Jane, 165
Addison, Joseph, 28, 30, 31, 32, 42, 51;
Cato, 28, 29; and Steele, The
Spectator, 30, 31; The Tatler, 30, 31
Adler, Mortimer, How to Read a Book,
248
Advancement of Learning (Bacon), 6,
14
Adventures (Davis), 225
Adventures of François (Mitchell), 199
Age of Innocence, The (Wharton), 231
Age of Reason, The (Paine), 35, 36, 37,
46
Agnes Sorel (James), 78
Aguilar, Grace, Home Influence, 98
Aiken, George L., dramatization of
Uncle Tom's Cabin, 111
Ainsworth, Henry, 9; transl. of the Psalms,
6
Ainsworth, William Harrison, 122

Airy, Fairy Lilian (Hungerford), 257
Alabama (Thomas), 202
Alarm to Unconverted Sinners, An
(Alleine), 12-13
Alcott, Louisa May, criticism of Samuel
Clemens, 150; Flower Fables, 97;
Little Women, 97
Alden, Isabella, 213; 'Pansy' series, 208
Alderbrook (Forester), 97
Alger, Horatio, 178, 187; Bound to Rise,
161; Strive and Succeed, 161
Alhambra, The (Irving), 83
Alice of Old Vincennes (Thompson), 204
All Quiet on the Western Front
(Remarque), 226
All This, and Heaven Too (Field), 259
Alleine, Joseph, An Alarm to Unconverted
Sinners, 12-13
Allen, Ethan, 36, 37; Reason the Only
Oracle of Man, 36
Allen, Frederick Lewis, Only Yesterday,
266
Allen, Hervey, 264; Anthony Adverse,
261-3
Allen, James Lane, 205, 216; The Choir
Invisible, 203, 257; John Gray, 203;
A Kentucky Cardinal, 210
Almanacs, 14, 24, 32, 36, 42, 43, 48; and
the rebellion, 42-3
Alonzo and Melissa, or the Unfeeling
Father (Jackson), 65
Alsop, Joseph and Kintner, Robert,
American White Paper, 270
American Bible Society, 118
American Claimant, The (Twain), 150
American Conflict (Greeley), 151
American Crisis, The (Paine), 45, 46,
285
American Female Poets, The (May), 126

319

Date Due
